THE PERFORMANCE OF EUROPEAN BUSINESS
IN THE TWENTIETH CENTURY

The Performance of European Business in the Twentieth Century

Edited by
YOUSSEF CASSIS, ANDREA COLLI,
and HARM G. SCHRÖTER

OXFORD
UNIVERSITY PRESS

OXFORD
UNIVERSITY PRESS

Great Clarendon Street, Oxford, OX2 6DP,
United Kingdom

Oxford University Press is a department of the University of Oxford.
It furthers the University's objective of excellence in research, scholarship,
and education by publishing worldwide. Oxford is a registered trade mark of
Oxford University Press in the UK and in certain other countries

Published in the United States of America by Oxford University Press
198 Madison Avenue, New York, NY 10016, United States of America

British Library Cataloguing in Publication Data
Data available

Library of Congress Control Number: 2016930261

ISBN 978-0-19-874977-6

Printed in Great Britain by
Clays Ltd, St Ives plc

Foreword

Franco Amatori

The origins of this book can be traced back to an iconoclastic will. The aim of the 'creator' of the project on the performance of European enterprises in the twentieth century, Youssef Cassis, was in fact to get rid of the Chandlerian infrastructures and to go directly to a topic that is at the very heart of business history: the performance of companies. Indeed, it is basically the aim to achieve a good performance—which, in a first approach, could be defined as the ability to make profits—that encourages firms to adopt particular managerial styles, strategies, and structures rather than others. At the same time, in the final analysis, the performance of a firm is the main indicator that makes it possible to judge the effectiveness of a company's behaviour.

In his work *Big Business: The European Experience in the Twentieth Century*, Cassis clearly states his position, moving from a famous comparison included in Alfred Chandler's *Scale and Scope*. Chandler compares two very similar companies: the German firm Stollwerck and Britain's Cadbury. They had similar beginnings: both were established just a few years apart (respectively 1839 and 1831), both operated in the same industry (making chocolate), both strongly expanded in the last quarter of the nineteenth century, and both were family-owned. Yet, in the Chandlerian narrative, Stollwerck was much more dynamic and successful than Cadbury, at least from the time that Ludwig Stollwerck decided to abandon a patriarchal and familistic style of managing the firm in favour of enlarging and strengthening its managerial hierarchy. Stollwerck's executives made some courageous choices, transforming the firm into a multinational with subsidiaries in the US and improving the company's position in research and development (for instance pioneering the development of vending machines as a cheap way to distribute its products). These efforts strongly improved Stollwerck's competitive position.

By contrast, in those same years, Cadbury did not abandon its personal way of management; the company remained a family-owned and run business. It did not establish subsidiaries abroad, its distribution system was not innovative at all, and it became a holding that exchanged shares with other companies with which it did not merge. In describing this history, Chandler does not hide a certain favouritism for the German company, seen as a successful case of a dynamic and well-run firm, even more so when compared with its more conservative British competitor.

Nonetheless, history was quite cruel with Stollwerck, and things took an unpredictable turn when most of Stollwerck's US subsidiaries were expropriated in the 1920s as a consequence of the First World War. In his book, Cassis points out that by 1929 Stollwerck had become a medium-sized company, basically disappearing from the international competitive scene. On the other hand, almost two centuries after its establishment, its more conservative and less innovative rival, Cadbury, is one of the major players in the food industry and far more famous than Stollwerck. In Cassis' opinion, Chandler's analysis has been thus unable to properly explain business performance.

Yet, getting rid of Chandlerian categories is not an easy task. The real meaning of 'performance' is difficult to define—and it is even more challenging to compare the concept among different European countries and over an entire century. When trying to measure the performance of a company, 'old' criteria and instruments largely used in the Chandlerian analysis (such as the size of a firm, its market share, and its rate of survival) come back. In addition, analysis of the performance of firms is made more complex by the fact that it is very difficult to separate the performance of a single firm from the external environment in which the company itself operates.

Despite these problems and challenges, this research on European companies' performance from a comparative perspective has been of paramount importance. The project brought together scholars from different countries, and its aim to understand the features and outcomes of European companies on a well-structured population of firms was reasonable and sound.

Summing up the experience of this very ambitious research project that lasted more than ten years, two challenges need to be mentioned.

The first is related to the difficulty of keeping together and coordinating scholars coming from different countries over the course of several years. The entire project was based on the voluntary involvement of all: no special funding was available for participants. In the early stages, the discussions proposed examining many more issues, and it took time to reduce the dimensions and shift to a more workable list of issues. In a certain way, this survey brings to mind the challenges of a much larger project—that of a unified Europe. Also complicating the picture was that some entered the project years after its start, while others left before it was finished. Only a minority were able to participate from the beginning to the end, including some of those contributing to this volume. Consequently, one issue should be kept in mind for future projects: without special financial support, there is a greater need to be realistic concerning the scale and scope of a cooperative initiative.

In spite of these challenges, a pan-European database on enterprises was assembled measuring all firms with the same parameters. On that basis, direct comparisons across countries based on quantitative information became possible. Though it was clear from the outset that it would not be possible to cover all issues and countries, and we later realized that for pragmatic reasons additional ones had to be excluded, this volume represents a first attempt to tackle European history on a strictly integrated European base of information and not in the traditional way based on national parameters.

National peculiarities, changes in the scholars involved, and other issues led to a second problem, a disappointing 'performance' of cooperation. Information on specific companies was not always shared within the team in a timely and efficient manner. Lukewarm collaboration prolonged the research beyond acceptable limits, leading to a reduction in the enthusiasm that characterized the group in its early stages.

Still, this research on the performance of European firms in the twentieth century represents a very big undertaking and offers a remarkable work by some determined scholars. For this reason, even if the project took longer than expected and has been subjected to serious resizing (when compared with the initial ambitions), there is reason to celebrate that this volume is now out and that the research on which it is based is available to scholars around the world. The volume's aims have been streamlined (when compared with the original concept). The work suggests various ways by which different scholars deal with pan-European information—further research in the field is called for. To enable that, the database is openly accessible. Furthermore, a Wikipedia-like approach has been chosen so that in future years the database can be expanded with compatible data, for instance, on countries or industries, inserted by the project's administrator.

Acknowledgements

This book is the outcome of a collective European research project, involving scholars from thirteen universities. They include, with some additions as well as some withdrawals in the course of the project, the London School of Economics and Political Science and the University of Bristol in the United Kingdom; the University Pierre Mendes France Grenoble II and the University Paris IV-Sorbonne in France; the University of Cologne in Germany; Bocconi University, Milan, in Italy; Pompeu Fabra University, Barcelona, in Spain; the Free University of Brussels and the University of Antwerp in Belgium; the University of Uppsala in Sweden; the University of Helsinki in Finland; the University of Bergen in Norway; and the University of Geneva in Switzerland.

The project was based at the London School of Economics and Political Science and benefited from a three-year grant from the Leverhulme Trust (F/07 004/J), which the authors of this book gratefully acknowledge. They would also like to thank the Centre National de la Recherche Scientifique and the Maison des Sciences de l'Homme Alpes in France, Bocconi University in Italy, and the University of Bergen in Norway for their financial support.

The project was coordinated by Youssef Cassis with the administrative and technical support of first Camilla Brautaset and then Michele D'Alessandro, who established the database. But it was above all a genuinely collective effort. Data were collected by teams of researchers in most of the participating universities, while theoretical and methodological issues were discussed at regular workshops—in Grenoble, London, Paris, Barcelona, Milan, Cologne, and Geneva.

This book would never have been possible without the exceptionally harmonious and highly productive cooperation between established scholars and young researchers. We would like to thank all those who contributed to the success of this project, including those who, for one reason or another, were not able to co-author one of the book's chapters—Dominique Barjot, Camilla Brautaset, Greta Devos, Ginette Kurgan van Hentenrijk, Isabelle Lescent-Giles, Andrea Lorenz-Wende, Francesca Polese, Peter Wardley, and Hans Willems. Although we cannot name them all, we would also like to thank all those who provided invaluable advice—especially Leslie Hannah and Margaret Levenstein—and all the participants in seminars, conferences, and congresses who commented on the papers related to our project. The responsibility for the views expressed in the volume rests of course entirely with its authors.

Youssef Cassis
Andrea Colli
Harm G. Schröter

October 2015

Contents

List of Figures

List of Tables

Notes on Contributors

Edoardo Altamura is a Postdoctoral Fellow (on scientific leave) at the Paul Bairoch Institute of Economic History of the University of Geneva. Currently he is a Visiting Scholar at the Faculty of History of the University of Cambridge and a Visiting College Research Associate at Wolfson College. He is the author of *European Banks and the Rise of International Finance: The Post-Bretton Woods Era* (Routledge Explorations in Economic History). His interests lie mainly in post-war international financial and banking history in the West and in the developing world.

Franco Amatori is Professor of Economic History at Bocconi University in Milan. His field of research is business history, a discipline in which he specialized at Harvard under the guidance of Alfred Chandler and David Landes in the late 1970s. He has published extensively on Italian and international business history. A member of the editorial boards of the most important journals in his area of expertise, he has also served as President of the European Business History Association.

Anna M. Aubanell-Joubany is Professor of Economic History in the Department of Economics and Economic History at the Universitat Autònoma de Barcelona. She has published on different aspects of the history of public utilities, including the analysis of the natural monopoly condition of the electricity industry in the interwar period, industrial welfare in electricity firms, cartel stability, and, lately, the history of the gas industry in Catalonia in the nineteenth and twentieth centuries.

Veronica Binda is a Lecturer in Economic History at Bocconi University in Milan. She previously taught at the University of Parma and at Pompeu Fabra University in Barcelona. Her main research interests focus on business history in Southern European countries, global economic history, and the history of international business. Her main publications include the book *The Dynamics of Big Business: Structure, Strategy, and Impact in Italy and Spain* (New York: Routledge, 2013) and articles in *Business History*, the *Business History Review*, the *European Journal of International Management*, *Revista de Historia Industrial*, *Información Comercial Española*, and *Imprese e Storia*.

Carlo Brambilla is Lecturer in Economic History at the University of Insubria, Varese. Among his works are *Investment Banking History: National and Comparative Issues (19th–21st Centuries)*, edited with H. Bonin (Brussels: P.I.E. Peter Lang, 2014); 'Miscarried innovation? The rise and fall of investment banking in Italy, 1860s–1930s', *Entreprises et Histoire*, 67, 2 (2012), 97–117; with G. Conti, 'Ownership structure and control, regulation and performance in Italian banking. A long-term perspective', in I. Elferink et al., eds., *Corporate Governance in Financial Institutions: Historical Developments and Current Problems* (Frankfurt: EABH, 2011); and with C.A. Ciampi, R. Prodi, and A. Manzella, *La sfida internazionale della Comit* (Bologna: Il Mulino, 2013).

Frans Buelens is Senior Researcher at the University of Antwerp. He received his PhD degree in applied economics. In the past he has been responsible at SCOB (Study Centre for Companies and the Stock Exchange) for the digitization of the Brussels stock exchange, and at present he is supervising the digitization of the Antwerp Stock Exchange. His main research interest is financial history. He has studied the history of the Belgian stock exchanges, the Belgian Congo, and Belgian (private) railroad companies. He has published books on these topics, as well as articles in journals such as the *Economic History Review*, the *European Journal of Economic History*, *Explorations in Economic History*, and *Cliometrica*.

Albert Carreras is Professor of Economics at Universitat Pompeu Fabra, Barcelona. Previously, he has held positions at Universitat de Barcelona and the European University Institute. He has served as Dean of the UPF School of Economics and Business and as Secretary General of the Spanish Economic History Association. His research focus is on comparative business and economic history, historical national accounting, industrialization, and the service economy. He has published many books and articles, including *Estadísticas Históricas de España: Siglos XIX y XX* (Madrid: Fundación BBVA, 1989), *Industrialización Española: Estudios de Historia Cuantitativa* (Madrid: Espasa Calpe, 1990), and *Historia Económica de la España Contemporánea* (Barcelona: Critica, 2004).

Youssef Cassis has been Professor of Economic History at the European University Institute, Florence since 2011. He previously worked at the Universities of Geneva and Grenoble. He has held visiting professorships at the Cass Business School, the Graduate Institute in Geneva, and the University of St Gallen. His work focuses on financial history and business history. His books include *City Bankers, 1890–1914* (Cambridge: Cambridge University Press, 1994), *Big Business: The European Experience in the Twentieth Century* (Oxford: Oxford University Press, 1997), *Capitals of Capital: A History of International Financial Centres, 1780–2005* (Cambridge: Cambridge University Press, 2006), and *Crises and Opportunities: The Shaping of Modern Finance* (Oxford: Oxford University Press, 2011). He was cofounder of the *Financial History Review*. He is a member of several learned societies and is past President of the European Business History Association.

Andrea Colli is Professor at Bocconi University, Milan. His research includes the history of Italian large, medium-sized, and small enterprises, including family firms and foreign direct investment during Italian industrialization. He has published articles in the main business history journals and acts as an associate review editor of *Family Business Review*. His most recent books reflect some of these research interests. He has edited, with Michelangelo Vasta, *Forms of Enterprises in 20th Century Italy: Boundaries, Structures and Strategies* (Cheltenham: Edward Elgar, 2010) and, with Abe de Jong and Martin Iversen, *Mapping the European Corporations: Strategies, Structures, Ownership and Performance* (Abingdon: Routledge, 2011), and he has written, with Franco Amatori, *Business History: Complexities and Comparisons* (Abingdon: Routledge, 2011).

Ludo Cuyvers is Emeritus Professor at the University of Antwerp, Professor Extraordinary at the North-West University (Potchefstroom Campus), South

Africa, and Associate Research Fellow of the United Nations University—Centre for Regional Integration Studies in Bruges. He has published five textbooks and edited three volumes with international publishers, and has scholarly articles in academic journals, including, among others, *Economica*, the *European Economic Review*, the *Economic Journal*, the *Asian Economic Journal*, the *Review* of *World Economics*, the *Journal* of *Asian Economics*, and the *International Business Review*.

Michele D'Alessandro holds a PhD from Bocconi University, Milan. He teaches there and at Ca' Foscari University of Venice. His research interests are business history, banking history, and global economic history. His publications cover the history of Italian multinational banking business, company histories, and international economic governance through the League of Nations in the 1920s.

Anne Dalmasso is Professor of Economic History at the University Grenoble-Alpes and a research associate of LARHA (Laboratoire historique Rhône-Alpes, UMR 5190). Her work focuses on business history, especially the fields of energy, hydro-electricity, and aluminium, as well as the social and economic history of alpine communities. Her comparative approach extends to areas where these activities have developed, such as Quebec.

Diane Dammers graduated in economics (2003) and business management (2005) from the University of Cologne. From 2003 to 2008, she was employed as a research assistant at the Department of Economic and Social History at the same university. Since 2009, she has worked at the Statistical Office of the Rhineland-Palatinate in Bad Ems, Germany. Among other things, she has been responsible for a project on collecting historical statistical data about the territory now belonging to the Rhineland-Palatinate.

Marc Deloof is a Professor of Finance at the University of Antwerp. He received his PhD degree from the Free University of Brussels in 1996. He has held part-time positions at the the universities of Louvain, Ghent, Hasselt, Hull, Calabria, and Beijing. His research focuses on financial history, corporate finance, and governance. He has published in a wide range of international academic journals on economic history, small business, management, and economics.

Hendrik K. Fischer studied economics, political sciences, medieval and modern history and journalism in Cologne. He worked in the Department of Economic and Social History at the University of Cologne as a research assistant and then took his PhD there in 2009 as Assistant Professor. In addition, he has taught microeconomics, macroeconomics, and economic policy at the European University of Applied Sciences in Brühl. Since 2010, he has worked for the German Space Agency (Deutsches Zentrum für Luft- und Raumfahrt, DLR), currently as Deputy Head of the Space Strategy Programme.

Terry Gourvish is a Fellow in the Economic History Department at the London School of Economics and Political Science. Until recently, he was Director of the LSE's Business History Unit, Chairman of the Business Archives Council, and President of the Association of Business Historians. He has written extensively in the business history field, notably on railways and brewing.

Riitta Hjerppe is Emerita Professor of Economic History at the University of Helsinki. She is the former President and now the Honorary President of the International Economic History Association. Her main research interests are Finland's economic growth, the economic and social history of large and small enterprises, foreign direct investment, economic integration, and trade policy.

Mats Larsson is Professor in the Department of Economic History at the University of Uppsala and Head of the Uppsala Centre for Business History (UCBH). He has mainly worked within the fields of business and financial history. His current research interests concern big business in Sweden, insurance and banking history, the Stockholm Stock Exchange, and the Swedish film industry. Among his most recent publications are, with Mikael Lönnborg, *SCOR Sweden Re: 100 Years of Swedish (Re)Insurance History* (Stockholm: Dialogos, 2014) and, as author and editor, *Det svenska näringslivets historia 1864–1914* [*The History of Swedish Industry and Trade 1864–2014*] (Stockholm: Dialogos, 2014).

Toni Pierenkemper started his studies in Münster and at the London School of Economics in 1966, receiving his PhD in 1977 and his Habilitation in 1984. Since 1972, he has taught at the universities of Münster, Saarbrücken, Frankfurt, and Köln. As a guest professor, he has worked at the Oskar Lange Akademie für Wirtschaftswissenschaften Breslau/Polen, at Georgetown University, Washington DC, and at the Katholische Universität Eichstätt.

Harm G. Schröter received his PhD in 1981. He has worked at ten different universities, since 1998 at the University of Bergen. His main interest is in European economic and business history. His books include *Americanization of the European Economy: A Compact Survey of American Economic Influence in Europe since the 1880s* (Dordrecht: Springer, 2005), *The European Enterprise: Historical Investigation into a Future Species* (as editor) (Berlin: Springer, 2008), and *The Cooperative Business Movement, 1950 to the Present* (as editor, with Patrizia Battilani) (New York: Cambridge University Press, 2012). He has served as President of the European Business History Association, and acts as a referee for many international journals and publishing houses. He is a member of the editorial boards of several journals.

Helma De Smedt is an Emerita Professor at the University of Antwerp, where she has taught contemporary economic history and financial and monetary history. She has also conducted seminars on historical issues of the contemporary period and on economic history. She has published mostly on the history of banking and banks, but also on entrepreneurial history and the history of the manufacturing industry.

Xavier Tafunell is Professor of Economics at Universitat Pompeu Fabra, Barcelona. His research focus is on capital formation, economic growth, business history, and the long-run development of Latin America. He has published several books, including *Historia Económica de la España contemporánea* (Barcelona: Crítica, 2003 and 2010) and *Estadísticas Históricas de España: Siglos XIX y XX*, 2nd edition (Madrid: Fundación BBVA, 2005). He is the author of many articles in *Revista de Historia Económica—Journal of Iberian and Latin American Economic History*, the *Journal of Economic History*, *Investigaciones de Historia Económica*, the *Journal of Latin American Studies*, and the *Australian Economic History Review*.

Pierre Vernus teaches modern history at the University Lumière Lyon 2, France. He is the author of *Art, luxe et industrie: Bianchini Férier, un siècle de soieries lyonnaises, 1888–1992* (Presses universitaires de Grenoble, 2006), and has co-edited several books on trade and employers' associations in Europe in the nineteenth and twentieth centuries.

Part I
Overview and Methodology

1

The Performance of European Enterprise during the Twentieth Century

General Overview

Youssef Cassis, Andrea Colli, and Harm G. Schröter

STUDYING BUSINESS PERFORMANCE

This book originated from a very simple idea—that in the last analysis, performance is what really matters in business and thus in business history. After all, the object of business history is to explain the success or failure of a company or an entire industry, or, at a more global level, to explain the relationship between business performance and economic performance. Yet, surprisingly, the analysis of performances has been neglected by economic and business historians. Of course, most company histories include some data, and sometimes some discussion, of profits or profitability. The performances of entire industries have been considered.[1] There have also been a few national analyses, especially in France, with the studies inspired by Jean Bouvier in the 1960s and Jacques Marseille in the 1990s.[2] In Germany, Mark Spoerer has reassessed business profitability under the Weimar Republic and the Nazi regime.[3] At the European level, Youssef Cassis attempted a comparative analysis of the performance (defined in terms of net profits, returns on equity, and survival) of the leading British, French, and German companies in the course of the twentieth century as part of his study of big business in the three major European economies.[4]

The contributions from economics and business strategy, though important, do not fill the existing gap in the literature. Neoclassical economics works on the

---

[1] See for example W. Feldenkirchen, *Die Eisen- und Stahlindustrie des Ruhrgebiets 1879–1914: Wachstum, Finanzierung und Struktur ihrer Großunternehmen* (Wiesbaden, 1978); Y. Cassis, *City Bankers, 1890–1914* (Cambridge, 1984); G. Jones, *British Multinational Banking, 1830–1990* (Oxford, 1993); T. Gourvish and R.G. Wilson, *The British Brewing Industry, 1830–1980* (Cambridge, 1994).

[2] J. Bouvier, F. Furet, and M. Gillet, *Le mouvement du profit en France au XIXème siècle* (Paris, 1965); J. Marseille, dir., *Les performances des entreprises françaises au XXème siècle* (Paris, 1995).

[3] M. Spoerer, *Von Scheingewinn zum Rüstungsboom: die Eigenkapitalrentabilität der deutschen Industrieaktiengesellschaften, 1925–1941* (Stuttgart, 1996).

[4] Y. Cassis, *Big Business: The European Experience in the Twentieth Century* (Oxford, 1997).

assumption that in a competitive environment expected profits converge in the long term and has thus paid little attention to the performances of individual companies. On the other hand, institutional economics has paid great attention to firms but has not directly addressed the question of performance. A number of major research projects on company profits have been undertaken within the field of applied economics, especially in Britain. P.E. Hart's work on the interwar years and beyond, based on Inland Revenue data and figures from the Central Statistical Office, provided aggregate data by industry and considered a number of issues such as the appropriation of profit and the effects of the size of the firm.[5] Geoffrey Whittington's analysis of company profits in the 1950s, based on the published accounts of all United Kingdom quoted companies engaged in manufacturing and distribution, was more directly interested in the profitability of firms, though at an aggregate level.[6] Similar studies have been undertaken in Continental Europe.[7] A more recent comparative study, coordinated by Dennis Mueller, has acknowledged the importance of firms' characteristics to explain the persistence of diverging profit rates, without, however, going beyond the level of aggregate figures at a national level.[8]

The business strategy literature has more directly addressed the question of the relationship between organizational structure and performance at company level, at least since Richard Rumelt's classic work on the largest American companies in the 1950s and 1960s. In the heyday of Chandlerian studies, Rumelt's conclusions pointed to strong performance for firms combining a strategy of diversification with a structure of divisional organization.[9] Interestingly, similar conclusions have been drawn by Richard Whittington and Michael Mayer in their recent analysis of the top 100 British, French, and German companies in the 1980s and 1990s.[10] One increasingly influential view of performance has been the measure of organizational longevity, notably the work of James Collins and Jerry Porras on American firms[11]—an issue that has interested business historians, in the first place Leslie Hannah, who has compared the world's largest 100 firms in 1912 and 1995.[12]

---

[5] E. Hart, *Studies in Profit, Business Saving and Investment in the United Kingdom, 1920–1962*, 2 vols. (London, 1965–8).

[6] G. Whittington, *The Prediction of Profitability and Other Studies of Company Behaviour* (Cambridge, 1971).

[7] See for example G. Echevarria and J.L. Herrero, 'La evolución de la economia española durante el período 1940–1988 a partir de un indicator de la tasa de beneficio del sector industrial', *Información Comercial Española* (1989), 665; X. Taffunell, 'Los beneficios empresariales en España, 1881–1980. Estimación de un índice annual de excedente de la gran empresa', in *Rivista de Historia Económica*, 16, 3, (1998), 707–46; H. Bruse, *Wettbewerbsbeurteilungen auf statistischer und dynamischer Basis, illustriert anhand der Aktiengesellschaften der 'Bonner Stichprobe'* (Bonn, 1981).

[8] D.C. Mueller, ed., *The Dynamics of Company Profits. An International Comparison* (Cambridge, 1990).

[9] R. Rumelt, *Strategy, Structure and Economic Performance* (Boston, 1974).

[10] R. Whittington and M. Mayer, *The European Corporation: Strategy, Structure and Social Science* (Oxford, 2000). Whittington and Mayer's aim was to extend the Harvard programme of the early 1970s, which included studies by Rumelt on the United States, Channon on Britain, Dyas on France, Thanheiser on Germany, and Pavan on Italy.

[11] J. Collins and J. Porras, *Built to Last* (London, 1994).

[12] L. Hannah, 'Marshall "Trees" and Global "Forest": were "Giant Redwoods" Different?', in N. Lamoreaux, D. Raff, and P. Temin, eds., *Learning by Doing in Markets, Firms and Countries* (Chicago, 1999). See also Howard Gospel and Martin Findler, "The long-run dynamics of big firms: the one hundred largest employers from the United States, the United Kingdom, Germany, France, and Japan, 1907–2002", in Giovanni Dosi et al., eds., *The Third Industrial Revolution in Global Business* (New York, 2013), pp. 68–90.

More recently, Christian Stadler has attempted to draw some lessons from 'outstanding corporations'—very large European companies combining survival (100 years or more) with performance, measured by total shareholder return.[13] There is undoubtedly a lot to take from the business strategy literature, especially for the analysis of performance in the last two or three decades. Nevertheless, it does not replace the long-term perspective and human dimension brought by the historical approach.

DEFINING BUSINESS PERFORMANCE

For all that, the word 'performance' is ever present in the title of economic and business studies. The problem is that there is no general agreement about what business performance actually means. For Alfred Chandler, for example, whose influence on an entire generation of historians has been enormous, the most successful firms are those that have made the 'three-pronged investment' in production, management, and marketing, with longevity being the only approximate measure of actual performance.[14] Business performance can be assessed at a firm, industry or national level, as in Michael Porter's notion of 'international competitive advantage', which is measured through the exports record of industries based in a particular country.[15] From a macroeconomic perspective, performance tends to be measured in terms of productivity growth. For others, performance is best assessed by a firm's innovative capacity. Performance can also be measured in a more qualitative or even subjective way, using such criteria as job creation—a major issue for trade unions—or contribution to national greatness.

At a firm level, performance can be defined according to four broad criteria. The first is size (whether measured by market capitalization, turnover, workforce, or total assets). This could be considered as an indirect measure of performance, since growth is usually, though not necessarily, the outcome of strong competitive results. The second, rates of return (like return on equity and holding return) is in many respects the most direct measure. Value added has recently tended to be considered as the key measure of business performance,[16] but its calculation is highly problematic for most of the twentieth century. A third criterion includes aspects related to survival and longevity. These should be considered as partial measures of performance, in the sense that, depending on a specific context, they can be indicators of success or failure. The sale of a company might be in the shareholders' best interest or part of an industry's necessary reorganization, while survival may be the result of a Malthusian policy. The fourth criterion, competitiveness, includes physical measures of performances, including market share, production per worker, and so on. It is a direct measure, which can be extremely

---

[13] C. Stadler, *Enduring Success. What We Can Learn from Outstanding Corporations* (Stanford, 2011).

[14] A. Chandler, *Scale and Scope. The Dynamics of Industrial Capitalism* (Cambridge, Mass., 1990).

[15] M. Porter, *The Competitive Advantage of Nations* (New York, 1990).

[16] See for example J. Kay, *Foundations of Corporate Success* (Oxford, 1993).

useful for comparative purposes, though only within a homogeneous group of industries. Innovative capacity, though important, should be considered as a factor rather than a measure of performance.

Nevertheless, profits and profitability remain the most common way of assessing business performance, and it is these measures that we have used in this project. There are many possible ratios of profitability (return on equity, return on assets, return on capital employed, and others). We have chosen two of them. The first, probably the most widely used, is return on equity (ROE), which is the ratio, expressed as a percentage, of net profits to shareholders' equity. Net profits are profits after tax, while shareholders' equity comprises paid-up capital, reserves, balance carried forward, and other undistributed profits. The second is holding return (HR), in other words the return realized by a hypothetical investor who bought a share in a company and sold it a year later. It is the ratio, also expressed as a percentage, of the difference between the selling and buying prices plus dividend to the buying price. ROE and HR can thus be seen as providing a complementary measure of profitability, the former as seen from a firm's perspective, the latter from an investor's perspective. In constructing the database used in this volume, ratios have been calculated around five benchmark periods (1911–13, 1927–9, 1954–6, 1970–2, and 1998–2000), on the basis of a three-year average in order to even out possible erratic deviations of one exceptional year.

There has been much discussion, and also much criticism, about the relevance of profits in economic and business history. The main criticism concerns the reliability of the figures published in balance sheets and profit-and-loss accounts, which is what we have used in our study. There is a serious risk that published figures are distorted, either optimistically or pessimistically, and many historical studies have revealed differences between published and actual profits. As far as comparative studies are concerned, there is the added problem of differences among accountancy practices in each country.

We are, of course, fully aware of these problems. But we are also convinced that studying business performance is not only possible, but highly desirable. Published profits provide, for all countries, at best a fairly accurate picture, at worst a rough idea of a company's state of affairs. That is already something. However distorted, published profits do reflect the image a company wishes to project, and there is no reason to assume that discrepancies between published and unpublished profits are more pronounced in one country than in another. For HR, the challenge is the fact that a company share price incorporates expectations about future profits, while the historian is concerned with past performance. But the figures are accurate in the sense that they reflect market expectations and have not been massaged by creative accountancy.

ANALYSING BUSINESS PERFORMANCE

The analysis of business performance is based on a sample of 1,225 companies, belonging to eight countries: the three major European economies (Britain, France, and Germany), two large south European latecomers (Italy and Spain), two smaller north-western countries (Belgium and Sweden), and one small

Nordic country (Finland). Lists of companies have been established for five benchmark averages each made of three years, referred to in the following as 1913, 1927, 1954, 1972, and 2000.

A major characteristic of the project is its comparative perspective, and a serious comparative approach requires putting all the countries involved on the same footing. This, in turn, requires that the sample of companies on which the analysis is based should be established very carefully, in order to capture the depth and breadth of European business. Simply selecting the 100 or 200 largest European firms, or even the 50 or 100 largest in each country, would not have done the job. Consequently, firms have been selected on the basis of both size (measured by assets until the 1950s and turnover thereafter) and industries, while national representation has been weighted according to the size of the country's economy. Methodological details regarding our selection procedure are provided in Chapter 2.

This book has been conceived as a specific contribution of history to the analysis of business performance, as distinct from that of accountancy, finance, economics, or business strategy. In the first place, we do not start with a series of theoretical hypotheses that we endeavour to test by using econometric methods. On the other hand, we do question the validity of a number of widely held and often controversial assumptions regarding business and economic performance (ownership and control of the firm, balance between 'old' and 'new' industries, role of banks and capital markets, state intervention, entrepreneurship and innovation, or superiority of one 'model' of capitalism over another) in the light of the actual performances of a sample of European companies.[17]

Profit ratios thus represent a point of departure from which we try to explain why certain companies, in certain sectors, in some countries, at a given period in time, have been particularly successful—or particularly unsuccessful. For this purpose, we combine a quantitative analysis of profits and profitability with qualitative data on individual firms. In this way, the study of performance is as much a starting point, to better understand businesses and their interaction with their economic environment, as a point of arrival whose prime objective would be measuring profit with 100 per cent accuracy.

The results presented in this book must be seen in this context. Rather than a comprehensive study of business performance in Europe in the twentieth century, our aim is to provide a first set of results that should generate essential discussions within the discipline and form a launching pad for further research. In the remaining part of this introduction, we first present the broad results of our

---

[17] There have been long-standing debates on most of these issues. See for example Chandler, *Scale and Scope*; W. Lazonick, *Business Organisation and the Myth of the Market Economy* (Cambridge, 1991); A. Chandler, F. Amatori, and T. Hikino (eds.), *Big Business and the Wealth of Nations* (Cambridge, 1997); L. Hannah, 'Survival and size mobility among the world's largest 100 industrial corporations, 1912-1955', *American Economic Review*, 88, 2 (1999), 62–5 and 'Marshall "trees" and global "forest"'; G. Jones and M.B. Rose, eds., *Family Capitalism*, special issue of *Business History*, 35, 4 (1993); A. Colli, *The History of Family Business, 1850-2000* (Cambridge, 2003); Y. Cassis, G.D. Feldman, and U. Olsson, eds., *The Evolution of Financial Institutions and Markets in Twentieth Century Europe* (Aldershot, 1994); J. Edwards and S. Ogilvie, 'Universal banks and German industrialisation: a reappraisal', *Economic History Review*, 49, 3 (1996), 427–46; M. Collins, 'English bank development within a European context', *Economic History Review*, 51, 1 (1998), 1–24.

project (measures of business performance at a European aggregate level and a preliminary assessment of the main determinant of business performance), before introducing the chapters of the book and suggesting some avenues for further research.

THE OVERALL PERFORMANCE OF EUROPEAN BUSINESS

The overall performance of Europe's leading companies displays a surprising degree of stability throughout the twentieth century.[18] Let us first consider ROE (Table 1.1). The median stood at around 8.5 per cent for three out of the five benchmark years (1913, 1929, and 1972); it was lower in the mid-1950s (6.7 per cent) and higher at the height of the second globalization, in 1998–2000 (12.7 per cent). Arithmetic averages, while recording greater variations, confirm this general trend. However, even during these latter years, rates of return remained on average below the 15 per cent benchmark, which, throughout the twentieth century, appears to have been the level that European companies have endeavoured to attain.[19]

However, only a minority reached that target. The proportion of Europe's 125 leading companies achieving an ROE of 15 per cent or more rose from 15 per cent in 1911–13 to 17 per cent in 1927–9; then fell to just under 10 per cent in 1954–6, and further to 7 per cent in 1970–2; before rising to a staggering 31 per cent—nearly a third—in the last years of the twentieth century. Interestingly, a comparatively high proportion amongst them were based in a small country (Belgium, Sweden, Spain, or Finland)—nearly half in 1954–6 and 1998–2000, whereas they made up only a quarter of Europe's leading companies.

Table 1.1. Overall performance, ROE (in %)

	Mean	Median	Minimum	Maximum	Standard deviation	N
1911–13	10.09	8.77	−0.60	37.80	6.12	118
1927–9	10.18	8.68	−6.35	42.53	7.18	123
1954–6	10.43	6.70	−10.56	153.77	19.35	123
1970–2	7.69	8.50	−45.24	38.89	8.94	123
1998–2000	14.20	12.73	−110.78	91.58	17.28	122
Total						609

N = Number of valid observations.

Source: The Performance of European Business, Small Sample

[18] The discussion that follows is based on the analysis of the 125 leading European companies in 1913, 1927, 1954, 1972, and 2000—defined as the 'Small Sample' for the purpose of this project, as opposed to the 'Large Sample', which has been established on a sectoral basis. The Small Sample includes the largest companies of the eight countries selected for this project: 30 for Great Britain, 25 for Germany, 20 for France, 15 for Italy, 10 for Spain, Belgium, and Sweden, and 5 for Finland. See Chapter 2 for more details on the selection procedure.

[19] See Cassis, *Big Business*, p. 86.

It is also noticeable that the best-performing companies were only occasionally the largest. Only three amongst the twenty largest (British American Tobacco, Krupp, and J. & P. Coats) managed an ROE of 15 per cent or more in 1911–13, four in 1927–9 (Union Minière, British American Tobacco, Imperial Tobacco, and Shell), a single one in 1954-6 (BP), two in 1970–2 (Daimler-Benz and VEBA), and none in 1998–2000. Companies from the 'old industries' were most likely to rank amongst the top performers during the first half of the century ('free-standing' mining companies were especially profitable before 1914), the 'Chandlerian firms' on the eve of the First World War as well as at the turn of the twenty-first century, and those from 'finance and services' during most of the century.

Only two non-financial companies (De Beers Consolidated and British American Tobacco) attained a 15 per cent ROE in three of the five benchmark periods, and another six (LKAB, Michelin, Petrofina, Prudential, Siemens, and Union Minière) managed to do so in two periods. This lack of consistency can be partly ascribed to changes in the composition of the group of leading companies, with some disappearing from the top 125 and new ones acceding to it. On the other hand, there were a number of major companies (in banking and the new industries of the Second Industrial Revolution) that remained amongst Europe's largest during fifty to eighty years, or even more, but they were not the most profitable.[20]

From an investor's point of view and considering HR, the picture is somewhat unexpected. Investors in European large companies made their day in the 1950s and 1990s, two periods in which median HRs were close to 20 per cent (Table 1.2). In these two periods, the number of over-the-average performers increased impressively: while only seven companies managed an HR higher than 15 per cent in 1911–13, their number reached forty-five in 1927–9, fifty-five in 1954–6, twenty-eight in 1970–2, and forty-five again in 1998–2000.

The highest returns also reached impressive levels, especially in the 1920s (above 96 per cent for Nord-Est and Générale Transatlantique and more than 77 per cent for Sofina), the 1950s (more than 300 per cent for Esso France and more than 80 per cent for Banque de l'Indochine, Shell, and Pétroles BP), and the

Table 1.2. Overall performance, HR (in %)

	Mean	Median	Minimum	Maximum	Standard deviation	N
1911–13	3.97	4.20	−36.45	60.72	10.46	104
1927–9	13.73	11.20	−30.37	98.23	21.96	117
1954–6	24.34	20.73	−28.94	311.12	36.54	99
1970–2	7.16	6.61	−23.10	46.15	14.58	102
1998–2000	18.43	12.76	−56.33	264.66	38.50	100
Total						522

N = Number of valid observations.

Source: The Performance of European Business, Small Sample

[20] See Cassis, *Big Business*, pp. 117–18. The best known include, amongst others, Barclays Bank, Lloyds Bank, Deutsche Bank, Société générale, Shell, BP, Unilever, RTZ, Michelin, Renault, Peugeot, Daimler Benz, RWE and Siemens.

turn of the twenty-first century (264 per cent for Anglo American, 158 per cent for Nokia, and 124 per cent for Finmeccanica).

Interestingly, the top performers in terms of HR were not the same as when measured by ROE: this happened with only one company in 1913 (BASF), five in the 1920s (Sofina, Cockerill, Forges de la Providence, Alais Froges Camargue, and Rhône-Poulenc), two in the 1950s (Union Minière and Saint-Gobain), and three in each of the last two benchmarks (Hawker Siddeley, Thorn, and Associated British Food in 1972 and Nokia, Vodafone, and WPP Group in 2000). Companies with substantial HRs were likely to be based in a large rather than in a small country—between 80 and 90 per cent of the 'top twenty' in all benchmark years except for the early 1970s, and around 70 per cent of those with an HR higher than 15 per cent. They were also less likely to be amongst Europe's largest companies—excluding banks. And finally, they were more likely to belong to the new than the old technology industries—motor cars (Citroën) and electricity (Sofina, Thomson-Houston, and Siemens) in the 1920s, oil (Esso Standard, Shell, and Compagnie Française des Pétroles) and motor cars (Fiat, Citroën) in the 1950s, and information technology (Nokia, Alcatel, Vodafone, and Olivetti) in the late 1990s.

The fact that high HRs were more often generated by companies based in large countries might be due, amongst other reasons, to the existence of a wider market for their shares—and hence the likelihood of a greater demand for the shares of big managerial enterprises. The fact that some of the best performers, in terms of HR, were the new technology industries is not surprising: in booming periods, such as the 1920s and the 1990s, the markets tend to take an optimistic view of their future prospects, irrespective of their actual profits, with often painful consequences.

Sectoral Performance

Beyond European-wide overall business performance and the results of individual firms, looking at sectors is essential in order to understand economic and business performance in the twentieth century. Sectors will be approached from two different angles: five broad sectors (old industries, 'Chandlerian firms', finance and services, utilities, and knowledge industries) on the one hand and, when necessary, their various branches on the other.[21]

Let us first consider performance in terms of ROE (Table 1.3). Firms belonging to the broad sector of finance and services consistently outperformed the other sectors in the three central benchmark years and exhibited one of the highest performances at the end of the twentieth century. They also persistently displayed higher returns than the leading companies' average, except in 1913. Manufacturing industry taken together, i.e. both the 'old industries' and the 'Chandlerian firms', outperformed the whole sample only at the height of the two globalization periods. Returns tended to be somewhat higher in the 'old industries' during their period of predominance (the first half of the twentieth century) and the

---

[21] See Chapter 2 for a definition of these five broad sectors.

Table 1.3. Sectoral performance, ROE (in %)

	1911–13		1927–9		1954–6		1970–2		1998–2000	
	Mean	Median	Mean	Median	Mean	Median	Mean	Median	Mean	Median
Old industries	11.19	8.49	10.19	8.11	11.74	5.80	4.12	6.65	12.43	12.88
Chandlerian firms	11.49	9.30	10.01	9.53	7.69	6.71	7.86	8.81	16.06	12.71
Finance and services	10.19	9.54	12.81	10.12	17.36	8.90	11.07	10.15	14.49	12.88
Public utilities	7.84	7.24	7.89	6.96	5.12	4.87	4.68	5.95	10.20	12.44
Knowledge industries	—	—	—	—	—	—	7.40	7.40	13.93	16.03
Total	10.09	8.77	10.18	8.68	10.43	6.70	7.61	8.28	14.21	12.73

Source: The Performance of European Business, Small Sample

Chandlerian firms during theirs (the second half). On the other hand, returns were consistently low in public utilities, though they regained momentum in the late 1990s. The knowledge industries, which are present only in the later benchmark years, showed significantly high returns.

These general trends are confirmed, complemented, and explained by looking at the subsectors. Returns were regularly high in banking and in insurance and commercial activities during the last quarter of the century. By contrast, returns were low in railways (only included in the earlier benchmark years). They declined in transport and communications and also in metal production. On the other hand, they increased in utilities for electricity and gas supplies. In the Chandlerian industries—chemicals, electrical engineering, oil, machine building, and transport equipment—returns moved more or less downwards until the 1970s, while they significantly recovered at the end of the century. Some subsectors somewhat deviated from this pattern: in oil and rubber, ROE rose in the 1920s, driven by firms such as Michelin (26.4 per cent) and Shell (16.7 per cent); in transport equipment, rates of return improved in the 1950s, owing especially to car makers such as Ford Motor (14.9 per cent) and British Motor (13.8 per cent), and the Swedish shipyard Götaverken (10.7 per cent). However, they stagnated afterwards. Firms such as Siemens, AEG, Bosch, GEC, CGE, BASF, Bayer, ICI, Unilever, Shell, BP, Michelin, Daimler-Benz, Peugeot, and Fiat only occasionally figured amongst the top performers, but they combined size, longevity, and steady profitability.

For all sectors, HRs were higher in the 1950s and 1990s than at other benchmark years, with particularly low yields in 1911–13, mainly as a result of a general bear market in 1913, with a particularly sharp fall in the securities of the Chandlerian firms (Table 1.4). The knowledge-based industries not only performed better than the other sectors in the last two benchmark years, but actually displayed the highest returns in the sample (in excess of 35 per cent). This is no surprise, since the sector comprises some of the subsectors (services to business and media) that greatly benefited from the information technology revolution of the last decade of the twentieth century and were partly involved in the 'dot com' bubble. Chandlerian firms and public utilities, on the other hand, were the main

Table 1.4. Sectoral performance, HR (in %)

	1911–13		1927–9		1954–6		1970–2		1998–2000	
	Mean	Median	Mean	Median	Mean	Median	Mean	Median	Mean	Median
Old industries	4.18	3.29	10.63	7.93	17.57	17.24	3.80	−1.42	26.13	14.86
Chandlerian firms	2.15	9.07	17.18	16.83	32.74	21.69	6.65	5.07	18.88	12.08
Finance and services	3.20	3.80	11.86	11.22	19.88	10.60	10.69	9.79	11.32	11.52
Public utilities	5.18	4.84	15.68	12.09	23.40	27.34	4.63	10.08	7.97	5.42
Knowledge industries	—	—	—	—	—	—	19.02	19.02	35.62	32.01
Total	3.97	4.20	13.73	11.20	24.34	20.73	7.67	7.35	18.17	13.00

Source: The Performance of European Business, Small Sample

drivers of the overall increase in HRs in the 1950s, whereas the old industries, whose performance had been below average for most of the century, significantly rebounded in 1998–2000. HR was less remarkable in finance and services, which only managed to outperform the whole sample in the early 1970s. Median figures confirm the general pattern as far as knowledge industries, Chandlerian firms, and public utilities are concerned, but finance and services did better on that count, with higher-than-sample yields not only in the 1970s, but also in the 1920s and 1990s.

The analysis of subsectors refines the picture further. Car makers (Citroen, with a return of 63.4 per cent) together with electrical engineering (Thomson-Houston, 49.5 per cent, and Siemens-Schuckertwerke, 48 per cent, being amongst the best performers) and chemical companies (Produits chimiques d'Alais, 40 per cent, and Kali-Industrie, 33.5 per cent) go a long way towards explaining the performance of the Chandlerian industries in the late 1920s, whereas oil companies (71.6 per cent) and again chemicals (34 per cent) account for the successes in the mid-1950s. Electricity companies (26.5 per cent) were mostly behind the outstanding performance of the utilities sector at mid-century, while mining (78.8 per cent) and food, drink, and tobacco firms (21.3 per cent) explain the impressive recovery of the old industries in 1998–2000, to a large extent driven by the substantial demand triggered by world economic growth and the rise of the BRIC countries. Insurance was a major determinant of the high returns of the finance and services sector in the last two benchmark periods—a sector otherwise penalized by the poor performance of retailing at the end of the century. Finally, electrical engineering yielded the highest returns of any industry at any period, with firms like Nokia, Alcatel, Marconi, and Ericsson—all close to the 'knowledge economy'.

Country-Level Performance

So far, Europe has been considered as a single entity, in the same way as business performance would be considered in the United States, Japan, or Australia. Is such an inclusive approach justified? Or should greater attention be paid to the performance achieved by businesses within individual countries? There are some arguments in favour of considering Europe as an economic unit after the creation of the Common Market in 1958 (despite a gradual enlargement and persisting obstacles to full integration), but arguably also before 1914—in terms of communication, transport, and fairly modest trade barriers. On the other hand, each country retained, for most if not all of the twentieth century, a strong economic identity, in terms of size, level of development, policies, and, most importantly from our point of view, business organization—all of which can help explain national variations in business performance.

Comparing business performance at national level, however, poses a number of problems. In the first place, it must be clear that the average ROE or HR of a given country should in no way be seen as any kind of measure of that country's economic performance—it only reflects the performance of its largest firms. Second, national results are likely to be affected by the uneven distribution of companies, in terms of number, size, and sectors, between countries. This is a direct consequence of the way the list has been assembled, but it has to be taken into account when comparing, say, Finland and France, or Spain and Germany. Nevertheless, an analysis of European business performance would not be satisfactory without integrating the national dimension.

Starting, once again, with return on equity and judging from median values, firms based in smaller countries (Belgium, Finland, Spain, and Sweden) tended to perform better than their counterparts in larger countries (Table 1.5). Belgium, in particular, hosted some of the most profitable companies in the 1920s (with Sofina, Forges de la Providence, and Union Minière), the 1950s (Banque Nationale and Union Minière), and at the end of the century (Colruyt and Petrofina), just as Spain did most notably before the start of the First World War (with the mining companies Rio Tinto and Tharsis, together with Banco de España) and at mid-century (again with Banco de España). A host of Swedish and Finnish firms fared comparably well in the 1950s (LKAB) and in 2000 (Nokia, Skanska, Ericsson, UPM-Kymmene, Volvo, and Electrolux). Greater variation can be observed within the group of the larger economies, with Great Britain showing ROEs rather stable at around 10 per cent until the surge of the late 1990s (20 per cent), while Germany and France followed a path of decreasing yields until the 1950s, and

Table 1.5. Country performance, ROE (in %)

	1913		1927		1954		1972		2000	
	Mean	Median	Mean	Median	Mean	Median	Mean	Median	Mean	Median
Belgium	8.71	8.55	18.45	17.54	17.85	11.31	10.25	8.53	18.02	17.65
Germany	13.27	10.24	8.87	8.24	4.31	4.69	6.99	8.79	12.72	12.44
Spain	15.20	11.95	11.75	9.70	23.81	7.56	9.55	10.34	18.95	14.57
Finland	10.60	10.60	7.62	8.11	7.61	6.82	5.74	6.24	18.01	14.52
France	8.79	7.61	9.72	9.08	6.46	5.30	8.41	7.88	9.48	10.84
Britain	9.82	8.05	10.62	9.24	10.85	9.06	9.84	9.65	21.38	1545
Italy	5.60	5.70	7.16	8.08	5.63	4.53	0.81	3.59	−0.06	9.06
Sweden	9.16	8.96	8.03	7.14	21.63	8.88	8.73	9.06	16.29	16.11
Total	10.09	8.77	10.18	8.68	10.43	6.70	7.69	8.50	14.20	12.73

Source: The Performance of European Business, Small Sample

Table 1.6. Country performance, HR (in %)

	1913		1927		1954		1972		2000	
	Mean	Median	Mean	Median	Mean	Median	Mean	Median	Mean	Median
Belgium	4.84	2.56	21.11	20.14	17.27	14.58	14.44	13.15	9.76	10.67
Germany	3.72	3.50	0.93	−2.72	25.63	27.56	−3.89	−4.44	9.82	8.96
Spain	5.05	2.50	13.01	11.63	26.43	27.16	2.91	0.76	−3.22	−2.85
Finland	—	—	−5.11	−7.95	13.95	16.25	29.41	27.90	57.98	38.03
France	3.93	5.82	42.44	40.56	54.47	37.47	7.49	8.57	21.86	19.22
Britain	6.24	5.10	3.65	4.27	13.08	12.13	14.63	16.02	19.11	12.52
Italy	−3.26	−0.67	14.10	14.81	26.80	30.75	−7.61	−4.42	31.04	15.42
Sweden	5.35	6.33	17.58	19.90	7.97	7.03	5.96	5.07	15.55	13.48
Total	3.97	4.20	1373	11.20	24.34	20.73	7.15	6.61	18.43	12.76

Source: The Performance of European Business, Small Sample

then recovered to levels closer to, if still below, the European average. Remarkably disappointing was, on the other hand, the performance of Italian big business, which proved almost consistently the lowest.

From the point of view of investors, the picture differs and is more varied (Table 1.6). No clear pattern differentiates the performances of smaller and larger countries. Median HRs of Belgian and Spanish companies rose in concert through the first half of the century, then declined more or less sharply. Swedish firms followed their continental peers, but declined earlier and bounced back more pronouncedly in 2000, whereas Finnish companies showed a reverse trend. Within large economies, French and German returns moved in opposite directions until the 1950s—with yields reaching their highest values in France (26.5 per cent) and negative values in Germany (−4.7 per cent) in the 1920s. On the other hand, British investors had to be content with relatively low returns (between 3.8 and 5.4 per cent), lower than the European average except in the last two benchmark years. Finally, Italian yields fluctuated widely, displaying both the lowest (in the 1970s, −11.7 per cent) and highest (in 2000, 28.6 per cent) levels recorded in the sample.

THE DETERMINANTS OF BUSINESS PERFORMANCE

Behind an overall stability and homogeneity, the performance of European business at the level of individual companies displays enormous disparities. High or low returns can be attributed to a number of factors—sector, period, competition, regulation, and others. However, this is not enough. Significant differences can be observed among companies operating at the same time in the same industry. Explaining these differences requires combining quantitative data on performance with qualitative data integrating the main elements of a firm's history—variables related to ownership, strategy, structure, governance, foreign direct investment, industrial relations, political lobbying, and so on. We have not been able to systematically analyse all these variables within the framework of this

Table 1.7. ROE by ownership category, 1911–2000 (in %)

	1911–13	1927–9	1954–6	1970–2	1998–2000
Family firms	14.87	11.08	17.65	8.02	12.71
State-owned enterprises	11.60	8.79	13.49	2.15	3.15
Widely dispersed ownership	10.01	9.15	7.92	10.02	16.45
Ownership by financial groups	9.74	14.33	7.79	10.90	16.89
All	10.09	10.18	10.54	7.69	14.05

Source: The Performance of European Business, Small Sample

project, and this will hopefully be the next stage in the study of business performance. However, our database enables us to consider the relevance of some of them.

Forms of ownership throw interesting light on business performance. Concentrated ownership, whether in family hands or in financial groups, has been a strong feature of European big business throughout the twentieth century, with the possible exception of Great Britain.[22] Dispersed ownership has of course increased, but family firms have persisted, while the data show quite clearly the impressive rise and fall of the state-owned enterprise in Europe. In terms of performance, the widely held view that dispersed ownership is conducive to better financial results is not confirmed by our analysis. In Europe, family-owned companies, as well as those controlled by financial institutions, achieved consistently high ROEs, even from the 1970s onwards—in sharp contrast with the poor returns of state-owned enterprises (Table 1.7). Dispersed ownership, on the other hand, seems to have had beneficial effects on long-term survival—another measure of business performance.

Scholars have continued to regard strategy and structure as significant variables of business performance ever since Alfred Chandler's groundbreaking work on the topic.[23] In the case of the companies included in this project, the database does not allow a precise measurement and analysis of the relationship between these two crucial dimensions of the corporate identity. The qualitative evidence available from the chapters, however, seems to point—consistently with the existing literature—in the direction of an increasing diffusion of branches of industry within European large firms. We observed strategies of diversification, especially since the 1970s, that were more pronounced in the case of companies belonging to industries characterized by a declining trend in ROEs, as in the case of both the 'old industries' and the 'Chandlerian' firms. The direct relationship between diversification strategies and declining returns is also a similarity between European and American large corporations, though with some differences in timing. As far as organizational structures are concerned, however, neither the quantitative nor the qualitative data permit further generalization. We are leaving this area of analysis for future research.

To what extent should a firm's international orientation be considered as a significant determinant of business performance? The database does not contain any coded information about companies' foreign activity—in terms of either

---

[22] This point is discussed in greater detail by Andrea Colli in Chapter 3.

[23] See Chandler, *Strategy and Structure* and, for a more recent appraisal, Whittington and Mayer, *The European Corporation*.

exports or foreign direct investments. Of course, the vast majority of the large companies included in the list had some kind of foreign activity, and here we suggest that higher foreign activity is directly correlated with higher profitability and returns. The propensity for international activity is clearly higher in some industries than others—one can expect low foreign activity in some branches of public utilities such as transport. Another element directly influencing the propensity for international activity is the dimension of the home market. From this perspective, the incentive to go abroad is higher for large companies based in small markets than for those with huge domestic outlets. In a similar way, a low propensity to internationalize activities can be explained by the possibility for companies to tap the advantages of monopolistic positions at home, something that discourages the search for (maybe risky) profits abroad.

The international dimensions can explain some sharp differences between the performances (in terms of ROEs) of companies based in different countries. An explanation of the persistent lower performances of Italian big business, for instance, can be connected to a comparatively low level of foreign activity among Italian firms, which were enjoying favourable conditions in the domestic market in terms of monopolistic rents. The contrary can be said, for instance, for Belgian companies, which were very active from the beginning on foreign markets.

A company's size is clearly the result of its past performance, but it can in turn act as a positive—and sometimes negative—factor in future performance. In this respect, our analysis reveals sharp difference between countries. As a rule, the largest companies in the sample belong to the core countries. Looking at the first deciles (by total assets), in 1913, six companies were British, five French, and one German. In 1927, eight were British, one Spanish, one German, and two Belgian, while in 1954, seven companies in the first decile were British, two Spanish, one Italian, one French and one Belgian. At the 1970–2 benchmark, four British companies were in the first decile, three Italian, three French, and two German. Finally, Germany led only in 2000, with five companies, as against four for Great Britain. The steady relevance of Britain among the largest companies, together with the 'weakness' of the German presence, look quite surprising, as does the French 'variability'. Peripheral countries—with to some extent the exception of Italy and Spain—are characterized by the presence of smaller companies, and one could of course be tempted to correlate this with the size of the domestic market.

Dimensional variance is straightforward and larger in Europe than in the United States. In 1913, the French railway company P.L.M. (Europe's largest company) was 150 times larger (by assets) than Oy W. Gutzeit, the Finnish wood and paper firm (the smallest of the 125 leading European companies). By comparison, in 1917 U.S. Steel, and, for that matter, the Pennsylvania Railroad Company, were about 57 times larger than Lehigh Valley Coal Company. In 2000, DaimlerChrysler, the largest manufacturing company in the sample, was more or less 200 times larger in asset size than the Belgian chemical firm U.C.B. The differences reflect as much the limited degree of European economic integration as the greater size and higher number of American giant companies. The fact that they have persisted throughout the twentieth century is no doubt a consequence of having included in the sample a quota of companies from smaller European countries—but this represents the diversity of European business—a very European characteristic indeed.

Other structural variables should be taken into consideration in the analysis of business performance. They include senior management (education and training, and stability), workforce (skills, turnover, and unionization), cartel agreements, research and development (innovation and technological intensity), socio-political networks (overlapping directorships and political lobbying), and also reputation—in a way a synthesis of them all. Here again, we hope to have lain the ground for their integration into a new generation of long-term analyses of business performance.

However, one should not dismiss the effect of the economic and political conjuncture. Our sample has been built in a way that eliminates major shocks, such as world wars or severe depressions—mainly because their effects can vary considerably from country to country and thus render meaningless any tentative comparison. Nevertheless, their long-term effects should be perceived. The study's first three benchmark periods correspond more or less to the 'Thirty Years War of the Twentieth Century'—the period extending from 1914 to 1945 and comprising two world wars and the most severe depression in modern history. However, what is perhaps most striking at this point is that, as a whole, the sample displays an impressive continuity in ROE levels across the first and most tormented part of the century, followed by a decline in the 1970s, at the end of the 'golden age' of economic growth, and a recovery on the eve of the new millennium. Of course, in the case of single countries, the variance is more pronounced, reflecting specific historical conditions. Germany, for example, seems to have suffered more from the Second than the First World War, while others, such as Belgium, prospered steadily across the century—in terms of their leading companies' returns.

An analysis of European business performance cannot ignore the effects of regulation and economic and industrial policies, and in the end state intervention. Regulation affected some industries more than others. The comparatively low performances (in terms of ROE) of public utilities, in particular transport and communications, may well be the result of persisting regulatory regimes in these industries, probably coupled with their position as domestic natural monopolies, very often under direct state ownership. Alternative reasons could include state intervention in order to reduce the daily-life expenditure of voters, or the choice to provide the highest standards and levels of security in such large technical systems. Both aims would be likely to reduce profitability. In any case, finding out the reasons requires additional qualitative case-studies.

The longitudinal analysis of the available data provides, to a certain extent, a contribution to the ongoing debate on the so-called 'varieties of capitalism'. This is true with respect, for instance, to ownership structures, with clear evidence of the persistence and prevalence of concentrated control in Continental Europe, with family capitalism in some countries and bank-centred systems in others, and Britain's peculiarity with an (apparent) precocious diffusion of widely held ownership structures. The effects of these 'varieties' on business performance are, however, far from clear-cut.

The same can be said about the 'competitive advantage of nations', their specialization in some sectors, which at the same time reflects their level of economic development. The composition of the Small Sample in 1913 reveals significant differences between Britain and Continental Europe. British capitalism had already reached a high level of maturity, being diversified into a wide range of manufacturing and service industries (railways, mining, textiles, financial inter-mediation, and food and beverage) when other countries were still in relative infancy, with industrial structures markedly oriented towards natural resources, old industries, and utilities. In other cases, the data confirm what we already know from the existing literature, for instance the prominence, until at least the 1950s, of Germany and Sweden in investment goods such as electric engineering.

INTERPRETING BUSINESS PERFORMANCE

The issues that we have raised here are discussed in greater depth, and elaborated with further details and examples, in the rest of this book. The book is divided into three parts, in addition to this general introduction. Part I, including Chapters 2 and 3, deals with thematic issues. Chapter 2, by Michele D'Alessandro, discusses the methodology adopted in this study, in particular the procedure for selecting the companies included in the sample, and problems related to sources, standard classification, and the reliability of published accounts. Chapter 3, by Andrea Colli, assesses the relationships between the ownership structures of Europe's largest companies (family or individual, widely held, financial institution, holding, state, foreign, and shareholders' agreement) and their performance in a long-term perspective. The analysis has been conducted with reference to four main analyt-ical frameworks: 'varieties of capitalism', corporate governance, ownership and control, and strategies and organizational patterns.

Part II is concerned with country performances, with seven chapters (4–10): one each for Belgium, Britain, France, Germany, Italy, and Spain, and one for Sweden and Finland, which are jointly dealt with in a single chapter. Each chapter has been constructed along the same broad lines and addresses, in turn, three main issues: first, overall business development, with specific reference to the country's leading companies, in other words those included in the sample, especially in terms of industries' representation, size, survival, and so on; second, performance measured in terms of ROE; and, third, performance measured in terms of HR. Results are discussed at aggregate, industry, and company levels, and considered in a long-term perspective. Despite this common framework, each chapter retains its own characteristic and flavour, because of the personality and style of its author(s) and the specific configuration of business prevailing in each country.

Part III is made up of four chapters (11–14), each covering a key group of industries. They represent the first cross-country analysis founded on a common data base and are consequently much more valid than previous comparisons. As we have already indicated, four broad groups of industries have been defined, partly on the basis of the nature of their activity and partly in terms of historical stage of industrial development. Two groups are concerned with manufacturing industry: the first with the 'old industries' of the First Industrial Revolution (coal, iron and steel,[24] textiles and leather goods, food, drink, and tobacco, and wood

---

[24] Steel, as part with coal and iron of the 'heavy industries', has been grouped with the 'old industries', even though it belongs to the industries of the Second Industrial Revolution. However,

and paper); the second with the 'Chandlerian firms', characteristic of the Second Industrial Revolution (chemicals and pharmaceuticals, electrical engineering, mechanical engineering, oil, rubber and other non-metallic products, and transport equipment). The 'knowledge-based industries' emerging with the third industrial revolution (information technology, telecom, services to business, media, and leisure and tourism) have had to be left out, as they only appeared in the last of our five benchmark periods (1998–2000). The third group includes 'finance and services' companies (banking, insurance, and commercial activities) and the fourth 'public utilities' companies (transport, electricity, gas, and water).[25] Three of these four chapters have been jointly written by two, sometimes three, contributors combining expertise on both a given field of business activity and one or several of the countries involved in the analysis—thus facilitating meaningful comparisons, at both industry and company levels.

The chapters that follow present the results of entirely new research—comparative, comprehensive and longitudinal. They combine a wealth of statistical material with innumerable narrative accounts of all aspects of the life of Europe's major businesses throughout the twentieth century. Above all, they provide a much needed discussion of these companies' successes and failures, with both intra- and extra-European comparisons, at European-wide, national, and firm levels. They represent a new and hopefully inspiring way of writing business history.

FURTHER RESEARCH ON BUSINESS PERFORMANCE

Post-Chandlerian business history is still at a crossroads, somewhat torn between several trends—institutional approach, theory of information, business and management tools, and culture and value systems. Looking at business activity through the lenses of performance provides a unifying platform, encompassing all types of approaches, from the economic to the cultural. By highlighting, over the long term, the main determinants of business performance, business history should provide a major contribution to the reflection on the competitiveness of European enterprises in a global economy, and more generally to the evolution of

---

the crisis it went through in the mid-1970s was more typical of the 'old' than the other 'new' industries, such as the electrical or motor industries.

[25] There are, of course, some overlaps between the groups. For example, food, drink, and tobacco could in many respects be considered as belonging to the 'Chandlerian firms' of the Second Industrial Revolution. Moreover, the industrial economics literature has produced useful taxonomies of industries and sectors. In particular, the OECD's distinction between low, medium, and high technological level industries has been further elaborated by economic historians in order to cope with the phenomenon of technological maturity. See R. Giannetti and M. Velucchi, 'The demography of manufacturing firms, 1911–1971', in R. Giannetti and M. Vasta, eds., *Evolution of Italian Enterprises in the 20th Century* (Heidelberg, 2009), which elaborates on T. Hatzichronoglou, *Revision of the High-Technology Sector and Product Classification*, STI Working Papers, 2, OECD (Paris, 1997). See also K. Pavitt, 'Sectoral patterns of technical change: towards a taxonomy and a theory', *Research Policy*, 13 (1984), 323–73. However, our proposed classification is more useful from a business history perspective, since it explicitly refers to the organizational typologies linked to the macro-sectors.

industrial capitalism, stability, crises and recoveries, regulation and deregulation, corporate governance, and increasing social inequalities.

A considerable amount of information has been gathered in the project's database—yet an even greater amount of work remains to be done in order to properly understand the dynamics of business performance. Nevertheless, we believe that we are offering a good starting point. In the first place, the database will be hosted at Bocconi University, and will be made available to everybody through open access. We hope that it will be not only widely used, but also updated and augmented—with data on still missing countries, missing years, and missing variables of business performance.

In particular, there is room for extending existing data into long-term time series suitable for econometric analysis. There is also room for complementing existing, mainly quantitative, data with systematically collected qualitative data integrating the main elements of a firm's history. Such data, related in particular to ownership, strategy, structure, governance, multinational expansion, industrial relations, political lobbying, and others, could be processed by making use of the prosopographical method, mainly employed by social historians.

Another extension could be geographical, with the inclusion of enterprises from European countries omitted in this project, such as the Netherlands and Switzerland, as well as Austria, Norway, Denmark, Portugal, and Greece, and—though with a gap during the communist period—the Eastern European countries.[26] More complicated but also more rewarding would be a supplement covering the space of the former socialist countries.

And a third direction would be to widen and deepen the comparative dimension of the study. The 'natural' comparison would obviously be with the United States and/or Japan. A less natural one, with the performance of large firms in planned economies, would also be interesting. Here, to the lack of research in the field would be added the problem of 'language', that is, of measuring returns in a non-capitalist environment, where firms produced with other objectives than profitability, ROE, or HR. Another comparative exercise could finally be to include in the analysis small and medium-size enterprises, in order to understand if, and to what extent, there is a correlation between measures of performances and the dimensional attributes of companies in different sectors.

We do know our efforts are just one step into the direction of an integrated European business history based on one common ground. However, we feel that though this volume represents a modest and limited approach, it is at the same time a necessary one. In any case, we strongly invite scholars to make use of and deepen and extend our somewhat Wikipedia-like database under the address of: http://www.crios.unibocconi.eu/wps/wcm/connect/cdr/centro_criosen/home/databases/european+business+performance+database.

---

[26] A list of Europe's leading companies could be established on the following distribution principles: Britain would have thirty companies, Germany twenty-five, France twenty, and Italy fifteen. The first tier of small European countries (Austria, Belgium, the Netherlands, Spain, Sweden, and Switzerland) would have ten each, and the second tier of small European countries (Denmark, Finland, Greece, Norway, and Portugal) five each—making a total of 175 Western European companies. The division between 'first tier' and 'second tier' small European countries is based on the size of each country's economy as measured by GDP.

2

Methodology and Traps

Michele D'Alessandro

Investigating the long-term evolution and performance of big business in Europe in the course of the twentieth century inescapably entails dealing with a considerable degree of diversity. Indeed, figuring as a prominent feature of the industrialization and growth patterns of individual European countries,[1] diversity has purposefully been sought in this study in order to offer as close as possible a representation of the variety of national historical developments. On a different level, variety has inevitably added to the difficulty usually inherent in collecting, using, and interpreting company data about a large number of firms from different countries. This chapter sets out to illustrate the criteria adopted to build the sample by focusing on the choice of countries to be included, sector and company selection, benchmark years, size and performance indicators, and issues related to the possible impact on data of different institutional contexts.

The sample draws companies from eight European countries: Belgium, Finland, France, Germany, Great Britain, Italy, Spain, and Sweden. The selection was intended to have a cross-section as representative as possible of European historical development and growth experiences. From a quantitative point of view, taken together, these countries make up a substantial proportion of European GDP, their share persistently accounting for above 80 per cent throughout the twentieth century (see Table 2.1). From a qualitative perspective, the countries included in the sample also cover a fairly wide variety of features that populate the economic history literature under well-known labels and established dichotomies: first-movers as opposed to latecomers, core and peripheral countries, large and small economies. Basically, some of these countries definitely entered the era of modern economic growth in the nineteenth century, while another group did not undergo a process of convergence until after the Second World War. Moreover, countries entering our sample span a rather broad spectrum of the institutional diversity upon which varieties-of-capitalism studies have more recently focused. Indeed, each of them could well fit one or another of the typologies carved out by this strand of socioeconomic literature, from the dualistic models of Michel Albert[2]

---

[1] See for instance G. Toniolo and R. Sylla, eds., *Patterns of European Industrialization* (London, 1991).

[2] M. Albert, *Capitalism vs. Capitalism* (New York, 1993).

Table 2.1. GDP level of sampled countries as a percentage of thirty European countries' GDP

	1913	1927	1954	1972	2000
Belgium	3.6	3.7	3.1	2.9	2.8
Finland	0.7	0.8	1.2	1.2	1.4
France	16.0	16.1	15.3	16.7	16.6
Germany	26.3	23.9	21.6	23.3	20.7
Italy	10.6	10.7	12.6	14.1	14.4
Spain	4.6	5.6	4.6	6.3	8.3
Sweden	1.9	2.2	3.1	2.8	2.4
United Kingdom	24.9	22.8	22.8	16.3	16.1
Total	88.6	85.8	84.3	83.7	82.6

Source: Calculations from Maddison Project Database

and of Hall and Soskice[3], to the more elaborated analytical categories identified by Bruno Amable, namely the market-based, the social-democratic, the Continental European, and the Mediterranean models.[4]

Each country contributes to the sample a fixed number of the largest of its companies from both the manufacturing and services sectors. This procedure ensures the representation in the sample of smaller countries and latecomers that would otherwise be excluded from a ranking of European firms based on just size. In fact, for most of the twentieth century, in any list of the 100–200 largest European companies, measured by whichever criterion of size (turnover, market capitalization, assets, or employment), British, German, and French companies, in this descending order, would make up a good three-quarters of the total. The introduction of country quotas avoids a bias in favour of larger countries and first-movers and offers a more balanced picture of European big business. Individual country contributions are weighted by a combination of the level of development (as captured by GDP per capita figures) and the size of the economy. Accordingly, Great Britain provides 30 firms, Germany 25, France 20, Italy 15, Belgium, Spain, and Sweden 10 companies each, and Finland 5. Taken together, these companies—which add up to 125 at each benchmark year—form what throughout the following chapters is referred to as the 'Small Sample'.

To delve further into the multifaceted phenomenon of big business in Europe, though, a second, broader sample (called the 'Large Sample') has been designed, gathering the largest firms by industry in each country. To this sample, countries contribute a number of companies proportionate to the size of their economy: Britain, Germany, and France each supply three companies per industry, Italy two, and Spain, Belgium, Sweden, and Finland one. Overall, the Large Sample

---

[3] P.A. Hall and D. Soskice, eds., *Varieties of Capitalism: The Institutional Foundations of Comparative Advantage* (Oxford, 2001).

[4] Actually, in his work Amable singles out five distinct models of capitalism, the last being the Asian one. The author defines models on the basis of the characteristics and regulation of five institutional areas, notably product-market competition, labour market institutions, financial markets and corporate governance, the welfare state, and education. See B. Amable, *The Diversity of Modern Capitalism* (Oxford, 2003).

Table 2.2. Number of companies in the Large Sample

	1913	1927	1954	1972	2000	Total
Belgium	17	19	19	17	23	95
Finland	5	15	14	17	17	68
France	44	45	47	54	49	239
Germany	42	48	45	50	52	237
Italy	30	32	30	32	38	162
Spain	19	21	18	23	23	104
Sweden	15	16	15	17	19	82
United Kingdom	43	49	43	49	54	238
Total	215	245	231	259	275	1,225

Note: Including wildcards

comprises 1,225 companies (see Table 2.2), of which about half concurrently belong to the Small Sample. It should be noted that, with respect to its a priori definition, the Large Sample presents a number of gaps, since companies could not always be found meeting the sampling criteria. This is due to several reasons. In the instance of smaller, less diversified economies or latecomers—as is the case of Finland at the beginning of the century—certain industries did not exist or, if they did, firms in those industries were too small to leave traces in official publications. Most often, however, companies could simply not be identified or the relevant financial data obtained.

It should be pointed out that, departing slightly from a strictly quantitative approach to sampling, allowance has been made for inclusion in the Large Sample of a limited number of 'wildcard' companies (up to five per country and benchmark) that for some reason did not satisfy sampling rules but that research teams believed ought to be taken into account, especially because of their historical importance.

All in all, the dataset counts 1,347 firms. Of these, 625 firms make up the Small Sample and 1,225 the Large Sample, with 503 companies belonging to both. This leads up to 1,289 companies, with the final figure being rounded out by taking account of 58 companies entering the Large Sample in the form of 'wildcards'.[5] A list of the companies included in the Large Sample (with assets, turnover, ROE, and HR for each benchmark year) can be found in the Appendix to this volume.

Built around different rules, the two samples pursue rather different research goals. On the one hand and in line with established international research on various leagues of the top largest firms in one or more countries, the Small Sample emphasizes matters of size and is meant primarily to compare the dimensions, industry distribution, and performance of the largest firms in each country. On the other hand, the Large Sample extends—notably downwards—the notion of 'bigness' and has a bias in favour of industry distribution: it is especially aimed for the systematic cross-country analysis revolving around industries that is carried out in the third part of the book. Needless to say, in neither case has a minimum threshold been imposed on the size of selected companies.

---

[5] Eventually, only five countries supplied 'wildcards', though not by the same amount at each benchmark: Belgium, Finland, France, Great Britain, and Spain.

Another major issue concerns the definition of industries. Certainly, the business history literature presents a considerable amount of variance in the labelling of economic activities. While some studies do not adopt any standard classification or do not use aggregated categories,[6] others rely on nationally defined standards,[7] broad categories,[8] or customized hybridizations of existing classification systems.[9] In addition, the longitudinal dimension of the analysis complicated further the choice of a suitable classification. The option eventually taken was to adopt an approach that is flexible with regard to the historical context, but robust when defining business activities. On the one hand, any company entering either sample has been classified according to the two-digit International Standard of Industrial Classification.[10] This provides a solid anchor for future use of the database by other scholars working both within and outside Europe, particularly the United States and Japan.[11] Moreover, as the standard is continuously updated, it allows the database to be kept up to date in the years to come according to applied and accepted international standards of classification.

On the other hand, individual firms have been aggregated into industry definitions that are broad enough to ensure that at any point in time they will effectively encompass the structure of the economy within a manageable set of categories, varying between fifteen at the beginning of the century and nineteen at century-end.[12] This procedure comes at the cost of diluting the specificity of individual industries, but at the same time strengthens the otherwise weak statistical evidence available. Certainly, industries are geared to tracking the evolution of big business in the wake of technological innovation and institutional change so that their number and labels vary over time. For instance, 'Post and telecommunications' and 'Services to business' are among the most notable new entries in the last three decades of the century. By the same token, in the process of time, 'Railways', 'Basic and fabricated metals', and 'Wood and paper products'—to name but a few—are dropped and subsumed under such headings as 'Transport and communication' and 'Mature industries'.[13] In order to facilitate the task of comparing performance

---

[6] L. Payne, 'The emergence of the large-scale company in Great Britain, 1870–1914', *The Economic History Review*, 20, 3 (1967), 539–42.

[7] A.D. Chandler, *Scale and Scope; The Dynamics of Industrial Capitalism* (Cambridge, Mass., 1990).

[8] For instance, in his comparative study of British, German, and French big business, Youssef Cassis groups firms under the comprehensive labels of Industry, Finance, and Services, in their turn further broken down into a few industries. See Y. Cassis, *Big Business: The European Experience in the Twentieth Century* (Oxford, 1999).

[9] Peter Wardley, 'The anatomy of big business: aspects of corporate development in the twentieth century', *Business History*, 33, 2 (1991), 281. In his analysis of the world's leading industrial companies, Christopher Schmitz does not specify the basis of his definition of industrial sectors, moving between broad categories and the core activity of the firm: C. Schmitz, 'The world's largest industrial companies of 1912', *Business History*, 37, 4 (1995), 85–96.

[10] The standard adopted is ISIC Rev. 3.1 and companies are classified according to divisions.

[11] The United Nations Statistics Division provides correspondence tables between successive versions of the North American Industry Classification System (NAICS) and ISIC. Much the same is done by the Japanese government's Statistics Bureau to match its national standard to the UN's.

[12] This is done by merging several ISIC divisions. For instance, we combine manufacture of food products and beverages (ISIC code 15) and manufacture of tobacco products (ISIC code 16) into one single industry. For a complete list see Table 2A.2 in the Appendix at the end of this chapter.

[13] For a complete list see Tables 2A.1 and 2A.2 in the Appendix.

across countries and longitudinally, the analysis also avails itself of five much broader categories resulting from further aggregation and representing both a macro-sectoral subdivision of economic activities and, as far as manufacturing is concerned, an indication of technological change. Thus, 'Old industries' by and large comprises First Industrial Revolution technologies: basic and fabricated metals; food, drink, and tobacco products; mining; textiles and leather goods; and wood and paper products. 'Chandlerian firms' coincides largely with the technologies of the Second Industrial Revolution: chemicals and pharmaceuticals; oil, rubber, and other non-metallic mineral products; mechanical and electrical engineering; and transport equipment. 'Knowledge industries' assembles the new knowledge-based activities that developed in the last third of the twentieth century: leisure and tourism; media; post and telecommunications; and services to businesses. 'Finance and services' includes banking, insurance, and commercial activities. Finally, 'Public utilities' covers transport and communication, and electricity, gas, and water supply.

The study hinges on size and performance measurements at five benchmark years. It starts with 1913, the culmination of the first episode of globalization in modern history and arguably of the long nineteenth century, and jumps to 1927— when the world economy, after returning to its pre-war level of production, was eventually enjoying a measure of international macroeconomic stability and growth. The years 1954 and 1972—our third and fourth benchmarks—portray European big business at the end of the phase of reconstruction after the Second World War and at the end of the golden age, whereas the year 2000, in the midst of a renewed process of globalization, represents the obvious final observation.

Coming to size and performance issues, this is the area where the choice of suitable indicators has been most constrained by the actual possibility of obtaining the relevant historical data. As for size, companies are selected on the basis of total assets in the first three benchmarks and of turnover in 1972 and 2000. This is because in the early part of the century, turnover figures are rarely provided in published repertories of company data.[14] An exception has been made for banks and insurance companies, which enter both samples according to their assets throughout the period under consideration. Because, especially for banks—whose assets are closely related to collected deposits and therefore provide a distorted indication of size with respect to firms in other industries—this carried the risk of overrepresentation in the Small Sample, a cap has been set limiting their number to 20 per cent of total national companies. As a result, at each benchmark we have six banks from Great Britain, five from Germany, four from France, three from Italy, two each from Belgium, Sweden, and Spain, and one from Finland. Both assets and turnover historical data were collected in national currencies and then converted to US dollars at the year-average exchange rate.

With respect to performance, the reasons for targeting profitability and choosing return on equity (ROE) and holding return (HR) (or total shareholder return) as performance indicators have already been discussed in Chapter 1. This leaves

---

[14] It must be stressed that company information could not always be collected according to sampling rules. Most notably in 1913, Finnish non-financial firms are ranked by turnover instead of assets. Conversely, in the fourth benchmark, Belgian firms are ordered by assets instead of turnover.

room to add just a few remarks concerning the use of these ratios in a cross-country comparison, since it cannot be excluded that they are affected by systematic, country-specific factors.[15] Starting with ROE, both its numerator and denominator are likely to be subject to this kind of influence. Corporate and income tax regimes varying from country to country, for instance, can be expected to have an impact on the level of net profit. Similarly, national business cycles not fully synchronized and country endowments affecting factor prices may be reflected in firms' financial performances. On the other hand, the balance between equity and debt in the composition of the capital structure may vary substantially not only across firms and industries, but also more generally according to institutional aspects characteristic of national financial systems[16] and labour markets.[17] Last, but not least, as is typical of accounting measures of performance, ROE is subject to the vagaries of idiosyncratic accounting practices and standards at the firm, industry, and national levels, and possibly to the not too infrequent practice of window-dressing.[18] Of course, all of this has the potential to affect ROE and hence invites caution in comparing and interpreting cross-country data. The same goes for HR, which is no less exposed to country-specific institutional variation. The ability of capital markets to assess and reflect in share prices the actual potential of a firm to generate future cash flows depends on the level of disclosure of company financials, on the effectiveness of information processing by market participants, and on the extent of herding behaviour. Furthermore, the amount of dividend

---

[15] The international business strategy, international economics, and international finance literature provide ample evidence that country-specific, in addition to firm- and industry-specific, factors affect a firm's performance. While agreement is wide on this score, more contentious are the importance of the country effect in explaining variance in performance and the question of what constitute the key determinants of the country effect. See for instance M. Blaine, 'Comparing the profitability of firms in Germany, Japan, and the United States', *Management International Review*, 34, 2 (1994), 125–48; S. Makino, T. Isobe, and C.M. Chan, 'Does country matter?', *Strategic Management Journal*, 25, 10 (2004), 1027–43; G. Hawawini, V. Subramanian, and P. Verdin, 'The home country in the age of globalization: how much does it matter for firm performance?', *Journal of World Business*, 39, 2 (2004), 121–35; and R.G.B. Goldszmidt, L.A.L. Brito, and F.C. de Vasconcelos, 'Country effect on firm performance: a multilevel approach', *Journal of Business Research*, 64, 3 (2011), 273–9.

[16] See Raghuram G. Rajan and Luigi Zingales, 'What do we know about capital structure? Some evidence from international data', *The Journal of Finance*, 50, 5 (1995), 1421–60; Asli Demirgüç-Kunt and Vojislav Maksimovic, 'Institutions, financial markets, and firm debt maturity', *Journal of Financial Economics*, 54, 3 (1999), 295–336; and Abe de Jong, Rezaul Kabir, and Thuy Thu Nguyen, 'Capital structure around the world: the roles of firm- and country-specific determinants', *Journal of Banking & Finance*, 32, 9 (2008), 1954–69. The institutional aspects typically regarded as responsible for variation in capital structure are legal enforcement, shareholder and creditor right protection along with bankruptcy legislation, the tax code, the market- as opposed to bank-oriented nature of the financial system, and stock market development.

[17] Daniel Folkinshteyn, Ozge Uygur, and Gulser Meric, for instance, maintain that the higher profitability of US versus German manufacturing firms in the early 2010s stems from, among other things, lower levels of unionization. See D. Folkinshteyn, O. Uygur, and G. Meric, 'A comparison of the financial characteristics of U.S. and German manufacturing firms', *International Journal of Business and Finance Research*, 8, 5 (2014), 9–22. It is worth stressing that in the early stages of this research, attempts were made to collect company data on long-term debt in addition to equity, but the limited availability of historical figures eventually led to a change in course and to this variable being dropped.

[18] For a general discussion of performance measurement, see Pierre J. Richard, Timothy M. Devinney, George S. Yip, and Gerry Johnson, 'Measuring organizational performance: towards methodological best practice', *Journal of Management*, 35, 3 (2009), 718–804.

paid out—the other component of HR—may vary substantially, among other things, according to established business customs, the nature and structure of ownership, and the maturity of firms and industries. In a cross-country study, it is all too easy to see how these issues are heightened by the diversity of national institutional contexts.

In light of this, while an attempt to fully account for the influence of institutional factors on the performance of firms is beyond the scope of this study, some of the country-specific effects arising from institutional diversity are separately addressed in Chapter 3. In order to reduce the impact of possible misalignments in national business cycles, it was decided that at each benchmark, company performance measurements would span three consecutive years. This has the additional advantage of helping smooth out the impact of stochastically determined record highs and lows in financial results. Finally, by combining an accounting-based and a financial-market-based measure, each incorporating different perspectives on and emphasising different aspects of performance, an attempt is made to offer a more balanced picture than is usually obtained through one single indicator. Overall, the database gathers 3,690 valid ROE and 2,905 valid HR observations, the rates of missing data being 7.6 and 27.3 per cent, respectively.[19]

To conclude, the sources tapped for this research—of which a comprehensive list is provided in the Appendix to this chapter—are mainly published annual stock exchange yearbooks collecting financial data of listed firms. Other official publications, quite often from various economics ministries, have allowed the inclusion of unlisted companies in the samples. Sometimes, companies that, though ranking among the largest in their home country, were not in joint-stock form could not be selected for want of financial data. This is especially the case for Germany, where company law did not require partnerships and limited liability companies to publish their balance sheets and income statements, most particularly in the first two benchmarks.[20] More often, and to the maximum feasible extent, gaps in the data have been filled in by drawing on collections of company balance sheets held at several university libraries and by consulting first-hand sources at large historical banking archives.

---

[19] The relatively high rate of missing holding return data is to be attributed to a significant extent to the appreciable number of companies that, although in joint-stock form, were not listed.

[20] For instance, Diana Dammers and Hendrik Fischer point out that 12 out of the 100 largest German companies in 1927 were in the form of either partnerships or limited liability companies. See Chapter 7 of this volume, footnotes 4 and 5.

APPENDIX

Table 2A.1. Synoptic table of Large Sample industries

Industry	1913	1927	1954	1972	2000
Basic and fabricated metals	X	X	X		
Chemicals and pharmaceuticals		X	X	X	X
Commercial activities	X	X	X	X	X
Construction and property companies				X	X
Electrical engineering	X	X	X	X	X
Financial intermediation[a]	X	X	X	X	X
Food, drink, and tobacco products	X	X	X	X	X
Insurance				X	X
Leisure and tourism				X	X
Mature industries[a]				X	X
Mechanical engineering	X	X	X	X	X
Media				X	X
Mining	X	X	X	X	X
Oil, rubber, and other non-metallic mineral products		X	X	X	X
Oil, rubber, chemicals, and other non-metallic mineral products	X				
Post and telecommunications					X
Railways	X	X			
Services to business				X	X
Textiles and leather goods	X	X	X	X	X
Transport					X
Transport and communication[b]	X	X	X	X	
Transport equipment	X	X	X	X	X
Utilities; Electricity, gas, and water supply	X	X	X	X	X
Wood and paper products	X	X	X		

[a] Includes 'Basic and fabricated metals' and 'Wood and paper products'
[b] Includes 'Railways'

Table 2A.2. ISIC codes and industries

Industry	ISIC code
Basic and fabricated metals	27. Manufacture of basic metals 28. Manufacture of fabricated metal products, except machinery and equipment
Chemicals and pharmaceuticals	23. Manufacture of coke, refined petroleum products, and nuclear fuel 24. Manufacture of chemicals and chemical products
Commercial activities	51. Wholesale trade and commission trade, except of motor vehicles and motorcycles 52. Retail trade, except of motor vehicles and motorcycles; repair of personal and household goods 55. Hotels and restaurants
Construction and property companies	45. Construction 70. Real estate activities
Electrical engineering	31. Manufacture of electrical machinery and apparatus n.e.c. 32. Manufacture of radio, television and communication equipment and apparatus

Financial intermediation	65. Financial intermediation, except insurance and pension funding
	66. Insurance and pension funding, except compulsory social security
Food, drink, and tobacco products	15. Manufacture of food products and beverages
	16. Manufacture of tobacco products
Insurance	66. Insurance and pension funding, except compulsory social security
Leisure and tourism	55. Hotels and restaurants
	63. Supporting and auxiliary transport activities; activities of travel agencies
	93. Other service activities
Mature industries	10. Mining of coal and lignite; extraction of peat
	20. Manufacture of wood and of products of wood and cork, except furniture; manufacture of articles of straw and plaiting materials
	21. Manufacture of paper and paper products
	27. Manufacture of basic metals
	28. Manufacture of fabricated metal products, except machinery and equipment
Mechanical engineering	28. Manufacture of fabricated metal products, except machinery and equipment
	29. Manufacture of machinery and equipment n.e.c.
	30. Manufacture of office, accounting, and computing machinery
	31. Manufacture of electrical machinery and apparatus n.e.c.
	33. Manufacture of medical, precision, and optical instruments, watches, and clocks
Media	22. Publishing, printing, and reproduction of recorded media
	92. Recreational, cultural, and sporting activities
Mining	2. Forestry, logging, and related service activities
	10. Mining of coal and lignite; extraction of peat
	13. Mining of metal ores
	14. Other mining and quarrying
	27. Manufacture of basic metals
Oil, rubber, and other non-metallic mineral products	11. Extraction of crude petroleum and natural gas; service activities incidental to oil and gas extraction, excluding surveying
	23. Manufacture of coke, refined petroleum products, and nuclear fuel
	25. Manufacture of rubber and plastics products
	26. Manufacture of other non-metallic mineral products
Oil, rubber, chemicals, and other non-metallic mineral products	23. Manufacture of coke, refined petroleum products, and nuclear fuel
	24. Manufacture of chemicals and chemical products
	26. Manufacture of other non-metallic mineral products
Post and telecommunications	64. Post and telecommunications
Railways	60. Land transport; transport via pipelines
Services to business	71. Renting of machinery and equipment without operator and of personal and household goods
	72. Computer and related activities
	74. Other business activities
Textiles and leather goods	17. Manufacture of textiles
	18. Manufacture of wearing apparel; dressing and dyeing of fur
	19. Tanning and dressing of leather; manufacture of luggage, handbags, saddlery, harness, and footwear
Transport	60. Land transport; transport via pipelines
	61. Water transport

(*continued*)

Table 2A.2. Continued

Industry	ISIC code
	62. Air transport
Transport and communication	60. Land transport; transport via pipelines
	61. Water transport
	62. Air transport
	64. Post and telecommunications
Transport equipment	34. Manufacture of motor vehicles, trailers, and semi-trailers
	35. Manufacture of other transport equipment
Utilities; Electricity, gas, and water supply	40. Electricity, gas, steam, and hot water supply
Wood and paper products	20. Manufacture of wood and of products of wood and cork, except furniture; manufacture of articles of straw and plaiting materials
	21. Manufacture of paper and paper products
	22. Publishing, printing, and reproduction of recorded media

Sources

Belgium

- Bourse de Bruxelles, *Cours authentique* (1900–2000).
- *Recueil Financier* (Bruxelles: Editions Bruylant, 1900–75).
- Memento der Effecten (1975–2000).

Finland

- Banker och Aktiebolag i Finland 1912–1915 [Banks and Limited Liability Companies in Finland 1912–1915].
- Firmor i Finland 1927–1929 [Companies in Finland 1927–1929].
- Riitta Hjerppe, *Suurimmat yritykset Suomen teollisuudessa 1844–1975* [*Major Companies in Finnish Manufacturing Industry 1844–1975*], Bidrag till kännedom av Finlands natur och folk, utgivna av Finska Vetenskaps-Societeten, H. 123 (Helsinki: Societas Scientiarum Fennica, 1979).
- Kauppalehti [Commercial Journal], 1926–9.
- Gunhard T. Kock, *Osakesäästäjän käsikirja 1972* [*Stock Savers' Handbook 1972*] (Helsinki: Tietoteos, 1973).
- Gunhard T. Kock, *Pörssitieto 1977: Osakesäästäjän käsikirja* [*Stock Exchange Information 1977: Stock Savers' Handbook*] (Helsinki: Tietoteos, 1976).
- Kotimaisen teollisuuden albumi [Album of Domestic Manufacturing Industry], I and II.
- PricewaterhouseCoopers Global Forest and Paper Industry Survey, 2005 Edition, Survey of 2004 Results.
- Suomen pankit ja osakeyhtiöt 1957 [Finnish Banks and Limited Liability Companies 1957].
- *Talouselämä* [*Economic Life*], 1955–7, 1971–3, 1999–2001. *Talouselämä* has share capital, balance sheets, and income statements of the largest banks and limited liability companies.

France

- Annuaire Desfossés: valeurs cotées en banque à la Bourse de Paris (Paris: E. Desfossés et Fabre frères).
- Crédit Agricole Historical Archives.

Germany

- *Salings Börsen-Jahrbuch: Ein Handbuch für Bankiers und Kapitalisten* (Berlin/Leipzig/ Hamburg, Verlag für Börsen- und Finanzliteratur, 1881/82 onwards).
- Handbuch der Grossunternehmen: Anerkannt durch den Adressbuchausschuss der Deutschen Wirtschaft, Darmstadt, Hoppenstedt, (1952 onwards).
- *Handbuch der Deutschen Aktien-Gesellschaften: Das Spezial-Archiv der Deutschen Wirtschaft* (Darmstadt, Wien, Zürich: Verlag für Börsen- und Finanzliteratur, 1896/ 97 onwards).
- *Hoppenstedt Auskunfts-CD Grossunternehmen* (Darmstadt: Hoppenstedt, 1996 onwards).
- *Hoppenstedt Aktienführer, CD* (Darmstadt: Hoppenstedt, 1998 onwards). The balance sheet data were mostly gathered from Hoppenstedt Aktienführer 2002 (2001), which contains the balance sheets and other key data of all German joint-stock companies. If the required data were not available in these periodical publications, they were directly extracted from the published balance sheets, which are collected at the 'Wirtschafts-archiv' (Economic Archive) of the University of Cologne.

Great Britain

- Stock Exchange Yearbook (1876 onwards).
- *The Financial Times.*
- *The Economist.*
- London Stock Exchange Archives.
- Guildhall Library.

Italy

- Italian Ministry of Industry, Bollettino Ufficiale delle Società per Azioni—Bilanci (BUSA).
- Assonime (Associazione Nazionale delle Società per Azioni), Notizie Statistiche.
- R&S, a research company owned by Mediobanca that conducts studies on the Italian economy, stock markets, and enterprises on a regular basis.
- Imita.db ('IMprese ITaliane. Data base'), database built by Reanto Giannetti and Michelangelo Vasta for their work on Italian business in the twentieth century. Built starting from data provided by Notizie Statistiche, it collects various information on 38,182 Italian companies for the period 1911–72.
- Banca Italiana Bilanci (BIB), bibliographical database listing enterprises' balance sheets kept in different historical archives and repositories.
- Intesa Sanpaolo Historical Archives.

Spain

- Anuario financiero de Bilbao que comprende el historial de valores públicos y de sociedades anónimas de España.
- Anuario financiero y de sociedades anónimas de España.

- Anuario oficial de valores de la Bolsa de Madrid.
- Anuario oficial de valores de las Bolsas de Madrid y Barcelona.
- Fomento de la producción, Las Mayores empresas españolas.
- Agenda financiera del Banco de Bilbao.
- Anuario estadístico de la banca privada.
- Informe del Mercado—Apéndice Estadístico Bolsa de Madrid.
- Informe del Mercado—Apéndice Estadístico Bolsa de Barcelona.

Sweden

- Annual reports for relevant companies, 1998–2000.
- *Svenska aktiebolag och enskilda banker* (Stockholm: Norstedts Förlag, 1911–13, 1927, 1928–9, 1954–6, 1977).
- *Sveriges 500 största företag* (Sollentuna: Ekonomisk Litteratur, 1979).
- *Sveriges 500 största företag* (Stockholm: Veckans affärer, 2000).

3

Ownership and Performance in European Big Business

The Longitudinal Perspective

Andrea Colli

INTRODUCTION

This chapter assesses the relationship between the prevalent ownership structures of the largest European companies and their performance from a long-term perspective. It explicitly refers to the main analytical frameworks dealing with the subject:

(a) The 'varieties of capitalism' approach,[1] which emphasizes the persistence over time of different typologies of capitalist systems and thus of ownership structures generated from different institutional frameworks.

(b) The corporate governance approach, dealing with the models of governance proper of the large corporations—basically the shareholder-value theory and the stakeholder models.[2]

(c) The corporate finance approach, which focuses on the causal relation between ownership structure and performances—an approach going back to Berle and Means' seminal research.[3]

(d) The 'strategy–structure–ownership' approach, which emphasizes the relevance of strategic and structural/organizational variables in determining the outcome in terms of performance—whatever its measure.[4]

---

[1] See for instance Peter A. Hall and David Soskice, *Varieties of Capitalism: The Institutional Foundations of Comparative Advantage* (Oxford: Oxford University Press, 2001).

[2] Thomas Clarke, ed., *Theories of Corporate Governance: The Philosophical Foundations of Corporate Governance* (London: Routledge, 2004).

[3] Adolf Berle and Gardiner C. Means, *The Modern Corporation and Private Property* (New York: MacMillan, 1932).

[4] Richard Whittington and Michael Mayer, *The European Corporation: Strategy, Structure and Social Science* (Oxford: Oxford University Press, 2000); Andrea Colli, Abe De Jong, and Martin Iversen, eds., *Mapping European Corporations: Strategy, Structure, Ownership and Performance* (London: Routledge, 2012).

In the light of these approaches, the main research questions in this chapter can be summarized as follows:

1. Is it possible to talk of a 'European model' of big business, or is it better to talk of European 'corporations'? What are the main differences with the US model of managerial control?

2. Across Europe, is there an ongoing process of convergence among different national patterns, or do 'regional' peculiarities still prevail? Are there general trends, common to different country models?

3. Is there any relationship between ownership structures and economic performance?

From a methodological point of view, it is worth mentioning three main issues.

(a) As far as the ownership structures of the largest European corporations are considered, information on a systematic basis and in detail is scarce for at least four of the five benchmarks considered. A proper methodology—the investigation of primary and secondary sources, including the help of 'national experts'—has thus been developed in order to fill the information gap for at least the companies included in the Small Sample.

(b) A second relevant methodological issue concerns the concept of perform-ance itself. The Small and Large Samples (see the Appendix to Chapter 2) provide information about return on equity (ROE) and holding returns for shareholders (HR), which is useful to assess the financial performance of companies with a particular emphasis on the shareholders' perspective. With regard to European corporations in particular, however, it is necessary to bear in mind that financial measures of performance have to be considered from a 'broad' perspective, particularly in the case of companies whose owners can be inclined towards goals other than purely financial ones, as in the case of families or governments. In the analysis in this chapter, financial performance will be considered as absolutely relevant but at the same time as something that has to be carefully framed in a wider perspec-tive, including that of longevity in the sample, a non-financial measure of efficiency.[5]

(c) The data available in the Small Sample, completed with information about ownership structure, could, in principle, constitute good material for econometric analysis aimed at investigating causal relationships be-tween structural variables such as size, ownership, or technological inten-sity on the one hand and economic performance on the other. However, the chapter does not move in this direction. The identification of causal rela-tionships will be explored through qualitative analysis and only to a minor extent through quantitative description. First, this is homogeneous with the other chapters in this book. Second, since this work is a business and economic history, the identification of causal relationships goes beyond the scope of the research.

---

[5] Youssef Cassis, *Big Business: The European Experience in the Twentieth Century* (Oxford: Oxford University Press, 1998), pp. 102ff.

Finally, since this book is mainly composed of country-specific studies dealing with single companies and industries, the discussion here will be based on the examination of general aggregates. References to single cases will be limited in order to avoid overlapping with material in other chapters.

The chapter is structured as follows. After a review of the various theoretical approaches to the study of the ownership structures of the largest European companies following the different research perspectives mentioned earlier, a qualitative analysis of the evidence collected in the Small Sample will be presented to shed some light on the crucial question concerning the existence of a 'European' corporation. Then an assessment of the regional differences in company ownership across Europe will be presented. To conclude, the relationship between the structural features of the largest European corporations and their performances will be discussed.

OWNERSHIP AND PERFORMANCE OF EUROPEAN BIG BUSINESS: THEORETICAL APPROACHES

The relationship between prevailing ownership structures and the performances of European corporations has been analysed in various ways.

A first stream of research, situated between political science and sociology, explicitly refers to the 'varieties of capitalism' approach.[6] The basic idea is to relate different levels of performance at the macro-level of the national economy to institutional and legal variables as 'foundations of competitive advantage'. Institutions matter since they are a decisive element in shaping the environment in which firms are located, grow, and take form. Enterprises survive in a given environment if they adapt to it, and among the relevant components of this process are ownership structures, which do change over space and time, according basically to institutional changes. Obviously, this is not only an exogenous process, endogeneity—the ability of firms to orientate institutional building—plays a relevant role as well. The relationship between ownership structures and macroeconomic performances has been variously interpreted, for instance by those who contrasted the 'European' capitalistic model—based upon concentrated ownership, long-term commitment, and stakeholder involvement—to the US short-term shareholder orientation.[7] A similar, even if more articulated, perspective is that of economic sociology. Richard Whitley[8] individuates a number of 'business systems' in which dominant forms of organizations are again shaped by a mix of cultural and institutional factors, characterized by a broad array of prevalent ownership structures. In all the mentioned examples, however, performances are basically considered at the macro-level, that of the general efficiency of the system,

---

[6] Hall and Soskice, *Varieties of Capitalism*.

[7] Michel Albert, *Capitalisme contre capitalisme* (Paris: Seuil, 1991); Wolfgang Streeck, *Social Institutions and Economic Performance: Studies of Industrial Relations in Advanced Capitalist Economies* (London: Sage, 1992); Suzanne Berger and Ronald Dore, eds., *National Diversity and Global Capitalism* (New York: Cornell University Press, 1996).

[8] Richard Whitley, *Divergent Capitalisms: The Social Structuring and Change of Business Systems* (Oxford: Oxford University Press, 2000).

also in terms of welfare. Only seldom is the analysis of ownership structures relative to different institutional settings and their effects on performance made more explicit.[9]

An in-depth comparative analysis of ownership structures at the microeconomic level is carried on in scholarly research in the field of corporate governance. Data allowing a systematic and comparative analysis of ownership structure of the largest European listed corporations have been available from the beginning of the 1990s, after the issuance of the large holdings European directive (E.E.C. 88/627). Detailed information about ownership stimulated a number of comparative cross-sectional studies.[10] In a large number of cases, however, the main focus of the analysis is the variation of prevailing ownership structures across different capitalist systems[11] as well as the reasons for the persistence of concentrated ownership as a prevailing feature of Continental Europe's large corporations.[12]

The relationship between ownership and performance is more closely addressed by another area of research in the field of corporate finance—one that is interested in the issue of firms' value. Put simply, its main research question concerns which ownership structure generates the best economic performance, which in turn maximizes the firm's value. Predictably, this question has spawned a great number of research papers based on more or less sophisticated datasets. Whatever their structure, the basic ingredients of these studies[13] are the definition of ownership (including the controversial threshold distinguishing between concentrated and dispersed ownership structures) and that of performance, variously defined in terms of returns or Tobin's Q.[14] Nowadays, country studies of a pure empirical nature are widely available, with an almost endless series of mixed results.[15]

[9] Neil Fligstein, *The Architecture of Markets: An Economic Sociology of Twenty-First-Century Capitalist Societies* (Princeton: Princeton University Press, 2002).

[10] See for instance Fabrizio Barca and Marco Becht, eds., *The Control of Corporate Europe* (Oxford: Oxford University Press, 2001).

[11] Rafael La Porta, Florencio Lopez de Silanes, Andrei Shleifer, and Robert Vishny, 'Corporate ownership around the world', *Journal of Finance*, 54, 2 (1999), 471–517; Barca and Becht, *The Control of Corporate Europe*; Mara Faccio and Jerry P. Lang, 'The ultimate ownership of Western European corporations', *Journal of Financial Economics*, 65, 3 (2002), 365–95.

[12] Mark J. Roe, *Political Determinants of Corporate Governance* (Oxford: Oxford University Press, 2003); Lucian Bebchuk and Mark J. Roe, 'A theory of path dependence in corporate ownership and governance', *Stanford Law Review*, 52, 1 (1999), 127–70; Randall Morck, ed., *A History of Corporate Governance Around the World* (Chicago: University of Chicago Press, 2007); Mary O'Sullivan, *Contests for Corporate Control—Corporate Governance and Economic Performance in the United States and Germany* (Oxford: Oxford University Press, 2000).

[13] Starting from Harold Demsetz and Kenneth Lehn, 'The structure of corporate ownership: causes and consequences', *Journal of Political Economy*, 93, 6 (1985), 1155–77.

[14] See for instance Harold Demsetz and Belen Villalonga, 'Ownership structure and corporate performance', *Journal of Corporate Finance*, 7, 3 (2001), 209–33; Ronald G. Anderson and David M. Reeb, 'Founding-family ownership and firm performance: evidence from the S&P 500', *Journal of Finance*, 58, 3 (2003), 1301–28; Raphael Amit and Belen Villalonga, 'How do family ownership, control, and management affect firm value?', *Journal of Financial Economics* 80, 2 (2006), 385–417.

[15] Michael Lemmon and Karl Lins, 'Ownership structure, corporate governance, and firm value: evidence from the East Asian financial crisis' *Journal of Finance* 58, 4 (2003), 1445–68; Emma García-Meca and Juan Pedro Sánchez-Ballesta, 'Firm value and ownership structure in the Spanish capital market', *Corporate Governance*, 11, 1 (2011), 41–53; Jeremy Grant and Thomas Kirchmaier, 'Corporate ownership structure and performance in Europe', CEPDP, 631 (London: Centre for Economic Performance, London School of Economics and Political Science, 2004).

As far as Europe is considered, Thomsen and Pedersen explore the relationship between ownership structure and firms' value.[16] As ownership typologies, they consider institutional investors, banks, (non-financial) companies, single individuals/families, and governments; the measures of performances used are market-to-book value of equity, return on assets, and sales growth. After the usual number of controls—by sector and country—they stress the existence of an inverse-U-shaped relationship between the degree of ownership concentration and performances. Another example is the research by Barontini and Caprio,[17] who emphasize the benefits of family involvement and direct ownership on performances, employing Tobin's Q as their privileged measure.

Whatever the results of these analyses—and they are largely dependent on the nature of the sample and on ownership thresholds—a common feature is basically their cross-sectionalism and the absence of a longitudinal perspective.

Slightly different is the perspective of management studies that have focused on the relationship between strategies, organizational structures, and ownership patterns. Systematic comparative studies on these issues have been carried on from the 1970s at Harvard Business School by a group of PhD students coordinated by Bruce Scott and supervised, among others, by Alfred Chandler. The group has produced a number of country studies, largely focusing on Europe, the aim of which was to investigate the strategy–structure relationship (the process of diversification of the large corporation coupled with an increasing diffusion of the multidivisional form) in various countries such as the UK,[18] France and Germany,[19] and Italy[20] in order to compare European developments with the American benchmark.[21] The results of this joint effort are well known: compared with US companies, European enterprises were slower in adopting strategies of related and non-related diversification, and even slower in shifting to the associated managerial structures. The determinants that explained this gap, as the Harvard researchers recited from case after case, were the role of the state, the prevalent business culture, and the absence of a efficient, motivated, and properly trained managerial elite. But the origin of the problem was mainly in concentrated ownership, which prevented the evolution of organizational structures towards the archetype of the M-form. Thus, ownership structure was the root cause of the relative backwardness of European corporations. In the studies of the 'Harvardians', however, a careful analysis of the relationships between strategy, structure, ownership, and performance is hard to find. In the works of Chandler and

[16] Steen Thomsen and Torben Pedersen, 'Ownership structure and economic performance in the largest European companies', *Strategic Management Journal*, 21, 6 (2000), 689–705.

[17] Roberto Barontini and Lorenzo Caprio, 'The effect of family control on firm value and performance: evidence from Continental Europe', EFA 2005 Moscow Meetings Paper. Available at SSRN: http://ssrn.com/abstract=675983.

[18] Derek F. Channon, *The Strategy and Structure of British Enterprise* (London: Macmillan Press, 1973).

[19] Gareth Dyas and Heinz Tanheiser, *The Emerging European Enterprise* (London: Macmillan Press, 1976).

[20] Robert J. Pavan, *Strategies and Structures of the Italian European Enterprises*, Unpublished Dissertation, Harvard Business School (1976).

[21] Richard P. Rumelt, *Strategy, Structure and Economic Performance*, (Cambridge, Mass.: Harvard University Press, 1974).

Penrose, performance is basically measured in terms of size, market shares, or even longevity.

A step forward was subsequently made by Richard Whittington and Michael Mayer in their longitudinal and comparative analysis of the largest French, German, and British corporations.[22] As a measure of performance, the two British scholars use return on assets, 'a good measure of efficiency and the most popular financial performance measure in the strategy field'.[23] Needless to say, their data confirm the direct relationship between the adoption of multidivisional structures and better financial performance. Other recent collaborative research combines the strategy–structure–ownership framework with more detailed measures of performances ranging across physical, market, and financial measures.[24]

To sum up, the various theoretical approaches assess the issue of the performance of big business in different ways, in some cases privileging the macroeconomic effect of ownership distribution or focusing on agency issues. Those taking explicit account of financial performances at the microeconomic level are normally cross-sectional, totally lacking—with few exceptions—a longitudinal perspective.

By combining relatively simple measures of financial performance with other structural features in the long run, the present research moves a step forward in the direction of an analysis of the ownership–performance relationship among large European companies from both a cross-sectional and a longitudinal perspective.

OWNERSHIP STRUCTURES: EVIDENCE FROM THE LARGEST EUROPEAN COMPANIES IN THE LONG RUN

Before proceeding with the analysis, some further methodological caveats are necessary, pertaining to the quality of the data available and to the methodology of analysis followed. As business historians know well, one of the main challenges of research in the field of ownership structure and corporate performance is the wide variability in the quality and reliability of the data, which very often have to be collected through time-consuming prosopographic research. Thus, inevitably, all research, even the most accurate, suffers from some flaws:

(a) It is difficult, and in some cases almost impossible, to ascertain the effective block-holding quota (the amount of ownership quotas, both direct and indirect) before the late 1980s and in some cases before the 1990s. Disclosure practices have been improving enormously, but only during the last two decades. Additionally, differences across countries—in terms of the availability of information—are still considerable, and were much more so in the past. Even the available business history literature about single

---

[22] Richard Whittington and Michael Mayer, *The European Corporation: Strategy, Structure and Social Science* (Oxford: Oxford University Press, 2000).

[23] Whittington and Mayer, *The European Corporation*, p. 151.

[24] Andrea Colli, Abe De Jong, and Martin Iversen, eds., *Mapping European Corporations: Strategy, Structure, Ownership and Performance* (London: Routledge, 2012).

companies, based on primary sources and company archival information, rarely mentions the exact distribution of ownership quotas. A first, severe, limitation is that in comparative historical research such as that carried out in this book, only the nature of ownership can be established with a good degree of accuracy, but rarely the exact amount of the controller's shareholdings.

(b) The historical evidence shows that ownership categories in use in corporate finance research have to be enriched—or rather made more 'historical'—in order to take into account typologies widely in use in the past, such as shareholder agreements, coalitions, managerial self-control, holdings, and even cartels. Cartels, in particular, were legal in interwar Europe and also for some years after the Second World War. Their survival was often made possible through the establishment of cross-shareholdings among the members of the cartel itself, which makes the analysis of ownership distribution in some cases quite complicated.[25]

(c) Some ownership structures found in the past are difficult to standardize. This applies, for instance, to Italy's largest banks before their nationalization in 1933 and to many of the country's largest companies in utilities. Their share ownership was apparently fragmented, with no holdings exceeding a few percentage points. This, however, was accompanied by the presence of tacit agreements among major shareholders plus the widespread willingness of small shareholders to delegate their administrative rights to the management, which thus was de facto able to maintain a stable control over the company. In such a situation is clearly not possible to talk of a shareholder agreement or of public ownership. A group of a *happy few* (managers and an inner circle of shareholders) were enjoying the benefits of entrenchment in terms of value extraction. In order to avoid an excessive fragmentation of the analysis, however, these deviant cases have been forced into one of the existing taxonomies—in this specific case, that of pacts and agreements.

A realistic (and historically acceptable) classification of ownership categories is thus the following: widely held (WID), family/individuals (FAM), state (SOE), financial institution (bank/insurance company) (FIN), holding/foundation (HOL), other non-financial company (ONF), foreign (FOR), and shareholders' agreement (including cartels) (SHA). For the purposes of this chapter, ownership has been ascertained on the basis of secondary sources: available business history literature, directories of company histories, websites, and interviews with national experts.[26] In uncertain cases, information has been double-checked. In line with the prevalent practice in corporate governance and finance research, the threshold between concentrated and diffuse ownership has been set at 10 per cent. Information about ownership has been added to those already present in the Small

[25] Jeffrey Fear, 'Cartels', in Geoffrey Jones and Jonathan Zeitlin, eds., *Oxford Handbook of Business History* (Oxford: Oxford University Press, 2007).

[26] I want here to express my gratitude to Franco Amatori, Veronica Binda, Frans Buelens, Youssef Cassis, Terry Gourvish, Riitta Hjerrpe, Hervé Joly, Mats Larsson, Andrea Schneider, Harm G. Schroeter, and Tony Pierenkemper for their invaluable support.

Table 3.1. Sample composition: number of companies by country

Country	No. of companies[a]
Belgium	10
Finland	5
France	20
Germany	25
Italy	15
Spain	10
Sweden	10
United Kingdom	30
Total	125

[a] For the criteria for company selection and country quotas, see Chapter 2

Table 3.2. Ownership categories in the entire sample, 1913–2000 (absolute numbers)

	1913		1927		1954		1972		2000	
SOE	6	0.05	9	0.07	33	0.26	26	0.21	18	0.14
HOL	3	0.02	6	0.05	5	0.04	11	0.09	7	0.06
FIN	14	0.11	10	0.08	12	0.10	9	0.07	11	0.09
FOR	12	0.10	10	0.08	5	0.04	4	0.03	9	0.07
SHA	8	0.06	10	0.08	4	0.03	5	0.04	3	0.02
ONF	6	0.05	3	0.02	6	0.05	9	0.07	2	0.02
WID	56	0.45	57	0.46	48	0.38	50	0.40	59	0.47
FAM	20	0.16	20	0.16	12	0.10	11	0.09	16	0.13
N	125	1	125	1	125	1	125	1	125	1

Source: Small Sample, own elaborations

Sample. Table 3.1 presents the number of companies for each country considered in each benchmark year.

Table 3.2 shows the distribution of the whole sample by ownership category. Some trends are quite evident: the rise and fall of state-owned enterprises, and the predominance of widely held companies, which constitute the largest ownership category in the sample throughout the whole period under consideration. Family ownership—the second ownership category by number of companies—declines in relevance in the period following the Second World War and rises again in the last benchmark, the same trend shown by foreign ownership. Ownership by financial institutions is constantly around 10 per cent of the sample. These trends are consistent with qualitative evidence about the history of European capitalism,[27] including the expansion of state direct intervention in the economy in the post-war decades.[28]

[27] Harm Schroeter, ed., *The European Enterprise: Investigation into a Future Species* (Berlin: Springer-Verlag, 2007); Franco Amatori and Andrea Colli, *Business History: Complexities and Comparisons* (London: Routledge, 2011).

[28] Pierangelo Toninelli, ed., *The Rise and Fall of State-Owned Enterprise in the Western World* (Cambridge: Cambridge University Press, 2000).

The main novelty revealed by the data in Table 3.2 is the overwhelming presence of widely held companies, companies that lack block-holdings exceeding 10 per cent of the share capital. Given the common view that European capitalism is historically characterized by concentrated ownership, this is a quite surprising result. It also diverges from the available research in the field of corporate finance, which emphasizes the relevance of families and governments as corporate owners.[29] To some extent, this outcome is the result of the research methodology used here. For one, British companies make up around a quarter of the sample, and they are largely widely held. Additionally, the sample is clearly biased towards the largest companies of each country, thus increasing the probability of dispersed ownership also in other countries. Indeed, even if British companies are excluded from the sample, widely held companies are still the largest group among the Continental European corporations in all benchmark years. The high prevalence of widely held companies is quite impressive, in particular for the first three benchmarks, in which it was expected that the ownership of the British corporations would be characterized by a higher incidence of personal and family ownership.[30] A further explanation for the high number could be the ownership threshold used. Ten per cent is a relatively high cut-off threshold, which risks labelling as widely held companies that are in fact characterized by concentrated control. A final potential source of bias that would increase the number of companies in the widely held category is the 'federal' nature of many large companies, especially British: mergers were often a formality, and former owners went on with their business without much interference from the new headquarters.[31] The new firm, a result of the merger of several companies, was thus apparently characterized by dispersed ownership but was de facto an agglomeration of family firms.

As far as family ownership is concerned, basing the categorization solely on data reporting direct family ownership may be misleading. It is known from qualitative research that in the European tradition families could exert effectively dominant control through the use of various mechanisms such as shareholders' agreements and holdings. Yet to consider all data reported under these two categories as actually indicating family ownership would also be misleading. Nonetheless, the possible link between the three characteristics increases the potential importance of family ownership as a category of company ownership.

Figure 3.1 shows the distribution of total assets according to the most important ownership typologies. The predominance of widely held companies is clearly evident, but the figure indicates an evident partial reciprocity with state-owned companies; the U-shaped curve of widely held ownership is crudely mirrored in the inversely U-shaped curve of state ownership. In terms of assets, corporate

---

[29] La Porta et al., 'Corporate ownership', Table II; Whittington and Mayer, *The European Corporation*, pp. 90ff.; Faccio and Lang, 'The ultimate ownership', Table 3.

[30] Cassis, *Big Business*. Recent research tends, however, to confirm the precocious separation between ownership and control in Britain; see Brian Cheffins, *Corporate Ownership and Control: British Business Transformed* (Oxford: Oxford University Press, 2008) and James Foreman-Peck and Leslie Hannah, 'Extreme divorce: the managerial revolution in UK companies before 1914', *Economic History Review*, 65, 4 (2012), 1217–38.

[31] John F. Wilson, *British Business History* (Manchester: Manchester University Press, 1995), p. 103.

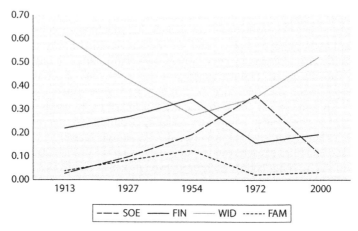

Figure 3.1. Distribution of assets under control by ownership category, 1913–2000
Source: Small Sample, own elaborations

control by financial institutions is considerably important as well, notwithstanding the small number of companies involved. The trend line of roughly 15–30 per cent of assets confirms the European feature of powerful financial institutions able to control important industrial players (see also Table 3.8). Company assets under personal or family control rose steadily until the 1950s, after which they declined. A key reason for this development is again the sample composition, which privileged the largest companies. A second reason is linked to the transition across technological paradigms. The technologies of the First Industrial Revolution, which prevailed in the first benchmark and were still central in the second, were consistent with a relatively reduced company size. The congruency between technology and organizational size could explain not only the diffusion of family ownership up to the Second World War and immediately after, but also its decline from the 1970s as the optimal company size associated with newer technologies increased beyond the control capabilities of individuals and/or families.

The distribution of assets by ownership, in sum, basically confirms the trends shown by the absolute number of companies presented in Table 3.2. But the numerical predominance of widely held companies was not always reflected in a similar predominance in assets. In the mid 1950s, banks controlled the largest proportion of company assets, and in the early 1970s the assets of state-owned companies were as large as those of widely held companies, a reflection of the widespread nationalization in the 1950s and 1960s. The database also allows a look behind the aggregate curves. Companies controlled by financial institutions were, before the Second World War, by far the largest companies in terms of capital assets, whereas family-controlled or widely held companies were generally smaller.

The overview offers, in sum, mixed evidence about the existence of a 'European' model of company ownership. On the one hand, the notion of a persistent presence of concentrated patterns of control is out of the question. On the other hand, widely held companies—as defined by a 10 per cent cut-off—seem to constitute a much more important and widely diffused ownership category than commonly suggested in the history of European big business.

In terms of national origin, 71 of the 180 widely held companies present in at least one benchmark are British, 38 French, 37 German, 16 Scandinavian (Swedish and Finnish), 9 Spanish, 3 Belgian, and 1 Italian. In Italy, Spain, and Sweden, the majority of companies are family-owned, whereas there are no family-owned companies in the British sample. There are thus clear differences among European countries in terms of prevailing ownership patterns, differences that the longitudinal perspective sharpens even further. In order to test the extent of these differences, the following analysis will divide the whole sample into two groups: the 'core' countries—Great Britain, Germany, and France, which industrialized first and fastest as well as having the largest GDPs, internal markets, and generally the greatest economic dynamism, and the 'European peripheries'—in this case the late industrializers Italy, Spain, Sweden, and Finland together with Belgium, which industrialized early but has a very small domestic economy. The basic idea is to investigate if differences emerge between these two groups that can shed light on the effective existence of a 'European model' of big business.

OWNERSHIP: REGIONAL DIFFERENCES IN THE LONG RUN

Table 3.3 shows the relationship between assets and ownership type in the core European economies of Britain, France, and Germany throughout the twentieth century. The data confirm—and in some cases accentuate—the general trend described in the previous paragraphs. Widely held companies are always the most numerous category, constituting more than 50 per cent of businesses. Their predominance in terms of assets is clear but less absolute; in 1954–6, they controlled only one-third of the group's assets rather than the customary over 50 per cent. At the other end of the scale, family firms never have much weight either numerically or in terms of assets controlled. The position of the other two

Table 3.3. Ownership and distribution of total assets in the core: UK, France, and Germany, 1913–2000 (as a fraction of the total; $N = 75$ each year)

	1913		1927		1954		1972		2000	
	No.	Assets	No.	Assets	No.	Assets	No.	Assets	No.	Assets
SOE	0.05	0.01	0.05	0.01	0.17	0.10	0.15	0.26	0.11	0.10
FIN	0.09	0.24	0.09	0.39	0.08	0.50	0.05	0.22	0.07	0.21
WID	0.68	0.70	0.68	0.58	0.55	0.34	0.56	0.42	0.65	0.58
FAM	0.12	0.03	0.11	0.02	0.08	0.02	0.07	0.01	0.07	0.01
OTH	0.05	0.02	0.07	0.01	0.12	0.04	0.17	0.09	0.11	0.09
Of which										
FOR	0.01	0.00	0.03	0.00	0.07	0.02	0.05	0.02	0.04	0.08
HOL	0.00	0.00	0.01	0.00	0.00	0.00	0.05	0.03	0.03	0.00
SHA	0.01	0.01	0.01	0.00	0.01	0.01	0.01	0.02	0.03	0.01
ONF	0.03	0.01	0.01	0.00	0.04	0.01	0.05	0.01	0.01	0.00

Source: Small Sample, own elaborations

Table 3.4. Ownership and distribution of total assets in the periphery: Belgium, Finland, Italy, Spain, and Sweden, 1913–2000 (fraction of the total; $N = 50$ each year)

	1913		1927		1954		1972		2000	
	No.	Assets	No.	Assets	No.	Assets	No.	Assets	No.	Assets
SOE	0.04	0.12	0.10	0.29	0.40	0.36	0.30	0.55	0.20	0.16
FIN	0.14	0.13	0.06	0.02	0.12	0.05	0.10	0.03	0.12	0.12
WID	0.10	0.07	0.12	0.11	0.14	0.17	0.16	0.21	0.20	0.34
FAM	0.22	0.08	0.24	0.22	0.12	0.31	0.12	0.05	0.22	0.10
OTH	0.50	0.59	0.48	0.35	0.22	0.11	0.32	0.16	0.26	0.28
Of which										
FOR	0.22	0.23	0.16	0.11	0.00	0.00	0.00	0.00	0.12	0.02
HOL	0.06	0.06	0.10	0.07	0.10	0.06	0.14	0.10	0.10	0.24
SHA	0.14	0.28	0.18	0.09	0.06	0.04	0.08	0.04	0.02	0.03
ONF	0.08	0.03	0.04	0.08	0.06	0.01	0.10	0.02	0.02	0.00

Source: Small Sample, own elaborations

ownership categories varies a good deal. Financial institutions never control more than 10 per cent of the companies, yet they controlled 50 per cent of the assets in 1970–2 and 39 per cent in 1954–76. State-owned companies have a marginal presence until the mid-1950s, but in the early 1970s they jump into second place in terms of assets controlled before falling back by the end of the century.

Table 3.4 presents data for the so-called European periphery—here Belgium, Finland, Italy, Spain, and Sweden—that reveal substantial differences from the core country dynamics for almost all ownership typologies.

(a) In the peripheral countries, widely held companies are much less numerous and control a smaller fraction of the top companies' total assets. Whereas in the core countries they show a marked U-shaped trend, in the periphery they show a steady, increasing penetration, which confirms the positive correlation between the diffusion of companies characterized by a highly dispersed share ownership and the affirmation of highly capital-intensive industries. In sum, in the long run, the peripheral countries tend to converge with the core countries as regards the importance of widely held companies.

(b) The role of financial institutions as controllers of companies and assets is very limited, much less than in the core countries.

(c) The trend in the role of state-owned enterprises is similar to that found in the core countries (and to the general one), but more pronounced: peripheral countries show a very high degree of government intervention, even before the Second World War, in terms of the number of state-owned corporations and of the assets under their control. Similarly, family ownership is more widely present than in the core countries, reflecting the relative scarcity of widely held companies and the relatively smaller size of the large companies in the periphery.

(d) Finally, it is worth noting that corporations with ownership structures different from the main four categories (SOE, FIN, WID, and FAM) are quite rare in the core countries, but rather frequent in the periphery. This wider variety in ownership structures can be explained by various elements. For instance, foreign ownership is higher in peripheral countries in the first two benchmarks, disappearing after 1927–9 and reappearing in 1998–2000, which is perfectly understandable given the backwardness of these national economies at least until the 1950s. Holdings and shareholder agreements—structures that can be seen as an 'intermediate' stage on the continuum between highly concentrated and dispersed ownership—are definitely much more prevalent in the smaller peripheral countries than in the central core countries, which confirms the fact that ownership structures roughly reflect the general maturation of domestic big business. A further confirmation of this interpretation is that the relevance of these 'particular' categories of ownership in peripheral countries seems to decline over time.

To summarize, the long-term perspective emphasizes the existence of relevant differences in terms of ownership across Europe. While in the core countries the overwhelming presence of widely held companies and the importance of owner- ship by financial institutions are the evident consequence of a faster maturation of capitalist enterprise, the picture is much more variegated in the peripheral countries.

Additional insight into these results is provided in Table 3.5, which compares the average company size by total assets in the countries investigated, using the British average as the base number. With some notable anomalies, the divide between core and peripheral countries is confirmed. The most evident exception is Spain, where the average size of large companies grew steadily in the first half of the century and since the 1950s has even exceeded the British base number. The primary reason for this development—which is partly seen also in Italy—is the emergence of state-owned enterprises in strategic capital intensive industries.

In general, however, the smaller size of companies in the peripheral countries is consistent with the persistence of concentrated control; as noted above, in a long-term perspective, the convergence in size across European big business is accompanied by a convergence in ownership structures. Still, from a historical perspective, it is hard to identify, at least in terms of ownership structures, a general type of 'European big business'. During a large part of the twentieth century, in fact, national differences prevail, mainly because of the structural features of national big firms, which are in turn determined by the opportunities for growth in the domestic market, by governmental support to big business, and by the timing in shift to the technological paradigm of the Second Industrial Revolution.

Table 3.5. Average company size by total assets, 1913–2000 (UK = 100)

	1913	1927	1954	1972	2000
Belgium	30	76	40	37	18
Finland	14	4	10	11	23
France	110	29	25	79	108
Germany	64	28	27	79	152
Italy	34	25	36	120	77
Spain	30	66	104	104	105
Sweden	17	17	26	37	46

Source: Small Sample, own elaborations

OWNERSHIP AND PERFORMANCE:
EVIDENCE FROM EUROPE

As suggested earlier, the relationship between ownership structures and performances is quite controversial in the existing literature, and results are far from
unambiguous. In this section, both financial (measured by return on assets[32]) and
structural (by longevity) performances will be taken into account.

Table 3.6 shows the trends in the aggregate three-year average return on equity
(ROE) for the companies in the Small Sample according to regional category.
A relative stability characterizes the first three benchmarks (the end of the Belle
Époque, the growth of the 1920s, and the beginning of the European 'economic
miracle'), while the turbulences of the 1970s are quite evident in the fourth
benchmark, and the values in the last benchmark confirm the economic revival
of the 1990s. The core countries yield generally better performances, but ROE in
the peripheral countries increases steadily in the first half of the century, a result of
the acceleration of industrialization process as well as the increasing dynamism
in the respective domestic markets.

What has to be demonstrated is that the persistence of variegated ownership
structures and of concentrated control has some impact on the level of financial
performance, or, better still, that different ownership structures lead to significant
variations in the ability of firms to generate good financial returns. In order to
maximize the reliability of the analysis, only the ownership categories for which a
reasonable number of observations are available will be considered, namely state-
owned companies, firms under family control, those controlled by financial
institutions, and widely held companies.

Table 3.7 reports the aggregate profitability of companies in the Small Sample
according to ownership category. The analysis is limited to the aggregate level,
since the individual country chapters of this book provide much more detailed
assessments of the trends at the 'local' level.

In short, the data are mixed and do not support unambiguous conclusions. First
of all, some trends are evident that confirm general tendencies discussed earlier as
well as already widely analysed in the literature—for instance, the dramatic drop
in the performances of state-owned enterprises in the last three decades of the
century. As far as the other categories are concerned, all show a clear tendency to
follow the macroeconomic cycle—a decline in the interwar years, a resurgence in

Table 3.6. Aggregate three-year average ROE by regional category, 1911–2000 (in %)

	1911–13	1927–9	1954–6	1970–2	1998–2000
All	10.09	10.09	10.54	7.69	14.05
Core	6.38	5.85	4.45	5.04	8.98
Periphery	3.38	4.16	5.97	2.61	4.88

Source: Small Sample, own elaborations

---

[32] Information on holding returns is too lacunose to allow an acceptable analysis.

Table 3.7. Aggregate three-year average ROE by ownership category, 1911–2000 (in %)

	1911–13	1927–9	1954–6	1970–2	1998–2000
FAM	14.87	11.08	17.65	8.02	12.71
SOE	11.60	8.79	13.49	2.15	3.15
WID	10.01	9.15	7.92	10.02	16.45
FIN	9.74	14.33	7.79	10.90	16.89
All	10.09	10.09	10.54	7.69	14.05

Source: Small Sample, own elaborations

Table 3.8. Average assets by ownership category, 1913–2000 (widely held = 100)

	1911–13	1927–9	1954–6	1970–2	1998–2000
FAM	20	56	182	14	22
SOE	43	145	101	53	76
WID	100	100	100	100	100
FIN	145	354	496	117	188

Source: Small Sample, own elaborations

1950s, and a decline in the troubled early 1970s—with the notable exception of companies controlled by financial institutions, which show a countercyclical behaviour, at least for the first three benchmarks. Given the scarcity of the available information, however, it is hazardous to put forward any ambitious hypothesis. What can be noticed when comparing the curves of individual categories with the general curve is that family-controlled firms tend to outperform the rest in the first three benchmarks when the size factor is probably not so very determinant and then drop behind widely held corporations and companies controlled by financial institutions in the last two benchmarks. It thus appears that family firms can perform well so long as maintaining technological efficiency does not demand an immoderate enlargement of company size. Once size becomes a crucial variable—with the predominance of scale-intensive industries and the advent of the Third Industrial Revolution, widely held companies and companies controlled by financial institutions, which in theory have more ready resources to support larger establishments—perform better. As Table 3.8 shows, except in 1954–6, the average size by assets of family-controlled firms is always smaller than that of the other types of company. A hypothesis of the growing importance of firm size—at least among the very large corporations—for profitability would explain quite well the decline in the overall performance of family-controlled firms, since such companies are seldom able to grow enough to cope with the requirements of new technological paradigms. However, such a hypothesis is far from being verified. A correlation analysis between size (in terms of total assets) and ROE reveals little or no statistical relationship, indicating that financial performance is not generally a function of firm size.

The search for causal relationships between ownership categories and company performance can be deepened by investigating the role of the technological intensity of companies. Technological intensity is measured according to the

Table 3.9. Technological intensity of companies in the Small Sample, 1913–2000 (absolute numbers)

	1913	1927	1954	1972	2000
High-tech	5	17	22	23	30
Medium-tech	76	66	66	58	44
Low-tech	19	16	10	10	10
Other	25	26	27	34	41
Total	125	125	125	125	125

Source: Small Sample, own elaborations

classification proposed by Thomas Hatzinchronoglou,[33] which has four broad categories: high-, medium-, and low-tech and 'others', namely, finance, insurance, leisure, and tourism.[34] The results of a breakdown of the Small Sample by technological intensity are reported in Table 3.9.

The data show quite well the shift across different technological paradigms towards the increasing importance of the tertiary sector (essentially, financial services). Low- and medium-tech industries decline in number over time, a decrease mirrored in the growing number of high-tech companies and of those in financial services and insurance. These trends, which are perfectly consistent with the literature on the impact of technological change on the composition of the population of large firms,[35] confirm that European enterprises as a whole follow the US pattern of development. Unsurprisingly, there are differences in the timing of the process between core and peripheral countries. The adoption of new technological paradigms and the abandonment of obsolete ones occur much more rapidly in the core than in the periphery. A further though indirect confirmation of the lag between the regional categories is given by the data showing the relationship between size and technological intensity (see Table 3.10). Companies in low-tech industries are generally smaller than those in medium- and high-tech. Notably, medium-tech companies generally have the largest firm size in three of the five benchmarks.

Nevertheless, it is difficult to single out a clear causal relationship between financial performances and technological intensity. Table 3.11 gives a breakdown of technological intensity and ROE over the whole of the century.

Apart from the already-noted general decline in the level of performances in 1970–2, the only evident trend is that companies in finance and insurance tend to perform better in almost all the benchmarks considered. The differences among high-, medium-, and low-tech companies in terms of ROE are clearly not great.

---

[33] Thomas Hatzichronoglou, 'Revision of the high-technology sector and product classification', *OECD Science, Technology and Industry Working Papers*, 1997/02 (Paris: OECD Publishing, 1997), p. 5.
[34] Low-tech: construction; food, drink, and tobacco; textile and leather products; wood and paper products; media and entertainment. Medium-tech: transport equipment; oil, rubber, and other non-metallic mineral products; utilities; electricity, gas and water supply; railways; mining; basic and fabricated metals. High-tech: post and telecommunications; electrical engineering; chemicals and pharmaceuticals; mechanical engineering.
[35] Alfred Chandler, *Scale and Scope: The Dynamics of Industrial Capitalism* (Cambridge, Mass.: Harvard University Press, 1990).

Table 3.10. Average size by total assets and technological intensity, 1913–2000 (high-tech = 100)

	1913	1927	1954	1972	2000
High-tech	100	100	100	100	100
Medium-tech	195	184	94	116	81
Low-tech	77	79	116	59	36

Source: Small Sample, own elaborations

Table 3.11. Three-year average ROE by technological intensity, 1911–2000 (in %)

	1911–13	1927–9	1954–6	1970–2	1998–2000
High-tech	12.38	10.00	6.90	6.78	17.99
Medium-tech	10.62	9.27	9.68	5.76	11.06
Low-tech	8.67	10.21	8.31	10.47	16.08
Other	10.19	12.81	18.05	11.34	15.73

Source: Small Sample, own elaborations

Remarkably, companies in low-tech industries seem to perform better in the long run than those in medium- and even high-tech sectors. Since financial performances seem to be poorly related to size, this is not totally surprising.

As pointed out in other research on European big business,[36] longevity can be considered another relevant dimension of a company's economic performance. In the sample there are ten companies that can be considered 'very long survivors', that is, present in all five benchmarks, and twenty-one 'long survivors' present in at least four of five. Thus, around 7.5 per cent of the companies in the Small Sample are quite long-lived, even though the absence of analogous research on an European scale makes these results incomparable with similar evidence. However, it is hard to determine any causal relationship between longevity and company economic activity: almost all the industries present in the sample— manufacturing, banking, and services—are represented in the group of 'long survivors' (Table 3.12). By far the most frequent ownership category among the 'long survivors' is the widely held company, followed at a distance by companies controlled by financial institutions. A much less frequently found ownership category is state ownership, which is consistent with the limited lifespan of nationalization in Europe. Almost completely absent from the group is the family firm, which is represented by a single company, namely Fiat, constantly under the control of the Agnelli family for the whole of the twentieth century. A closer look at the 'long survivors' also reveals that many of them remain, notwithstanding even frequent changes in ownership: for example, Spanish Telefónica goes from foreign ownership (second benchmark) to state ownership (third and fourth) and finally to dispersed ownership; French Credit Lyonnais goes from widely held ownership (first and second benchmarks) to state ownership (third and fourth); Italian Montecatini goes from control by the Donegani family to the control of a

---

[36] Cassis, *Big Business*, pp. 103ff.

Table 3.12. 'Long survivors': companies present in at least four of the five benchmarks

	Country	Company name[a]	Industry
1	DE	Allgemeine Elektricitäts-Gesellschaft (AEG)	Electrical engineering
2	DE	Badische Anilin- & Soda-Fabrik (BASF)	Oil, rubber, chemicals, and other non-metallic mineral products
3	DE	Farbenfabriken vorm. Friedrich Bayer & Co. (Bayer)	Oil, rubber, chemicals, and other non-metallic mineral products
4	DE	Bayerische Hypotheken- und Wechsel-Bank	Financial intermediation
5	DE	Commerz- und Privat-Bank Aktiengesellschaft (Commerzbank)	Financial intermediation
6	DE	Deutsche Bank	Financial intermediation
7	DE	Dresdner Bank	Financial intermediation
8	DE	Fried. Krupp AG	Basic and fabricated metals
9	DE	Rheinisch-Westfälisches Elektrizitätswerk AG (RWE)	Utilities; Electricity, gas, and water supply
10	SE	Skandinaviska bank	Financial intermediation
11	GB	Anglo-Persian Oil (British Petroleum)	Oil, rubber, and other non-metallic mineral products
12	GB	Barclays Bank	Financial intermediation
13	GB	British-American Tobacco Co	Food, drink, and tobacco products
14	GB	Guest, Keen & Nettlefolds	Basic and fabricated metals
15	GB	Imperial Chemical Industries (ICI)	Chemicals and pharmaceuticals
16	GB	Imperial Tobacco Company [of Great Britain & Ireland]	Food, drink, and tobacco products
17	GB	Lever Brothers (Unilever)	Oil, rubber, chemicals, and other non-metallic mineral products
18	GB	Lloyds Bank	Financial intermediation
19	GB	Shell Transport and Trading Company	Oil, rubber, chemicals, and other non-metallic mineral products
20	IT	Banca Commerciale Italiana	Financial intermediation
21	IT	ILVA	Basic and fabricated metals
22	IT	FIAT	Transport equipment
23	IT	Montecatini (Montedison)	Chemicals and pharmaceuticals
24	FR	Thomson-Houston (Alsthom)	Electrical engineering
25	FR	Banque de Paris et des Pays-Bas (Paribas)	Financial intermediation
26	FR	Crédit Lyonnais	Financial intermediation
27	FR	Saint-Gobain	Oil, rubber, chemicals, and other non-metallic mineral products
28	FR	Société Générale	Financial intermediation
29	ES	Telefonica Nacional de Espana, CIA., 'CTNE' (Telefonica)	Transport and communication

[a] This is the name with which the company first appear in the dataset. The most commonly used abbreviations are shown in parentheses

shareholder coalition and finally comes under the control of a holding (Gemina), which in turn is controlled by Mediobanca, a financial institution. Such evidence suggests strongly that longevity can be positively associated with dispersed ownership, even though there are a number of cases in which 'long survivors' show the capability to pass through different ownership regimes without any problem, as well as a very few cases in which 'long survivors' are under the control of a financial institution.

In sum, the long-term relationship between financial performance and structural characteristics in European big business remains quite obscure.[37] The common view, which considers that a dispersed ownership structure leads to better financial performances, does not seem confirmed in the European case, at least not by the evidence found in the Small Sample. Companies under the control of families and financial institutions also show good performances after the 1970s, especially so when compared with the poor returns of state-owned enterprises. Financial performance seems also to be uninfluenced by technological intensity or company size (measured in terms of total assets), two variables that can in turn be determined by the ownership typology. Dispersed ownership does seems to influence a different kind of performance though, namely survival. In the midst of these negative or weak relationships, however, there is a clear positive association: country location. Geography seems to matter a good deal: companies on the periphery perform more poorly than those in core countries, presumably because of the low dynamism of the respective domestic markets.

CONCLUSIONS

As far as ownership is concerned, the evidence emerging from the database confirms the historical predominance of concentrated control among the largest European corporations. Families and individuals, financial institutions, and the state are the most frequent owners throughout the entire twentieth century. Other ownership types whose relevance changes over time and place can be added: shareholders' agreements and control exerted via other companies, both manufacturing and financial (holdings). The distribution of ownership typologies proves remarkably resilient over time. The 'control of corporate Europe' today is still fundamentally grounded in the same categories of block-holders already widely used in the past.[38]

Public companies are, however, much more important than suggested by existing research, and not only in countries, such as Britain, that are characterized

---

[37] This may obviously be due to the structural features of the sample, the choice of benchmarks, and the number of observations. The availability of a wider amount of empirical evidence can provide more solid results, as shown by Michelangelo Vasta, 'Firm performance (1900–1971)', in Renato Giannetti and Michelangelo Vasta, eds., *Evolution of Italian Enterprises in the 20th Century* (Heidelberg: Physica Verlag, 2006); however, his research is limited to Italy and does not consider ownership as a relevant determinant of performance.

[38] Barca and Becht, *The Control.*

by a precocious separation between ownership and control.[39] The data confirm in fact a process of convergence in ownership structures particularly during the last decades of the twentieth century, with widely held corporations exceeding in absolute number all other ownership categories.

On a closer view, however, it is difficult to talk of a single type of 'European corporation', at least in terms of ownership structures. *Rheinisch* capitalism is not only different from Anglo-Saxon capitalism, but is also widely differentiated in itself according to the individual countries' path of industrialization. The state's role in the economies of the European periphery, for instance, and its influence on big business performance there, are very different from the role the state plays in the economies of the 'core' countries, and the same can be said for foreign-controlled firms. Widely held companies spread earlier in some areas than others, introducing different goals and managerial philosophies.

As for the relationship between ownership and performance, the evidence in the database is mixed. At the aggregate level and in the long run, financial performance seem unrelated to a specific ownership structure as well as to other structural variables such as technology and firm size. Yet there are a few reasonably firmly established findings: financial institutions tend to perform better than companies in manufacturing and in the primary sector; companies in core countries perform better than those in the periphery; ROEs are more a function of the macroeconomic cycle than of the structural characteristics of individual companies. The sole performance criterion in some way influenced by ownership is longevity, which is positively related to dispersed ownership.

ACKNOWLEDGEMENTS

In writing this chapter, I have benefited from suggestions and helpful comments by Franco Amatori. He was originally intended to be a co-author, but personal reasons prevented him from doing so. I obviously bear the sole responsibility for any errors or omissions.

---

[39] Cheffins, *Corporate Ownership and Control.*

Part II
Countries' Performance

4

The Performance of Belgian Enterprises in the Twentieth Century

Frans Buelens, Ludo Cuyvers, Marc Deloof,
and Helma De Smedt

INTRODUCTION

After the Industrial Revolution in Britain, Belgium was the first country to take part in the Industrial Revolution on the European continent. From the 1830s onwards, numerous investments were made in the sectors of textiles, coal mining, non-ferrous metals (zinc), glass, iron (and later steel), breweries, and transport equipment, and in the metalworking industry. Under the leadership of the mixed banks Société Générale and Banque de Belgique, industrial development in Belgium proceeded at a rapid pace. In the last quarter of the nineteenth century, these investments spread out to other countries, at first in Western Europe (France, Germany, Spain, and Italy, among others), then later on in Central and Eastern Europe (with Russia having more than 100 Belgian enterprises) and overseas, such as in Argentina, Brazil, China, Egypt, the Congo Free State, and others. Several multinational companies (Vieille Montagne and Asturienne des Mines for the zinc industry and Cockerill for steel) took the lead.[1]

In our survey of the five benchmark periods for Belgium, we focus on two samples: the top ten companies sample (Table 4.1) (henceforth referred to as the Small Sample) and the sample with the single largest companies in each industry (transport and financial companies included) (Table 4.2) (the Large Sample). The former is a narrow list of the most important companies, in contrast to the latter, which provides a more diversified picture of the economy, also including companies in the less concentrated industries.

---

[1] For a general view, see R. Leboutte, J. Puissant, and D. Scuto, *Un siècle d'histoire industrielle: Belgique, Luxembourg, Pays-Bas: Industrialisation et Sociétés 1873–1973* (Paris: Sedes, 1998).

Table 4.1. Small Sample composition of Belgian companies: ranking order

Company	Industry	1911–13	1927–9	1954–6	1970–2	1998–2000
Banque Nationale de Belgique	Financial intermediation	1	2	1		
Société Générale de Belgique	Financial intermediation	2	3			2
Compagnie internationale des Wagons-Lits	Railways	3	6			
Dniéprovienne du Midi de la Russie	Basic and fabricated metals	4				
Société d'Ougrée-Marihaye	Basic and fabricated metals	5	5			
Lothringer Hütten Verein 'Aumetz Friede'	Basic and fabricated metals	6				
Tramways de Buenos-Ayres	Railways	7				
Cockerill	Basic and fabricated metals	8	10		3	
Eclairage et Chauffage par le Gaz	Utilities; Electricity, gas, water	9				
Transports et Entreprises	Utilities; Electricity, gas, water	10	7	8		
Société Nationale des Chemins de Fer Belges	Railways		1	3	4	
Union Minière	Mining		4	4		6
Vieille Montagne	Basic and fabricated metals		8	9		
Forges de la Providence	Basic and fabricated metals		9	10		
Banque de la Société Générale	Financial intermediation			2	1	
ACEC	Electrical engineering			5		
Intercommunale Belge d'Électricité	Utilities; Electricity, gas, water			6	7	
Petrofina	Oil, rubber and mineral products			7	6	5
Banque de Bruxelles	Financial intermediation				2	
Solvay	Chemicals and pharmaceuticals				5	4
La Royale Belge 'Vie Accidents'	Insurance				8	
Ebes (Electrabel from 1990 on)	Utilities; Electricity, gas, water				9	3
AG Financière	Insurance				10	
Dexia	Financial intermediation					1
Delhaize	Commercial activities					7
Bekaert	Mature industries					8
U.C.B.	Chemicals and pharmaceuticals					9
Colruyt	Commercial activities					10

Note: Companies are arranged according to assets in decreasing order from 1 to 10

Table 4.2. Large Sample composition of Belgian companies (1913–2000): assets, ROE, and HR

Year	Company	Assets (US$)	ROE (%)	HR (%)
1913	Ateliers Construction Electriques de Charleroi	6,766,260	6.43	10.33
1913	Banque Nationale de Belgique	252,906,985	15.42	−2.80
1913	Blaton-Ath (Canal de)	1,579,917	9.01	−11.35
1913	Brasseries et Laiteries d'Haecht	442,821	19.77	1.16
1913	Carrières de Porphyre de Quenast	3,872,562	10.08	3.02
1913	Charbonnages de Bascoup	2,811,572	38.37	−0.10
1913	Compagnie internationale des Wagons-Lits	35,585,395	7.24	−3.91
1913	De Naeyer	3,172,394	12.61	−9.12
1913	Dniéprovienne du Midi de la Russie	34,211,605	6.79	30.96
1913	Fabrique Nationale	3,176,539	28.46	28.09
1913	Germania (Glaces)	3,091,344	56.93	4.17
1913	Grands Hôtels Belges	1,968,268	14.11	9.01
1913	Linière La Lys	3,241,343	16.29	6.28
1913	Minerva Motors	2,772,003	32.85	11.85
1913	Glaces Nationales Belges	3,817,985	10.95	5.08
1913	Transports et Entreprises	12,025,002	11.52	7.77
1913	Val-Saint-Lambert à Seraing	2,292,947	8.33	6.37
1927	Assurances Générales	44,852,282	37.13	34.23
1927	Ateliers Constructions Electriques de Charleroi	38,148,753	9.34	27.42
1927	Banque Nationale	1,581,172,072	24.22	−18.42
1927	Cimenteries et Briqueteries Réunies	44,649,818	8.07	5.61
1927	Cockerill	62,292,767	18.34	45.21
1927	Compagnie Belge pour les Industries Chimiques	9,793,688	8.82	27.82
1927	Compagnie Maritime du Congo Belge	23,013,452	8.28	16.40
1927	De Naeyer	11,675,404	50.07	44.93
1927	Fabrique Nationale d'Armes de Guerre	32,922,668	7.07	72.93
1927	Glaces Nationales Belges (Glaces de Saint Roch)	13,070,218	61.38	23.10
1927	Grands Hôtels Belges	4,976,688	36.08	4.16
1927	Manufacture Liégeoise de caoutchouc souple	21,646,740	16.42	204.44
1927	Minoteries et Élévateurs à Grains	17,789,135	36.68	20.43
1927	Ougrée-Marihaye	169,080,523	10.85	34.42
1927	Société Financière des Caoutchoucs (Socfin)	47,284,126	11.87	−15.13
1927	Société Nationale des Chemins de Fer Belges	1,792,527,381	3.91	12.09
1927	Soie Artificielle de Tubize	24,002,866	16.34	54.41
1927	Transports et Entreprises Industrielles (Sofina)	112,926,549	29.91	77.71
1927	Union Miniere	187,127,597	25.09	7.93
1954	Asturienne des Mines	49,173,355	15.61	26.11
1954	ACEC	104,814,122	6.80	−2.88
1954	Banque Nationale de Belgique	2,234,924,552	60.18	18.87
1954	Brufina	21,946,574	17.20	20.61
1954	Ciments d'Obourg	14,550,547	21.89	27.80
1954	Chemins de Fer et d'Entreprises	7,388,426	12.05	12.42
1954	Fabrique Nationale d'Armes de Guerre	28,528,247	9.58	15.49
1954	Gevaert Photo Producten	37,448,141	15.93	15.29
1954	Grands Magasins à l'Innovation	16,175,675	12.68	31.40
1954	Intercommunale Belge d'Électricité	80,154,914	9.67	10.28
1954	Glaces de Saint Roch	14,066,891	8.07	59.31
1954	Papeteries de Belgique	16,499,558	8.84	27.38
1954	Petrofina	73,517,621	17.71	7.14
1954	Société Générale de Belgique	101,881,076	16.75	22.05
1954	Société Nationale des Chemins de Fer Belges	623,217,528	−3.29	2.97
1954	Tabacofina	19,235,635	11.05	16.93
1954	Union Cotonnière	17,052,212	4.54	22.24

(*continued*)

Table 4.2. Continued

Year	Company	Assets (US$)	ROE (%)	HR (%)
1954	Union Minière	359,678,261	45.06	38.79
1954	Vieille Montagne	60,415,166	10.05	48.98
1972	ACEC	209,065,302	6.82	17.09
1972	Banque de la Société Generale de Belgique	6,878,790,763	11.49	8.09
1972	Cimenteries et Briqueteries Réunies (CBR.)	98,354,700	8.54	20.32
1972	Cockerill Ougrée Providence Espérance Longdoz	1,174,742,477	1.98	−1.57
1972	Compagnie d'Entreprises C.F.E.	47,655,389	14.99	10.03
1972	Femmes d'Aujourd'hui	20,521,654	−4.27	−33.80
1972	G.B. Entreprises	153,129,430	10.88	5.76
1972	General Biscuit Company	38,621,566	8.01	27.52
1972	Helchteren et Zolder	25,332,753	1.30	28.09
1972	Intercom Belge d'Electricité	925,506,460	7.98	13.68
1972	La Royale Belge 'Vie Accidents'	812,394,424	38.89	15.62
1972	Petrofina	904,099,882	10.17	44.86
1972	Pieux Franki	31,482,016	23.33	8.96
1972	Société Nationale des Chemins de Fer Belges	1,135,378,447	−0.37	12.62
1972	Solvay	1,053,167,019	4.89	10.45
1972	Union Cotonnière	115,167,421	3.85	25.73
1972	Wagon Lits	108,203,558	5.79	35.82
2000	Almanij	3,399,355,613	12.30	3.98
2000	Barco	676,600,812	8.54	−7.40
2000	Bekaert	1,493,222,858	12.73	1.57
2000	CMB	1,103,301,329	18.48	22.35
2000	Cofinimmo	1,218,748,154	6.68	5.12
2000	Creyf's	131,694,055	29.80	52.39
2000	Delhaize	1,974,291,913	16.93	11.19
2000	Dexia	123,728,449,040	20.46	18.25
2000	Electrabel	10,596,546,344	18.38	17.62
2000	Electrafina	2,415,066	0.71	24.99
2000	Fortis AG	404,434,091,581	17.30	22.54
2000	GBL	5,462,163,959	14.22	25.43
2000	Nationale Portefeuille maatschappij	2,474,119,276	22.59	22.47
2000	Petrofina	7,719,225,443	25.23	25.15
2000	Quick Restaurants	244,702,733	7.33	−14.35
2000	Sabca	194,293,759	6.45	−11.98
2000	Sait Electronics	152,184,269	3.81	−0.67
2000	Sioen Industries	98,985,414	8.89	78.02
2000	Sofina	1,176,214,919	26.15	12.34
2000	Solvay	4,950,906,573	8.33	10.15
2000	Spadel	54,934,453	25.86	11.32
2000	Telindus	203,912,482	153.57	23.81
2000	Union Minière	2,026,235,229	7.92	−6.79

BUSINESS DEVELOPMENT

First Benchmark: 1911–13

Around 1900, finance, tramway, and railway industries dominated economic life in Belgium. First, since the start of Belgian capitalist development in the early nineteenth century, the 'mixed banking' (universal banking) system had systematically grown in importance, with the Société Générale at the top, followed by some other mixed banks. Second, the bulk of fixed capital investment during most of the nineteenth century was in the transport industry, first in railways and later on in tramways. At the turn of the century, Belgian capitalism was undergoing dramatic expansion internationally, with the universal banks extensively financing foreign direct investments, ranking Belgium in the top five foreign direct investors in the world. Among the main areas of Belgian foreign investment, mention should be made of the international transport industry (e.g. Compagnie Internationale des Wagons-Lits and Compagnie Générale des Tramways de Buenos-Ayres).

Other industries (especially basic and fabricated metals), as well as utilities, were also increasing rapidly in importance. Although never absent (as early as the 1830s, there was a broad industrial diversification into coal mining, pig iron companies, glass, breweries, textiles, zinc companies, etc.), their fixed capital needs were not of the same order of magnitude as those of the railways. This situation gradually changed, so that by the turn of the century, 'basic and fabricated metal' had conquered an important position, as is reflected in the first benchmark period 1911–13, with four out of ten companies in that industry in the Small Sample (Table 4.1): Dniéprovienne du Midi de la Russie (a daughter company of Cockerill), Ougrée-Marihaye, Cockerill, and Lothringer Hütten Verein 'Aumetz Friede'. In fact, these companies were often vertically integrated conglomerates, with Cockerill being a typical example, owning coal and ore mines, producing iron and steel, running (later on) its own shipping company, and exporting a wide variety of metal products such as rail equipment. Utilities also held a prominent position in the Small Sample, with companies such as Eclairage et Chauffage par le Gaz (gas industry) and Société Financière de Transports et d'Entreprises Industrielles (Sofina) (transport and electricity industry).

Other important activities (e.g. textiles, glass, zinc, and coal mining) were, however, absent from the Small Sample, although some companies owned assets that were nearly as big as these of the Small Sample, with companies such as Vieille Montagne, Asturienne (zinc), and Tramways Bruxellois (tramways). Some industries were absent because of the smaller size of the companies, even though, as a whole, they were rather important (e.g. textiles, coal mining, and glass). This evidently implies that the Small Sample does not provide an accurate picture of the Belgian economy, especially in the case of coal mines. Coal mining companies were absent from the sample, in spite of belonging to an important industry in Belgium. Indeed, at the start of the nineteenth century, the Belgian Industrial Revolution had to a large extent been fuelled by the coal mines in the valley of the Meuse (Charleroi and Liège) and in the Borinage (La Louvière and Mons). Geographically, the entire region was part of the coal basin that stretched from Northern France to the *Ruhrgebiet* in Germany. Coal mining was profitable throughout the whole of the nineteenth century and remained important until the mid-twentieth century. Even in the first years of the twentieth century, new mines were opened in the Limbourg province (the north-eastern part of Belgium) and new companies were established.

The Large Sample illustrates the wide diversity of the Belgian economy at the time of the first benchmark period (Table 4.2). Besides the companies already mentioned, others appear in a wide variety of industries, such as the automotive sector (Minerva Motors), breweries (Brasseries et Laiteries d'Haecht), high-performing metallic construction (FN, Fabrique Nationale d'armes de Guerre), metal engineering (ACEC—Ateliers de Constructions Electriques de Charleroi), the paper industry (De Naeyer), textiles (La Lys), and coal mining (Charbonnages de Bascoup). No company in the Belgian Congo, however, belonged to that sample. This would soon change.

Second Benchmark: 1927–9

The 1927–9 samples reflect four important changes in the Belgian economy, mainly as a consequence of the Congo colonization (the Congo Free State becoming the Belgian Congo in 1908), as well as the First World War and its aftermath. First, as the war was followed by a vast merger movement during the 1920s, the largest mixed bank at the time, the Société Générale, merged with the largest colonial mixed bank, the Banque d'Outremer.[2] Second, since the Belgian government had nationalized nearly all the private railway companies, a large state-owned railway company was established in 1926 (Société Nationale des Chemins de Fer Belges—SNCB/NMBS[3]). Third, many Belgian-owned foreign companies had disappeared owing to nationalization programmes in foreign countries, among which were Russia and Italy.[4] Fourth, in the 1927–9 sample, the most important newcomer was Union Minière, a mining company that would play a dominant role for decades to come. Belgium had a long-standing tradition in mining, and the exploitation of the mineral riches of the Belgian Congo would reinforce this position. Founded in 1906, Union Minière made its first profits only after the First World War, based on the mineral wealth of the Belgian colony.

---

[2] After the First World War, the mixed banks had started to enlarge their capital basis. This favoured a remarkable merger movement, greatly stimulated by generous tax incentives (reducing by two-thirds registration and transcription fees on documents concerning mergers of companies and with tax exemption on the income of joint-stock companies that liquidated their assets by merger within a three-year period) by an Act of 23 July 1927. In 1928, the merger of the largest (mixed) bank, Société Générale de Belgique with the Banque d'Outremer (which controlled the Compagnie du Congo pour le Commerce et l'Industrie, the owner of the vast majority of Congo companies) made Société Générale one of the biggest European banks at the time (G. Kurgan-Van Hentenryk, 'De Société Générale van 1850 tot 1914', in H. Van der Wee, ed., *De Generale Bank 1822–1897* (Tielt: Lannoo, 1997), pp. 69–301).

[3] SNCB (Société Nationale des Chemins de Fer Belges) or NMBS (Nationale Maatschappij der Belgische Spoorwegen) was a semi-governmental company (founded in 1926 in order to reduce public debt) whose stocks were listed on the stock market. In fact, there were already earlier state railways, but they were directly exploited by the state and had no legal company status as such. SNCB would soon fall into a permanent state of loss-making and would be heavily subsidized for decades to come (F. Buelens and J. van den Broeck, *Financieel-institutionele analyse van de Belgische beursgenoteerde spoorwegsector, 1836–1957* (Antwerp: Garant, 2004), pp. 194–204).

[4] For example, in Italy, Société des Tramways de Turin had to give its concession back to the town of Turin in 1923 in exchange for some annual payments (*Recueil Financier* (Brussels: Bruylandt, 1937), Vol. 2, p. 476). The same was true for Tramways de Bologne and other companies elsewhere, for example Tramways de Budapest (Hungary) (*Recueil Financier* (Brussels: Bruylandt, 1926), Vol. 2, p. 1656).

Union Minière even succeeded in competing with the most advanced (American) copper-ore-producing companies in the world.[5]

Railways held a strong position in the Small Sample, with Société Nationale des Chemins de Fer Belges being the largest company in the sample, with US $1,792,527,381 of assets. So did the banking industry, with Société Générale (which succeeded in doubling its assets during 1927–9) and the National Bank of Belgium (Banque Nationale de Belgique), one of the few national banks quoted on the stock exchange. The same holds for basic and fabricated metals, with the steel companies Ougrée-Marihaye, Cockerill, and Providence. Compared with the previous benchmark, non-ferrous ores companies had grown in importance (Vieille Montagne). Utilities were also in the Small Sample, with Sofina. One of the most important newcomers was the mining company Union Minière.

The Large Sample at the time illustrates, again, the diversified nature of the Belgian economy, with companies from construction (Cimenteries et Briqueteries Réunies, later on CBR, one of the largest European cement oligopolies),[6] mechanical and electrical engineering (ACEC and FN), and textiles (Tubize), a rapidly concentrating sector, as well as the transport industry, with Compagnie Belge Maritime du Congo in 1930 becoming CMB (Compagnie Maritime Belge), the largest Belgian shipping company. As the mining business was dominated by Union Minière, other (Belgian) coal mining companies are not in the sample, such as Charbonnages André Dumont, a coal company in the Limbourg province.

The Belgian economy also witnessed the rise of Belgian-based multinational agro-business and related activities (Minoteries et Élévateurs à Grains), including tropical products (Socfin). Minoteries et Élévateurs à Grains was founded in 1901 by Edouard Bunge (who also founded the Bunge Company) and was mainly active in Argentina (in 1934 Minoteries et Élévateurs à Grains would be liquidated and the activities brought into the Argentine Company Molinos Rio de la Plata). On the other hand, Socfin was established in 1909 for the exploitation of tropical products in the Belgian Congo; it would soon extend its activities to South-East Asia.[7]

Chemicals (Compagnie Belge pour les Industries Chimiques), wood and paper industries (De Naeyer), glass (Glaces Nationales Belges), insurance (Assurances Générales), and commercial activities (Grands Hôtels Belges) were also significant. Some of these industries were (or would soon become) involved in big merger movements. In the glass industry, Glaces Nationales Belges, for example, would merge in 1929 with Glaceries Germanie and change its name to Glaceries de Saint Roch. The reasons for this merger were obvious, since the glass industry, having always played an important role in Belgium, was characterized by low capitalization. Participating in the merger movement of the time offered possibilities for growth and survival. Other examples in other industries are the 1928 merger of Société Générale with Banque d'Outremer, and in the same year a big merger movement in the chemicals sector led to Union Chimique Belge (UCB).

[5] R. Brion and J.-L. Moreau, *Van Mijnbouw tot Mars: De ontstaansgeschiedenis van Umicore* (Tielt: Lannoo, 2006).

[6] P. Joye, *Les Trusts en Belgique: La concentration capitaliste* (Brussels: Société popularie d'éditions, 1961), pp. 54–60.

[7] The Bunge Company as well as Socfin survived and are even today two important multinational companies.

Some mergers of companies that are not in the 1927–9 sample are nevertheless important to mention, such as that of Société Générale des Chemins de Fer Economiques, Société Générale Belge d'Entreprises Electriques, and Compagnie Générale pour l'Eclairage et le Chauffage par le Gaz (20 November 1929). The new company took the name of Electrobel and would acquire a strong position in the utilities industry.

Third Benchmark: 1954–6

The 1954–6 benchmark illustrates that the structure of the Belgian economy had not changed fundamentally after the Second World War. The Small Sample still reflects a Belgian economy heavily involved in the basic industries such as basic and fabricated metals (Providence), zinc (Vieille Montagne), and minerals (Union Minière). Banking also maintained a strong position.

However, two new important industries entered the Small Sample for the first time: electricity and utilities and the petroleum business.

Utilities had grown in importance, with Sofina no longer being the only utilities company in the sample, which now included the electricity industry (Intercommunale Belge). In fact, within the public utilities industry, a concentration process started around this time, leading to the creation of three large electricity companies, which finally merged into Electrabel by the end of the century. But in 1954–6, the industry was still characterized by relatively large companies, in spite of the first mergers. For example, Electricité de l'Escaut (founded in 1905, becoming EBES later on) merged in 1956 with Centrales Electriques des Flandres et du Brabant and later on would be involved in a lot of other mergers before becoming Electrabel in 1990.

The Petrofina Oil Company also entered the Small Sample. Founded in 1920, Petrofina was initially the heritage of Belgian foreign direct investments in Romania. It expanded into a highly profitable oil-producing company that would finally be acquired by Total (France) in 2000. Petrofina succeeded in nearly doubling its assets in the period considered.

Other things changed too. Banking, for one, had experienced important changes in the 1930s with the abolition of the universal banking system in 1934–5. As a consequence, Société Générale was split up into a holding company and a commercial bank (Banque de la Société Générale). The total assets of Banque de la Société Générale amounted to US$727,330,794, somewhat higher than the railway company NMBS/SNCB (US$623,217,527), which was still present in the Small Sample. ACEC also entered the Small Sample. As a consequence of deliveries of Congolese uranium to the US government during and after the Second World War, the Belgian government had obtained privileged treatment.[8] ACEC would collaborate with the American-based Westinghouse in developing nuclear technology, transforming ACEC into a multinational player with strongly diversified activities.

---

[8] J. Helmreich, *United States Relations with Belgium and the Congo, 1940–1960* (Newark: University of Delaware Press, 1998).

The other companies in the Large Sample reflect the diversity of the Belgian economy, with companies such as Union Cotonnière (textiles, founded in 1919), Tabacofina, a world player in tobacco (founded in 1928), Compagnie Belge de Chemins de Fer et d'Entreprises (transport equipment), Ciments d'Obourg (cement), Papeteries de Belgique (wood and paper products), and Gevaert Photo Producten (chemicals). The arms producer FN held on to its position.

New tendencies can be observed, and for the first time a retail company, Grands Magasins à l'Innovation, entered the sample (later on, this activity will become among the major ones in the next samples).

Fourth Benchmark: 1970–2

From the 1960s, the Belgian economy went through a process of change. First, the Belgian Congo had become independent, inducing colonial companies to look for a new future. Second, European integration (as well as a worldwide GATT-inspired trade liberalization process) enlarged markets, but also increased competition. Third, foreign multinational companies made vast investment inroads in Belgium. American companies invested in modern industries such as (petro) chemicals, electro-mechanics, and car manufacturing, which were activities in which Belgium was lagging behind other Western countries. Foreign investments were mainly oriented towards industries characterized by relatively high capital intensity and high value added per worker. Fourth, it became clear that the overall structure of the economy was going to change. 'Old industries' such as steel, glass, coal, shipbuilding, and textiles ran into serious difficulties during the 1970s. Service industries became more important.

The 1970–2 benchmark samples, however, do not yet fully reflect these general tendencies, since they show the last upheaval of the economy before the world-wide oil crisis of 1973–4 and the monetary chaos after the collapse of the Bretton Woods system, stagflation, and the globalization process and increased international division of labour. During the next decades, these tendencies would become clearly visible.

The Small Sample already reflects the move into the dominant position of the service sector (banks, insurance, and department stores) and utilities (gas, oil, water, and electricity), away from industry, as well as the exit from Congo. Only one steel company remained in the sample, namely Cockerill, which had evolved into a mega company (Cockerill Ougrée Providence Espérance Longdoz) after many mergers with other Belgian steel companies.[9] The steel producers were, however, dramatically hit by the crisis of the 1970s.

As before, the composition of the Large Sample shows that industrial diversification was still ongoing, owing to the presence of, for example, the General Biscuit Company (food), Wagons Lits (leisure and tourism), Pieux Franki (mechanical engineering), Compagnie d'Entreprises C.F.E. (formerly Chemins de Fer et d'Entreprises), Union Cotonnière (textiles), and Cimenteries et Briqueteries

---

[9] H. Askenazy, *Les grandes societes europeennes* (Brussels: Centre de Recherche et d'Information Socio-Politiques, 1971), p. 119.

Réunies (CBR). The coal mining company Helchteren et Zolder also entered the sample, but, like steel, the coal mining industry would be hit hard by the coming crisis. Union Minière, however, was no longer in the sample, because of the difficulties encountered after the independence of Congo.

Fifth Benchmark: 1998–2000

The crisis of the 1970s put an end to the old industrial base of Belgium founded on steel, coal mines, glass, shipbuilding, and textiles. The government took drastic measures, such as the devaluation of the BEF in 1982, the Cooreman–De Clercq law, which provided fiscal stimuli for issuing new stocks and investing in stocks, and the Royal Decree on coordination centres, which provided fiscal stimuli for multinational corporations. Many companies in the traditional industries were forced to close down (shipbuilding, coal mining, and textiles), whereas others received massive state support. Many Belgian companies (Cockerill, Glaverbel, Banque Bruxelles-Lambert, etc.) were acquired by foreign multinational companies. There was a real shift away from traditional ('old') industries towards new ones, and Belgium, being a small open economy, became increasingly involved in the rapid process of globalization of the world economy. 'Belgian' capitalism received a final blow from the takeover of Société Générale by the French company Suez in 1988, which marked the end of the 'old industries'-based Belgian capitalism.

Not surprisingly, the composition of the Small Sample in Belgium for 1998–2000 shows a very different picture compared with that of the earlier benchmarks. The Small Sample consists now of companies in banking (Dexia and Fortis AG), retail (Colruyt and Delhaize), chemicals, oil, and pharmaceuticals (Solvay, UCB, and Petrofina), and electricity, gas, and water supply (Electrabel), besides mature industries (Bekaert). Union Minière had also restored its position again in the Small Sample; the company was in the middle of a transformation process towards a highly specialized minerals-transforming company (it would change its name to Umicore in 2001).

The Large Sample no longer reflects the real diversification pattern of the Belgian economy as before. This is partly due to the composition methodology of our sample, which is based on stock exchange quoted companies (the number of companies listed at the Brussels stock exchange had strongly decreased), but also to the higher number of multinational companies active in Belgium (such as BASF, Bayer, etc.) that are not in the sample.

ROE PERFORMANCE

A performance measure often used is return on equity (ROE), which is defined as the percentage ratio of net profits on shareholders' equity.[10] Table 4.3 shows the

---

[10] In the early twentieth century, few legal rules limited the discretionary power of management to dress up the annual report, which led to a substantial heterogeneity in the structure of the reported

Table 4.3. ROE for the Small and Large Sample of Belgian companies: mean and median

Period	ROE (Small Sample) (%)		ROE (Large Sample) (%)	
	Mean	Median	Mean	Median
1911–13	8.71	8.55	17.95	12.61
1927–9	18.45	17.54	22.10	16.42
1954–6	17.85	11.31	15.81	12.05
1970–2	10.25	8.53	9.07	7.98
1998–2000	18.02	17.61	20.55	14.22

ROE in the various periods for the Large and Small Samples. Mean and median ROE are reported for each benchmark of three years. Over the whole period, median ROE remains relatively stable, with average median values oscillating between 12.61 and 16.42 per cent (for the Large Sample), with the exception of the 1970–2 period.

We will discuss the mean and median values for the three-year averages for ROE in this section and then for holding return (HR) in the next section. Unless otherwise stated, all data discussed are three-year data, although we discuss also the yearly evolution if this allows a better understanding of the changes over time (this is especially the case in the discussion on HR performance).

For the 1913 and 1927 benchmarks, the ROE levels should be interpreted with caution, as some companies, for various reasons, reported artificially low book values for share capital. One example is Charbonnages de Bascoup, which reported in the 1911–13 period a zero share capital. The Belgian legislation allowed companies to pay back the nominal value of shares to shareholders, thereby reducing the reported share capital. When the shares were paid back, the shareholders were often allowed to keep the shareholder's rights. They continued to receive dividends, were permitted to assist and vote at the shareholders general meeting, could be elected to the board of directors, etc. In many cases, the shareholders received a different type of shares ('*actions de jouissance*') with zero nominal value to mark the difference with the original situation. Another reason for caution, which relates to all benchmark periods, is the presence of outliers, leading to large differences between average and median ROE.

First Benchmark: 1911–13

For 1911–13, the ROE (Large Sample) has a median value of 12.61 per cent, although the mean is considerably higher (17.95 per cent), reflecting the presence of some outliers such as Glaces Germania (56.93 per cent) and Charbonnages de Bascoup (38.37 per cent), Minerva Motors (32.85 per cent), Fabrique Nationale d'Armes de Guerre (28.46 per cent), and Brasseries et Laiteries d'Haecht (19.77 per cent). As most of these companies are not in the Small Sample, the median

balance sheets and income statements. Fortunately, even before the First World War, the law provided some guidelines about the depreciation of assets and the distribution of profits (C. Lefebvre and J. Flower, *European Financial Reporting: Belgium* (London: Routledge, 1994), pp. 81–120).

ROE for that sample, as well as the average, is considerable lower (8.55 and 8.71 per cent respectively). The dominant companies of the basic and fabricated metals sector seem to be responsible for these more moderate ROE levels.

Second Benchmark: 1927–9

For the 1927–9 period, the ROE (Large Sample) shows a median value of 16.42 per cent, which, not surprisingly, is the highest of the five benchmark periods, reflecting the boom of the 'roaring twenties'. Also in this case, the mean ROE is considerable higher (22.10 per cent), indicating the presence of some outliers in the sample, such as Glaces Nationales Belges (61.38 per cent), Compagnie Maritime du Congo Belge (50.07 per cent), Assurances Générales (37.13 per cent), Minoteries et Élévateurs à Grains (36.68 per cent), and Grands Hôtels Belges (36.08 per cent). For the Small Sample, the median ROE is of the same order of magnitude, although somewhat higher (17.54 per cent). All companies in the Small Sample (except SNCB) succeeded in obtaining at least 10 per cent ROE.

These results have to be situated in their time frame. The years 1925 and 1926 had brought stagnation and even a decline in industrial production, as well as financial instability and downward-spiralling international trade. The stabilization (devaluation) of the Belgian franc in the autumn of 1926 was a great success. The undervaluation of the franc boosted industrial production, restored confidence in the Belgian financial market, and excluded trouble in financing expansion by issuing shares. Foreign capital and Belgian capital that had been invested abroad flowed back into the country. The stabilization of the franc was also accompanied by fiscal policy measures such as revaluation of the value of companies' fixed assets and the reduction of taxes on mergers by two-thirds. The result was a booming period for mergers. Unemployment reached very low levels. Production could only be expanded by investing on a large scale. In addition, Belgium, as a small open economy, benefited from the international economic upswing of the late 1920s. ROEs during this period were thus very high and even in 1929 substantial profits were reported.

Third Benchmark: 1954–6

For 1954–6, the ROE (Large Sample) has a median value of 12.05 per cent, with a mean that is somewhat higher (15.87 per cent). For the Small Sample, the ROE median of 11.31 per cent hardly differs, whereas the ROE average for that sample is considerably higher (17.85 per cent), indicating also here the presence of some important outliers in the sample, such as Banque Nationale de Belgique (60.18 per cent) and Union Minière (45.06 per cent). The performance of several other companies in the Small Sample was, however, rather low, which is probably due to Belgian corporate taxation. Whereas colonial companies could enjoy tax exemption, companies in Belgium were confronted with higher tax rates.

These results reflect the post-war economic conditions. During the 1930s (not in our benchmark periods), the ROE had declined. The period 1954–6 witnessed a strongly recovering economy (at least compared with the 1930s). After the Second

World War, the economy recovered spectacularly, owing to the Korean War, strategic stockpiling of raw materials, and reconstruction efforts, which clearly influenced performance. For Belgium, an additional factor was the booming economy of the Belgian Congo. In fact, the ROE results for 1954–6 are strongly influenced by Belgian companies active in the Belgian Congo. Evidently, the Belgian companies present in the Congo gained from Cold War-induced international demand for strategic stockpiling, not only of traditional minerals as copper and tin, but also of uranium, radium, cobalt, and other minerals.

Fourth Benchmark: 1970–2

Regarding the 1970–2 benchmark, the ROE (Large Sample) has a median value of 7.98 per cent with a mean of only 9.07 per cent. Both figures are the lowest ROEs of the five benchmark periods. Only a few outliers, such as La Royale Belge 'Vie Accidents' (38.89 per cent) and Pieux Franki (23.33 per cent), are found in that sample. In contrast, most companies are performing far below the historical average, such as ACEC (Ateliers de Constructions Electriques de Charleroi) (6.82 per cent) or Helchteren et Zolder (1.30 per cent). For the Small Sample, the ROE median is 8.53 per cent, while the ROE average for that sample is hardly higher (10.25 per cent).

All this seems to announce the coming economic crisis of the 1970s. The benchmark period 1970–2 relates to the years immediately following the 'golden sixties', but before the first worldwide oil shock of 1973–4. For a number of reasons, the performance of the Belgian economy improved dramatically in the 1960s. Small open economies, like Belgium, benefited from European economic integration, following the creation of the ECSC (1951) and the EEC (1957), which enlarged markets through tariff reductions, the abolition of various trade barriers, and standardization. Whereas subsidizing of the old, loss-making coal mining companies in the Walloon area was phased out, the geographical location of Belgium and the prospects of a large unified European market attracted American companies to set up subsidiaries. As a consequence, Belgium's old and outdated economic industries declined in importance. By the end of the decade, dark clouds had gathered, however, owing to increasing international financial instability. Performance dropped accordingly. For example, at the lower end of the sample, the problem companies of the next decades are already visible: SNCB, Helchteren et Zolder (coalmining), Cockerill (steel), and Union Cotonnière (textile) all show rather low profits, or even losses. ACEC offers a quite different picture, hesitating between profits and losses, but eventually not surviving.

Fifth Benchmark: 1998–2000

For 1998–2000, the ROE (Large Sample) indicates that the crisis years of the 1970s were past. Historical high ROE figures, comparable to these of the 1920s, were obtained. The ROE (Large Sample) has a median value of 14.22 per cent with a mean of 20.55 per cent and is in line with the results of the Small Sample: ROE median (17.65 per cent) and ROE average (18.02 per cent). As before, also now some outliers are observed. As to the ROE (Large Sample), a majority of results (such as those of Petrofina, Sofina, and others) were in the range of 20–30 per cent, explaining the overall good results.

By the end of the twentieth century, the Belgian economy had survived two major oil shocks and dramatic business downturns. A series of government measures had reformed the economy. As a small open economy, depending immensely on international trade and international investment, Belgium followed most other countries in the world in riding the wave of globalization. As a consequence, Belgium had by the close of the twentieth century a business climate that was much more favourable towards investments, profits, and stock market transactions. Therefore, companies could reach higher levels of performance.

HR PERFORMANCE

Through changes in stock price, HR also captures the influence of the stock market's assessment of a company's current and future profitability. Not surprisingly, HR is typically more volatile than ROE.

Avoiding repetition, we will restrict ourselves here largely to highlighting elements that have not yet been mentioned in the discussion of ROE performance. Table 4.4 shows the changes in mean and median HR per benchmark period for the Small and Large Samples. In general, it can be observed that, over the century, HR moves upwards and downwards from one benchmark period to another, more or less in the same way as ROE, although the figures are evidently different.

First Benchmark: 1911–13

The average HR of the Small Sample companies during the first benchmark period of 1911–13 is rather low (4.84 per cent) and the median HR even lower (2.56 per cent), reflecting the performance of some outliers that we identified before. The same holds for the Large Sample, with a median HR of 5.08 per cent and an average HR of 5.69 per cent. In fact, HR is the lowest for all the benchmark periods (for both samples). HR seems to reflect rather pessimistic expectations about the future during that period.

Table 4.4. HR for the Small and Large Sample of Belgian companies: mean and median

Period	HR (Small Sample) (%)		HR (Large Sample) (%)	
	Mean	Median	Mean	Median
1911–13	4.84	2.56	5.69	5.08
1927–9	21.11	20.14	35.77	27.42
1954–6	17.27	14.58	22.17	20.61
1970–2	14.44	13.15	14.66	13.68
1998–2000	9.76	10.67	15.11	12.34

It can also be observed that HR performance is declining rapidly during 1911–13, as is evidenced for example by the average HR in the Large Sample, which drops from 9.8 per cent in 1911 to nearly 1.2 per cent in 1913, and by the median HR, which drops from 4.1 per cent in 1911 to 1.8 per cent in 1913. In general, the year 1913 seems to reflect the most pessimistic expectations for the three years.

Second Benchmark: 1927–9

During the years 1927–9, HR followed a similar pattern to ROE. HR (median) for the Large Sample is 27.42 per cent, with HR (average) even higher (35.77 per cent). The same can be observed, although with lower HR, for the Small Sample, with an HR (median) of 20.14 per cent and an HR (average) of 21.11 per cent. The reasons behind this have been identified earlier. The stock market was the epitome of a bubble economy at the time, ending in the dramatic Wall Street Crash.

Interestingly, when analysing the evolution throughout these three years, it can be observed that, after a spectacular rise, although with initial bad signals for some companies in 1928, HR fell dramatically in 1929. All the companies in the Small Sample witnessed share price losses. For example the price of Sofina went down from 89,500 BEF (October 1928) to 23,500 BEF by the end of December 1929. Such share price losses should, however, be assessed in the light of the extremely high HR values of, for example, 258.8 per cent for Sofina in 1927 (the share price was still 25,900 BEF in January 1927). Looking at individual HRs in the Large Sample, most companies also witnessed large negative values in 1929, with for example, Compagnie Belge pour les Industries Chimiques having an HR in 1928 of 57.2 per cent and an HR in 1929 of −45.4 per cent.

Third Benchmark: 1954–6

During the years 1954–6, HR in the Large Sample was at a rather high level and a more moderate level in the Small Sample. The stock market at the time reflected the bright perspectives of the real economy (see earlier). HR (median) for the Large Sample was 20.61 per cent and HR (average) 22.17 per cent. The Small Sample HR (median) was 14.58 per cent and HR (average) 17.27 per cent.

For the whole period, HR was not significantly different from ROE for both the Small and Large Samples. This masks, however, dramatic changes within the period. Stock prices were still increasing in 1954 owing to the Korean War boom, which, together with the high profits, was leading to median HRs of 34.8 per cent (Small Sample) and 22.5 per cent (Large Sample) in 1954. These high HR levels fell to 3.3 and 6.6 per cent, respectively, in 1956, announcing the economic downturn of 1957–8.

In the 1954–6 period, HR of the Large Sample also shows large volatility. In 1954, many companies experienced an HR of more than 25 per cent. For example, the retail store chain Grands Magasins à l'Innovation reached an HR of 54.9 per cent. Only a few stocks in the sample produced an HR of less than 5 per cent, but none of these had negative results. Towards the end of the period, however, HR was already diminishing. For example, Petrofina had an HR of 31.49 per cent in 1954 but −26.61 per cent in 1956.

Fourth Benchmark: 1970–2

The movements and evolution of HR in the period 1970–2 are at first also much dominated by stock price increases. HR performance indicates the booming economy of the early 1970s, at the eve of the oil crisis of 1973 and the severest world economic crisis after the Second World War. For the Large Sample, HR (median) amounted to 13.68 per cent and HR (average) 14.66 per cent, whereas for the Small Sample, these figures were 13.15 and 14.44 per cent, respectively. For example, the General Biscuit Company, with a poor HR of 0.41 per cent in 1970, reached as high as 67.04 per cent by the end of 1972. This would not, however, last for long (see earlier).

Fifth Benchmark: 1998–2000

For the period 1998–2000, HR witnessed the new stock market mania of the time (largely triggered by ICT stocks). In 1998, the median HR of the Small Sample was some 48 per cent in 1998 (with an average of 42.9 per cent), but dramatically declined in the years after. In 1998, numerous companies in the Small Sample achieved an HR higher than 10 per cent. In 1999, however, few of them could report a positive HR.

HR in the Large Sample showed a similar movement over time, reaching median values of 23 per cent in 1998 (with an average of 45 per cent), in contrast to the dramatic declines in 1999 and 2000. This picture has to be qualified, however, since some companies of the Large Sample were suffering losses in the stock market during the boom of 1998, such as Union Minière (HR−48.4 per cent), the maritime transportation company CMB (HR−41.6 per cent), Sabca, active in transport equipment (HR−34.2 per cent), and the steel wire manufacturer Bekaert (HR−21.3 per cent). Moreover, also in the next two years, the stocks of some companies in this sample held positive returns, and others negative ones, without any consistent movement per stock. Consequently, the overall three-year result summarizes this evolution. HR (median) for the Large Sample is 12.34 per cent and HR (average) is 15.11 per cent. For the Small Sample, HR is even lower: HR (median) is 10.67 per cent and HR (average) is 9.76 per cent. These rather moderate figures are correct in their own way, but do not fully reflect the booming stock market of the 1990s.

SUMMARY AND CONCLUSIONS

The twentieth century was characterized by changes in importance of 'Belgian capitalism' as well as of the industrial composition of activities in Belgium. Whereas 'Belgian capitalism' was highly dominant in 1900, in the home country and also with heavy investment abroad, at the end of the twentieth century it was pushed into a minority position, with foreign multinational companies having become dominant players. The independence of the Belgian Congo in 1960 and the takeover of the Société Générale in 1988 by the French Suez company dealt it an important blow.

Around 1900, 'old industries' such as steel, coal, and textiles dominated the Belgian economy. Their position gradually declined, however, and around 2000, it was rather telecommunications, gas and electricity, retail distribution, and petro-chemical industries that played a major role. Nevertheless, during most of the twentieth century, the presence of the 'old industries' in industrial activities remained overwhelming.

ROE performance throughout the century had its ups and downs, but remained by and large remarkably stable, with ROE (median) around 10–12 per cent. In some periods, ROE (median) was higher (e.g. during the 1920s or the 1990s) or lower (e.g. during the 1970s). ROE (average) was most of the time higher, in general as a result of outliers.

In spite of some differences, ROE performances (median) in the Small and Large Samples were similar. Differences were mostly due to the different compositions of the two samples. The Small Sample contained the most concentrated companies, whereas the Large Sample rather reflected the overall composition of industrial activities.

In the five periods considered, the Small Sample was dominated by old indus-tries. Consequently, ROE (median) performance was higher than that of the Large Sample during times when these 'old industries' were flourishing. In contrast, in times when these industries were in transformation (the 1970s), their ROE (median) performance was lower.

In contrast to ROE performance, HR performance reflects prospective views on the future of the economy and the companies involved, and is characterized by high volatility. Even during the three years per benchmark period, this volatility can clearly be observed. Within several of these periods, HR reached rather high and low (if not negative) levels.

5

The Performance of British Business in the Twentieth Century

Youssef Cassis and Terry Gourvish

THE DEVELOPMENT OF BRITISH BIG BUSINESS

On the eve of the First World War, British big business broadly reflected the development of the British economy during the long nineteenth century with, in particular, its status as the first industrial nation and its phenomenal formal and informal expansion overseas.[1] As a result, it is unsurprising to find that most of the companies featured in the country's thirty largest[2] were in textiles (J&P Coats, Fine Cotton Spinners, Bleachers' Association, and Calico Printers), or consumer goods, especially those in the food, drink, and tobacco sector (Imperial Tobacco, British American Tobacco, and Watney), or were 'free-standing' concerns, operating abroad or in the empire (De Beers, Consolidated Gold Fields of South Africa, and Rio Tinto).[3]

Nevertheless, as in France and the US, the largest companies were the railway companies—the nine largest if measured by assets. The largest commercial banks came next in terms of assets, for obvious reasons, since banks work with their clients' deposits, though they were smaller than the top ten industrial companies in terms of share capital. For the purpose of this study, only the top three banks and railway companies in 1913 (respectively London City & Midland, Lloyds

---

[1] Peter Mathias, *The First Industrial Nation: An Economic History of Britain 1700–1914* (London, 1969).

[2] The first part of this part is based on the project's 'Small Sample', in other words on the thirty largest British companies, as opposed to the 'Large Sample', which has been assembled on a sectoral base and includes around forty to fifty-five companies, depending on the years. For a methodological discussion of these two samples, see Chapter 2.

[3] A path-breaking study of the corporate sector in Britain was P.L. Payne, 'The emergence of large-scale company in Great Britain, 1870–1914', *Economic History Review* (1967), followed by Leslie Hannah, *The Rise of the Corporate Economy* (2nd edn, London, 1983) and John F. Wilson, *British Business History, 1720–1994* (Manchester, 1995). On the companies identified in the text, see also D.A. Farnie, *The English Cotton Industry and the World 1815–1896* (Oxford, 1979), B.W.E. Alford, *W.D. & H.O. Wills and the Development of the UK Tobacco Industry 1786–1965* (London, 1973), Howard Cox, *The Global Cigarette: The Origins and Evolution of British American Tobacco, 1880–1945* (Oxford, 2000); Hurford Janes, *The Red Barrel: A History of Watney Mann* (London, 1963); H.A. Chilvers, *The Story of De Beers* (London, 1939), and C.E. Harvey, *The Rio Tinto Company: An Economic History of a Leading International Mining Concern, 1873–1954* (Penzance, 1981).

Bank, and London County & Westminster Bank, and Midland Railway, London & North Western Railway, and Great Western Railway) have been included in the sample.

Amongst the new industries, oil (with Shell) and chemicals (Lever Brothers, United Alkali, and Brunner Mond) were well represented in British big business, though no company in electrical engineering featured in the top thirty.[4] The largest firms in the heavy industries (Vickers, Armstrong, and John Brown) were mainly involved in shipbuilding, the major exception being Guest, Keen & Nettlefolds.[5] From services, shipping companies (P&O and Cunard) and a single utility company (Gas Light & Coke, the country's largest firm excluding banks and railways) completed the group of the 'top thirty'.[6]

Fifteen years later, in the late 1920s, British big business displayed two main features. The first was the sheer size of the largest companies: the top twenty-five industrial companies all had assets exceeding £15 million, a size reached by only seven companies in Germany (but by 110 in the US), while the 'Big Five' banks had become the largest in the world following the mega mergers of 1918.[7] And the second was the weight of the 'new' industries—with ICI and Lever Brothers in chemicals, GEC and AEI in electrical engineering, Austin, Morris, and Ford in motor cars, Shell and Anglo-Persian Oil in oil, Dunlop in rubber and tyres, and Courtaulds and British Celanese in artificial fibres, to which should be added those in branded packaged products, namely Imperial Tobacco (the world's second largest firm measured by market capitalization in 1938) and British American Tobacco, as well as the alcoholic drinks firms Distillers, Guinness, and Watney Combe Reid. The railway companies, now reduced to four enlarged businesses following government-directed mergers (London, Midland & Scottish, London & North Eastern, Great Western, and Southern) were still the country's largest firms, though by a smaller margin than before the war, while the clearing banks strengthened their position. Again, only the three largest in each of these latter two sectors have been considered here. Nevertheless, despite the structural crisis suffered by the staple industries, J&P Coats and Fine Cotton Spinners in textiles, and Vickers, GKN, and Harland & Wolff in the heavy industries (including shipbuilding) were still present amongst the country's largest companies. All in all, British big business reached a degree of modernity and maturity not yet reached elsewhere in Europe.

---

[4] Joost Jonker et al., *A History of Royal Dutch Shell*, 4 vols. (Oxford, 2007); Charles Wilson, *The History of Unilever*, 2 vols. (Oxford, 1954); W.J. Reader, *Imperial Chemical Industries: A History*, 2 vols. (Oxford, 1970).

[5] J.D. Scott, *Vicker: A History* (London, 1962); C. Trebilcock, *Vickers Brothers: Armaments and Enterprise, 1854–1914* (London, 1977); Edgar Jones, *A History of GKN*, 2 vols. (Basingstoke, 1987–1990).

[6] T.L. Williams, *A History of the British Gas Industry* (Oxford, 1981); Gordon Boyce, *Information, Mediation and Institutional Development: The Rise of Large-Scale Enterprise in British Shipping, 1870–1919* (Manchester, 1995).

[7] In 1918, the country's ten largest banks merged, two by two, to give birth to five giant clearing banks, immediately christened the 'Big Five': Midland Bank, Lloyds Bank, Barclays Bank, Westminster Bank, and National Provincial Bank. Based in London, they each had a national and, usually, international network of branches at their disposal, while collectively controlling more than 90 per cent of the country's deposits.

British big business continued to mature during the 1930s and 1940s, with the Second World War giving a further boost to the new industries. With the nationalization of the railway companies and the clearing banks tightly controlled by the Treasury and the Bank of England and somewhat marking time, big business came to be largely dominated by the 'Chandlerian' firms of the Second Industrial Revolution. On the whole, the same firms maintained their dominance: ICI and Unilever in chemicals, GEC and AEI in electrical engineering, Shell and Anglo-Persian in oil, BMC (the product of the merger between Austin and Morris) in motor cars, Dunlop in rubber and tyres, Courtaulds in artificial fibres, Imperial Tobacco, British American Tobacco, and Distillers in branded packaged products/food, drink and tobacco, as well as Vickers and GKN in the heavy industries. A few others made it into the top thirty: English Electric and BICC in electrical engineering and Hawker Siddeley in aerospace. Continuity also characterized the service industries, in particular with P&O and Cunard in shipping. Even more than in the late 1920s, all these companies were significantly larger than their counterparts in Continental Europe, though some might have become less dynamic.[8]

The contour of British big business hardly altered during the golden age of European capitalism. With the 'new' industries reaching full maturity, the large firms that had established themselves in the 1920s—Shell and BP, ICI and Unilever, GEC (reinforced after its merger with AEI and English Electric), Dunlop, Courtaulds, Imperial Tobacco and British American Tobacco, British Leyland (about to enter a crisis that would prove terminal), and GKN (the only survivor of the old iron and steel companies)—all retained their dominant position, together with the clearing banks (reduced to four after the merger between National Provincial and Westminster). A number of other firms that entered the 'top 30' in later decades, such as Hawker Siddeley, BICC, Marks & Spencer, and Great Universal Stores, also remained prominent. This left little space for newcomers, though there were some, mainly in food, drink, and tobacco (Grand Metropolitan, Associated British Foods, Allied Breweries, and Gallaher), at the bottom end of the 'top 30'. These were companies that increased in size through merger as much as internal growth.[9]

The changes that took place in British big business during the last three decades of the twentieth century were undoubtedly the most momentous in the country's corporate history. The combination of the advent of the Third Industrial Revolution, the globalization of the world economy, and the market policies initiated by the Thatcher government led to a profound rationalization of the industrial base, the most far-reaching in Western Europe, even if it did not reach the same scale as in the US. With the exception of BP, Shell, and British American Tobacco, the giant firms that had dominated British business for half a century or more—ICI, Unilever, GEC, Dunlop, Courtaulds, Imperial Tobacco, and British Leyland and its forerunners—were no longer amongst the country's top thirty companies, if they were still in existence. Some disappeared (Dunlop, Courtaulds, and British

---

[8] See Y. Cassis, *Big Business: The European Experience in the Twentieth Century* (Oxford, 1997), pp. 33, 34, 35–46.

[9] Derek F. Channon, *The Strategy and Structure of British Enterprise* (London, 1973).

Leyland), others reinvented themselves before disappearing (GEC), others moved down in the ranking as a result of a major de-merger (ICI) or of the rise of newcomers (Unilever).

In their place came firms more closely linked to the new economy: pharmaceuticals (GlaxoSmithKline and AstraZeneca) replaced chemicals, telecoms (BT) replaced the old utilities (though Centrica, formerly British Gas, was still in the top thirty), defence (BAE Systems) replaced the 'mature' industries, and services to business gave birth to large firms (WPP). Retailers (Tesco, Sainsbury's, and Kingfisher) continued to grow, while the clearing banks and some remnants of British business tradition (Anglo-American in mining and Diageo in consumer goods) kept their place amongst Britain's largest companies.

PERFORMANCE: RETURN ON EQUITY

Measured in terms of return on equity (ROE), the performance of British business was fairly stable during most of the twentieth century (Table 5.1). In the first four benchmark years, the average rate for a sample of leading companies[10] fluctuated between 8.6 and 11.1 per cent, and the median between 8.1 and 9.2 per cent; minima and maxima were also fairly stable: between −4 and 3 per cent for the former, and 26 and 29 per cent for the latter. The exception was the final benchmark period, 1998–2000, when the mean shot up to over 20 per cent and the median to 16 per cent; and with extreme minimum (−21.7 per cent) and maximum (91.6 per cent). Business performance was thus particularly strong at the very end of the twentieth century, in the context of both the British and the European historical experiences. Conversely, the early 1970s were, not surprisingly, difficult years; while returns were of the same order of magnitude in the early 1910s, late 1920s, and mid-1950s.

Before the First World War, the average return for British companies (9.7 per cent) was slightly below the mean of those of the seven countries included in the study (10.04 per cent). This is partially explained by the performance of the railway companies, whose ROE was, not unexpectedly, rather low (4.6 per cent). Banks, on the other hand, did well (13.2 per cent): as deposit banks, they had a low equity ratio and were able to make the most of their basic activities (discount

Table 5.1. Leading British companies: ROE, 1913–2000 (in %)

Year	Mean	Median	Minimum	Maximum	Standard deviation	N
1913	9.70	8.13	2.84	29.23	5.44	43
1929	8.57	8.52	−2.26	26.35	6.28	49
1956	11.12	9.07	4.25	27.70	6.06	43
1972	9.08	9.18	−4.07	26.34	6.37	44
2000	21.01	16.03	−21.72	91.58	19.09	53

Source: Performance project, Large Sample

---

[10] See footnote 2. The next two sections are based on the Large Sample.

and short-term loans). However, as Crafts has pointed out, Britain's growth rested upon an ultimately unsustainable specialism in export industries, and its vulnerability reflected the comparative advantage it had developed in low-wage activities.[11] Thus, the most profitable companies were those operating abroad or in the empire (British American Tobacco, De Beers Consolidated, and Consolidated Gold Fields of South Africa) with an ROE on average over 20 per cent (27.4 per cent for De Beers). Strong performances (13.6 per cent) were also achieved by firms in mechanical engineering (Babcock & Wilcox and Howard & Bullough)— another case of high returns by medium–large firms.[12] Textile firms also did well (10.1 per cent), especially J&P Coats (15.8 per cent), one of the country's best performing firms. Five other industrial companies—Imperial Tobacco (13.3 per cent), Shell (13.2 per cent), Metropolitan Carriage Wagon & Finance Co. (13.1), Guinness (11.2 per cent), and Stewarts & Lloyds (10.1 per cent)—together with the commercial banks achieved an ROE above 10 per cent.

The overall performance of British business was slightly weaker in the late 1920s than on the eve of the First World War, with an average of 8.57 per cent— though it stood at 10.62 per cent for the country's thirty largest companies, amongst which fewer of the least profitable firms featured. However, the mainstays of the UK's nineteenth-century Industrial Revolution were now experiencing more difficult trading conditions. Railway companies did worse than average (3.9 per cent), while the heavy industries (coal, iron and steel, and shipbuilding) were poorer, with less than 2 per cent; the leading firms in textiles, on the other hand, held their own fairly well (13 per cent for J&P Coats, 11.3 for Courtaulds, and a lower 6.2 per cent for Fine Cotton Spinners). The performance of the new industries was not always superior to that of the old; indeed, the sector presents a picture of contrasts. Chemicals were somewhat disappointing, with an ROE of 7.2 per cent for ICI and 9.4 per cent for Lever Brothers (which became Unilever in 1929). Electrical engineering did not do much better, with 4.4 per cent for AEI and 9.1 per cent for GEC. Motor cars, oil, as well as rubber and tyres, not surprisingly, proved stronger: 19.4 per cent for Austin, 17.1 per cent for Morris, 16.7 per cent for Shell, 14.4 per cent for Anglo-Persian, and 11.3 per cent for Dunlop. Food, drink, and tobacco (with an ROE of 16.4 per cent) did even better, with, in particular, 20.3 per cent for Watney Combe Reid, 18.3 for Guinness, 15.1 for Distillers, 19.4 for British American Tobacco, and 17.1 per cent for Imperial Tobacco. The service industries, especially commercial activities (department stores) and wood and paper products (newspapers), combined rapid growth with high profitability, with ROEs of respectively 10.6 and 13.4 per cent on average. Finally, banks (with an ROE of 9.3 per cent) were near the national average.

British business did better in the mid-1950s (11.2 per cent) than in the late 1920s, possibly because the newly nationalized railway companies are no longer taken into account. Looking at sectors and individual companies, services, especially commercial activities, continued to produce high returns (27.6 per cent for

---

[11] N.F.R. Crafts, *British Economic Growth during the Industrial Revolution* (Oxford, 1985), pp. 156, 160.

[12] Babcock & Wilcox and Howard & Bullough did not rank amongst Britain's thirty largest companies, but were the country's two largest mechanical engineering firms.

Woolworth and 16.4 per cent for Great Universal Stores), as did food, drink, and tobacco, with an ROE averaging 10.2 per cent—two strongholds of British business. Good performances (nearly 15 per cent) were also achieved, perhaps more surprisingly, by the iron and steel industry (Stewart & Lloyds and United Steel), though this was partly the result of the decision by the new Conservative government to privatize it (it had been nationalized by Labour in 1951), since the companies had to be made attractive to potential investors,[13] and by transport equipment, especially motor cars, with 14 per cent for a still profitable BMC. With the exception of Unilever (27.7 per cent) and BP (17 per cent), the 'Chandlerian' firms of the new industries showed poorer results, with an ROE between 6 and 9 per cent for GEC, AEI and English Electric, ICI and British Oxygen, Shell, Dunlop, and Courtaulds. The clearing banks, for their part (8.1 per cent), continued their slide.

Rates of return (9.1 per cent) were not much lower in the early 1970s, but firms operated in a far more inflationary context. Traditionally strong sectors such as commercial activities (the best performing sector with 18.3 per cent) and food, drink, and tobacco (a little lower with 13 per cent) continued to do well. The ROE of the giant firms in the established 'new' industries was in the 9–11 per cent range. Newcomers tended to do better—Thorn, for example, in electrical engineering, with 22.4 per cent. The clearing banks (11.9 per cent), recently freed from direct control, somewhat recovered in a buoyant City. State-owned companies, on the other hand, performed very poorly during a difficult decade for the British economy, with losses for British Steel (with an ROE of −4.1 per cent) and British Rail (−1.16 per cent), and no profits for British Gas, the Electricity Board (−0.5 per cent), and the Post Office (−0.3 per cent). This had a negative impact on both the national average and sectors such as mining, utilities, transport and communications, and 'mature' industries.

Performances reached a higher level in the closing years of the twentieth century. ROEs climbed to 21 per cent (mean) and 16 per cent (median), with particularly strong performances from pharmaceuticals (GlaxoSmithKline and AstraZeneca), engineering (GKN, Smiths Group, and Tomkins), services to business (Hays and WPP), media (Pearson and Reuter), and post and telecommunications (Vodafone, Cable & Wireless, and BT), with ROEs well above 20 per cent.

PERFORMANCE: HOLDING RETURN

From the perspective of the market, as measured by the holding return (HR), the performance of British business was less impressive than from the accounting perspective provided by the ROE (Table 5.2). With the exception of the early 1970s, and, to a far less extent, the mid-1950s, HR was lower—sometimes significantly so, as in the late 1920s—than return on equity, whether mean or

---

[13] Kathleen Burk, *The First Privatisation: The Politicians, the City and the Denationalisation of Steel* (London, 1988).

Table 5.2. Leading British companies: HR, 1913–2000 (in %)

Year	Mean	Median	Minimum	Maximum	Standard deviation	N
1913	8.72	6.22	−36.45	79.17	17.99	41
1929	1.92	3.30	−36.32	29.35	13.58	48
1956	11.46	11.29	−28.94	84.10	18.41	40
1972	13.07	15.36	−20.31	48.39	16.45	39
2000	16.14	10.74	−56.38	264.66	43.12	53

Source: Performance project, Large Sample

median. Swings between minima and maxima were also far sharper, especially, once again, in the last benchmark period (1998–2000).

For British and, more generally, European investors, returns were comparatively low during the three years preceding the First World War. The mean HR stood at 8.72 per cent and the median at a lower 6.22 per cent. Out of a total of forty-two companies, fifteen produced a return of more than 10 per cent, and another eleven a return of more than 5 per cent. Investors in only four companies suffered a hypothetical loss. Companies in transport and communications (shipping firms such as Cunard, Royal Mail, and P&O), engineering (Howard & Bullough, Kynoch, and Metropolitan Carriage Wagon & Finance), and metals (Bolckow Vaughan and Guest, Keen & Nettlefolds) were the most likely to produce a positive return. Exceptional returns were realized by shareholders in British Westinghouse and Watney Combe Reid (respectively 79 and 61 per cent), two companies recovering from poor performance earlier in the decade.[14] 'Free-standing' companies, on the other hand, did far worse in terms of HR than in terms of ROE, with just over 5 per cent for De Beers and a negative return for Consolidated Goldfields. Railways, as expected, were a very conservative investment, with returns in the range 2–3 per cent. Banks were fractionally more attractive, with 4.5 per cent. The biggest losses were, perhaps unsurprisingly, suffered by investors in United Alkali—a company linked from its inception to an obsolete technology. Returns were on the whole lower in 1913 than during the previous two years.

Returns on investment were much lower in the late 1920s, with a mean of only 1.92 per cent, though the median was somewhat higher at 3.30 per cent. Compared with the pre-war years, a smaller proportion of companies (thirteen out of forty-seven) yielded more than 10 per cent and, especially, a far greater number (seventeen) offered negative returns. Banks (Lloyds and Midland), food, drink, and tobacco (Distillers, Watney Combe Reid, and British American Tobacco), chemicals (ICI and Lever Brothers), electrical engineering (GEC and AEI), as well as utility companies (County of London Electric Supply and Gas, Light & Coke) all had returns above or at about 10 per cent. Amongst the 'new' industries, oil, rubber and motor cars were disappointing (with negative returns for Anglo-Persian, Dunlop, and Morris), usually, and for most firms, as a result of HR falling dramatically in 1929. The highest losses, also mostly suffered in 1929, were experienced, not surprisingly, in the old industries: coal (Powell Duffryn with

[14] T.R. Gourvish and R.G. Wilson, *The British Brewing Industry 1830–1980* (Cambridge, 1994), pp. 284, 295–8; R. Jones and O. Marriott, *Anatomy of a Merger: A History of GEC, AEI and English Electric* (London, 1970), pp. 51–67.

−24.6 per cent), shipbuilding (Harland & Wolff with −8.4 per cent), and cotton (Fine Cotton Spinners with −9.4 per cent).

Holding return was higher in the mid-1950s than in earlier periods, with a mean of 11.46 per cent and a median of 11.29 per cent. The top performer was Shell, with 84 per cent, but another nine companies, including P&O, Hawker Siddeley, Stewarts & Lloyds, United Steel, Bowater, Distillers, AEI, and BP, achieved an HR higher than 20 per cent. All in all, this reflected the bull market that started in 1953.[15] There was a clearer match between ROE and HR, and investors in only two companies (Dunlop and Rank) recorded a substantial hypothetical loss (more than 20 per cent).

HR continued to improve, reaching an average of 12.49 per cent for the years 1970–2, though the median was once again lower at 5.69 per cent. For investors in twenty companies out of thirty-eight,[16] HR was higher than 15 per cent, with Tube Investments, Hawker Siddeley, Boots, and Trafalgar House all higher than 30 per cent. Banks (Natwest, Barclays, and Midland) were also strong, with returns exceeding 20 per cent. BP, Unilever, Courtaulds, GEC, and GKN performed creditably, with HRs between 10 and 15 per cent, ICI was lower (6.3 per cent), and Shell even lower (2.6 per cent). Troubles were clearly apparent for Vickers and BMC, with negative HRs of respectively −6 and −1 per cent.

HR was also high at the turn of the twenty-first century, with 18.63 per cent (mean), despite the burst of the IT bubble in spring 2000, though the median was significantly lower at 5.39 per cent. Eighteen companies (out of fifty-three) recorded an HR higher than 20 per cent, but the same number suffered negative returns. Anglo-American was the outlier, with an HR of 265 per cent, but high returns were produced by firms in IT, service to business, and media (Logica, Vodafone, WPP, Aegis, Pearson, Reuters, and Cable & Wireless), some of them fairly new business undertakings, thus confirming the mutation of British business during the previous decades. However, this buoyancy was not to be sustained, and companies such as EMI, Vodafone, and Pearson all experienced difficulties in the new century. At the other end of the scale, the more established companies (ICI, BP Amoco, BA, P&O, GKN, and Corus) were amongst the weakest performers.

CONCLUSION

Three points can be made in concluding this brief survey of the performance of British business in the twentieth century. The first concerns the relative stability of rates of return throughout the period under review. ROE has remained constant within the 9–11 per cent range, with the exception of the turn of the twenty-first century, when it shot up to over 20 per cent. And HR has also been fairly stable at around 10 per cent, with the exception of the mid-1920s, when it fell to just over 1 per cent and, again, at the turn of the twenty-first century, when it approached

---

[15] George G. Blakey, *The Post-War History of the London Stock Market* (Didcot, 1994), pp. 30–7.

[16] No HR is available for the seven state-owned companies and the two subsidiaries of foreign firms included in the sample for the benchmark period 1970–2.

20 per cent. While the fall of the stock market in 1929 partly explains the poor returns realized by investors in the late 1920s, the inordinately high ROE and HR in 1998–2000 reflect the new climate within which businesses operated in a market-oriented type of capitalism.

The second point relates to the variations observable within this stable environment. Not surprisingly, ROE displayed less variation than the more volatile HR, which reflects market expectations. This can be seen in the disparity between ROE and HR for some companies, and, at a more general level, in the much narrower difference between mean and median and the much lower standard deviation for ROE.

The third point concerns sectoral performance. Even though no clear pattern can be established, it appears that the food industry, including drinks and tobacco, and commercial activities have tended to produce the strongest performances. The 'old industries', i.e. textiles and metals, performed somewhat better than expected, especially the former, although the latter suffered badly in times of crisis, most markedly in the 1920s. The 'Chandlerian' firms of the Second Industrial Revolution were not, at any time in the twentieth century, the best performing ones: some occasionally did very well, but, as a group, they remained more or less around the national average. The same can be said of utilities, with two exceptions: on the one hand the railways, which displayed conservative results before the First World War and in the late 1920s, and on the other hand the state-owned companies, whose performance was dismal in the early 1970s. Finally, banks performed well above average in periods of globalization and below average under state regulation.

6

The Performance of French Business in the Twentieth Century

Youssef Cassis, Anne Dalmasso, and Pierre Vernus

THE DEVELOPMENT OF FRENCH BIG BUSINESS

The structure of French big business on the eve of First World War, while characteristic of that of the leading industrialized countries, also reflected the specificity of French industrial capitalism. The largest French companies were, by a wide margin, the railways companies—the PLM (Paris–Lyon–Méditerranée), Europe's largest company measured by total assets (over $1200 million), the Paris–Orléans (596), the 'Est' (583), the 'Nord' (500), and the 'Midi' (425).[1] The other firms making up the top ten non-financial companies were transport (the two shipping companies Messageries Maritimes and Compagnie Générale Transatlantique)[2] and utility (Compagnie Parisienne de Distribution d'Electricité, Compagnie Centrale d'Eclairage par le Gaz, and Compagnie Générale des Eaux)[3] companies, with assets between $30 and $60 million. No manufacturing company thus ranked among the country's top ten, the two largest (Saint-Gobain in glass and chemicals and Thompson-Houston in electrical engineering)[4] being respectively twelfth and thirteenth, with assets around the $25–30 million mark, followed by the metallurgical concerns Marine Homécourt and Schneider,[5] with assets just above $20 million. Because of their huge assets, since banks work with their clients' deposits, the large commercial banks (Crédit lyonnais, Société générale, Comptoir national d'escompte de Paris) all ranked amongst the country's ten

---

[1] F. Caron, *Histoire des chemins de fer en France*, 2 vols. (Paris, 1997–2005) and *Les grandes compagnies de chemin de fer en France, 1823–1937*: études présentées par François Caron, Archives économiques du Crédit Lyonnais, 5 (Geneva, 2005).

[2] M.-F. Berneron-Couvenhes, *Les Messageries maritimes: L'essor d'une grande compagnie de navigation française—1851–1894* (Paris, 2007).

[3] A. Beltran, *L'électricité dans la région parisienne 1878–1946* (Paris, 2002); J.-P. Williot, *L'Industrie du gaz à Paris au XIXe siècle* (Paris, 2010).

[4] J.-P. Daviet, *Une Multinationale à la française: Histoire de Saint-Gobain, 1665–1989* (Paris, 1989); P. Lanthier, *Les constructions électriques en France: financement et stratégie de six groupes industriels internationaux, 1880–1949*, Thèse de doctorat, Université de Paris-X Nanterre (1988).

[5] J.-M. Moine, *Les barons du fer* (Nancy, 1989); M.J. Rust, *Business and Politics in the Third Republic: The Comité des Forges and the French Steel Industry, 1896–1914*, PhD Thesis, Princeton University (1973).

largest companies, but this was also the case when using such criteria as share capital and market capitalization.[6]

French big business was thus clearly dominated by finance and services, which made up fourteen out of the country's twenty largest companies.[7] This trend was reinforced by the emergence of large enterprises in commercial activities, especially department stores (in the first place Bon Marché, which, with $26 million in assets, ranked in the top twenty, but also Printemps and Nouvelles Galeries). Within the manufacturing sector, the heavy industries, including ship-building, held sway.[8] Apart from Saint-Gobain and Thomson, large companies in the major industries of the Second Industrial Revolution (chemicals, electrical engineering, and mechanical engineering) remained on the fringe of big business and were only fractionally larger than firms in food or textiles.

The structure of French big business altered after the First World War. The railway companies remained the country's largest. More significant, however, was the rise of the industries of the Second Industrial Revolution, which had taken off fairly slowly before 1914. The rise was not as strong as in Britain, but still significant and particularly noticeable in motor cars, where France enjoyed an early lead before being overtaken by the US in 1906, though it still retained first place in Europe until the depression of the 1930s. By 1929, Citroën was France's largest manufacturing company (with assets reaching $67 million) and Renault was not far behind, though data are unavailable because the company remained in family ownership.[9] It was followed by Saint-Gobain ($51 million) and two newcomers: Michelin in rubber ($42 million) and Produits chimiques et métallurgiques d'Alais (Pechiney) in aluminium and chemicals ($41 million). In electrical engineering, the largest firm, CGE ($33 million), just about made it into the top twenty, with Thomson-Houston ($25 million) a little behind.

Nevertheless, big business was still dominated by the heavy industries, with the large collieries of Northern France such as Mines de Lens ($55 million) and Mines de Vicoigne-Noeuds & Drocourt ($44 million) on the one hand, and the iron and steel concerns such as Nord Est ($38 million) and Longwy ($36 million) on the other. Forward integration for the former and backward integration for the latter mainly took place through cross-shareholding or joint ownership of subsidiary companies.

In finance and services, shipping companies, such as Compagnie générale transatlantique ($54 million) and utility companies, such as Lyonnaise des eaux ($38 million), Energie électrique du littoral méditerranéen ($35 million), and Union d'électricité ($34 million) remained prominent. Taken individually, they were now smaller than the largest industrial concerns. However, especially in

[6] B. Desjardins, M. Lescure, R. Nougaret, A. Plessis, and A. Straus, dir., *Le Crédit lyonnais 1863–1986* (Geneva, 2003).

[7] The first part of this part is based on the project's 'Small Sample', in other words on the twenty largest French companies, as opposed to the 'Large Sample', which has been assembled on a sectoral base and includes around 40–55 companies, depending on the years. For a methodological discussion of these two samples, see Chapter 2.

[8] Y. Cassis, *Big Business: The European Experience in the Twentieth Century* (Oxford, 1997).

[9] P. Fridenson, *Histoire des usines Renault*, i: *Naissance de la grande entreprise* (Paris, 1972); S. Schweitzer, *Des engrenages à la chaîne: Les usines Citroën, 1915–1935* (Lyon, 1982); J.-L. Loubet, *La maison Peugeot* (Paris, 2009).

electricity, they were at the heart of vast business groups (Union d'électricité, for example, was linked to seventy-five other companies, including Lyonnaise des eaux and Compagnie parisienne de distribution d'électricité) which, taken as a whole, would reach a much larger size.[10] With the odd exception, such as Saint-Frères in textiles and Galeries Lafayette in distribution, other industries, both traditional and new, such as oil, were left behind. Banks, for their part, were weakened by war and inflation, but in spite of their decline remained an integral part of French big business.

Perhaps surprisingly, French big business was not fundamentally transformed by depression, war, occupation, and reconstruction. It was rather its organization, in particular its form of ownership, that was altered through the nationalization of some of its key components. The railway companies had already been national-ized by the Popular Front in 1937. They were followed in 1945–6 by the com-mercial banks (which retained, however, their corporate identity), the insurance companies, the coal mines, the electricity and gas (though not water) companies, air transport, and the car maker Renault, following accusations of collaboration with the German war effort made against its head and founder, Louis Renault.[11]

Leaving aside the state-owned monopolies—SNCF (railways), EDF (electricity), GDF (gas), and Charbonnages de France (coal mining)—French big business was henceforth dominated by the industries of the Second Industrial Revolution. Oil finally took off with the Compagnie Française des Pétroles (CFP): created in 1924 on the state's initiative, it had become France's largest industrial company by 1956 (with $248 million assets). The subsidiaries of the two 'Anglo-Saxon' giants, Esso-Standard ($170 million) and Pétroles BP (132 million), were also in the country's top twenty companies. Concentration in the iron and steel industry led to the formation of two groups of European dimensions: Sidelor ($207 million) and Usinor ($208 million),[12] with Le Creusot ($181 million) and de Wendel ($168 million), the latter still largely in family hands,[13] likewise in the top twenty. Saint-Gobain ($164 million), Pechiney ($161 million), and Ugine ($104 million) in chemicals, Alsthom ($141 million) and CGE ($106 million) in electrical engin-eering,[14] Renault ($188 million) and Citroën ($131 million) in motor cars, and SNECMA ($98 million) in aerospace, as well as the Messageries Maritimes ($190 million) in shipping, completed, together with the four leading banks, the group of the country's twenty largest companies. Commercial banks, however, now in state ownership, continued their decline. In terms of capital (though not of course of assets), not a single one featured amongst France's twenty largest companies. Only the privately owned Banque de Paris et des Pays-Bas (investment banks had not been nationalized) still managed to do so.

---

[10] H. Morsel, 'Les groupes dans les industries électriques en France avant les nationalisations', *Cahiers d'histoire*, 26, 4 (1981), 365–76; C. Vuillermot, *Pierre-Marie Durand et l'Energie industrielle: L'histoire d'un groupe électrique 1906–1945* (Paris, 2001).

[11] C. Andrieu, L. Le Van, and A. Prost, *Les nationalisations de la Libération: de l'utopie au compromis* (Paris, 1987).

[12] E. Godelier, *Usinor–Arcelor: du local au global* (Paris, 2006).

[13] J. Marseille, *Les Wendel, 1704–2004* (Paris, 2004); H. James, *Family Capitalism: Wendels, Haniels, Falcks, and the Continental European Model* (Cambridge, Mass., 2006).

[14] J. Marseille and F. Torres, dir., *Alcatel Alsthom—Histoire de la Compagnie Générale d'Electricité* (Paris, 1992).

By the early 1970s, after thirty years of sustained economic growth, French big business had reached new dimension, both in quantitative and in qualitative terms. Quantitatively, the sizes of the leading French companies were comparable to those of their main European competitors in Britain and Germany.[15] Qualitatively, in each of the main sectors of the Second Industrial Revolution, which reached full maturity during the three decades following the Second World War, France had one or two companies capable, or supposedly capable, of competing in the world markets: Renault (with a turnover of $2,429 million in 1972), Peugeot ($2,134 million), and Citroën ($2,089 million) in motor cars; Total ($2,806 million) and Elf ($1,854 million) in oil; CGE ($2,164 million) and Thomson ($1,521 million) in electrical engineering; Pechiney-Ugine-Kuhlmann ($2,651 million) and Rhône-Poulenc ($2,479 million) in chemicals; Usinor ($1,046 million) and Wendel-Sidelor ($1,099 million) in iron and steel; Michelin ($1,681 million) in tyres; Saint-Gobain-Pont-à-Mousson ($2,690 million) in building materials—all of fairly comparable size. These companies, which, with the state-owned monopolies (SNCF, EDF, and GDF) and the big commercial and investment banks (BNP, Crédit lyonnais, Société générale, and Paribas), made up the bulk of France's top twenty, were often the result of wide-ranging mergers encouraged by the French government as part of its policy of 'national champions'.[16]

In terms of corporate identity, the core of French big business did not change very much during the last thirty years of the twentieth century. The giant firms that dominated the field in 1970 were still present in 2000: Total, now merged with Elf (and Petrofina of Belgium), the country's largest firm measured by turnover ($115 billion); Peugeot, now merged with Citroën ($41 billion); Renault ($37 billion); CGE, now called Alcatel ($29 billion); Générale des Eaux, now called Vivendi ($42 billions); Saint-Gobain ($27 billions); BNP and Paribas, now merged ($51 billion); EDF ($34 billion); Rhône-Poulenc, now called Aventis following its merger with Hoechst of Germany ($21 billion).

Three major changes, however, best characterize the profile of French big business at the end of the twentieth century, shaped by the globalization of the world economy and the advent of the Third Industrial Revolution. First, with or without a change of name, a shift took place in the domains of activity of the country's leading firms, usually as a result of mergers and/or de-mergers. The best known examples are those of Alcatel focusing on telecommunications, Vivendi on media and telecommunications, and Aventis on pharmaceuticals and biotechnology. Second, a number of newcomers, all in services, emerged at the top: Axa in insurance ($94 billion); Carrefour ($60 billion), from a large company in commercial activities to one of the giants of French and European business; France Telecom ($31 billion); Adecco ($27 billion) in business services (temporary employment); Pinault-Printemps-Redoute ($23 billion), the commercial and luxury goods group set up by François Pinault. And third, a change took place within the hierarchy of French business, with a number of 'big names' (Usinor, Michelin,

---

[15] Cassis, *Big Business*, pp. 65–71.

[16] See G. Dyas and H. Thanheiser, *The Emerging European Enterprise: Strategy and Structure in French and German Industry* (London, 1976); M. Bauer and E. Cohen, *Qui gouverne les groupes industriels?* (Paris, 1981).

Danone, Pechiney, L'Oréal, Thalès, and others) no longer in the top twenty, though still large and influential.

PERFORMANCE: RETURN ON EQUITY

Measured in terms of return on equity (ROE), the performance of French business was fairly stable across the twentieth century.[17] With the exception of the mid-1950s, when it fell under 7 per cent, ROE hovered around the 9–10 per cent mark, with a peak of 11.3 per cent before 1914 and a trough of 8.4 per cent in the early 1970s. Mean and median only deviated with some significance in 1911–13, the only benchmark period when the highest rate of return achieved by one company (*Le Petit Parisien*) reached an inordinate level. Losses, on the other hand, were never abysmal. And, unlike in Britain, for example, returns were in the European norm in the years 1998–2000 (Table 6.1).

The mean ROE for the leading French companies in 1911–13 stood at 11.3 per cent, the highest of the five benchmark periods. The median, on the other hand, was only 8.7 per cent, since the arithmetic average was inflated by the profits of the family-owned newspaper company *Le Petit Parisien* (69 per cent), whose share capital was a mere 14.6 million francs ($2.9 million) but whose circulation exceeded one million by the turn of the twentieth century. The performance of the largest companies—the highly regulated railway companies and the rather conservative commercial banks—remained fairly modest, around 7–8 per cent. Conversely, the performance of another component of French big business, the iron and steel industry, was much stronger: its ROE averaged more than 20 per cent, with individual companies such as Châtillon-Commentry (33 per cent) and Longwy (24 per cent) being particularly profitable. Such high profits might have derived, at least in part, from the sale of iron ore from Meurthe-et-Moselle. However, the most profitable companies were to be found, on the one hand, amongst those operating in the colonial empire or abroad (the Chemin de fer de Gafsa, for example, with an ROE of 47 per cent) and, on the other, in sectors on the fringe of big business, at least in the first half of the twentieth century, such as newspapers.

Table 6.1. Leading French companies: ROE, 1913–2000 (in %)

Year	Mean	Median	Minimum	Maximum	Standard deviation	N
1911–13	11.26	8.65	0.30	68.99	10.83	39
1927–9	10.42	9.30	−0.32	30.24	6.61	43
1954–6	6.73	5.84	−1.09	23.35	4.84	46
1970–2	8.38	7.68	−9.09	26.34	6.37	44
1998–2000	9.69	10.35	−13.62	23.06	6.14	46

Source: Performance project, Large Sample

[17] See footnote 7.

Rates of return were slightly lower in the late 1920s than on the eve of the First World War, with an average 10.4 per cent for the a sample of forty-three firms. The best performing firms were in industries dominated by medium–large companies: in food, drink, and tobacco (Raffinerie et sucrerie Say, in sugar refining, achieved 30.2 per cent); media and publishing (wood and paper products in this study's industrial classification) with Agence Havas (21.8 per cent) and Hachette (19.4 per cent); commercial activities, with the department stores Bon Marché (15.2 per cent) and Galeries Lafayette (14.1 per cent); and even textile (16.1 per cent for Dollfuss Mieg). With the exception of Michelin (26.4 per cent) and Rhône-Poulenc (25.2), the new industries were disappointing: 9.6 per cent for chemicals, 8.7 per cent for electrical engineering, 6 per cent for transport equipment (though Peugeot achieved 12.9 per cent); banks and the heavy industries had rates of return of the same order of magnitude. Interestingly, a similar trend can be observed in Germany, especially as far food and department stores are concerned.

Rates of return were low in the early to mid-1950s, mainly as a result of high investment undertaken during the years of reconstruction. ROE stood on average at 6.7 per cent (and the median at 5.8 per cent), once again with strong performance from media and publishing: 23.4 per cent for Havas and 18.8 per cent for Hachette. Somewhat surprisingly, the commercial banks also did well (11.7 per cent on average and 14.5 per cent for the Comptoir National d'Escompte de Paris), though this must be attributed to the very low level to which their shareholders' equity had fallen following nationalization. Food, drinks, and tobacco (Say and Lesieur) were above average at about 10 per cent (10.3 and 9.5 per cent, respectively). Amongst the large firms in oil, chemicals, motor cars, and electrical engineering dominating French big business, Rhône-Poulenc, Renault, and the CFP stood out, with ROE between 9.5 and 10 per cent. Basic and fabricated metals, for their part, only averaged 1.7 per cent, with a maximum of 2.3 per cent for Usinor and a minimum of 1.6 per cent for Longwy.

The effects of the industrial policy conducted in France during the 'Trente Glorieuses'—the thirty years following the Second World War—marked by a high degree of state intervention, cannot be discussed within the scope of this chapter. Economic growth was spectacular—at an annualized rate of 5.05 per cent for GDP and 4.05 per cent for GDP per capita between 1950 and 1973.[18] In terms of business performance, however, the results were somewhat disappointing, with mean ROE standing at 8.4 per cent and median slightly lower at 7.7 per cent. Aggregate returns were no better for the top twenty companies (mean at 6.5 per cent and median at 5.3 per cent) with, at an individual level, a high 20.1 per cent for Michelin and a low 5.1 per cent for Rhône-Poulenc. Interestingly, the strongest performances came from firms forming the outer circle of French big business and often consisting of newcomers in new activities: supermarket chains (commercial activities in this study's industrial classification), which experienced tremendous growth in the 1950s and 1960s, with Carrefour (41.8 per cent) and, to a lesser extent, Casino (16.1 per cent); construction and property companies, with Bouygues (21.8 per cent) on its way to becoming the world's largest construction company a decade or so later; leisure and tourism,

---

[18] A. Maddison, *The World Economy: A Millennial Perspective* (OECD, 2006), pp. 186–7.

with Jacques Borel International, the chain of motorway restaurants (22 per cent), and Club Méditerranée (15.3 per cent); media, with Hachette (13.9 per cent) and Publicis (12.0 per cent); and specialized fields within chemicals and pharmaceuticals, such as l'Air liquide (22.1 per cent) in industrial gases and l'Oréal (18.1 per cent) in cosmetics. At the other extreme, the performances of the state-owned enterprises were particularly poor: whether in transport (Air France, RATP, and SNCF), energy (Gaz de France), insurance (AGF, GAN, and UAP), or motor cars (Renault), ROE was around 0 per cent. The worst performer belonged to the 'mature' industries: Agache-Willot, in textiles, suffered a 9.1 per cent loss and was soon to go bankrupt after an ill-fated attempted at restructuring the sector.

French business did not experience a surge in profitability in the closing years of the twentieth century. At 9.7 per cent (mean) and 10.35 per cent (median), ROE was fractionally higher than in the early 1970s. As for earlier benchmark years, the largest companies were not the most profitable. Most of them performed creditably, with ROE in the 10–15 per cent range: Société générale (13.6 per cent), Total (13.5 per cent), Carrefour (13.4 per cent), France Telecom (12.3 per cent), Alcatel (11.9 per cent), Saint-Gobain (11.1 per cent), BNP Paribas (10.9 per cent), and Renault (10.8 per cent). On the other hand, Publicis, in media and communication, achieved 23.1 per cent, Hermes, in luxury goods, 19.2 per cent, and Atos Origin, in information technology, 18.5 per cent. Medium to large firms in new business activities thus tended to be more profitable than giant firms, without, however, being at the frontier of the new technologies. Moreover, the gap between the two was not exceptionally wide, while the only firm suffering a substantial loss (13.6 per cent) was Adecco Travail, in services to business (job recruitment and employment agency).

PERFORMANCE: HOLDING RETURN

From an investor's point of view, the holding return (HR) on the securities of French leading companies was higher than the European average during the three first benchmark periods, and, indeed, together with the return on Belgian stock, it was significantly higher in the late 1920s and the mid-1950s—with 38.4 and 33.7 per cent, respectively. On the other hand, it was comparatively poor in the early 1970s (4.1 per cent), but more or less within the norm, with 15.1 per cent, in the years 1998–2000 (Table 6.2).

Table 6.2. Leading French companies: HR, 1913–2000 (in %)

Year	Mean	Median	Minimum	Maximum	Standard deviation	N
1911–13	6.56	4.87	−31.39	51.10	14.66	40
1927–9	38.43	33.36	−7.81	160.49	30.22	41
1954–6	33.65	24.83	−18.36	311.12	50.49	41
1970–2	4.14	4.46	−29.80	56.95	16.55	37
1998–2000	15.12	10.16	−53.72	84.36	31.49	31

Source: Performance project, Large Sample

As in all European countries, HR was comparatively low in France in 1913 (6.6 per cent), even though the rate was second only to that achieved in Britain. Like ROE, HR was on average lower for the largest companies (3.9 per cent for the top twenty)—though the reverse was true for median HR (5.8 per cent for the top twenty). Investors in such large companies as Saint-Gobain, the Messageries Maritimes, the Compagnie Générale Transatlantique, or the Mines d'Anzin— the country's worst performing firms—suffered heavy losses, with a negative return of around −10 per cent. By contrast, shareholders in medium–large companies such Alais, Froges, Camargue (Pechiney) in aluminium, Alsacienne de constructions mécaniques in mechanical engineering, and the Raffineries et sucreries Say in food—the best performing ones—enjoyed a return of some 50 per cent. Railway, banking, and iron and steel companies were around the national average, a little lower for the first, a little higher for the last two—with PLM, Crédit lyonnais, Comptoir National d'Escompte de Paris, and Schneider standing out at more than 7 per cent.

HR was much higher in the bull market of the late 1920s (the index of French share more than doubled between 1926 and 1929), averaging 35 per cent for the years 1927–9. Returns reached their peak, at 59.99 per cent, at the end of December 1928, before collapsing to 4 per cent the following year. HR was nevertheless very volatile, with a standard deviation of 30.2 per cent (51.26 per cent in 1928), as against 6.6 per cent for ROE. The more capital-intensive industries yielded the highest returns: basic and fabricated metals and utilities with more than 50 per cent, mining and electrical engineering with more than 40 per cent, and chemicals and pharmaceuticals, transport equipment, and financial intermediaries with more than 30 per cent—partly as a result of a more active market, because of the large amount of public issues offered in the late 1920s, and partly because their returns fell more sharply than those of the more traditional industries in 1929. The highest returns were made by investors in the Société alsacienne de constructions mécaniques, an engineering company, with 160 per cent, while another eleven companies yielded between 50 and 100 per cent.

HR was nearly as high, and even more volatile, in the mid-1950s, with a 33.65 per cent mean and a 24.83 per cent median, despite the pretty sluggish state of the stock market.[19] Eight companies yielded a return of more than 50 per cent, including three in oil (Esso Standard, with a staggering 311 per cent, Pétroles BP, and Compagnie Française des Pétroles), two in chemicals (Pechiney and Ugine), and two in services (Havas and Galeries Lafayette), as well as the leading investment bank, the Banque de Paris et des Pays-Bas. HR was higher than 25 per cent for another twelve companies, while at the other end of the spectrum, it was particularly low for utilities (in this case the water companies Lyonnaise des eaux and Compagnie Générale des Eaux, the latter with a negative return) and the building and construction companies (Grands travaux de Marseille and Société générale d'entreprises).

---

[19] O. Feiertag, 'The international opening-up of the Paris Bourse: overdraft-economy curbs and market dynamics', in Y. Cassis and E. Bussière, eds., *London and Paris as International Financial Centres in the Twentieth Century* (Oxford, 2005).

Uncharacteristically, HR was lower than ROE in the early 1970s: 4.14 per cent on average and a very close median of 4.46 per cent. The best performers were, once again, outside the group of the twenty largest companies, with Carrefour (56.95 per cent), Lainière de Roubaix (36.74 per cent), Club Méditerranée (22 per cent), and the Compagnie des compteurs, part of the Schlumberger group (15.2 per cent); and so were the worst—the mining companies Le Nickel and Peñarroya, with negative returns of some 25 per cent, the construction companies Bouygues and Auxilière d'entreprises, as well as the heavy loss-making textile concern Agache-Willot, all around −10 to −15 per cent. Collectively, however, the largest companies did fractionally better, with 7.5 per cent mean and 8.6 per cent median, respectively, though the figures do not include the loss-making state-owned enterprises whose stock was not traded on the stock exchange. Peugeot (28.6 per cent) and Michelin (14.9 per cent), two family-owned firms, stood out, while another nine were in the 5–10 per cent bracket. Investors in Citroën, on the other hand, soon to be taken over by Peugeot, suffered a loss of 7.95 per cent.

With a mean of 15.12 per cent and a median of 10.16 per cent, HR was just below the European average at the close of the twentieth century and still fairly high despite the burst of the IT bubble in spring 2000. As in previous benchmark periods, with the exception of the pre-1914 years, the return was higher for the group of the twenty largest companies—with a mean of 21.86 per cent and a median of 19.22 per cent, the third highest in Europe after Finland and Italy in terms of mean and the second after Finland in terms of median. Investors in Alcatel, France's eleventh largest company, enjoyed the highest return (84.36 per cent), followed by Bouygues (eighteenth), with 65.90 per cent. The country's two largest companies, Total Fina Elf (22.60 per cent) and Axa (35.82 per cent), also proved a lucrative investment. Amongst the medium–large firms, high returns were obtained by investors in firms in services to business (Cap Gemini Ernst & Young with 65.9 per cent and Adecco, with 58.53 per cent), high-tech industries (CEA-Industries, with 45.5 per cent), media (Lagardère Groupe, with 32.85 per cent), and luxury goods (Hermes, with 39.39 per cent). But it was equally amongst these medium to large firms in new businesses that investors suffered the heaviest losses—negative returns in Accor (hotel management), Atos Origin (services to business), and Christian Dior (luxury goods) were all in double digits.

CONCLUSION

This brief survey of the performance of French business in the twentieth century does not entirely square with the idea of a 'specificity' of France's economic and business development. In many respects, France has been very much in the European norm, including in the emergence of large firms. During the three first benchmark periods, until the mid-1950s, French big business was closer to its British and, especially, German counterparts than is often assumed, it had virtually caught up by the early 1970s, and undertook similar changes during the globalization of the late twentieth century. In terms of performance, rates of return have been close to the European average, with one major exception: an HR level in the late 1920s far higher than that of other European countries, except for Belgium—no doubt a reflection of the boom enjoyed by the French economy following the stabilization of the franc by Raymond Poincaré in 1926.

The performance of French big business, in the narrow sense of the country's twenty largest firms (the Small Sample), proved stronger than that of a larger sample of about forty-five companies, spectacularly so if measured by HR in the late 1920s. Nevertheless, in terms of individual results, the best performers have tended to be firms on the fringe of big business, medium to large companies in the service industries, especially distribution and luxury goods, a fact already noticed by Jacques Marseille[20]—though it is by no means certain that this constitutes a French specificity.

---

[20] J. Marseille, ed., *Les performances des entreprises françaises au XXème siècle* (Paris, 1995).

7

The Performance of German Big Business in the Twentieth Century

Diane Dammers and Hendrik K. Fischer

INTRODUCTION

The industrialization of the Western Hemisphere since the nineteenth century and the extraordinary growth of the European economies were accompanied by the emergence of large-scale enterprises, often referred to collectively as big business. Considering its important role in the modern German economy, it is surprising that—except for some listings of big companies[1]—the history of German big business in the nineteenth and twentieth centuries has not yet been written. This chapter will trace the development of the Chandlerian modern business enterprise in twentieth-century Germany by examining the evolution of its structure and economic performance.[2]

---

[1] M. Fiedler, 'Die 100 größten Unternehmen in Deutschland—nach Zahlen ihrer Beschäftigten—1907, 1938, 1973 und 1995', *Zeitschrift für Unternehmensgeschichte* 44 (1999), 32–66; M. Fiedler, 'Die 100 größten Unternehmen von 1938—ein Nachtrag', *Zeitschrift für Unternehmensgeschichte* 44 (1999), 235–42; J. Kocka and H. Siegrist, 'Die hundert größten Industrieunternehmen im späten 19. und 20. Jahrhundert. Expansion, Diversifikation und Integration im internationalen Vergleich', in N. Horn and J. Kocka, eds., *Recht und Entwicklung der Großunternehmen im späten 19. und 20. Jahrhundert* (Göttingen: Vandenhoeck & Ruprecht, 1979), pp. 55–122; H. Siegrist, 'Deutsche Großunternehmen vom späten 19. Jahrhundert bis zur Weimarer Republik. Integration, Diversifikation und Organisation bei den 100 größten deutschen Industrieunternehmen (1887–1927) in international vergleichender Perspektive', *Geschichte und Gesellschaft* 6 (1980), 60–102; D. Weder, *Die 200 größten deutschen Aktiengesellschaften. Beziehungen zwischen Größe, Lebensdauer und Wettbewerbschancen von Unternehmen*, PhD Dissertation, Johann Wolfgang Goethe-Universität, Frankfurt am Main (1968); Youssef Cassis, *Big Business: The European Experience in the Twentieth Century* (Oxford: Oxford University Press, 1997); W. Feldenkirchen, 'Concentration in German industry 1870–1939', in H. Pohl, ed., *The Concentration Process in the Entrepreneurial Economy since the Late 19th Century: Lecture Held at the 9th International Congress of Economic History in Berne, Switzerland, on August 28, 1986* (Stuttgart: Franz Steiner, 1988), pp. 113–46.

[2] See A.D. Chandler, *Scale and Scope: The Dynamics of Industrial Capitalism*, 3rd edn (Cambridge, Mass.: Belknap Press, 1994), *The Visible Hand: The Managerial Revolution in American Business* (Cambridge, Mass.: Belknap Press, 1977), and *Strategy and Structure: Chapters in the History of the American Industrial Enterprise* (Cambridge, Mass.: MIT Press, 1962). Chandler's impact on business history was indubitably huge; see M.J. Iversen, 'Measuring Chandler's impact on European business studies since the 1960s', *Business History Review* 82, 2 (2008), 279–92.

The study's focus is quantitative, with an emphasis on size of capital assets, business turnover, and profitability. The main sources for balance sheet data on German companies were *Salings Börsen-Jahrbuch* for the first two benchmark periods (1911–13 and 1927–9) and the *Handbuch der Deutschen Aktien-Gesellschaften* for the third and fourth benchmark periods (1954–6 and 1970–2). For 1970–2 and 1998–2000, the *Handbuch der Großunternehmen* was also used. With the help of this encyclopaedia, it was possible to identify companies not listed at the stock exchange and to include them systematically in the samples. For the last benchmark period (1998–2000), an electronic database was available, which facilitated the selection process.[3]

PECULIARITIES OF THE GERMAN CASE

Before proceeding with the analysis, we must recall some special features of German big business. In contrast, for example, to the British case, in Germany, large companies are not necessarily organized as joint-stock companies (Aktien-gesellschaft, AG). Certainly, at the beginning of the twentieth century, the majority of German large-scale enterprises were joint-stock companies, but in 1927, 12 of the 100 biggest companies listed by Hannes Siegrist[4] were organized as business partnerships or limited corporations. Others were joint-stock companies in a formal sense, but they were controlled by an entrepreneurial family and their shares were not listed on the stock exchange.[5]

According to German law, only joint-stock companies were obligated to publish accounts of assets and liabilities. That is why, in the early benchmark periods, it was impossible to include in the samples companies that were not listed on the stock exchange. In the later benchmark periods, those companies could be taken into account, but mostly their data were incomplete. In particular, holding return (HR) could not be calculated, because share prices did not exist. Thus, we concentrate on return on equity (ROE) to measure economic performance and neglect HR. Especially in the 1998–2000 sample, several gaps are caused by companies not publishing balance sheets. In some industries, it was hardly

---

[3] *Salings Börsen-Jahrbuch. Ein Handbuch für Bankiers und Kapitalisten* (Berlin/Leipzig/Hamburg: Verlag für Börsen- und Finanzliteratur, 1881/82ff.). *Handbuch der Großunternehmen. Anerkannt durch den Adreßbuchausschuß der Deutschen Wirtschaft* (Darmstadt: Hoppenstedt, 1952ff.); *Handbuch der Deutschen Aktien-Gesellschaften. Das Spezial-Archiv der Deutschen Wirtschaft* (Darmstadt/Wien/ Zürich: Verlag für Börsen- und Finanzliteratur, 1896/97ff.); *Hoppenstedt Auskunfts-CD Großunternehmen* (Darmstadt: Hoppenstedt, 1996ff.); *Hoppenstedt Aktienführer, CD* (Darmstadt: Hoppenstedt, 1998ff.). The balance sheet data were mostly gathered from Hoppenstedt Aktienführer 2002 (2001), which contains the balance sheets and other key data of all German joint-stock companies. If the required data were not available in these periodical publications, they were extracted directly from the published balance sheets, which are collected at the 'Wirtschaftsarchiv' (Economic Archive) of the University of Cologne.

[4] Siegrist, *Großunternehmen*, 86.

[5] See Andrea Colli, *The History of Family Business, 1850–2000* (Cambridge: Cambridge University Press, 2003), pp. 36–7; Hans Pohl, 'Zur Geschichte von Organisation und Leitung deutscher Großunternehmen seit dem 19. Jahrhundert', *Zeitschrift für Unternehmensgeschichte (ZUG)* 26 (1981), 143–78, 165.

possible to identify the biggest companies because most large-scale enterprises even today do not publish their figures, for example in the sectors of leisure and tourism and of media.

Consequently, our choice of companies is distorted to a certain extent. In the early benchmark periods, the selection is less representative because only joint-stock companies could be taken into account, but their data are almost complete. In the later benchmark periods, it is more likely that the biggest companies are identified, but the material is less complete.

The second peculiarity is the central role of the state in German big business. Right from the beginning of the period under consideration, all big railway companies were state-owned, so they were not included in the sample. The same is true for the German broadcasting stations. The biggest ones were not organized as private companies, but as so-called *öffentlich-rechtliche Unternehmen* (enterprises under public law). These companies were run autonomously, but they were financed by taxes, so they were not included in the sample either.

Finally, it must be remembered that Germany had different currencies throughout the twentieth century. Until 1923, the old Mark (the former Goldmark) was still valid. After the great inflation, a currency reform was undertaken, which resulted in the implementation of the Reichsmark (RM). After the Second World War, the Reichsmark was replaced by the Deutsche Mark (DM) in 1948 (in West Germany). Because of the changing currency, it does not make sense to compare absolute values of different benchmark periods.

THE PERFORMANCE OF GERMAN BIG BUSINESS

Because of the changing economic structure, the composition of the sectoral tableau was modulated from one benchmark period to the next. Some new sectors such as media or business services were added in the course of time, while others disappeared, for example free-standing companies. Other sectors were divided or merged. So the sectors 'reflect the economic structure of the time of the benchmark years; however, each firm will be uniquely identified according to its core business activities by an ISIC code. Thus, while the sectors are flexible, the company identification is not and the ISIC codes are the same for all observation years.'[6]

In the last years of the Kaiserreich, big business in Germany was dominated by heavy industry, disregarding the banking sector, which cannot be compared with the others because of differing balance sheet structures.[7] In 1911–13, six of the twenty-five biggest companies belonged to the mining or metal industry.[8] Heavy

---

[6] Cassis, Youssef and Camilla Brautaset, 'The Performance of European Business in the Twentieth Century', Paper presented at the International Colloquium on Business Performance in the 20th Century: A Comparative Perspective, Milan 14–16 October 2004, p. 8.

[7] See Ulrich Wengenroth, 'Germany: competition abroad—cooperation at home, 1870–1990', in Alfred D. Chandler, Franco Amatori, and Takashi Hikino, eds., *Big Business and the Wealth of Nations* (Cambridge: Cambridge University Press, 1997), pp. 139–75, 140–51.

[8] Assets/turnover and performance of all companies included in the top twenty-five, also called the Small Sample, can be found in the appendix.

industry represented 28.8 per cent of the total assets of all companies included in the Large Sample, exclusive of the financial companies. In second place was the transport sector with the huge shipping companies HAPAG and Norddeutscher Lloyd.[9] The four companies of land and water transport included in the Small Sample (top twenty-five) represented 17.6 per cent of the total assets. In third place was electrical engineering. The three companies of this industrial sector held 14.0 per cent of all assets. Other important sectors were utilities as well as oils and chemicals. Admittedly, the companies of these industrial sectors were not as large as those of the sectors already mentioned, but with respectively three (utilities) and two (oils and chemicals) companies in the top twenty-five, these two sectors still played an important role in German big business in 1911–13.

Considering the general development of the German economy between 1850 and 1913, these results are not surprising. However, in a European comparative perspective, it is remarkable that—unlike, for example, the British case—there are no railway companies in the German sample, although railways had played an important role in the economic development of the nineteenth century. This is due to the gradual nationalization of railways in Germany after 1870. By 1912, only about one-twentieth of the whole railway network of 60,521 kilometres was still run by private companies, which were too small to be included in the sample.

It is also not very surprising that the leading sectors of the Second Industrial Revolution, the electrical and chemical industries, are also well represented in the sample. The big players of these dynamic and modern industries (Bayer, BASF, Siemens, and AEG) all appeared in the top twenty-five sample; remarkably, two of them (Bayer and Siemens) were still among the biggest companies in the last benchmark period.

A quick view of the profitability of the top twenty-five companies shows that the performance of big business seems to mirror the general state of the economy. As can be seen from Table 7.1, the best-performing sectors in 1911–13 measured by ROE were the then modern industries like chemicals (average ROE 25.4 per cent) and electrical engineering (average ROE 15.8 per cent). But the companies of the leading sectors of the First Industrial Revolution in Germany—mining and metals—could also keep up with the others. Therefore, Youssef Cassis notes the importance of chemicals and electrical engineering, but warns 'of over-emphasizing their weight in the world of German big business before 1914'.[10]

According to company size, heavy industry was still the strongest sector of German big business; metal companies were even as profitable as the electrical engineering companies (average ROE 15.8 per cent). In fourth place came mechanical engineering (average ROE 12.5 per cent) followed by the utilities sector (average ROE 11.7 per cent), another branch with a promising future.

A look at the best-performing individual companies of the Large Sample confirms these observations (Table 7.2): the three best-performing companies come from the chemical industry, and the three biggest electrical engineering companies appear among the best performers as well.

After the Second World War, German business was affected by rationalization and the formation of big industrial conglomerates on the lines of American

---

[9] See Cassis, *Big Business*, p. 26.   [10] Cassis, *Big Business*, p. 24.

Table 7.1. German companies: average shares of total turnover and average performance (ROE) according to sector, 1911–13 (in %)

Sector	Average share of the sum of assets represented in the Large Sample	Average performance of all three companies represented in the Large Sample
1 Mining	11.6	8.5
2 Utilities	6.8	11.7
5 Construction and property	2.8	−11.8
6 Commercial activities	1.6	9.6
7 Financial intermediation		10.6
8 Food, drink, and tobacco	1.7	10.7
9 Textiles and leather	2.2	10.0
10 Mechanical engineering	4.0	12.5
11 Electrical engineering	14.0	15.8
12 Transport equipment	4.8	7.7
13 Metals	17.2	15.8
14 Wood and paper	2.4	7.0
16 Free-standing companies	7.3	6.4
17 Water transport	10.8	9.9
18 Land transport	6.7	8.1
22 Oils and chemicals	5.9	25.4

developments.[11] Therefore, it is not surprising that in 1927–9, as can be seen from Table 7.3, the sample is dominated by two industrial sectors: metals with 25.3 per cent and chemicals and pharmaceuticals with 19.5 per cent of the sum of assets represented in the Large Sample, excluding financial intermediation. In both sectors, the degree of concentration was very high: the biggest industrial company in the 1927–9 sample is Vereinigte Stahlwerke AG, with total assets of 2.073 billion RM in 1927. It exceeded Friedrich Krupp AG, the second-biggest company in the metal industry, by more than four times. The biggest chemical enterprise was IG Farbenindustrie AG, with a balance sheet total of 1.818 billion RM. It was even more than six times larger than the second-biggest chemical company, Kali-Industrie AG. These huge firms were established in the middle of the 1920s by merging most of the former biggest players in their respective industrial sectors. Vereinigte Stahlwerke included nearly all of the major metal and coal enterprises (e.g. Thyssen and Phoenix). Only Krupp, Hoesch, Klöckner, Gutehoffnungshütte, and Mannesmann remained independent.[12]

The history of the second big trust of the Weimar era started earlier. In 1904, three big chemical enterprises (Agfa, BASF, and Bayer) established the first so-called Interessengemeinschaft (IG, or community of interests). The intended purpose of this IG was to represent the common interests of its three members, which were still independent companies. In 1925 and 1926, these three companies

[11] Wengenroth, 'Germany', p. 152; Cassis, *Big Business*, pp. 48–9.

[12] For details, see Alfred Reckendrees, *Das 'Stahltrust'-Projekt. Die Gründung der Vereinigte Stahlwerke A.G. und ihre Unternehmensentwicklung 1926–1933/34* (Schriftenreihe zur Zeitschrift für Unternehmensgeschichte, Vol. 5) (München: C.H. Beck, 2000), esp. pp. 149–275.

Table 7.2. Best- and worst-performing German companies, Large Sample, 1911–13 (average ROE in %)

Rank	Company	Sector	ROE	Standard deviation
	Best-performing			
1	Bayer	Oils and chemicals	26.7	0.7
2	Hoechst	Oils and chemicals	26.7	5.5
3	BASF	Oils and chemicals	22.7	1.6
4	Phoenix AG für Bergbau und Hüttenbetrieb	Metals	22.3	2.5
5	Siemens & Halske AG	Electrical engineering	20.1	7.3
6	Krupp	Metals	16.8	2.5
7	Berliner Elektricitäts-Werke	Utilities	16.0	0.3
8	Maschinenbau-Anstalt 'Humboldt'	Mechanical engineering	15.1	0.9
9	Siemens-Schuckertwerke GmbH	Electrical engineering	14.3	0.2
10	AEG	Electrical engineering	13.0	0.6

Rank	Company	Sector	ROE	Standard deviation
	Worst-performing			
1	Berliner Terrain- und Bau AG	Construction and property	−42.2	37.3
2	Tapeten-Industrie AG	Wood and paper	0.3	0.1
3	Handelsgesellschaft für Grundbesitz	Construction and property	1.6	2.2
4	Ostafrikanische Eisenbahngesellschaft	Free-standing companies	1.8	1.6
5	Vulkan-Werke	Transport equipment	4.6	2.9
6	Neue Boden-AG	Construction and property	5.3	4.4
7	Blohm & Voss KGaA	Transport equipment	5.8	1.1
8	Gesellschaft für elektrische Hoch- und Untergrundbahnen	Land transport	6.3	0.4
9	Harpener Bergbau AG	Mining	7.3	1.0
10	Schantung Eisenbahn-Gesellschaft	Free-standing companies	7.6	0.7

merged with five other big chemical enterprises (including Hoechst) and founded the IG Farbenindustrie AG.[13]

The third-biggest industrial sector in the sample was electrical engineering, which represented 11.8 per cent of all assets in the Large Sample, excluding financial intermediation. But in contrast to the aforementioned branches in this sector, the three companies included in the sample were almost the same size.[14]

---

[13] For details, see Gottfried Plumpe, *Die I.G. Farbenindustrie AG: Wirtschaft, Technik und Politik 1904–1945* (Berlin: Duncker & Humblot 1990); Gottfried Plumpe, 'The political framework of structural modernisation: the IG Farbenindustrie AG, 1904–1945', in W. Robert Lee, ed., *German Industry and German Industrialisation* (London: Routledge, 1991), pp. 220–64; Cassis, *Big Business*, pp. 50–1.

[14] On the electrical engineering sector, see Wilfried Feldenkirchen, 'Competition and cooperation in German electrical industry in the home and world markets', in H. Pohl, ed., *Competition and Cooperation of Enterprises on National and International Markets* (Stuttgart: Franz Steiner 1997), pp. 13–34; Cassis, *Big Business*, p. 51.

Table 7.3. German companies: average shares of total turnover and average performance (ROE) according to sector, 1927–9 (in %)

Sector	Average share of the sum of assets represented in the Large Sample	Average performance of all three companies represented in the Large Sample
1 Mining	3.8	6.1
2 Utilities	8.4	10.7
5 Construction and property	0.8	−0.1
6 Commercial activities	3.8	15.6
7 Financial intermediation		11.4
8 Food, drink, and tobacco	2.3	12.5
9 Textiles and leather	4.3	8.8
10 Mechanical engineering	2.3	7.9
11 Electrical engineering	11.8	13.5
12 Transport equipment	1.7	0.3
13 Metals	25.3	10.4
14 Wood and paper	1.7	11.9
16 Free-standing companies	0.1	7.0
18 Land transport	3.3	4.7
19 Transport and communication	7.3	7.0
23 Oil and rubber	3.7	7.8
24 Chemicals and pharmaceuticals	19.5	8.5

A look at the performance of German large-scale enterprises in the 1927–9 benchmark period shows that the biggest companies were not necessarily the best-performing ones (Table 7.4). Measured by ROE, as shown in Table 7.3, the most profitable branch was commercial activities (average ROE 15.6 per cent). The significance of this value should not be overestimated, because it was partly due to the extraordinary good performance of the small Deutsch-Russische Handelsgesellschaft, with a balance sheet total of only 56 million RM in 1927. However, the two larger commercial companies (the department store companies Leonhard Tietz AG and Rudolph Karstadt AG) were also quite successful in these years.

In other industrial sectors, remarkable differences among the performances of individual companies occurred as well. For example, electrical engineering was the second best-performing sector, with an average ROE of 13.5 per cent. But the ROE of the individual electrical engineering companies varied between 20.0 per cent for the best-performing company, Siemens & Halske AG, and 7.8 per cent for the worst, AEG.

But what about the two giant firms, IG Farben and Vereinigte Stahlwerke? Looking at performance measured by return on equity, IG Farben came in the higher mid-range (average ROE 10.4 per cent) while Vereinigte Stahlwerke was in the lower (average ROE 6.6 per cent). It is noteworthy that both are beaten by a better-performing smaller company in their own sector: Kali-Industrie-AG achieved an average ROE of 11.2 per cent and Mannesmannröhren-Werke an average ROE of 19.1 per cent.

Regarding the worst performers among the large-scale enterprises in the late 1920s, it is eye-catching that all three companies of the transport equipment sector appear on that list. Their average ROE amounted only to 0.3 per cent.

Table 7.4. Best- and worst-performing German companies, Large Sample, 1927–9 (average ROE in %)

Rank	Company	Sector	ROE	Standard deviation
		Best-performing		
1	Deutsch-Russische Handels-AG	Commercial activities	22.4	12.5
2	Siemens & Halske AG	Electrical engineering	20.0	6.4
3	Mannesmannröhren-Werke	Metals	19.1	14.0
4	Schultheiss-Patzenhofer Brauerei AG	Food, drink, and tobacco	18.4	1.4
5	Hamburgische Electricitäts-Werke	Utilities	14.9	1.7
6	Rudolph Karstadt AG	Commercial activities	14.1	1.8
7	Jaluit-Gesellschaft	Free-standing companies	14.1	10.0
8	Feldmühle, Papier- und Zellstoffwerke AG	Wood and paper	13.2	1.3
9	Darmstädter und Nationalbank	Financial intermediation	13.1	2.3
10	Siemens-Schuckertwerke AG	Electrical engineering	12.8	0.7
		Worst-performing		
1	Industriebau-Held & Francke AG	Construction and property	−12.0	33.6
2	Henschel & Sohn AG	Transport equipment	−4.1	0.0
3	Adam Opel AG	Transport equipment	−3.7	0.0
4	Guatemala Plantagen-Gesellschaft	Free-standing companies	0.1	0.8
5	Rhenania-Ossag Mineralölwerke AG	Oil and rubber	1.5	5.8
6	Daimler-Benz AG	Transport equipment	1.6	0.2
7	Harpener Bergbau AG	Mining	3.9	2.3
8	Lübeck-Büchener Eisenbahn-Gesellschaft	Railways	4.2	0.1
9	Tempelhofer Feld AG für Grundstücksverwertung	Construction and property	4.3	9.6
10	Mansfeld AG für Bergbau und Hüttenbetrieb	Mining	4.5	2.9

The companies of the construction and property sector performed even worse (average ROE −0.05 per cent), but the average ROE of this sector is strongly influenced by the outlier Industriebau-Held & Francke AG, whose average ROE of −12.0 per cent was by far the lowest in the sample in this benchmark period. Without this outlier, the construction sector's performance would be in midfield, with an average ROE of about 8 per cent.

After the Second World War, the Western Allies, first and foremost the Americans, decartelized and deconcentrated German business. The 1954–6 sample is clearly affected by these policies. Three branches should be considered in more detail: the financial sector, iron and steel, and the chemical industry.[15]

Because of the forced divestiture of the banking sector, this is the only benchmark period in which the financial sector was not dominated by at least two of the three big universal banks: Deutsche Bank, Dresdner Bank, and Commerzbank.

---

[15] See Volker R. Berghahn, *The Americanisation of West German Industry, 1945–1973* (Cambridge: Cambridge University Press, 1986), pp. 94–100; Cassis, *Big Business*, pp. 50–1.

The Allies' original intention was to split them up into as many as thirty regional banks. But in 1952, after long negotiations, it was agreed to divide each of them into three regional banks. Four of the five banking companies included in our sample were former parts of the three big pre-war banks: Deutsche Bank AG West (total assets 2.675 billion DM)[16] and Süddeutsche Bank AG (total assets 2.538 billion DM) were parts of Deutsche Bank; Commerzbank-Bankverein (total assets 1.793 billion DM)[17] emanated from Commerzbank; and Rhein-Main-Bank (total assets 1.604 billion DM) was the biggest part of the former Dresdner Bank. However, the division of the three banks did not last long. In 1956, an agreement was reached between the banks and the German government so that by the beginning of 1957 they were reunited under their former names.[18]

The Allies also broke up the big firms that dominated the iron and steel and the chemical industries. This was done especially because these enterprises had played an important role in the Third Reich. IG Farben, for example, had exploited inmates of the Auschwitz concentration camp in their plants. As the country's biggest steel producer, Vereinigte Stahlwerke had profited from armaments in general and from forced labour in particular.

Vereinigte Stahlwerke was divided into eighteen independent companies, among them Gelsenkirchener Bergwerks-AG (total assets 1.746 billion DM), Dortmund-Hörder Hüttenunion AG (total assets 770 million DM), Hüttenwerke Phoenix AG (total assets 695 million DM), and August Thyssen-Hütte AG (total assets 637 million DM).[19] The other big companies of the mining and metal industry, like Krupp, Hoesch, and Klöckner, were also divided into different firms. The Allied policy of dividing the big integrated coal- and metal-producing companies into smaller firms explains why suddenly all nine companies from these Old Industry sectors appeared among the top twenty-five, whereas in 1927–9 there were only five. But the increase in number did not correspond to a similarly high increase in importance compared with other industrial sectors in the post-war German economy. Their weight among the top twenty non-financial companies grew indeed, but not as much as one might expect. In the 1954–6 benchmark period, coal- and metal-producing companies represented 45.1 per cent of all assets in the Small Sample, compared with 33.9 per cent in 1927–9. If we consult the Large Sample with three companies of each sector, there was no change at all in the relative weight of heavy industry (Table 7.5). The three biggest coal- and metal-producing companies represented 29.6 per cent of the sum of assets in 1954–6, compared with 29.1 per cent of all assets in 1927–9. Given the divestiture of Vereinigte Stahlwerke, this stability is surprising.

De-concentration policy was similar in the chemical industry. The former IG Farben was divided into four smaller units: Bayer AG (total assets 1.318 billion DM), BASF AG (total assets 990 million DM), Hoechst AG (total assets 823

[16] At the time of its foundation in 1952, it was called Rheinisch-Westfälische Bank AG.

[17] At the time of its foundation in 1952, it was called Bankverein Westdeutschland AG.

[18] See Manfred Pohl, 'Zerschlagung und Wiederaufbau der deutschen Großbanken, 1945–1957', *Beiträge zu Wirtschafts- und Währungsfragen und zur Bankgeschichte* 13 (1974), 21–32; Berghahn, *Americanisation*, p. 110; Cassis, *Big Business*, p. 48.

[19] Karl Heinrich Herchenröder et al, *Die Nachfolger der Ruhrkonzerne* (Düsseldorf: Econ-Verlag, 1953), pp. 57–118, esp. p. 110; Cassis, *Big Business*, p. 50.

Table 7.5. German companies: average shares of total turnover and average performance (ROE) according to sector, 1954–6 (in %)

Sector	Average share of the sum of assets represented in the Large Sample	Average performance of all three companies represented in the Large Sample
1 Mining	14.7	3.0
2 Utilities	17.9	4.6
5 Construction and property	0.8	7.1
6 Commercial activities	2.1	6.5
7 Financial intermediation		6.1
8 Food, drink, and tobacco	2.2	12.8
9 Textiles and leather	2.9	4.8
10 Mechanical engineering	3.4	5.4
11 Electrical engineering	11.5	5.4
12 Transport equipment	5.7	24.7
13 Metals	14.8	2.4
14 Wood and paper	1.8	4.8
19 Transport and communication	2.7	−9.9
23 Oil and rubber	5.4	3.0
24 Chemicals and pharmaceuticals	14.1	6.1

million DM), and the much smaller Casella AG, which is the only one of the IG Farben offspring not appearing among the top twenty-five companies. The companies of the chemical industry held 14.1 per cent of all assets in the Large Sample, financial intermediation excluded, so there is a loss in weight of about 5 per cent compared with 1927–9. It is noteworthy that the utilities sector gained importance in the 1954–6 benchmark period. The Rheinisch-Westfälische Elektrizitätswerke AG (RWE) was the biggest German company measured by total assets (2.930 billion DM). It was even bigger than the banks. Though this can be explained by the temporary division of the banks, it is still a striking fact. Two other utility companies also appear in the top twenty-five. So it is not astonishing that the utilities sector represents 17.9 per cent of all assets included in the 1954–6 Large Sample.

Concerning profitability, it is noteworthy that only one of the twenty-five biggest companies was among the ten best performers (Table 7.6): the Bayerische Hypotheken- und Wechselbank (average ROE 6.4 per cent). The performance of the companies of the transport equipment industry was extraordinarily high, with an average ROE of 24.7 per cent.[20] Daimler Benz and Adam Opel AG were among the ten best-performing companies of this benchmark period. Opel was even in the first place, with an average ROE of 61.4 per cent. Furthermore, the companies of the food industry (average ROE 12.8 per cent) and the construction sector (average ROE 7.1 per cent) were very profitable. These results correspond to the general economic situation of the 1950s, especially to the German reconstruction after the Second World War and the strong backlog of demand for food and consumer goods in general and for durable consumer goods in particular.

---

[20] Cassis, *Big Business*, p. 94, draws a different, less successful picture of the German transport equipment sector in the 1950s: they do not even appear in a list of the most profitable German companies.

Table 7.6. Best- and worst-performing German companies, Large Sample, 1954–6 (average ROE in %)

Best-performing				
Rank	Company	Sector	ROE	Standard deviation
1	Adam Opel AG	Transport equipment	61.4	36.7
2	Margarine-Union AG	Food, drink, and tobacco	26.8	1.8
3	Feldmühle, Papier- und Zellstoffwerke AG	Wood and paper	8.8	0.3
4	Rudolph Karstadt AG	Commercial activities	8.0	0.6
5	Philipp Holzmann AG	Construction and property	7.7	1.0
6	Beton- und Monierbau AG	Construction and property	7.6	0.7
7	Daimler-Benz AG	Transport equipment	7.5	0.8
8	Kaufhof AG	Commercial activities	6.7	0.8
9	Bayerische Hypotheken- und Wechsel-Bank	Financial intermediation	6.4	0.7
10	Vereinigte Glanzstoff-Fabriken	Textiles and leather	6.3	0.3
Worst-performing				
Rank	Company	Sector	ROE	Standard deviation
1	Deutsche Dampfschiffahrtsgesellschaft 'Hansa'	Transport and communication	−22.1	24.1
2	Hapag	Transport and communication	−7.7	6.7
3	Dortmund-Hörder Hüttenunion AG	Metals	−1.0	5.9
4	Gelsenberg Benzin AG	Oil and rubber	−0.2	0.0
5	Hamburger Hochbahn AG	Transport and communication	0.0	0.0
6	Aschaffenburger Zellstoffwerke AG	Wood and paper	1.4	0.8
7	Rheinische AG für Braunkohlenbergbau und Brikettfabrikation	Mining	2.3	0.3
8	Bergwerksgesellschaft Hibernia AG	Mining	2.4	0.4
9	Esso AG	Oil and rubber	2.6	2.4
10	Christian Dierig AG	Textiles and leather	3.3	0.6

In 1951, only 1.3 per cent of German households owned a car. This number increased to 8.1 per cent in 1961. So the good performance of industrial sectors such as transport equipment, construction, and food can easily be explained.[21] Amongst the worst performers, we find all companies of the transport sector and two out of the three mining companies.

The companies included in the 1970–2 sample were selected according to their turnover, except for banking and insurance companies, which were selected according to their assets. Most of the enterprises in the top twenty-five sample were already present in this group in 1954–6, so the structure of German big business seems to have remained quite stable in these years. The 1970–2 sample is

[21] See Werner Abelshauser, *Deutsche Wirtschaftsgeschichte seit 1945* (München: C.H. Beck, 2004), pp. 338–40.

Table 7.7. German companies: average shares of total turnover and average performance (ROE) according to sector, 1970–2 (in %)

Sector		Average share of the sum of turnover represented in the Large Sample	Average performance of all three companies represented in the Large Sample
1	Mining	6.2	−17.4
2	Utilities	6.9	13.3
5	Construction and property	2.4	25.7
6	Commercial activities	4.8	15.8
7	Financial intermediation		9.8
8	Food, drink, and tobacco	3.3	16.7
9	Textiles and leather	0.5	−1.0
10	Mechanical engineering	5.1	7.7
11	Electrical engineering	13.8	8.4
12	Transport equipment	15.3	13.2
15	Mature industries	12.2	8.2
19	Transport and communication	1.6	4.6
23	Oil and rubber	8.1	8.0
24	Chemicals and pharmaceuticals	16.9	9.2
25	Leisure and tourism	2.3	9.2
26	Insurance		26.7
27	Media	0.5	22.5

dominated by heavy industry, which gained 18.5 per cent of total turnover represented in the Large Sample and possessed 19.2 per cent of all assets, financial intermediation excluded.[22] Nevertheless, signs of the emerging decline of the Old Industries can already be observed: in 1969, many of the former integrated iron, steel, and coal companies divested their increasingly inefficient coal business, which suffered from overcapacity, and 'shifted it to the shoulders of the Ruhrkohle AG'.[23]

The top twenty-five sample shows that other industrial sectors gained importance and formed the backbone of German big business in the 1970s (Table 7.7). Five out of the twenty non-financial companies in the Small Sample belonged to the chemical and the oil and rubber industries. These two branches accounted for 25.0 per cent of total turnover and even 27.0 per cent of total assets represented in the Large Sample. The other prospering branches were transport equipment (15.3 per cent of total turnover, 9.7 per cent of all assets) and electrical engineering (13.8 per cent of total turnover, 12.8 per cent of all assets).[24]

In 1970–2, the overall profitability of German big business as measured by the average ROE of all companies in the Large Sample rose dramatically compared with the 1954–6 benchmark period. While the average ROE was 5.8 per cent in 1954–6, it increased to 10.6 per cent in 1970–2. In 1954–6, an ROE of 6.3 per cent was sufficient to put a company among the ten best-performing companies, whereas in 1970–2, Aral AG, with a ROE of 6.2 per cent, was among the worst

---

[22] All figures excluding financial intermediation.
[23] Wengenroth, 'Germany', p. 164, and see Abelshauser, *Deutsche Wirtschaftsgeschichte*, pp. 203–11.
[24] See Wengenroth, 'Germany', pp. 165–70.

Table 7.8. Best- and worst-performing German companies, Large Sample, 1970–2 (average ROE in %)

	Best-performing			
Rank	Company	Sector	ROE	Standard deviation
1	Victoria Lebens-Versicherungs-AG	Insurance	50.2	2.2
2	Strabag Bau-AG	Construction	41.9	1.8
3	Deutsche Unilever GmbH	Food, drink, and tobacco	24.6	7.2
4	Axel Springer Verlag AG	Media	22.5	17.9
5	Philipp Holzmann AG	Construction and property	20.8	6.0
6	Adam Opel AG	Transport equipment	19.1	1.6
7	Horten AG	Commercial activities	18.8	2.0
8	Gerling-Konzern Versicherung-Beteiligungs-Gruppe AG	Insurance	18.1	5.9
9	VEBA AG	Utilities	17.6	6.3
10	Karstadt AG	Commercial activities	14.6	0.4
	Worst-performing			
Rank	Company	Sector	ROE	Standard deviation
1	Ruhrkohle AG	Mining	−44.6	43.6
2	Deutsche Rhodiaceta AG	Textiles and leather	−10.9	10.3
3	Deutsche Lufthansa AG	Transport and communication	2.1	6.4
4	Salamander AG	Textiles and leather	3.8	1.2
5	Erba AG für Textilindustrie	Textiles and leather	4.2	2.7
6	Deutsche Dampfschifffahrts-Gesellschaft 'Hansa'	Transport and communication	4.2	0.6
7	AEG	Electrical engineering	5.2	1.8
8	Volkswagenwerk AG	Transport equipment	5.9	3.9
9	August Thyssen-Hütte AG	Mature industries	6.2	4.1
10	Aral AG	Oil and rubber	6.2	0.8

performers (Table 7.8). These findings correspond to the results of Cassis, who observed a doubling of the profit rates of German companies between the 1950s and the 1970s as well.[25]

Among the best-performing companies of the 1970–2 benchmark period (Table 7.8), we find only three of the twenty biggest non-financial corporations: two of them were the automobile manufacturers Opel (average ROE 19.1 per cent) and Daimler-Benz (average ROE 14.6 per cent), and the third was VEBA AG (average ROE 17.6 per cent), the biggest German utilities company at that time.

Highly profitable also were companies from other branches, in particular the insurance companies with an average ROE of 26.7 per cent and the construction companies with an average ROE of 25.7 per cent. Two out of the three companies of each of these branches included in the Large Sample appear on the list of best performers.

[25] Cassis, *Big Business*, p. 87.

Table 7.9. German companies: average shares of total turnover and average performance (ROE) according to sector, 1998–2000 (in %)

Sector	Average share of the sum of turnover represented in the Large Sample	Average performance of all three companies represented in the Large Sample
1 Mining	2.0	10.7
2 Utilities	11.8	13.4
3 Construction	1.6	−3.2
4 Property	1.3	16.2
6 Commercial activities	9.6	9.6
7 Financial intermediation		9.6
8 Food, drink, and tobacco	1.1	18.5
9 Textiles and leather goods	0.8	14.5
10 Mechanical engineering	2.5	15.1
11 Electrical engineering	10.7	14.9
12 Transport equipment	27.9	6.1
15 Mature industries	3.2	14.2
20 Transport	4.4	9.7
21 Post and telecom	6.8	17.2
23 Oil and rubber	3.9	34.3
24 Chemicals and pharmaceuticals	7.7	11.7
25 Leisure and tourism	1.5	15.4
26 Insurance		13.8
27 Media	1.8	19.2
28 Services to business	1.4	9.6
29 Public administration and health	0.1	21.1

Expectedly, Ruhrkohle AG heads the list of the worst-performing companies. Among the worst performers, all textiles and leather producers can be found as well. This shows how the shrinking fabrication of elementary textiles since the 1960s affected the structure of big business in Germany.[26]

Between the 1970s and our last benchmark period, 1998–2000, the composition of German big business changed dramatically. The transport equipment sector finally took the leading position (Table 7.9), with DaimlerChrysler AG[27] and Volkswagen AG as the biggest German enterprises. Together with the third-biggest car manufacturer, BMW, they represented almost 30 per cent of the sum of assets or turnover in the Large Sample. As before, the chemical industry and the related pharmaceutical, oil, and rubber industries are well represented with four companies in the top twenty-five sample. They generated 11.6 per cent of the total turnover in the Large Sample (without financial intermediation). But the utilities sector with three companies in the top twenty-five, which represented 11.8 per cent of the total turnover, was just as important. Again, electrical engineering played an important role, although only two electrical engineering companies were big enough to enter the top twenty-five. The larger one, Siemens, was the

---

[26] Stephan Lindner, *Den Faden verloren. Die westdeutsche und französische Textilindustrie auf dem Rückzug, 1930/45–1990* (Schriftenreihe zur Zeitschrift für Unternehmensgeschichte, Vol. 7) (München: C.H. Beck 2001), pp. 137–53.

[27] Daimler-Benz merged with the American car manufacturer Chrysler in May 1998.

third-biggest German company at that time, and the sector represented 10.8 per cent of the summarized turnover.

The trend of privatization is also visible in the Small Sample with the appearance of two former state-owned companies. Deutsche Telekom AG and Deutsche Post AG emerged from Bundespost, the former German Federal telecommunication and postal service. Bundespost was not included in the samples of the earlier benchmark periods, because it was state-owned and therefore was not run as a competitive business enterprise.

Also, a merger wave in the 1990s changed the structure of big business in Germany. Two new conglomerates appeared among the top twenty-five companies: the utility giant E.ON, resulting from the merger of VEBA and VIAG in 2000, and ThyssenKrupp, which combined three former big players of German heavy industry.[28]

Mergers were no longer a national phenomenon as large-scale enterprises were increasingly affected by the process of globalization at the end of the twentieth century. There was a huge rise in international mergers between 1998 and 2000, with German companies absorbing as well as being absorbed. Four mergers serve as examples here: first, the hostile takeover of Mannesmann—which had transformed itself from a heavy industry company into one of the leading cellular phone companies—by Vodafone in 2000; second, the acquisition of Chrysler by Daimler-Benz in 1998; third, Rhône-Poulenc's takeover of Hoechst in 1999; and fourth, Deutsche Bank's purchase of Bankers Trust in 1998.[29] In connection with globalization, the shareholder structure of many German companies changed since the 1990s. The consequence was the end of the old ownership structure called 'Deutschland AG' in which the greatest amount of shares was held by the big German banks or other German companies.

Only three of the twenty biggest non-financial companies performed well enough to be among the group of top ten performers (Table 7.10): Deutsche Post with an extraordinarily high ROE of 41.7 per cent, Deutsche Shell GmbH (average ROE 38.4 per cent), and Bertelsmann AG (average ROE 20.0 per cent). Among this group, we find all three of the sample's companies that operated in the oil business. The media sector was the second sector that appeared with more than one company: the journal publisher Gruner + Jahr and the big media holding Bertelsmann.

Among the worst-performing companies, we find two construction companies. Surprisingly, the carmaker BMW was in second place on the list of worst performers because it had incurred enormous losses in 1999 in connection with the fiasco of its merger with British carmaker Rover. After divesting itself of Rover in 2000, BMW recovered its profitability.

The general increase in the level of ROE compared with all the earlier benchmark periods is eye-catching: the average ROE of all companies represented in the Small Sample was 13.9 per cent, and a company had to generate an ROE of nearly 20 per cent to reach the top ten best performers, which is enormously high with regard to the German historical data. These figures illustrate the rationalization activities of German big business since the fall of the Iron Curtain in order to meet the challenges of increasing globalization.

---

[28] Hoesch merged with Krupp in 1992; Thyssen and Krupp merged in 1999. Prollius, Michael v., *Deutsche Wirtschaftsgeschichte nach 1945* (Göttingen: Vandenhoeck & Ruprecht, 2006), p. 271.

[29] See Dohmen, Frank, et al., 'Industriepolitik: "Kämpfen Sie!"', *Der Spiegel* 6 (2004), 22–5.

Table 7.10. Best- and worst-performing German companies, Large Sample, 1998–2000 (average ROE in %)

		Best-performing		
Rank	Company	Sector	ROE	Standard deviation
1	Deutsche Post AG	Post and telecommunications	41.7	3.7
2	Gruner + Jahr AG & Co.	Media	39.6	0.0
3	Deutsche Shell GmbH	Oil and rubber	38.4	7.3
4	Deutsche BP AG	Oil and rubber	38.0	6.6
5	Hugo Boss AG	Textiles and leather	29.3	4.6
6	RWE-DEA AG für Mineraloel und Chemie	Oil and rubber	26.5	2.9
7	SAP AG	Services to business	24.4	2.7
8	ZF Friedrichshafen AG	Mechanical engineering	22.6	9.7
9	Rhön-Klinikum AG	Public administration and health	21.1	3.5
10	Bertelsmann AG	Media	20.0	3.2
		Worst-performing		
Rank	Company	Sector	ROE	Standard deviation
1	Philipp Holzmann AG	Construction	−32.2	31.3
2	BMW AG	Transport equipment	−11.6	36.5
3	Infineon Technologies AG	Services to business	−5.2	23.5
4	Alcatel SEL AG	Post and telecommunications	0.5	16.8
5	Bilfinger + Berger Bau-AG	Construction	0.9	5.9
6	RAG Aktiengesellschaft	Mining	1.2	1.9
7	Deutsche Bahn AG	Transports	1.3	0.5
8	Adidas-Salomon AG	Textiles and leather	4.1	24.9
9	ThyssenKrupp AG	Mature industries	4.7	1.4
10	Bayerische Hypo- und Vereinsbank	Financial intermediation	5.3	1.3

CONCLUSION

Until now, we have analysed the structure and performance of German big business on the basis of the company data contained in the Large and Small Samples. What general facts can be distilled from these observations?

For that purpose, we can regard how the sectors' shares of all assets represented in the samples change during the twentieth century; additionally, in the last two benchmark periods, the sectors' percentage of total turnover can be observed (see Figure 7.1). What do those figures reveal? First of all, it is obvious that the importance of different industrial sectors within big business varies over time. German large-scale enterprises were dominated by heavy industry until the 1950s: mining and metal companies held almost one-third of all assets represented in the Large Sample in the three earlier benchmark periods.[30] From the 1920s onwards,

---

[30] The apparent decline of the mining industry relative to the metals sector in the 1927–9 benchmark period was triggered by the integration of mining and metalworking under the roof of

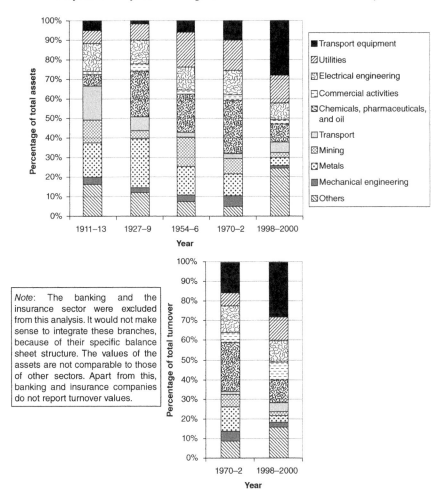

Figure 7.1. German companies: shares of total assets/turnover according to sectors, Large Sample, 1913–2000

we can trace the rise of the chemical industry and the related oil and rubber industry, which finally overtook all others in the 1970s—measured by assets and by turnover—and lost the top position to the transport equipment sector in 1998–2000. Another noteworthy point is the strong position of the utilities sector as measured by total assets, especially in the 1950s and 1970s, which was partly due to the high capital intensity of the power grid. However, the role of utilities within big business is not that crucial when measured by turnover.

Furthermore, the group of other industrial sectors not listed by name in the diagram in Figure 7.1 should also be considered briefly. They played an important

the Vereinigten Stahlwerke or the other big heavy industry companies, which led to a ballooning in the size of the metals industry.

Table 7.11. Profitability of German big business, 1911–2000 (ROE in %)

	Dammers/Fischer		Cassis[a]
1911	9.9		
1912	10.8	(average 9.9)	10.7
1913	8.9		
1927	8.0		
1928	10.0	(average 8.5)	7.2
1929	7.4		
1954	6.9		
1955	4.4	(average 5.8)	3.0
1956	6.2		
1970	13.8		
1971	9.9	(average 11.6)	7.2
1972	11.0		
1987–9	Not available		10.5
1998	13.0		Not available
1999	12.8	(average 13.9)	
2000	15.9		

[a] Cassis' benchmark periods differ a little from those in our study: instead of 1954–6, Cassis' data refer to the years 1953–5; additionally, he analyses the benchmark period 1987–9 (Cassis, *Big Business*, pp. 86–7).

role at the beginning and end of the twentieth century. In 1911–13, free-standing companies (i.e. German companies with exclusively business abroad) dominated the group of 'other' companies (7.3 per cent of all assets in the Large Sample). In 1998–2000, the companies of the post and telecommunications sector held about 18.6 per cent of all assets, which was mostly due to the former state-owned companies, Deutsche Post and Deutsche Telekom. Measured by turnover, the share of these branches was only 6.8 per cent; nevertheless, this sector takes the biggest part of the 'others' in this respect, too.

In the following, we give a general overview of the development of profitability of German big business throughout the observation period. Table 7.11 shows the average ROE of all companies in the Large Sample for each benchmark period. Our data are compared with the calculations of the return on shareholders' funds offered by Cassis, who analysed a varying sample of large-scale enterprises, chosen by a combined criterion of workforce, share capital, and turnover.[31]

[31] Cassis calls his measure of profitability 'return on shareholders' funds, but calculates it in the same way as ROE is calculated in this study, so the two measures should be equivalent (Cassis, *Big Business*, p. 86). For the first three benchmark periods, Cassis chose companies by workforce or share capital in order to include all top companies as well as to consider all sectors. For 1911–13, he included thirty-nine German companies. For 1927–9, he analysed forty-five companies, but only forty-one were integrated in the analysis of profits. For 1953–5, he also picked forty-five companies, but only thirty-two were used to calculate the profit ratio (Cassis, *Big Business*, pp. 238, 245–7, 255–7, 264–6). For his fourth benchmark period, Cassis chose thirty-two German industrial companies with a turnover greater than $500 million in 1972 (Cassis, *Big Business*, p. 96, note 37). He used the same criterion for his 1987–9 data, when thirty-three German industrial companies with more than $2.5 billion turnover were included (Cassis, *Big Business*, p. 238, note 2).

Both time series show the same tendencies: the late Kaiserreich was a period of high profitability for big business, whereas profitability in the Weimar Republic was significantly lower. But the difference between the two values is significantly higher in Cassis' data. In the 1950s, the period of the so-called Wirtschaftswunder, German large-scale enterprises performed with the lowest profitability ratios in the whole twentieth century. This general conclusion is supported by both studies. But again, the new data suggest that German big business had a much higher profitability than Cassis found. The difference between the figures is even greater than in the late 1920s: using the new data, profitability appears to be almost twice as high. The values for the 1970s show a similar tendency. Both data series reveal a rising trend, yet Cassis' results are again lower. However, both studies show a rising profitability of German large-scale enterprises by the end of the century. By the 1980s, German big business could match its success in the Kaiserreich, when it was the global market leader in many industrial sectors. In the years following German reunification in 1990, the profitability of large-scale enterprises reached a level it had never attained before.

In short, our findings lead us to believe that Cassis' evaluation of German big business was perhaps too pessimistic and that consequently his conclusion that 'British companies have consistently generated higher profits than their... German counterparts'[32] possibly has to be modified slightly.

---

[32] Cassis, *Big Business*, p. 233.

8

Big Business Performance in Twentieth-Century Italy

Carlo Brambilla and Andrea Colli

INTRODUCTION AND METHODOLOGICAL REMARKS

In this chapter, we assess the strategies, structures, and performances of the largest Italian corporations in manufacturing, utilities, and services during the twentieth century. The study employs a multifactorial definition of performances, both qualitative and quantitative.[1] Its contribution to the history of Italian big business follows the framework of the comparative studies in this collection. Thus, its structure and purposes, and the empirical evidence on which it is based, differ somewhat from those of other quantitatively based research on the strategy, structure, and performances of Italian enterprises.[2]

The statistics presented in this chapter come from the general database of the collective research project, and they are thus subject to the limitations and caveats discussed in Chapter 2. What are specific and peculiar about the Italian data are the sources used to identify sample companies and balance sheets. Data have been derived from a combination of sources: the official bulletin on joint-stock companies issued by the Ministry of Industry, the Bollettino Ufficiale delle Società per Azioni–Bilanci, and a repertoire of statistics, Notizie Statistiche, initially compiled by the Credito Italiano bank and later by Assonime (the Italian Association of Joint-Stock Companies). Data for the last three benchmarks (1954–6, 1970–2, and 1998–2000) have been obtained from the database on the largest Italian companies provided by R&S, the research branch of Mediobanca, another Italian bank.[3]

---

[1] A first attempt to measure performance using share capital as an indicator was set up by G. Federico, R. Giannetti, and P. Toninelli, 'Size and strategy of business enterprise in Italy (1907–1940): empirical evidence and some conjectures', *Industrial and Corporate Change*, 3, 2 (1994), 491–511. The most recent, which provides quantitative evidence at aggregate level, is that by Michelangelo Vasta, 'Firm performance, 1900–1971', in Renato Giannetti and Michelangelo Vasta, eds., *The Evolution of Italian Enterprises in the 20th Century* (Heidelberg: Springer-Verlag, 2006), pp. 153–90.

[2] Giannetti and Vasta, *The Evolution*; Andrea Colli and Michelangelo Vasta, *Forms of Enterprise in 20th Century Italy: Boundaries, Structure and Strategies* (London: Elgar, 2010).

[3] Additional information about total assets of the largest companies has been derived from Imita.db, an online dataset containing information on all the Italian joint-stock companies from the beginning of the century to 1972 (http://imitadb.unisi.it/, last accessed October 2013).

When dubious or controversial situations occurred, data have been cross-checked and completed through archival research.

The chapter is structured as follows. The next section provides a synthesis of the main stages of Italian industrial development throughout the twentieth century. This is followed by a review of company performance indicators in the five benchmarks and their relationship to Italian economic development. The fourth section focuses on company performance in four principal sectors: basic and fabricated metals; engineering and transportation equipment; electricity and telecommunications; and financial intermediation. The importance of these sectors for the country's development is made clear by the fact that they appear in the samples of top fifteen companies throughout the century. In the conclusion, we discuss some relevant issues such as bank–industry relationships and the role played by the state.

CORPORATE ITALY IN THE TWENTIETH CENTURY

In 1911, only a few years before entering the First World War, Italy celebrated the fiftieth anniversary of its political unification. In half a century, Italy had been able—alone among the Mediterranean countries—to engage successfully in a process of industrialization, which moved the country from Europe's economic periphery into the centre. The process, which started immediately after unification, was initially promoted by the state's infrastructural policy, and was rooted in the diffusion of artisanal manufacturing activities in both the countryside and the main cities of the North and the Centre, which was the result of a widespread integration between agriculture and manufacturing brought about by the production of raw silk.[4] Cotton production, the other main manufacturing activity— often carried on by foreign entrepreneurs—was located mainly in the North and carried out in both centralized plants and efficient putting-out networks. This situation lasted for at least two decades after national unification. In the 1880s, the international foodstuffs market began to be flooded by cheap products from Russia and the American Midwest, which led the Italian government to introduce policies to protect the country's primary sector. These protectionist policies were extended to manufacturing and assisted an effective take-off of the Italian secondary sector. From the beginning of the 1890s, industries such as metallurgy, mechanics, electromechanics, and steam engines and locomotives experienced a double-digit growth in output.[5]

During this phase, several ambitious first-movers—Fiat in automobiles, Ansaldo in shipbuilding, Pirelli in rubber, and Falck, Terni, and Piombino in steel—established superiority in their respective industries. In the same years, modern universal banks were founded, such as the Banca Commerciale Italiana

[4] Franco Amatori, Matteo Bugamelli, and Andrea Colli, 'Technology, firm size and entrepreneurship', in Gianni Toniolo, ed., *The Oxford Handbook of the Italian Economy since Unification* (Oxford: Oxford University Press, 2013), pp. 455–84.

[5] Franco Amatori and Andrea Colli, *Impresa e industria in Italia dall'Unità ad oggi* (Venice: Marsilio, 2000).

and the Credito Italiano, which channelled capital into the manufacturing sector. Over these years, regional economic divergence deepened, since the burgeoning industrial activity was mainly located in the north-western regions of the country.

The real take-off of the Italian industrial system, however, took place during the First World War. Energy- and scale-intensive industries, such as hydroelectricity, heavy mechanics, steel, and chemicals, expanded at maximum speed in order to meet the needs of the military. The existing first-movers consolidated their position and initiated a process of internal and external growth. Investments and acquisitions were encouraged by the favourable fiscal treatment of re-invested wartime profits. This policy persuaded, for instance, existing leaders such as Fiat (motor vehicle production), Montecatini (chemicals), SNIA (artificial fibres), and Ansaldo (heavy mechanics) to undertake ambitious projects of horizontal and vertical integration by creating large business concerns.

The consolidation of capital-intensive industries went on in the early years of the Fascist dictatorship and during the Great Depression. The world economic crisis and the strong protectionist and autarchic policies of the Fascist regime had two structural consequences for the Italian economy. First, they took Italy's largest corporations almost completely out of the global market while at the same time granting them a virtual monopoly in the internal market, although this market was not particularly large or dynamic at the time. This situation often led to suboptimal consequences: in steelmaking, real mass production could not be attained, since Italian plants did not use modern technologies. In other cases, internal demand dictated companies' commercial strategies: Montecatini, for instance, retained a strong leadership in fertilizers but undertook very little diversification in advanced chemicals.[6] The second structural consequence emerged from the way in which the effects of the Wall Street Crash were managed in Italy. In short, in order to avoid a massive disruption of both the banking and the industrial systems, the state bailed out the country's three largest banks—the Banca Commerciale Italiana, the Credito Italiano, and the Banco di Roma—and transferred their industrial holdings to a state agency, the Istituto per la Ricostruzione Industriale (Agency for Industrial Reconstruction), or IRI. Thus, in 1933, and almost overnight, the Italian government became one of the largest business players in the country's economy, owning or controlling hundreds of companies in almost all sectors. It has been calculated that with the creation of IRI, around one-quarter of the accumulated capital of all Italian joint-stock companies fell under the control of the state.[7]

After the Second World War, many of the constraints deriving from a small domestic market characterized by low dynamism were removed. The Italian economy (and society) joined the rest of Europe in what Jean Fourastié has called 'thirty glorious years' of growth and expansion. The affirmation of a consumer society together with a virtuous infrastructural policy carried on by successive governments mainly through state-owned enterprises had a crucial impact on Italian big business. Meanwhile, the process of European economic integration opened to Italian firms a market that was, at least in principle, much

---

[6] Amatori and Colli, *Impresa e industria*.
[7] Valerio Castronovo, ed., *Storia dell'IRI. Dalle origini al Dopoguerra* (Bari: Laterza, 2012).

larger than the domestic one. Italian big business became collectively stronger and the degree of concentration in capital-intensive industries increased. State intervention through direct ownership became pervasive. In 1953, Ente Nazionale Idrocarburi (ENI) was created, an agency for oil and gas exploration and exploitation, and in 1962, the whole electric sector was nationalized into the Ente Nazionale dell'Energia Elettrica (National Agency for Electric Power, or ENEL). Alongside the private sector, the state ran leading companies in air transport, motorways, cement, and other scale-intensive industries. The aggregate sales of the country's leading 200 companies in the 1960s accounted for about one-third of Italian GDP—a percentage similar to that found in the United States, Germany, or Britain, even though their organizational structures were substantially different.[8]

To understand what happened to the Italian economy during the last quarter of the twentieth century, it is crucial to turn again to the shift in technological paradigms introduced by the information and communications revolution that started after the Second World War. In 1960, Italian big business was at its zenith. Many of the largest firms crossed the new technological frontier—microcomputing (Olivetti), microelectronics (IRI-controlled SGS Ates), and telecommunications (STET, Alenia, and Telespazio, all IRI-controlled enterprises)—successfully established collaborative networks and joint ventures with the main foreign players in their respective fields. Only a handful of these initiatives, however, survived for very long. Most of them were always in a marginal position and not really able to reach a global exposure. Thus, Italy remained a marginal player in IT-dominated industries of the so-called Third Industrial Revolution. In the meantime, the gigantic state-controlled sector of the economy was crumbling under the combined pressure of corruption and inefficiency, a consequence of its having become more and more closely intertwined with political parties. This deterioration paved the way for a comprehensive privatization programme during the 1960s in which the state dismantled and sold off a huge section of Italian big business.

By the beginning of the new millennium, the overall contribution of big business to the growth of the Italian economy was steadily declining. While the backbone of the domestic economy was to be found in a multitude of small and medium-sized enterprises, often organized in industrial districts enjoying agglomeration economies, the few remaining Italian large firms were still concentrated in scale-intensive industries characteristic of the Second Industrial Revolution, such as automobiles, steel, oil and gas, electricity, and cement. In fact, at the beginning of 2000, Italy had only three companies (ENI in energy, Assicurazioni Generali in insurance, and Fiat in car production) among Europe's top fifty by revenue[9], whereas Germany had fourteen and the UK and France ten each.

---

[8] Robert J. Pavan, *Strategie e strutture delle imprese italiane* (Bologna: Il Mulino, 1977).

[9] http://money.cnn.com/magazines/fortune/global500/2006/europe/ (last accessed October 2013).

THE PERFORMANCE OF BIG BUSINESS IN ITALY:
A DIACHRONIC APPROACH

The 1911–13 Benchmark

The qualitative review just presented is confirmed by our quantitative data. In 1913, the increasing penetration of capital-intensive industries and the increasing production (and relevance) of capital goods are clearly seen in the composition of the country's top fifteen companies (see Table 8.1). Besides the three main banks or financial institutions, there are five firms belonging to 'basic and fabricated metals' and three 'utilities' (two electricity companies and one railway company).

Shifting our focus to the performance of the two best companies per sector (the Large Sample, see Table 8.2), the pervasiveness of the changes induced by the industrialization process in the country's industrial structure emerges equally clearly. The best ten performers in terms both of total assets and of return on equity (ROE) comprise largely companies producing industrial goods. The data confirm the weakness of Italy's machinery industry, whose backwardness—especially if one considers its most advanced and technologically innovative branches—is mirrored

Table 8.1. Top fifteen Italian companies, 1911–13: three-year averages of assets, ROE, and HR

Company	Sector	Assets (US$)	ROE (%)	HR (%)
Banca Commerciale Italiana	Financial intermediation	371,119,744	6.18	1.80
Credito italiano	Financial intermediation	209,593,941	5.97	3.23
Società italiana per le strade ferrate meridionali	Financial intermediation	147,107,090	0.69	−2.72
ILVA	Basic and fabricated metals	27,816,919	−0.60	
Navigazione generale italiana	Transport and communication	22,813,688	6.22	8.11
Società anonima italiana Gio. Ansaldo & C.	Transport equipment	21,881,804	5.70	
Società degli alti forni, fonderie ed acciaierie di Terni	Basic and fabricated metals	20,403,229	13.34	4.87
Società delle ferriere italiane	Basic and fabricated metals	18,544,021	2.42	−13.24
Compagnia reale delle ferrovie sarde	Railways	18,150,665	5.25	0.63
Società generale italiana Edison di elettricità	Utilities; Electricity, gas, and water supply	15,435,407	10.68	−1.98
Alti forni, fonderie e acciaierie di Piombino (D)	Basic and fabricated metals	14,633,052	5.44	−9.02
Elba. Società anonima di miniere e di alti forni	Basic and fabricated metals	11,256,907	5.30	−11.64
Società ligure-lombarda per la raffinazione degli zuccheri	Food, drink, and tobacco products	11,175,065	8.94	3.09
Elettricità Alta Italia	Utilities; Electricity, gas, and water supply	10,471,347	5.84	
Società italiana E. De Angeli per l'industria dei tessuti stampati	Textiles and leather goods	10,369,755	2.70	−22.19

Table 8.2. The Large Sample, Italy, 1911–13: three-year averages of assets, ROE, and HR

Company	Sector	Assets (US$)	ROE (%)	HR (%)
Banca Commerciale Italiana	Financial intermediation	371,119,744	6.18	1.80
Credito italiano	Financial intermediation	209,593,941	5.97	3.23
ILVA	Basic and fabricated metals	27,816,919	−0.60	
Navigazione generale italiana	Transport and communication	22,813,688	6.22	8.11
Società anonima italiana Gio. Ansaldo & C.	Transport equipment	21,881,804	5.70	
Società degli alti forni, fonderie ed acciaierie di Terni	Basic and fabricated metals	20,403,229	13.34	4.87
Compagnia reale delle ferrovie sarde	Railways	18,150,665	5.25	0.63
Società generale italiana Edison di elettricità	Utilities; Electricity, gas, and water supply	15,435,407	10.68	−1.98
Società ligure-lombarda per la raffinazione degli zuccheri	Food, drink, and tobacco products	11,175,065	8.94	3.09
Elettricità Alta Italia	Utilities; Electricity, gas, and water supply	10,471,347	5.84	
Società italiana E. De Angeli per l'industria dei tessuti stampati	Textiles and leather goods	10,369,755	2.70	−22.19
Società italiana per l'industria dello zucchero indigeno	Food, drink, and tobacco products	9,914,488	13.48	2.33
Società italiana per il carburo di calcio	Oil, rubber, chemicals, and other non-metallic mineral products	9,401,625	7.68	4.24
Società della ferrovia sicula occidentale Palermo-Marsala-Trapani (A)	Railways	9,278,237	3.09	−0.98
Società anonima Riccardo Gualino	Mining	8,705,901	−44.53	
Unione italiana fra consumatori e fabbricanti di concimi e prodotti chimici	Oil, rubber, chemicals, and other non-metallic mineral products	7,575,522	5.24	1.24
Lloyd italiano	Transport and communication	6,986,018	3.93	21.11
Società italo-americana pel petrolio	Commercial activities	6,973,027		
Lanificio Rossi	Textiles and leather goods	6,802,831	8.24	0.30
FIAT Fabbrica italiana automobili Torino	Transport equipment	6,514,103	8.42	−0.59
Società anonima delle miniere di Montecatini	Mining	4,831,000	6.53	11.63
AEDES Società anonima ligure per imprese e costruzioni	Construction and property companies	4,549,384	−3.18	−19.42
A.E.G. Thomson Houston	Electrical engineering	4,152,511	5.41	
Compagnia italiana dei grandi alberghi	Commercial activities	3,847,468	0.92	6.93
Società costruzioni A. Brambilla	Construction and property companies	3,295,154	5.53	

(*continued*)

Table 8.2. Continued

Company	Sector	Assets (US$)	ROE (%)	HR (%)
Tecnomasio italiano Brown Boweri	Electrical engineering	2,686,826	5.37	
Cartiera italiana	Wood and paper products	2,132,663	21.50	5.35
Officine meccaniche Stigler	Mechanical engineering	1,995,345	8.18	
Cartiere Pietro Miliani	Wood and paper products	1,852,758	5.84	
Officine Sesto San Giovanni & Valsecchi Abramo	Mechanical engineering	1,814,596	3.95	−13.57

in the fact that only one firm—Officine meccaniche Stigler—is present in the Large Sample. The electrical engineering companies, both of them ultimately under foreign control, are to be found in the bottom half of the ranking by ROE.

Data on holding return (HR) affirm Italy's incomplete economic transformation at the beginning of the twentieth century. First, less than one-half of companies (fourteen of thirty) generated a positive HR, among which are the country's two universal banks. Moreover, aside from the banks, the highest HR is achieved by firms belonging to more traditional sectors: shipping, mining, wood, and paper, as well as food, drink, and tobacco products, and hotels. It is also noteworthy that, with the important exception of banks, only three of the best-performing companies in terms of HR are in the top fifteen, of which only six record positive figures (see Table 8.1). Generally speaking, HR shows a decreasing trend between 1911 and 1913, with a widening gap between the highest and lowest ranks. In short, in 1911–13, the structure of Italian big business appears to be in a transitional phase.

The 1927–9 benchmark

The data on company performance at the end of the 1920s show clearly the growing relevance of capital-intensive industries in the years following the First World War. Among the top fifteen companies listed in Table 8.3, advanced sectors are well represented: five firms in utilities (electricity) and two in chemicals and pharmaceuticals. Although the biggest enterprises are still the three universal banks, the changes in Italy's industrial structure since 1913 are manifested by the disappearance of companies in 'food, drink, and tobacco', the reduction of firms in 'basic and fabricated metals' from five to three, and the increase in the number of firms in transport equipment and both electrical and mechanical engineering.

The distribution of ROE for companies in the Large Sample confirms the common view about Italian industrial history (see Table 8.4). The ten companies with the highest returns belong to financial intermediation and the just-mentioned capital- and technology-intensive sectors. In cases such as Montecatini and Fiat, their good earnings have been traditionally attributed to the ability of their respective leaders, Guido Donegani and Giovanni Agnelli, to focus on strategies of growth, both internal and external, and to avoid excessive speculation and sub-optimal use of the conspicuous profits made during the war. The good performance of both Montecatini and Fiat is also confirmed by their HRs, which placed them among the country's ten most profitable industrial companies (that is, excluding banks).

Table 8.3. Top fifteen Italian companies, 1927–9: three-year averages of assets, ROE, and HR

Company	Sector	Assets (US$)	ROE (%)	HR (%)
Banca Commerciale Italiana	Financial intermediation	809,513,404	8.28	20.37
Credito Italiano	Financial intermediation	550,619,376	8.70	14.81
Banco di Roma	Financial intermediation	224,228,512	7.08	10.39
Societa Generale Italiana Edison di Elettricita	Utilities; Electricity, gas, and water supply	96,942,196	8.08	26.46
SNIA-Viscosa	Chemicals and pharmaceuticals	91,513,874	4.97	−12.08
SIP	Utilities; Electricity, gas, and water supply	90,079,238	8.45	13.99
Terni	Basic and fabricated metals	75,812,175	4.48	9.29
Montecatini	Chemicals and pharmaceuticals	69,894,707	10.37	19.54
FIAT	Transport equipment	66,968,894	10.37	9.67
Navigazione Generale Italiana	Transport and communication	50,143,148	5.09	19.03
ILVA	Basic and fabricated metals	49,984,680	3.05	21.37
Societa Meridionale di Elettricita	Utilities; Electricity, gas, and water supply	43,220,702	14.68	16.11
Societa Generale Elettrica dell'Adamello	Utilities; Electricity, gas, and water supply	38,444,767	12.04	29.27
Societa Anonima Elettricita Alta Italia	Utilities; Electricity, gas, and water supply	37,624,022	5.04	4.05
Ansaldo	Mechanical engineering	34,777,125	−3.24	9.21

Table 8.4. The Large Sample, Italy, 1927–9: three-year averages of assets, ROE, and HR

Company	Sector	Assets (US$)	ROE (%)	HR (%)
Banca commerciale italiana	Financial intermediation	809,513,404	8.28	20.37
Credito italiano	Financial intermediation	550,619,376	8.70	14.81
Societa generale italiana edison di elettricita	Utilities; Electricity, gas, and water supply	96,942,196	8.08	26.46
Snia-viscosa	Chemicals and pharmaceuticals	91,513,874	4.97	−12.08
SIP	Utilities; Electricity, gas, and water supply	90,079,238	8.45	13.99
Terni	Basic and fabricated metals	75,812,175	4.48	9.29
Montecatini	Chemicals and pharmaceuticals	69,894,707	10.37	19.54
FIAT	Transport equipment	66,968,894	10.37	9.67
Navigazione generale italiana	Transport and communication	50,143,148	5.09	19.03

(*continued*)

Table 8.4. Continued

Company	Sector	Assets (US$)	ROE (%)	HR (%)
Ilva	Basic and fabricated metals	49,984,680	3.05	21.37
Ansaldo	Mechanical engineering	34,777,125	−3.24	9.21
Societa italo-americana pel petrolio	Commercial activities	30,359,352	2.20	
Societa italiana commercio materie tessili	Commercial activities	26,832,901	−131.08	
Societa italiana pirelli	Oil, rubber, and other non-metallic mineral products	23,039,546	10.57	14.45
Lloyd triestino	Transport and communication	22,783,414	−0.06	−11.02
Societa italiana ernesto breda per costruzioni meccaniche	Mechanical engineering	18,774,743	5.06	5.66
Linificio e canapificio nazionale	Textiles and leather goods	13,825,477	5.98	−5.83
Istituto di fondi rustici	Construction and property companies	13,226,407	4.93	1.81
Cantiere navale triestino	Transport equipment	12,962,688	4.90	1.42
Compagnia italiana dei cavi telegrafici sottomarini–italcable (soc. An. 'compagnia italiana italcable')	Electrical engineering	12,015,352	7.49	2.35
Distillerie italiane	Food, drink and tobacco products	11,799,941	6.40	32.93
Manifatture cotoniere meridionali[a]	Textiles and leather goods	11,574,740	2.58	−9.66
Aedes	Construction and property companies	10,722,800	4.33	−14.93
U.n.i.c.a. (d)	Food, drink, and tobacco products	10,493,289	5.46	
Societa anonima stefano pittaluga	Wood and paper products	9,947,455	5.98	−35.00
Ferrovie nord milano	Railways	8,211,333	7.29	
Officine elettriche genovesi	Electrical engineering	7,940,987	7.29	75.89
Cartiere burgo	Wood and paper products	7,544,828	7.37	
Societa mineraria e metallurgia di pertusola	Mining	5,463,999	−11.92	
Monte amiata	Mining	4,084,087	24.39	5.27
Unione italiana tramways elettrici	Railways	3,587,657	10.76	
Romsa	Oil, rubber, and other non-metallic mineral products	3,216,556	6.34	

[a] 1926.

A comparison of ROE in 1913 and 1927 for companies in the advanced sectors shows that their profitability increased only slightly, thus suggesting that in the last years of the 1920s the industrialization process in Italy was slowing down and losing dynamism, even though exogenous reasons related to the global business cycle played a considerable role here. An exception is the growth of firms in electrical engineering, which benefited from the steady expansion of hydroelectric supply. Another exception is financial companies, whose profitability in 1927 was higher than in 1913. The reasons for the high profits, however, can be found more in their attitude to speculation than in inherently superior efficiency.

The same picture of a reinforcement of Italian big business is seen in the HR data. In 1927, HR figures were on average higher than those of the previous benchmark, even though six of the thirty-one companies in the Large Sample recorded negative performances (see Table 8.4). The highest HRs in 1927 were mainly achieved by companies belonging to the advanced sectors, and there was no significant divergence between the top fifteen companies according to assets and the firms having the highest HR (see Tables 8.1 and 8.3).

The 1954–6 benchmark

The list of top fifteen companies for 1954 (Table 8.5) documents that the capital- and technology-intensive industries in manufacturing and utilities definitively

Table 8.5. Top fifteen Italian companies, 1954–6: three-year averages of assets, ROE, and HR

Company	Sector	Assets (US$)	ROE (%)	HR (%)
BNL (state-owned)	Financial intermediation	1,033,793,600	7.69	
Banca Commerciale Italiana (IRI)	Financial intermediation	904,980,800	14.94	
Banco di Roma (IRI)	Financial intermediation	870,406,400	20.36	
Edison	Utilities; Electricity, gas, and water supply	569,777,600	4.63	29.80
Fiat (IFI)	Transport equipment	502,745,600	7.21	53.58
Montecatini	Chemicals and pharmaceuticals	363,225,600	6.59	36.27
SIP (IRI)	Utilities; Electricity, gas, and water supply	247,683,200	4.36	25.15
SME–Società Meridionale Elettrica	Utilities; Electricity, gas, and water supply	230,355,200	4.07	37.95
Terni (IRI)	Basic and fabricated metals	215,070,400	2.25	36.99
Cornigliano (IRI)	Basic and fabricated metals	196,953,600	3.36	
SADE–Società Adriatica di Elettricità	Utilities; Electricity, gas, and water supply	187,992,000	4.10	26.06
Stipel–Società Telefonica Interregionale Piemontese e Lombarda (IRI)	Transport and communication	177,424,000	5.31	
Pirelli	Oil, rubber, and other non-metallic mineral products	141,057,600	6.64	31.71
Ansaldo (IRI)	Mechanical engineering	129,188,800	−10.56	−20.31
SNIA Viscosa	Textiles and leather goods	125,784,000	3.46	10.82

head Italy's economy immediately after the Second World War. The top three positions are once again occupied by financial companies owing to the peculiar structure of their balance sheets but also indirectly confirming the continuous reliance of Italian big business on the banks' assistance. But the top three non-financial firms belong to modern sectors: Edison (electricity), Fiat (automobiles), and Montecatini (chemicals) are leaders in their respective industries in the domestic market and they all have significantly larger assets than the companies ranked sixth to fifteenth.

Although the top fifteen companies in 1954 come from largely the same sectors as in 1927, there are some significant differences that attest to the emergence of the production of transport equipment (namely, Fiat, which accounts for 88.6 per cent of national production) and of chemicals as the major forces behind the country's post-war economic growth. In 1927, Fiat ranked only ninth out of fifteen, while in 1954, it ranked fifth. Similarly, Montecatini—the country's largest chemicals producer by far—rose from eighth position to sixth. The mechanical industry is represented in both benchmarks by a single company: Ansaldo, which improved its ranking slightly from fifteenth to fourteenth.

A slightly different picture emerges if one looks at the performance of the two best companies per sector that are included in the Large Sample (see Table 8.6). Among the ten companies with the highest ROE are, for the first time since the beginning of the century, two companies of the 'commercial activities' sector: Magazzini Standa and La Rinascente. Although they are at the bottom of the list according to size, their presence and performance are potent signals of the deep social changes underway in the country.

Table 8.6. The Large Sample, Italy, 1954–6: three-year averages of assets, ROE, and HR

Company	Sector	Assets (US$)	ROE (%)	HR (%)
BNL (state-owned)	Financial intermediation	1,033,793,600	7.69	
Banca Commerciale Italiana (IRI)	Financial intermediation	904,980,800	14.94	
Edison	Utilities; Electricity, gas, and water supply	569,777,600	4.63	29.80
Fiat (IFI)	Transport equipment	502,745,600	7.21	53.58
Montecatini	Chemicals and pharmaceuticals	363,225,600	6.59	36.27
SIP (IRI)	Utilities; Electricity, gas, and water supply	247,683,200	4.36	25.15
Terni (IRI)	Basic and fabricated metals	215,070,400	2.25	36.99
Cornigliano (IRI)	Basic and fabricated metals	196,953,600	3.36	
Stipel–Società Telefonica Interregionale Piemontese e Lombarda (IRI)	Transport and communication	177,424,000	5.31	
Pirelli	Oil, rubber, and other non-metallic mineral products	141,057,600	6.64	31.71
Ansaldo (IRI)	Mechanical engineering	129,188,800	−10.56	−20.31

SNIA Viscosa	Textiles and leather goods	125,784,000	3.46	10.82
Cantieri Riuniti Adriatico (IRI)	Transport equipment	106,667,200	−14.74	−5.17
Italia di Navigazione (IRI)	Transport and communication	104,737,600	0.44	
AGIP (ENI)	Mining	94,852,800	6.38	
Eridania	Food, drink, and tobacco products	77,195,200	7.54	16.14
Manifatture Lane G. Marzotto	Textiles and leather goods	77,102,400	0.44	
ENI (state-owned)	Mining	70,251,200	8.99	
Stanic (ENI; Esso Italiana)	Oil, rubber, and other non-metallic mineral products	59,299,200	7.30	
Generale Immobiliare	Construction and property companies	45,515,200	6.99	39.90
RIV–Officine di Villar Perosa	Mechanical engineering	35,944,000	3.81	
Italiana Industria Zuccheri	Food, drink, and tobacco products	30,963,200	11.82	22.33
Rai (IRI)	Wood and paper products	30,705,600	4.30	
Istituto Romano Beni Stabili	Construction and property companies	26,400,000	2.86	6.55
Ercole Marelli	Electrical engineering	24,876,800	4.43	14.47
Anic (ENI)	Chemicals and pharmaceuticals	23,961,600	5.74	31.65
Magneti Marelli (Ercole Marelli; Fiat)	Electrical engineering	21,800,000	7.22	102.63
La Rinascente	Commercial activities	16,776,000	7.91	70.94
Arnoldo Mondadori Editore	Wood and paper products	7,611,200	13.79	
Magazzini Standa	Commercial activities	4,792,000	22.76	

A comparison of the profitability of companies belonging to different industries in the two benchmark years 1927 and 1954 sheds further light on the country's shifting economy. Commercial activities show remarkable growth, while banking institutions demonstrate impressive stability, and chemicals fall off slightly. In the production of transport equipment, Fiat is beyond doubt the principal player in the industry, although its ROE decreased somewhat from 10.3 per cent to 7.2 per cent. One must also mention the good performance achieved by corporations in 'food, drink, and tobacco', once again represented by sugar-refining companies. Among the underperformers in 1954 are textile companies, although within the sector there was a considerable gap between SNIA Viscosa, the leader in the production of artificial fibres, whose ROE was about 3.5 per cent, and the second company, Manifatture Lane G. Marzotto, which produced mainly woollen fabrics and generated an ROE of only 0.44 per cent.

Data on HR are available for a smaller percentage of the companies in 1954 than in 1927, but even with the reduction of coverage, the figures confirms the positive performance of Italian industry in these years. No company recorded a negative HR in 1954, and overall HR rates are much higher than in the first half of the century.

The 1970–2 benchmark

The structural change of Italian big business continued apace in the 1950s and 1960s. Particularly noticeable in 1972 is the transformation of the electrical industry after the Nationalization Act of 1962 created ENEL, a state-owned monopoly that took over the business previously carried out by private companies. ENEL positioned itself as the second largest company among the top fifteen in 1972, surpassed only by Fiat (see Table 8.7). Several of the sectors that had fuelled the country's economic growth since the first decades of the century continued to occupy the first ranks of big business: chemicals (Montedison), basic and fabricated metals (Finsider), and mechanical engineering (Olivetti). The position of transport equipment was strengthened by Alfa Romeo joining Fiat among the top fifteen. Commercial activities are again represented by Standa and LaRinascente, which both moved upward in the size ranking.

At the same time, the ROE figures for the top fifteen companies show that the beginning of the 1970s was a greatly troubled time for Italian big business in general and especially critical for the chemical company Montedison and the state-owned airline Alitalia. The profitability of all fifteen leaders in 1972 was lower than

Table 8.7. Top fifteen Italian companies, 1970–2: three-year averages of turnover, ROE, and HR

Company	Sector	Turnover (US$)	ROE (%)	HR (%)
Fiat (IFI)	Transport equipment	3,669,559,705	3.10	−2.30
ENEL (state-owned)	Utilities; Electricity, gas, and water supply	2,338,661,984	0.00	
AGIP (ENI)	Mining	2,174,776,426	0.70	
Montedison	Chemicals and pharmaceuticals	1,410,351,208	−45.24	−23.10
Italsider (Finsider)	Mature industries	1,234,486,894	−6.34	−20.03
SIP (STET)	Transport and communication	1,161,502,484	5.69	2.67
Banca Commerciale Italiana (IRI)	Financial intermediation	724,038,033	7.00	−0.91
BNL (state owned)	Financial intermediation	666,239,507	3.59	
Magazzini Standa (Montedison)	Commercial activities	624,480,041	15.05	
Assicurazioni Generali	Insurance	590,793,216	9.06	9.79
La Rinascente	Commercial activities	504,956,313	7.81	−6.35
Alfa Romeo (IRI)	Transport equipment	480,003,426	3.57	
Alitalia (IRI)	Transport and communication	475,831,763	−5.52	−15.68
Ing. C. Olivetti & C.	Mechanical engineering	436,172,691	5.95	−17.67
Banco di Roma (IRI)	Financial intermediation	407,140,654	7.66	−2.49

in earlier benchmarks, and in some cases the figures were strongly negative: namely, in chemicals and pharmaceuticals and in electrical engineering. In the traditional textile sector, the replacement in the Large Sample of the artificial fibres producer SNIA Viscosa by Gruppo Finanziario Tessile (GFT), a large-scale producer and seller of ready-to-wear men's clothes, was a yet further signal of the adoption of modern managerial structures even within traditional sectors as well as of the modernization of consumption patterns within Italian society.

Because of the large number of missing companies, an evaluation of HR performance for 1972 is necessarily incomplete. The available data show a sharp decrease compared with 1954, thus providing even more evidence of the difficulties that Italian big business experienced during the 1970s (see Table 8.8). Among the firms recording an especially low HR in 1972 were a large number of state-owned companies, including Alitalia, Anic, Dalmine, and Italsider.

Table 8.8. The Large Sample, Italy, 1970–2: three-year averages of turnover, ROE, and HR

Company	Sector	Turnover (US$)	ROE (%)	HR (%)
Fiat (IFI)	Transport equipment	3,669,559,705	3.10	−2.30
ENEL (state-owned)	Utilities; Electricity, gas, and water supply	2,338,661,984	0.00	
AGIP (ENI)	Mining	2,174,776,426	0.70	
Montedison	Chemicals and pharmaceuticals	1,410,351,208	−45.24	−23.10
Italsider (Finsider)	Mature industries	1,234,486,894	−6.34	−20.03
SIP (STET)	Transport and communication	1,161,502,484	5.69	2.67
Banca Commerciale Italiana (IRI)	Financial intermediation	724,038,033	7.00	−0.91
BNL (state-owned)	Financial intermediation	666,239,507	3.59	
Magazzini Standa (Montedison)	Commercial activities	624,480,041	15.05	
Assicurazioni Generali	Insurance	590,793,216	9.06	9.79
La Rinascente	Commercial activities	504,956,313	7.81	−6.35
Alfa Romeo (IRI)	Transport equipment	480,003,426	3.57	
Alitalia (IRI)	Transport and communication	475,831,763	−5.52	−15.68
Ing. C. Olivetti & C.	Mechanical engineering	436,172,691	5.95	−17.67
Industrie Pirelli	Oil, rubber, and other non-metallic mineral products	434,954,600	−29.23	
Anic (ENI)	Chemicals and pharmaceuticals	363,004,968	−0.86	−14.09
Rai (IRI)	Media	314,572,554	0.39	
Industrie A. Zanussi	Electrical engineering	292,706,870	−24.79	
A.P.I.–Anonima Petroli Italiana	Oil, rubber, and other non-metallic mineral products	275,684,427	−4.43	
Dalmine (Finsider)	Mature industries	271,403,118	−7.35	−28.96
SAI	Insurance	255,917,423	2.42	−15.87

(*continued*)

Table 8.8. Continued

Company	Sector	Turnover (US$)	ROE (%)	HR (%)
Galbani	Food, drink, and tobacco products	213,270,516	5.07	
Ferrero	Food, drink, and tobacco products	210,382,046	4.79	
Arnoldo Mondadori Editore	Media	147,186,911	5.94	23.96
Magneti Marelli (Fiat)	Electrical engineering	145,401,747	1.30	48.51
Ansaldo Meccanico-Nucleare (IRI)	Mechanical engineering	124,418,366	−2.98	
Gruppo Finanziario Tessile	Textiles and leather goods	119,508,309	3.60	
Italgas (ENI)	Utilities; Electricity, gas, and water supply	114,253,898	1.91	11.70
Lanerossi (ENI)	Textiles and leather goods	104,044,886	0.00	4.10
Cogefar	Construction and property companies	98,346,753	2.83	
Costruzioni autostrade italiane–SCAI	Construction and property companies	88,783,622	4.88	
Società Mineraria e Metallurgica di Pertusola	Mining	49,429,501	3.32	19.00

The 1998–2000 Benchmark

The institutional changes of the 1990s, together with a radical transformation in the global economic framework, revolutionized the structure of Italian big business. Of the top fifteen companies in 1972, only six—Assicurazioni Generali, Alitalia, ENEL, Montedison, Pirelli, and Fiat (now part of the IFI group)—remained on the list in 2000 (see Table 8.9). Because of the disintegration of the vast state-owned enterprise system, private and family-owned companies took over prominent positions among the leading enterprises: Edizione Holding (Benetton family), Parmalat (Tanzi family), and IFI (Agnelli family). In principle, they represented 'traditional' sectors such as food and beverages, textiles, and transport equipment; in effect, they were conglomerates, especially IFI.

A closer look at the sectoral composition of the top fifteen companies reveals that Italian big business was shifting towards services at the end of the twentieth century. The highest ROE in 2000 was registered by the oil and rubber sector, thanks to the good performance of Pirelli and due especially to the production of cables for telecommunications. The next best ROE performance belonged to companies in 'services to business'. Other companies achieving high levels of profitability were in the utilities sector and in 'textiles and leather goods'. The latter indicates the growing importance of the so-called 'made in Italy' consumer goods industries. At the same time, the data for the Large Sample show the persistent relevance of traditional sectors in Italian industry throughout the entire century. Still among the best performers in

Table 8.9. Top fifteen Italian companies, 1998–2000: three-year averages of turnover, ROE, and HR

Company	Sector	Turnover (US$)	ROE (%)	HR (%)
IFI (Agnelli)	Transport equipment	61,648,818,316	1.07	15.42
ENI	Mining	44,255,908,419	17.27	14.86
Assicurazioni Generali	Insurance	41,003,508,124	10.24	24.84
Olivetti	Post and telecommunications	27,503,692,762	7.44	42.64
ENEL	Utilities; Electricity, gas, and water supply	22,790,805,022	12.41	4.63
Montedison	Food, drink, and tobacco products	12,900,664,697	1.48	55.78
IntesaBci	Financial intermediation	10,409,896,603	9.06	54.37
UniCredito Italiano	Financial intermediation	8,592,134,417	9.43	11.52
Pirelli & C.	Oil, rubber, and other non-metallic mineral products	7,067,946,824	10.36	54.40
Parmalat	Food, drink, and tobacco products	6,784,527,326	7.07	9.97
Edizione (Benetton)	Textiles and leather goods	6,592,503,693	13.02	
Poste Italiane	Post and telecommunications	6,368,168,390	−110.78	
Finmeccanica	Transport equipment	5,527,141,802	−0.10	124.20
Sanpaololmi	Financial intermediation	5,317,577,548	12.80	13.00
Alitalia	Transport	4,976,920,236	−1.70	−22.16

2000 are such well-known names as ENI, ENEL, and Riva Acciai, another family-owned company in the steel sector (see Table 8.10).

HR figures for 2000 are generally better than those for 1972, notwithstanding the downturn experienced by financial markets in the bursting of the dot-com bubble. Remarkably, the company with the highest HR (123.4 per cent) is Montedison, the long-time leader of the chemicals sector. This successful turnaround of its negative performance in the 1970s was closely related to the reorganization process started at the beginning of the 1990s. The firm divested much of its chemicals business (in which it was no longer in the top fifteen) and moved into the agro-food sector (20–40 per cent of national market share) and energy (almost 20 per cent of national market share). Among the companies recording a low HR are Fiat-IFI (−4.8 per cent), which was suffering from the crisis of Fiat Auto, and Finmeccanica (−4.8 per cent), which in 2000 was in the middle of major organizational changes (see Table 8.10).

THE PERFORMANCE OF BIG BUSINESS IN ITALY: A SECTOR-BASED ANALYSIS

This section gives an aggregate analysis of the trends of four core sectors: basic and fabricated metals, engineering and transportation equipment, electricity and communications, and financial intermediation (banking).

Table 8.10. The Large Sample, Italy, 1998–2000: three-year averages of turnover, ROE, and HR

Company	Sector	Turnover (US$)	ROE (%)	HR (%)
IFI (Agnelli)	Transport equipment	61,648,818,316	1.07	15.42
Fiat (IFI)	Transport equipment	49,115,583,456	3.64	−1.20
ENI	Mining	44,255,908,419	17.27	14.86
Assicurazioni Generali	Insurance	41,003,508,124	10.24	24.84
Olivetti	Post and telecommunications	27,503,692,762	7.44	42.64
ENEL	Utilities; Electricity, gas, and water supply	22,790,805,022	12.41	4.63
Montedison	Food, drink, and tobacco products	12,900,664,697	1.48	55.78
Snam (ENI)	Utilities; Electricity, gas, and water supply	12,897,895,126	27.67	
IntesaBci	Financial intermediation	10,409,896,603	9.06	54.37
UniCredito Italiano	Financial intermediation	8,592,134,417	9.43	11.52
Pirelli & C.	Oil, rubber, and other non-metallic mineral products	7,067,946,824	10.36	54.40
Pirelli SpA (Pirelli & C Group)	Oil, rubber, and other non-metallic mineral products	6,849,150,665	30.04	23.06
Parmalat	Food, drink, and tobacco products	6,784,527,326	7.07	9.97
Edizione (Benetton)	Textiles and leather goods	6,592,503,693	13.02	
Poste Italiane	Post and telecommunications	6,368,168,390	−110.78	
Enichem (ENI)	Chemicals and pharmaceuticals	5,555,760,709	−14.53	
Alitalia	Transport	4,976,920,236	−1.70	−22.16
Riva Acciaio	Mature industries	4,567,023,634	10.84	
La Rinascente (IFI)	Commercial activities	4,514,401,773	5.60	0.21
FS–Ferrovie dello Stato	Transport	4,399,926,145	−5.32	
Toro Assicurazioni	Insurance	4,152,511,078	5.38	25.53
Magneti Marelli (Fiat)	Mechanical engineering	4,109,121,123	8.50	
Supermarkets Italiani	Commercial activities	2,895,125,554	13.17	
Rai	Media	2,596,011,817	8.86	
CIR	Mechanical engineering	2,312,592,319	8.93	81.85
SMI	Mature industries	2,179,652,880	3.80	19.29
Mediaset	Media	2,136,262,925	15.89	56.99
Benetton Group	Textiles and leather goods	1,862,998,523	16.07	17.59
Stmicroelectronics (Finmeccanica)	Electrical engineering	1,841,765,140	7.37	
Impregilo	Construction and property companies	1,747,599,705	−2.81	−2.00
SNIA	Chemicals and pharmaceuticals	1,165,066,470	2.46	15.86
Finsiel (Olivetti Group)	Services to business	1,116,137,371	17.76	

Alpitour (IFI Group)	Leisure and tourism	942,577,548	8.12	
Italtel (Olivetti Group)	Electrical engineering	911,189,069	−19.88	
Astaldi	Construction and property companies	663,774,003	8.67	
Esprinet	Services to business	652,695,716	27.78	
Fincab	Leisure and tourism	394,202,363	−76.18	
Maffei	Mining	53,545,052	6.29	−2.81

Basic and Fabricated Metals

This sector was one of the key movers behind Italy's industrialization, but its performance data also highlight the considerable limitations of its development in the twentieth century. Steel companies are present among the top fifteen in all benchmarks. In 1913, five out of the top fifteen firms operate in the metal industry, and one of them, Ilva, is also the largest in terms of assets of all non-financial companies. However, the relevance of steel companies, in terms both of assets and of rank in the top fifteen, deteriorates thereafter (see Table 8.11). In 2000, they no longer figure in the list of Italy's fifteen largest enterprises.

The sector's best ROE was also achieved in 1913, when Terni generated profits of 14.69 per cent, the highest yield among the top fifteen companies. A double-digit profit did not return to the sector until 2000, when a private company, Riva Acciaio, returned 12.03 per cent, much higher than other firms in the sector after 1913, though still lower than companies in other industries. The worst performances came in 1972 when Italsider recorded an ROE of −5.76 per cent and Dalmine one of −13.56 per cent. With regard to variations in longevity or company survival, we see that what at first glance appear as 'new entries' to the sector are, in four out of the five benchmarks, merely reorganizations of pre-existing firms. Real new entries in the top fifteen, such as Riva Acciaio and SMI, another private company founded in 1886 and a holding company since 1976, appear only in 2000.

The large corporations in the Italian steel industry acquired their economic leadership in a protected environment under the aegis of the state. Although in the first two benchmarks the firms were privately owned and controlled by an interest group (basically a trust) or by another steel company, the role of the state should not be underestimated: government support included protective tariffs, procurement contracts, and repeated bailouts. In fact, the rescue operation carried out by the Bank of Italy in 1911 can indeed be seen as responsible for the good performance of the steel companies in the 1913 benchmark. State intervention encouraged the steel firms to establish a threefold financial, commercial, and managerial agreement. Ilva, which in 1911 had a lower ROE (−8.29 per cent) than the other steel firms, was in charge of managing the plants, while Terni did not take part in the agreement, even though it owned shares in most of these firms. However, the common management of the plants did not provide the companies involved with technological or organizational means that could implement the rationalization that the sector needed.

Table 8.11. Incidence of the total assets of the top two Italian companies (per industry) on the sum of the Large Sample's total assets (finance and insurance excluded) (100% = 1)

	1913	1927	1954	1972	2000
Basic and fabricated metals	0.18	0.14	0.12	0.14	0.01
Chemicals and pharmaceuticals	0.00	0.18	0.11	0.14	0.01
Commercial activities	0.04	0.06	0.01	0.01	0.01
Construction and property companies	0.03	0.03	0.02	0.01	0.01
Electrical engineering	0.03	0.02	0.01	0.01	0.01
Food, drink, and tobacco products	0.08	0.02	0.03	0.00	0.05
Leisure and tourism	0.00	0.00	0.00	0.00	0.00
Mechanical engineering	0.01	0.06	0.03	0.03	0.01
Media	0.00	0.00	0.00	0.00	0.01
Mining	0.05	0.01	0.05	0.00	0.09
Oil, rubber, and other non-metallic mineral products	0.06	0.03	0.06	0.03	0.04
Post and telecommunications	0.00	0.00	0.00	0.00	0.19
Railways	0.10	0.01	0.00	0.00	0.00
Services to business	0.00	0.00	0.00	0.00	0.00
Textiles and leather goods	0.07	0.03	0.06	0.01	0.03
Transport and communication	0.11	0.08	0.08	0.14	0.10
Transport equipment	0.11	0.09	0.18	0.10	0.32
Utilities; Electricity, gas, and water supply	0.10	0.21	0.24	0.36	0.11
Wood and paper products	0.02	0.02	0.01	0.00	0.00
Total	1.00	1.00	1.00	1.00	1.00

This failure might explain the sector's weak performance in 1927, as well as its lack of competitiveness in interwar Europe. In the 1927 benchmark, the Italian steel industry's only representative in the top fifteen is Terni (see Table 8.3). However, if we bring in information on industrial strategy, we see that a big change had occurred between 1913 and 1927. In 1913, the sector's five companies in the top fifteen either had steel production as the dominant activity or operated in related activities, such as shipbuilding. In 1927 by contrast, Terni—now named 'Terni. Società per l'Industria e l'elettricità'—had heavily diversified into unrelated activities such as electricity and electrochemicals. Ilva, the other steel firm present in the Large Sample and the only one whose core business is still steel production, performed quite poorly; its ROE was a feeble 0.46 per cent. The company's productive facilities were non-integrated, technologically heterogeneous, and geographically distant.

In the first post-war benchmark, 1954–6, a dramatic shift in the history of the Italian steel industry is evident: both of the large steelworks in the top fifteen, Terni and Cornigliano, were now under the control of Finsider, the holding company of state-owned IRI, which de facto owned 40 per cent of the steel industry's total capacity. Furthermore, the historical technological and organizational weakness of the Italian steel industry was partially overcome thanks to the adoption of continuous casting technology at Cornigliano. Cornigliano's performance is underestimated in our data, which derive from the years immediately following the company's foundation before the new facilities had reached their full capability. Yet, thanks to the Cornigliano steelworks, in the 1960s, Italy became the sixth largest steel producer in the world.

The symbiosis of the state and the large steel corporations, however, did not prevent the terrible performances in 1972 of Italsider (an outcome of the merger between Ilva and Cornigliano) and Dalmine (Finsider Group)—both under the umbrella of Finsider. Their losses at this time reflect the beginning of the crisis of the state-ownership system, which culminated in the 1988 bankruptcy of Finsider. In 2000, the sector is represented in the database by a private company, Riva Acciaio, a family-run firm founded in 1954 that had progressively expanded, adopting technological innovations in continuous casting (mini-mills). In 1989, it acquired the newly privatized Cornigliano plant, thus becoming the second largest steel producer in Europe, and in 2000, Riva Acciaio was the tenth largest producer of steel in the world. Nonetheless, at the beginning of the new millennium, the relative weight of steel companies in Italian big business was negligible (see Table 8.11).

Engineering and Transportation Equipment

In terms of technology, production, forms of ownership, and growth strategies, the Italian engineering industry was characterized by fragmentation. Although historians have stressed the sector's enormous growth in Italy during the twentieth century, its profits have been fairly diverse and overall lower than those of other sectors.

In 1913, no mechanical engineering company ranked in the top fifteen. Even in the Large Sample, the sector's two representatives, Stigler and Officine Meccaniche Valsecchi, were quite far down in the ranking (thirty-sixth and thirty-eighth, respectively). In 1927, Nuova Ansaldo qualified for inclusion in the top fifteen, remaining there also in the 1954 benchmark. In 1972, the Ansaldo Meccanico Nucleare was joined in the Large Sample by Olivetti, which also moved into the top fifteen. In 2000, Olivetti and Ansaldo Nucleare lost their places in the Large Sample to Magneti Marelli and CIR.

Italian big business in mechanical engineering is represented mainly by two types of firms with different performance trends. Such a distinction also mirrors the difference in behaviour between different types of engineering firms: (a) companies following a specific pattern of growth mainly in steelmaking and shipbuilding, which perform relatively well in the first half of the century; and (b) family-owned and market-oriented firms, which show good performance especially in the second half of the century.

The first type is represented by Ansaldo, which is present in all the benchmarks from 1913 to 1972 and whose declining profitability distorted the performance record of the entire industry between 1927 to 1972. Since the end of the nineteenth century, the Genoa-based company, in search of vertical integration, adopted a strategy of related diversification that moved it from shipbuilding into steel production, railway products, mechanical engineering, electromechanics, and weapons, thus progressively modifying its structure from functional with production activities to that of a pure holding. Like the steel companies, in the first half of the century, Ansaldo benefited from close links to the state (bailouts, protective tariffs, guaranteed pre-financing through military orders, and so on). In the early 1930s, it became a part of IRI. Yet not even the continual financial support of IRI enabled Ansaldo to improve its performance. However, the strategic importance of Ansaldo—which in the 1950s accounted for 45 per cent of Italian output in shipbuilding and 25 per cent in mechanical engineering—delayed its dismantling until 1966. In 1972, despite the reorganization of the mechanical complex (1966) and subsequent specialization in the production of nuclear power plants, performance was still negative.

Olivetti is representative of the second type of mechanical engineering enterprise. Founded at the end of the nineteenth century and owned by the same family for generations, Olivetti grew considerably in the interwar period, making significant advances in terms of technical and organizational modernization. The limits of the Italian economy in the interwar years, particularly in terms of market size and dynamism, forced Olivetti (and other similar companies) either to pursue growth strategies based on internationalization or to reduce production costs by a precocious modernization of facilities according to scientific management theories. The strategy ultimately paid off. After a major reorganization process that started in 1964, Olivetti qualified for the top fifteen in 1972 and yielded a good ROE of 4.97 per cent.

The Italian electrical engineering sector is characterized by different company strategies over the entire twentieth century. According to the data in our sample, the ROEs of the electromechanical firms are better, especially in 1927 and 1954, than those of other engineering firms. However, no electromechanical company makes it into the top fifteen in any benchmark. In 1913, moreover, there is no genuinely Italian firm even in the Large Sample, since both AEG Thomson Houston and Tecnomasio Italiano Brown Boveri are subsidiaries of foreign companies. Electrical engineering appears to be characterized by a high volatility: in each benchmark, there is a new entry, and only Magneti Marelli is present in two consecutive benchmarks (1954 and 1972). In 2000, the sector had yet again two new entries in the Large Sample: STMicroelectronics (chip production) and Italtel, a subsidiary of Telecom Italia (information technology); the first recorded excellent earnings (7.37 per cent), the second miserable (−19.88 per cent). What is clear is the technological transition from electrical engineering to electronics, which required a complete reorganization of the sector's companies and their production systems.

In the transport equipment industry, the pre-eminence of Fiat is uncontested. Fiat is the only company that ranked in the country's top fifteen enterprises in all benchmarks except 1913. Its ROE performance increased steadily in the first part of the century and was particularly high in the 1927–9 benchmark (10.37 per cent). From the 1920s, the family-owned company had adopted a strategy of diversification into related activities, which were managed through a strongly centralized functional structure, although, especially during the years of Vittorio Valletta's management (1946–66), the company strongly concentrated on its core production (automobiles) and related business. The good results of 1954–7 (ROE 7.21 per cent) attest to Fiat management's accurate assessment of future trends and its readiness to take advantage of the 'Italian economic miracle' and of the American model of mass production. However, after 1954, Fiat's performance fell off; its ROE collapsed to 1 per cent in 1970, but recovered to 4 per cent in 1972; similar figures were recorded in the 2000 benchmark. The poor profits of 1970–2 marked the beginning of a difficult decade for the company: increasing indebtedness, less favourable market conditions, and difficult industrial relations from the late 1960s. Furthermore, in 1972, Fiat started a process of reorganization that was completed only in 1979 with the creation of Fiat Auto s.p.a. (the holding in charge of the strategic and financial management of Fiat Group). The outcome of this process was the introduction of a multidivisional structure. The long gap between the benchmarks of 1972 and 2000 does not allow us to evaluate the successes that the reorganization and the launching of new models brought the company during the 1980s. However, the ROE for 2000 (1.07 per cent) indicates the beginnings of a renewed crisis for Fiat at the start of the new century.

Shipbuilding performed quite well in the first half of the century, but the sector entered into permanent decline starting from 1954, underscored by the negative performance (ROE −4.2 per cent) of Cantieri Riuniti dell'Adriatico (IRI).

Electricity and Communications Services

Not surprisingly, companies involved in the production and distribution of electricity have played a fundamental role in Italy's economic growth since the very beginning of the country's industrialization. To them, one must add communications services, which quite precociously featured among the country's most important industries. Data concerning all benchmark years seem to link the good performance maintained by these sectors' top companies with the favourable institutional framework and market regulation that shaped their activities and from which they benefited (for their incidence in terms of assets in the Large Sample, see Table 8.11).

Although there were over 250 electric companies in Italy on the eve of the First World War, the whole sector was firmly controlled by some 20 large firms. The latter acted as 'locally based' monopolies, which achieved a growing influence within the economy owing to the industrial and financial interests involved, the benevolent concessions granted by the state, and the huge investments and resources required. In the first benchmark year (1913), there were two companies from the 'utilities' sector (i.e. electricity, gas, and water supply) in the Small Sample of the top fifteen enterprises: Edison and Elettricità Alta Italia, ranking tenth and thirteenth respectively). In the following two benchmarks, Edison was again the largest non-financial company in the top fifteen. In 1927, the economic weight of public utilities was confirmed by the presence of electricity companies among the top fifteen, all of which yielded outstanding ROEs and HRs. One of them, SIP (ranked sixth), had large shareholdings in the telephone sector. In 1954, there were also five public utilities companies in the top fifteen: four in electricity and one, Stipel, in telephone services.

The peculiar structure of this industry deserves clarification. From the earliest stages of industrialization in Italy, electricity companies developed into big businesses with a very effective multifunctional managerial structure. The latter was, indeed, the solution chosen to manage these large 'industrial groups', or 'functional holdings', which pursued a strategy of growth through acquisitions or cross-shareholdings in other electricity companies or related industries. In 1927, for example, Edison controlled a second electricity company in the top fifteen, Società Generale Elettrica dell'Adamello, while the other two electricity enterprises in the Small Sample were controlled by SIP, the holding company for Società anonima Elettricità Alta Italia. The presence of an owning group of banks and/or investors as dominant shareholder, a single- or dominant-product business strategy, and the policy of alliances and agreements with other electricity producers were common features among the leading companies of this sector, at least for the first two benchmarks considered. By 1954, these features have changed somewhat. The banks are no longer among the shareholders; top managers now play a central role in exploiting the expansive opportunities of the post-war boom, and there are the beginnings of a diversification strategy provoked by fear of a nationalization of the electricity sector (for example, Edison moves into petrochemicals). However, even after the Second World War, the economic strength of the electric companies was largely rooted in their ability to act as regional monopolies linked by mutual agreements.

The presence of the electricity industry among the best-performing Italian sectors continued after the 1962 nationalization of all industrial activities involved in production, distribution, and sale of electric power. The state agency created by this legislation, ENEL (Ente nazionale per l'energia elettrica—National agency for electric power), made it into the Small Sample of the top fifteen companies in both 1972 (ranked second) and 2000 (ranked fourth). During the 1990s, following the liberalization programme started in 1992, ENEL became an industrial holding company with a completely revamped organizational model—the traditional core business of production, transmission, and distribution of electricity was spun off to service divisions as independent companies—and a deep involvement in new lines of business such as mobile telephony. The company's ROE in 2000 was 11.94 per cent, attesting to the success of the reorientation.

The nationalization of the electricity industry also opened a new chapter in the history of Italian telecommunications. In 1964, SIP (now part of IRI) moved into the telephone industry, becoming a de facto monopolist in that sector. Thus, studying the growth of telecommunications big business in the last decades amounts largely to the analysis of SIP's development. In 1972, SIP was among the top fifteen companies by turnover and its ROE and HR were among the best in this group. This performance is even more remarkable considering that the company was suffering great organizational and financial difficulties that would result in a first redesign of its structure in 1983–4 and then in the adoption of the multidivisional structure in 1991. The last benchmark in 2000, gives a picture of the telecommunications sector soon after the transformation of SIP into Telecom Italia (1994), the 1997 merger between Telecom Italia and STET (the state-owned holding for the telephone industry created in 1934), Telecom's privatization (1998), and its acquisition by Olivetti. These profound changes, which were still in progress in 2000, did not stop the corporation's good performance, however, thanks to the explosive expansion of the mobile telephone industry. Following its acquisition of Telecom, Olivetti jumped from fourteenth to fourth ranking in the top fifteen; if one looks only at the turnover of non-financial firms, this rise was even more impressive (from sixth to fourth ranking).

Financial Intermediation: The Banking System

In 1913, the universal banks Banca Commerciale Italiana (Comit) and Credito Italiano (Credit) ranked first in both the Large and Small Samples, followed in the latter by Società italiana per le strade ferrate meridionali (Bastogi), a former railway operator that invested the compensation received from the national-ization of the country's railways in 1905 in electrical and mechanical compan-ies. Their ranking clearly shows the great difference in terms of total assets between financial and non-financial companies across all benchmarks, even if in different proportions. In 1927, Bastogi falls out of the top fifteen, but is replaced by another financial intermediary, the Banco di Roma. The banks' performance indicators continue to be good throughout these years, with increasing ROEs and highly positive HRs, especially for Comit and Credit. During the second half of the 1920s, universal banks experienced a 'degener-ation', transforming themselves into something like holding companies with significant equity holdings.

The Bank Act of 1936 put an end to universal banking, driving financial intermediation into a functional specialization, while ownership of the three big banks was transferred to IRI. Indeed, the consequences of the regulatory changes are evident in 1954: Credit has exited the sample, while Comit and Banco di Roma have slipped behind the state-owned Banca Nazionale del Lavoro (BNL) that grew out of the cooperative movement. The redesign of the banking system, however, does not seem to have damaged the banks' performance, since their ROEs were higher than before the Second World War; Banco di Roma topped the group with a ROE just over 20 per cent. By contrast, the economic crisis that started in the early 1970s was reflected in the lower ROE values recorded by the three leading financial companies in the 1972 benchmark. Also in 1972, the group of financial intermediaries in the top fifteen includes for the first time the country's largest insurance company, Assicurazioni Generali, ranked tenth, affirming the evolution of Italy's financial sector according to a trend already present in other industrialized countries. The increasing differentiation and wealth of the individ-ual actors in the financial sector in the last quarter of the twentieth century led to Assicurazioni Generali reaching rank three in the top fifteen in 2000 (rank two by assets).

In the 1990s, growing integration of national and international financial markets, together with EU regulatory policies, fuelled rapid privatization and favoured concentration in the Italian banking system. The Bank Act of 1993 reintroduced the option of universal banking and the possibility for operators to merge into enormous financial groups. To a certain extent, these changes in ownership and strategy can be seen in the last benchmark of 1998–2000. The top two banks had become financial groups—IntesaBci and UniCredito Italiano—with high rates of ROE and HR even though their restructuring processes were not yet completed.

CONCLUSIONS

The results of the longitudinal analysis of the data available for the largest Italian companies provide general support for the 'convergence/divergence hypothesis'.[10]

By 1914, Italy had built—quite successfully for a latecomer country—an industrial structure in line with that of the advanced economies of north-western Europe, even though some inefficiencies remained. Big business was particularly present in steelmaking and electricity, while in the financial sector the largest banks had achieved a size capable of meeting the capital needs of an expanding industrial economy. The consolidation of big business continued in the interwar years, when firms belonging to sectors typical of the Second Technological Wave, such as chemicals, engineering, and motor vehicles, found their way into the country's top fifteen companies. The analysis of financial performance shows, in general, the positive correlation between profitability, returns, and growth in size. Apparently, the nature of ownership did not affect the dynamics of big business.

The convergence of the country's industrial structure speeded up again during the almost three decades of steady post-war economic growth, with the emergence of big business in energy and oil but also in mass distribution, a mirror of the social modernization of the country. Despite its defects, the comprehensive system of state-owned corporations played a major role in this transformation. However, the positive correlation between size and performance no longer held true. From the 1970s, the mounting pressure of the global economic slowdown coupled with turbulence in the domestic labour market had negative consequences for the performance of large firms especially.

The relatively 'positive' performance of Italian big business in the first three-quarters of the twentieth century, however, looks more controversial from the perspective of the last benchmark. Big business is still present, of course, but its structural composition harbours potential difficulties for future development. It is in fact evident that the country's industrial system has failed to catch the third technological wave. Only a couple of the largest firms in the 2000 sample could be considered meaningful representatives of cutting-edge technology, while the absolute majority of Italian big business was still devoted to products and skills characterizing the second technological wave. Moreover, the privatization policies of the 1990s pushed the country's big business in two directions: fragmenting the (once) largest companies under state control and leading to a higher diffusion of family control among the largest industrial enterprises, but they did not lead to a greater presence in the latest technologies.

ACKNOWLEDGEMENTS

A first version of this chapter was presented at conferences in Milan in 2004 and Copenhagen in 2006. The research from which the present chapter originates has already been

---

[10] Amatori, Bugamelli, and Colli, 'Technology'.

used in an earlier paper: Carlo Brambilla, Chiara Casalino, Valentina Fava, Francesca Polese, and Daniele Pozzi, 'Big business performance in the 20th century: Italy', in Camilla Brautaset, ed., *Essays in European Business Performance in the 20th Century* (London: LSE Business History Unit Occasional Paper, 2005). The authors express here our gratitude to all the above-mentioned scholars.

9

Spanish Business Performance in the Twentieth Century

Veronica Binda, Albert Carreras, and Xavier Tafunell

INTRODUCTION

At the dawn of the twentieth century, Spain was largely an agricultural country, which exported mainly primary goods—agricultural and mineral—to Western Europe. According to the interpretation of the distinguished economic historian Jordi Nadal, during the nineteenth century, Spain's First Industrial Revolution as well as the initial steps of the Second Industrial Revolution were for the most part failed developments. Some negative international circumstances as well as several disadvantageous characteristics of the Spanish economy hindered effective industrialization, although some big businesses were founded and in some industries new technologies were adopted quite rapidly.[1] A low degree of integration into the international economy, the country's agricultural backwardness, and a succession of unfavourable political events (such as the Spanish–American War of 1898 and the Francoist policy of autarky from the late 1930s to the mid 1950s) delayed Spanish industrialization and held back the country's economic growth until the end of the 1950s.[2]

Yet the achievements of the Spanish economy during the last forty years of the twentieth century were impressive. A favourable national and international economic framework enabled an 'economic miracle' during the 1960s, and the country's economic growth after the end of the Francoist dictatorship was very rapid. Spain's GDP per capita has quickly converged with those of the richest nations over the last few decades and, even though it has recently suffered a great number of setbacks, the Spanish economy retains a prominent position within the European Community.

Spanish corporations were important protagonists in this catch-up process, and it has been claimed that the contribution of big business to Spain's national

---

[1] J. Nadal, *El Fracaso de la Revolución Industrial en España, 1814–1913* (Ariel, 1975).

[2] A. Carreras, 'La industrialización Española en el Marco de la historia económica europea: Ritmos y caracteres comparados', in J.L. García Delgado, ed., *España, Economía* (Espasa Calpe, 1993); J. Nadal, A. Carreras, and C. Sudriá, eds., *La Economía Española en el Siglo XX: Una Perspectiva Histórica* (Ariel, 1994); G. Tortella, *El Desarrollo de la España Contemporánea: Historia Económica de los Siglos XIX y XX* (Alianza, 1994).

GDP during the twentieth century was very large.[3] Notwithstanding this importance, investigations into the economic performances of Spanish big business have been very few and of poor quality, with the notable exception of Xavier Tafunell's studies on the financial profitability of Spanish companies between 1880 and 1981.[4]

In this work, the performance of selected Spanish companies has been analysed on the basis of two samples over five benchmark periods (1911–13, 1927–9, 1954–6, 1970–2, and 1998–2000). The first sample (the 'Small Sample' or top ten) is made up of the ten largest Spanish firms. The second (the 'Large Sample') aims to provide a broader view of the country's business landscape and is made up of the largest company in each industry (transport and financial firms included) and up to five 'wildcards' (that is, other firms that the research team considered important). Information on performance has been gathered from joint-stock companies' yearbooks, stock exchange yearbooks, and companies' annual reports. The main yearbooks used are *Anuario Financiero y de Sociedades Anónimas de España, Anuario Financiero del Banco de Bilbao, Anuario Oficial de Valores de la Bolsa de Madrid, Anuario Oficial de Valores de la Bolsa de Barcelona, Fomento de la Producción—Las Mayores Empresas Españolas, Agenda Financiera del Banco de Bilbao, Anuario Estadístico de la Banca Privada, Informe del Mercado—Apéndice Estadístico Bolsa de Madrid*, and *Informe del Mercado—Apéndice Estadístico Bolsa de Barcelona* (various years).

DEVELOPMENT OF SPANISH BUSINESS

At the beginning of the twentieth century, despite the country's strong agricultural base, Spain had some large companies. Most of them were born in the 1880s, while other new big businesses emerged after a wave of mergers between the late nineteenth and early twentieth centuries.[5] However, their total number was quite small, and they were concentrated in particular industries such as railways, mining, and financial intermediation.[6]

In 1913, railway companies were absolutely dominant. Usually founded with foreign capital, the railways were by far the biggest corporations in Spain.[7] The

---

[3] A. Carreras and X. Tafunell, 'Spain: Big manufacturing firms between state and market, 1917–1990', in A. Chandler, F. Amatori, and T. Hikino, eds., *Big Business and the Wealth of Nations* (Cambridge University Press, 1997); V. Binda, *The Dynamics of Big Business: Structure, Strategy, and Impact in Italy and Spain* (Routledge, 2013).

[4] X. Tafunell, *Los Beneficios Empresariales en España (1880–1981): Elaboración de una Serie Anual*, Documento de Trabajo 9601, Fundación Empresa Pública, Programa de Historia Económica (1996); X. Tafunell, 'La rentabilidad financiera de la empresa española, 1880–1981: Una estimación en perspectiva sectorial', *Revista de Historia Industrial*, 18 (2000), 69–112.

[5] A. Carreras and X. Tafunell, *National Enterprise: Spanish Big Manufacturing Firms (1917–1990), between State and Market*, Economics Working Paper 93, Universitat Pompeu Fabra (1994).

[6] G. Tortella, *Los Orígenes del Capitalismo en España: Banca, Industria y Ferrocarriles en el Siglo XIX* (Tecnos, 1973).

[7] P. Tedde de Lorca, 'La expansión de las grandes compañías ferroviarias españolas: Norte, MZA y Andaluces (1865–1930)', in F. Comín and P. Martín Aceña, eds., *La Empresa en la Historia de España* (Civitas, 1996), pp. 265–301.

assets of the country's largest company, Caminos de Hierro del Norte de España (Caminos), were worth 3.5 times more than those of the biggest non-railway firm in the country and exceeded those of the smallest enterprises in the top ten sample by a factor of 15. Spain's second-largest railway of the country, Ferrocarril de Madrid a Zaragoza y Alicante (MZA), occupied a similarly dominant economic position in the country's top ten.

With the help of foreign capital, mining also fostered big businesses at the beginning of the new century, such as Río Tinto, Minera y Metallúrgica de Peñarroya (Peñarroya), and the Tharsis Sulphur and Copper Co. Ltd (Tharsis),[8] while financial intermediation firms, such as Banco de España and Banco Hipotecario de España, were predominantly national private-owned corporations.[9] Even though they were less frequently represented, manufacturing corporations in industries such as food (General Azucarera de España (Azucarera)) and metals (Sociedad Metalúrgica Duro Felguera) were not missing from this panorama, and new industries such as electricity (Riegos y Fuerzas del Ebro) were also starting up.

The Large Sample confirms that the largest companies at this time operated in industries such as metals, utilities, and food and tobacco, while enterprises in textiles, transport and communication, wood and paper products, mechanical engineering, oil, rubber, chemicals and other non-metallic mineral products, commercial activities, construction, and property, were definitely smaller in terms of assets. The companies that make up the Large Sample also make it possible to check two insights that are foreshadowed by the Small Sample. First, foreign capital and technologies were most significant in the newest and most capital-intensive industries—such as railways and utilities—and the exploitation of natural resources—such as the mining industry. Second, the country's big business was clearly geographically concentrated. The mining and food-producing industries were mainly concentrated in Andalusia, while practically all other large companies in Spain were located in Madrid, Barcelona, or the Basque Country.[10]

The impact of the First World War on Spanish business was emphatically positive in the short run. Until the end of the 1920s, Spain experienced strong economic expansion, which was particularly favourable for the development of native big business. Foreign-owned firms downsized or sold their shares to Spanish nationals, and a number of Spanish-owned companies were created from scratch. New industries, such as public utilities (electricity and telecommunications), appeared. During the war, Spanish banks enjoyed very good times, managing the excess liquidity of the economy and investing in bonds and shares. These developments are reflected in the panorama of large corporations, even though continuities are also detectable.

[8] M.A. Pérez de Perceval, M.Á. López Morell, and A. Sánchez Rodríguez, eds., *Minería y Desarrollo Económico en España* (Sintesis, 2006).

[9] J.L. Malo de Molina and P. Martín Aceña, eds., *The Spanish Financial System: Growth and Development since 1900* (Macmillan, 2011); P. Martín Aceña and M.Á. Pons, 'Estructura y rentabilidad de las empresas financieras en España, 1874–1975', in F. Comín and P. Martín Aceña, eds., *La Empresa en la Historia de España* (Civitas, 1996).

[10] J.L. García Ruiz and C. Manera, eds., *Historia Empresarial de España: Un Enfoque Regional en Profundidad* (LID, 2006).

Within the enterprises of the Small Sample, a few industries continued to dominate the group. Railways and financial intermediation remained the strongest, but their relative weights had changed. The railway companies Caminos and MZA, which had been Spain's largest enterprises in 1911–13, were overtaken in size by financial intermediaries. At the 1927–9 benchmark, Banco de España and Banco de Bilbao were by far the two largest firms in the country.

Mining, however, which had been incredibly grand in Spain during the fifty years that preceded the First World War, started its irreversible decline during the 1920s. Although three of the largest ten companies in Spain in the early 1910s belonged to the mining industry, there was not a single mining company in the top ten in the 1927–9 benchmark. The decline of the mining industry was counterbalanced by the inclusion of 'new' industries in the top ten, such as utilities, with Barcelona Traction, Light and Power Company Ltd and Compañía Hispano Americana de Electricidad (CHADE), and transport and communication, with Compañía Trasatlántica and Telefónica Nacional de España (CTNE).[11]

At the bottom of the top ten were manufacturing companies such as the shipbuilding firm Sociedad Española de Contrucción Naval and the tobacco corporation Compañía Arrendataria de Tabacos (Tabacalera), which had by this time overtaken Azucarera as the largest enterprise in the food, drink, and tobacco products industry.

The Large Sample reflects the continuities that characterized traditional industries during these years: Compañía Anónima de Hilaturas de Fabras y Coats remained the largest corporation in the textile industry, while Azucarera continued to be the biggest company in the food sector. However, some innovative industries, such as the chemical industry, did not have new big entries, and Unión Española de Explosivos (UEE) confirmed itself as the largest company in this field. Although dropping out of the top ten, mining continued to have a considerable presence in Spanish big business; the sector's largest companies were very often in foreign hands, as in the cases of the Río Tinto Company and Royale Asturienne des Mines. At the same time, new large companies were started in new industries. Compañía Arrendataria del Monopolio de Petróleo, S.A. (CAMPSA) was formed to manage the monopoly in the oil industry and promptly became one of Spain's biggest firms.[12] The number of large corporations in the electricity industry also grew, as did the importance and size of electromechanical and mechanical engineering enterprises such as Sociedad Española de Construcciones Electromecánicas and Sociedad Española de Construcciones Metálicas. The Large Sample in 1927–9 also included for the first time a Spanish-owned company in commercial activities: the family firm Almacenes Rodríguez S.A. This was one of the first department stores in the country and overtook, in terms of assets, the multinationals' sales subsidiaries in Spain.[13]

After 1929, Spain underwent years of economic crisis. This was partly an outcome of the collapse of international trade and partly the result of a collapse

[11] Á. Calvo, *Historia de Telefónica: 1924–1975* (Ariel, 2011).

[12] G. Tortella, 'El Monopolio del Petróleo y CAMPSA, 1927–1947', *Hacienda Pública Española*, I (1991), 171–90.

[13] P. Toboso Sánchez, *Grandes Almacenes y Almacenes Populares en España: Una Visión Histórica*, Fundación SEPI Documento de Trabajo 2002/2.

in investment caused by domestic political uncertainties. In contrast to some European countries, there was no recovery from the mid 1930s: the Civil War began in 1936, and the progress made during the good years was lost. And once the Civil War ended, the Second World War began. The Spanish economy was unable to benefit from neutrality during the war years. The Franco regime was politically so closely tied with Nazi Germany that most Spanish exports were pre-committed to Germany to pay back the German assistance received during the Civil War. Moreover, because of this political connection, Spain did not partici-pate in the Marshall Plan, which helped to rebuild the post-war European economy, and instead the government continued an autarkic policy that lasted until 1959. During the Korean War, the United States reassessed the geopolitical value of Franco's Spain and decided to support it. The military agreement of 1953 marked the recognition of Spain's new role in the Cold War world. For Franco, it enabled his own political survival. It also was a turning point for Spain's economy: the regime's economic policy switched from autarky to import substitution industrialization (ISI).

The study's third benchmark period of 1954–6 comes after the Civil War (1936–9) and in the middle of the autarkic period (1939–59), and the company make-up of the samples enables us to identify several continuities. The Small Sample in 1954–6 confirmed the definitive decay of Spanish mining and the decline of the private railway corporations, which were nationalized in 1941 and gathered into the state-owned company Red Nacional de Ferrocarriles Españoles (RENFE).[14] Banks continued to be by far the largest companies in Spain—indeed, their distance from other firms in terms of assets increased remarkably between 1927–9 and 1954–6. The assets of the biggest non-financial corporation in the Small Sample, CTNE, are fifteen times smaller than those of Banco de España and five times smaller than those of the country's second largest bank, Banco Español de Crédito (Banesto). The same trend detected at the end of the 1920s is also shown in this benchmark. Industries such as oil, electricity, shipbuilding, and transport had fostered by the early 1950s some of the biggest corporations in the country: CAMPSA, Empresa Nacional Calvo Sotelo (ENCASO), Hidroeléctrica Española (Hidrola), Iberduero,[15] Empresa Nacional Bazán de Construcciones Navales Militares, and Empresa Nacional Elcano.[16]

The main discontinuity discerned in 1954–66 had little to do with the economic sectors of the large companies, but rather with their ownership structures. Several of the largest firms in Spain were now state-owned, and most of them belonged to the state holding Instituto Nacional de Industria (INI), which had been founded in 1941. All the companies whose names begin with the words 'Empresa Nacional' (often shortened to 'E.N.') were unmistakably public. Additionally, the state started to establish big enterprises in those industries that were considered to be

[14] M. Artola, *Los Ferrocarriles en España, 1844–1853* (Banco de España, 1973–5); F. Comín, P. Martín Aceña, M. Muñoz Rubio, and J. Vidal, eds., *150 Años de Historia de los Ferrocarriles Españoles* (Fundación de los Ferrocarriles Españoles, 1995).
[15] F. Antolín. 'Iniciativa privada y política pública en el desarrollo de la industria eléctrica en España: La hegemonia de la gestión privada, 1875–1950', *Revista de Historia Económica*, 2 (1999).
[16] De Rodrigo, 'La construcción naval, la marina mercante y el desarrollo económico Español', *Información Comercial Española*, 470 (1972), 51–7.

'strategic' for the country's development. The metallurgical company Empresa Nacional Siderúrgica (Ensidesa), which had been founded in 1950 and in 1954 was already ranked among the top ten corporations in Spain, represents one of the best-known examples of this policy.[17]

However, as the Large Sample shows, not everything was state-owned, particularly in other industries. The largest company in construction, Dragados y Construcciones, S.A., was privately owned, as were the biggest firms in mechanical engineering (La Maquínista Terrestre y Marítima) and wood and paper products (La Papelera Española). The largest corporations in the food, textiles, and chemicals industries were the same as twenty-five years earlier, and they were privately owned: Azucarera, Hilaturas Fabra y Coats, and UEE. Moreover, private companies, mainly bank-owned and/or bank-controlled,[18] also continued to exist in industries in which the state had created a 'national champion', as for instance in the steel industry, where the private enterprise Altos Hornos de Vizcaya (AHV) competed with the INI company Ensidesa.

Even though several firms preserved their previous names, foreign presence nearly disappeared during the first years of Franco's regime when, in line with an autarkic plan of development and with the aim of promoting national industrialization, a new law forbade foreign investors from holding majority shares of the capital of a corporation in Spain (Ley de Ordenación y Defensa de la Industria Nacional (24 Noviembre 1939), apartado a del artículo 5°).

Between 1954 and 1970, the Spanish economy underwent rapid economic growth. The high growth rates were interrupted in 1959–60 by the negative effects of the government's tough stabilization and liberalization plan. The short recession was the price paid for the switch from autarky and ISI policies to a more liberal and market-oriented economic environment. Overall, the change in economic policy was a major success. It freed the Spanish economy from autarkic elements and allowed it to fully enjoy the enormous economic expansion that prevailed in the Western world and, more specifically, in Western Europe. Thanks to a combination of devaluation and convertibility, plus an open attitude to foreign investment in manufacturing, the Spanish economy boomed. Income from tourism, long-term capital investments, and the remittances from Spanish emigrants paid for an increasingly huge trade deficit caused by imports of all sorts of goods, including capital goods. The Spanish economy invested heavily and managed to grow at a rate of between 7 and 10 per cent for slightly more than a decade. All of this economic growth occurred within a relatively stable system of big firms.

The growth of the Spanish economy is only partly reflected in the Small Sample comprising the top ten companies. Looking at the sectors to which the largest

---

[17] P. Martín Aceña and F. Comín, *El INI: Cincuenta Años de Industrialización en España* (Espasa Calpe, 1991).

[18] On the debate over the role played by the banks in the dictatorship and earlier, see F. De la Sierra, 'La situación monopolística de la banca privada en España', *Revista de Economía Política*, 3 (1951); J. Muñoz, *El Poder de la Banca en España* (ZYX, 1969); J. Pueyo Sánchez, *El Comportamiento de la Gran Banca en España (1921–1974)*, Estudio de Historia Económica 48, Banco de España (2006); J. Pueyo Sánchez, 'Relaciones intercmpresariales y consejeros comunes en la banca espanola del siglo XX', *Investigaciones de Historia Económica*, 6 (2006).

enterprises belonged, a strong continuity can be found between the 1954–6 and 1970–2 benchmarks. Financial intermediation, oil, transport and communication, transport equipment, and metallurgy continue to dominate the Small Sample, with companies such as Banco Central and Banesto (financial intermediation), CAMPSA (oil), CTNE and Iberia (transport and communication), Astilleros Españoles and SEAT (transport equipment), and Ensidesa (mature industries— steel production).

Only three relevant changes can be detected. The first is the nature of the companies involved in transport and transport equipment production. At the beginning of the 1950s, these activities mainly involved sea transport and ship-building companies; during the 1970s, air transport (Iberia) and automobile construction (SEAT or Sociedad Española de Automóviles de Turismo) almost completely replaced them.[19] Second, the disappearance of large electricity companies from the top ten should be noted, while, third, two new industries entered the top ten: chemicals and construction, which were also favoured by the economic boom and the urbanization taking place at the time. Looking at the names of the largest companies in these industries, it can easily be detected that we are not observing new firms but rather corporations that were already the largest in their industry and grew in size to reach the top ten, such as Unión Española de Explosivos Río Tinto in chemicals[20] and Dragados y Construcciones (Draconsa) in construction.[21]

In addition, the 1970s Large Sample shows a strong continuity with the early 1950s sample. Out of the twenty-three corporations considered, fourteen were already present in 1954–6 and nine in 1927–9. A relative stability can be detected in, for instance, the steel industry, with AHV, which remained the main private rival to Ensidesa; in financial intermediation, where Banco de Bilbao, Banco Hispano Américano, and Banesto were among the main banks for almost the entire century; in electricity, whose main companies, even though they fall outside the top ten were still big and 'old' (companies such as Hidroeléctrica Española and Iberduero); in textiles, whose leading firm continued to be Hilaturas Fabra y Coats throughout this whole period; and in chemicals and construction, as already mentioned.

However, it has to be stressed that during the Spanish economic miracle, new companies and new industries entered the Large Sample. In some cases, old established corporations were able to get the top of the rankings in their respective sectors, such as El Corte Inglés in department stores and CEPSA, which was the main private rival to CAMPSA, in the oil industry. In other cases, large corporations emerged in new industries that were having increasing success in a country

---

[19] On the crisis of shipbuilding, see L. Portillo, 'La construcción naval española en el contexto de la crisis mundial del sector', *Información Comercial Española*, 577 (1981), 111–35. On the growth of Iberia, see J. Vidal Olivares, *Las Alas de España: Iberia, Lineas Aéreas (1940–2005)* (Publicacions Universitat de Valencia, 2008); on SEAT, see P. González de La Fe, *Seat: Fundación, Desarrollo y Privatización de una Empresa Automovilística en España*, Fundación Empresa Pública Documento de Trabajo 2001/01.

[20] R. Tamames, *Estructura Económica de España* (Alianza, 1990); N. Puig, *Bayer, CEPSA, Repsol, Puig, Schering y La Seda: Constructiores de la Química Española* (LID, 2003).

[21] E. Torres Villanueva, Origen, *Crecimiento e Internacionalización de las Grandes Empresas Españolas de la Construcción (1900–2008)* (Universidad de los Andes, 2011).

that was becoming more and more modern and rich and thus offered firms new opportunities for development. This was true in, for instance, the case of Victor Sagi Publicidad, which was established in the media advertising industry, and that of the hotel company Meliá, which grew quite quickly thanks to the increasing levels of tourism in the country.

The crisis of the 1970s and Spanish economic integration into the European Economic Community, which took place in 1986 after the demise of the Francoist dictatorship, radically transformed the Spanish economy and the dynamics of large corporations.[22]

However, quite surprisingly, a first glance at the top ten corporations in Spain in 1998–2000 reveals that most of the largest firms in 2000 were already in the group in 1972, even though they had undergone some significant transformations in the meantime. Financial intermediation remains at the top of the sample, which is led by two major banks, each of which is the result of a process of mergers and restructuring: Banco Santander Central Hispano (BSCH) and Banco de Bilbao Vizcaya Argentaria (BBVA).[23] Since the 1954–6 sample, the telecommunications company Telefónica has consistently been the largest non-financial company by size after the banks, and its recent history mirrors quite well two general changes that were common to several of the largest companies during the last quarter of the twentieth century. The first of these is privatization; the Spanish state divested its ownership of Telefónica in 1997.[24] The second trend that Telefónica shares with other firms is increasing international activity (or globalization), which is reflected by the high position in the rankings of its subsidiary Telefónica International España, which operates in Europe, Asia, and the Americas.

Other large corporations in current Spanish big business are not new at all, but have changed their names as a result of restructuring and privatization. Repsol-YPF, for instance, is now the Spanish national champion in the oil industry and is a direct heir of the merger between CAMPSA and the state-owned firms in the oil industry and that company's subsequent privatization. Altadis was the result of the restructuring and mergers that characterized Tabacalera in the tobacco industry. Empresa Nacional de Electricidad (Endesa), the state-owned champion in the electricity industry, still bore that name in 2000, but it too had undergone privatization.

---

[22] V. Binda, (2005). 'Entre el estado y las multinacionales: La empresa industrial española en los años de integración a la CEE', *Revista de Historia Industrial*, 28 (2005), 117–54; V. Binda and M. Iversen, 'Towards a "Managerial Revolution" in European business? The transformation of Danish and Spanish big business 1973–2003', *Business History*, 49, 4 (2007), 506–30; V. Binda and A. Colli, 'Changing big business in Italy and Spain, 1973–2003: Strategic responses to a new context', *Business History*, 53, 1 (2011), 14–39.

[23] J.L. García Ruiz, ed., *Revista de la Historia de la Economía y de la Empresa: Instituciones Financieras en España* (BBVA, 2007); C. García Ramos, *Una Visión Panorámica de las Entidades de Crédito en España en la Última Década*, Fundación de las Cajas de Ahorros Documento de Trabajo 283 (2006); M.F. Guillén and A. Tschoegl, *Building a Global Bank: The Transformation of Banco Santander* (Princeton University Press, 2008); M.F. Guillén, *The Rise of Spanish Multinationals* (Cambridge University Press, 2005); M.F. Guillén and E. García-Canal, *The New Multinationals: Spanish Firms in a Global Context* (Cambridge University Press, 2010).

[24] Á. Cuervo García, *La Privatización de la Empresa Pública* (Encuentro, 1997); L. Gámir Casares, *Las Privatizaciones en España* (Pirámide, 1999); J. Clifton, F. Comín, and D. Díaz Fuentes, *Privatization in the European Union: Public Enterprises and Integration* (Kluwer, 2003).

The almost complete disappearance of the state from the ownership of the largest companies in Spain in 2000 has been counterbalanced by the increasing role of foreign-owned corporations in the Small Sample. CEPSA had passed to French hands; French-owned company Renault was in the Small Sample[25] and Centros Comerciales Carrefour in the Large Sample.[26] However, it has to be stressed that Renault's sales had overtaken those of the previously Spanish-owned champion SEAT, which had been sold to Volkswagen in the 1980s, while the Spanish national champion in commercial activities, El Corte Inglés, was able to maintain its leadership position and even to grow further during this period.[27]

The broader panorama provided by the Large Sample allows us to claim that Spanish corporations exhibited a greater dynamism in the last quarter of the twentieth century than in previous periods, and that several new entries were able to grow and gain prominent positions. Some of the new entries included in the Large Sample were, as in the Small Sample, the result of mergers and restructuring that occurred in mature industries. For instance, the steel producer Aceralia emerged in 1997 out of a corporate restructuring that included a merger between the state-owned company Ensidesa and the private corporation AHV.[28] In other cases, mergers were carried out in order to create national champions that could compete in the new European and world context, such as Iberdrola and Gas Natural SDG in the utilities sector.[29] The Large Sample in 2000 acquired new members by several different processes: 'old' companies that had successfully grown (Grupo Iberostar in tourism and Bergé y Compañía in business services to business), relatively young Spanish companies that replaced old ones (Inditex in textiles[30] and Timón in media), or the takeover of Spanish corporations by subsidiaries of foreign multinationals (the national champion UEE, which had been Spain's leading company in chemicals since 1911–13, lost its leadership to the American giant Dow Chemicals).

COMPANY PERFORMANCE ACCORDING TO RETURN ON EQUITY

In this section, comparative in scope and pan-European in ambition, we are going to analyse how the return on equity (ROE) of Spanish companies evolved.

---

[25] E.M. Sánchez Sánchez, 'La implantación industrial de Renault en España: Los origines de FASA–Renault, 1950–1970', *Revista de Historia Económica*, 1 (2004), 147–75; T. Fernández de Sevilla, *Responses to a Crisis: FASA–Renault in Spain during the 1970s*, Documents de Treball de la Facultat d'Economia i Empresa, Universitat de Barcelona, E11/261 (2011).

[26] R. Castro Balaguer, *Génesis y Transformación de un Modelo de Inversión Internacional: El Capital Francés en la España del Siglo XX*, Doctoral thesis, Universidad Complutense, Madrid (2011).

[27] J. Cuartas, *Biografía de El Corte Inglés* (Dictext, 1992); P. Toboso Sánchez, *Pepín Fernández 1891–1982: Galerias Preciados: El Pionero De Los Grandes Almacenes* (LID, 2000).

[28] A. Carreras, X. Tafunell, and E. Torres, 'The rise and decline of Spanish state-owned firms', in P.A. Toninelli, ed., *The Rise and Fall of State-Owned Enterprise in the Western World* (Cambridge University Press, 2000), pp. 220–2.

[29] M.F. Guillén, *The Rise of Spanish Multinationals* (Cambridge University Press, 2005).

[30] E. Badía, *ZARA . . . y sus Hermanas* (LID, 2008).

Table 9.1. ROE for Spanish companies in the Small and Large Samples (in %)

Period	ROE (Small Sample)		ROE (Large Sample)	
	Mean	Median	Mean	Median
1911–13	15.20	11.95	10.99	8.95
1927–9	11.75	9.70	12.43	9.45
1954–6	23.81	7.56	18.96	10.37
1970–2	9.55	10.34	10.60	10.46
1998–2000	18.95	14.57	17.01	14.34

Table 9.1 shows the mean and median values of ROE in our two samples, which are reported for each three-year benchmark. Median ROE remained quite stable over time, oscillating between 8.95 and 14.34 per cent in the Large Sample and between 7.56 per cent and 14.57 per cent in the Small Sample. The mean values, however, oscillated more, and in both samples achieved particularly high values during the 1954–66 benchmark period.

During the first benchmark, the median ROE for the Large Sample is 8.95 per cent, not very different from the mean value of 10.99 per cent. In the Small Sample (the top ten), however, the difference between the median (11.95 per cent) and the mean (15.20 per cent) is greater, indicating that there were some relevant outliers whose performances were higher than those of the others, which represented the very top level of Spanish big business. These were the mining companies, which were subsidiaries of foreign-owned multinationals. To be precise, they were 'free-standing companies', such as Río Tinto, Tharsis, and Peñarroya. The attractive profitability expected from mining and metallurgical companies made sense in a less-developed economy that provided high returns in exchange for higher risks. The Spanish-owned companies were less profitable, but some of them fared pretty well. Banco de España, for example, came in third place. The worst performers were mostly Spanish. However, the two largest railway companies (Caminos and MZA), which were among the worst performers, also had a large share of foreign—mainly French—capital. Looking at the Large Sample according to sector, all the railway companies performed well below average, as did most of the banks. Only the Banco de España performed well. Compared with the performance of a larger group of Spanish firms previously studied by Xavier Tafunell, our sample displays much higher performance. It is fair to say that these data are much more in line with those from other countries such as the UK, Germany, and Sweden. The decision to study big firms has entailed the selection of very highly profitable firms, at this date concentrated in mining and metallurgy. The closest correspondence to these values is with those in the German study, which also has a strong mining and metallurgical bias in these early years.

In the 1927–9 benchmark, the ROE is almost identical to that of the previous period. Looking at the Large Sample, only a slight increase can be noted, both in the median (9.45 per cent) and in the mean (12.43 per cent). However, in the Small Sample, there is a slight decrease in both median and mean ROE: 9.70 and 11.75 per cent, respectively. Three companies in particular out-performed all the others. Banco de España achieved an ROE of 38.2 per cent while also being the largest firm in terms of market value. Fomento de Obras y Construcciones, a much smaller company, was the leading performer in the 'public works' area; UEE, also among the smallest in our sample, held assets more than 2.5 times greater than those of the construction company. The banks' returns were much better during this period than before the First World War, and the four selected were among the best performers in terms of ROE. Electricity firms also did quite well, but less so than the banks. Companies with close ties to the public administration, such as Tabacalera, CAMPSA, and CTNE, performed quite modestly, undoubtedly because they were legal monopolies whose markets were restrained by state regulations.

The difference between the ROE of our sample firms and the ROE of the larger Spanish sample studied by Xavier Tafunell[31] is smaller for the late 1920s than for 1913. This confirms that the 'bonanza' was widespread. However, the Spanish ROE data are more optimistic than those obtained from other European countries: not by very much, around two or three percentage points more. Again, the potential gains made from previous backwardness could explain a lot.

Whether based on the preference for autarky or on the policy of import substitution industrialization, the common purpose of economic policy during the first decades of Franco's dictatorship was to minimize the presence of foreign capital and to maximize the number of state-owned firms. Looking at company size by assets of the samples in 1954–6, this is clearly visible. However, when looking at the profitability ranking, the most salient firms disappear. The mean ROEs in 1954–6, namely 23.81 and 18.96 per cent for the Small and Large Samples, respectively, are significantly higher than the mean ROEs in 1927–9 (11.75 and 12.43 per cent, respectively). The median ROEs in 1954–6, however, show a very different picture, being lower than the value in the previous benchmark for the Small Sample (7.56 versus 9.70 per cent) and higher for the Large Sample (10.37 versus 9.45 per cent).

In order to understand these facts, it is first of all necessary to explain that the performance of the Banco de España, which significantly over-performed all other corporations in the Small Sample, skewed the sample's mean ROE and created an unrealistic value. Banco de España's astonishing ROE (153.77 per cent) was the result of an artificially reduced equity denominator. The Spanish government refused to sanction an increase either in share capital or in retained profits. Because the bank was still in private hands, the government wanted to restrain its size; at the same time, because it played a central role in state monetary policy, Franco's government could not permit it to accumulate retained profits.

The remaining firms in the Small Sample were mostly privately owned, but there were four state-owned companies in the bottom half of the ranking: Empresa Nacional Bazán, Empresa Nacional Elcano, Ensidesa, and Empresa Nacional Calvo Sotelo. The top positions in terms of profitability were taken by the big private commercial banks, which experienced their best performances during the 1950s. The combination of a strongly regulated banking market, an anti-foreign-capital stance, a very closed economic policy, and a very favourable (for the banks) nationalization of the Spanish railways produced a unique

---

[31] X. Tafunell, 'La rentabilidad financiera de la empresa española, 1880–1981: Una estimación en perspectiva sectorial', *Revista de Historia Industrial*, 18 (2000), 69–112.

opportunity for Spanish-owned private banks. They entered as shareholders into many manufacturing firms and harvested high rates of profit during the autarkic and import substitution years. Indeed, the data on ROEs show that performance during this period became higher and more homogeneous. Poor returns for private firms were quite rare. Below the banks came a wide array of industries from the traditional mining sector to chemistry (mining oriented: UEE), paper-making, public works, tobacco, electricity, shipbuilding, engineering, steelmaking, telephony, textiles, and sugar. No clear specialization pattern emerges other than the dominance of the banking sector. For banking, these were the years of maximum economic leverage. The data for 1954–6 provide the first instance of small-sample ROEs falling below those from the larger sample, which suggests that medium-sized firms were more profitable than bigger ones. Moreover, although the differences between countries' ROEs were often great, the Spanish case for the first time is quite in line with another European case, namely Sweden.

At the beginning of the 1970s, the median and mean ROE values are quite similar to those from 1927–9 and, except for the skewed mean values, also to those from 1954–6. If the Banco de España Banco, which was nationalized in 1962, is excluded, the mean ROE of the Large Sample (10.60 per cent) surpasses the mean return for the mid 1950s, but it is below those of the pre-war benchmarks. However, the median ROE of the Large Sample (10.46 per cent) is better than in all the previous benchmarks, although the range of profits is smaller.

Once again the private commercial banks outperformed most of the other firms. The only exceptions were an electrical engineering company (Standard Eléctrica), an unlisted commercial distribution firm (El Corte Inglés), an oil refining and distribution monopoly (CAMPSA), a textile enterprise (Hilaturas Fabra y Coats), and a construction and public works firm (Dragados y Construcciones). All other companies yielded an average or below-average ROE. Among them were the electricity giants (Hidroeléctrica Española and Iberduero), the largest firm by assets and market value (CTNE), state-owned firms (such as Ensidesa), monopolies (including Tabacalera), newly created car manufacturers (such as SEAT), and new firms in the financing of car acquisitions (Finanzauto y Servicios).

Spanish firms continued to have higher ROEs than corporations in the rest of Europe. Even the companies in Tafunell's larger sample[32] seem to have been more profitable than those in the UK, Germany, Italy, and Sweden. This should not surprise us, because Spain was enjoying high growth rates within quite a protected market and there was a lot of catching-up going on. Just as in 1913, the inflow of foreign capital was a clear signal that high profits were expected from investments in Spain.

By the end of the twentieth century, a significant increase in the ROE of many corporations is detectable in both the mean and median values of the Small and Large Samples. Average ROE in the Large Sample jumped to 17.01 per cent (from 10.60 per cent in 1970–2), while the median ROE was significantly lower (14.34 per cent), although this was still a large increase over the 1970s median of 10.46

---

[32] X. Tafunell, *Los Beneficios Empresariales en España (1880–1981): Elaboración de una Serie Anual,* Documento de Trabajo 9601, Fundación Empresa Pública, Programa de Historia Económica (1996); X. Tafunell, 'Empresa y Bolsa', in A. Carreras and X. Tafunell, eds., *Estadísticas Históricas de España* (Fundación BBVA, 2005).

per cent. The development of returns in the Small Sample was quite similar; the ROE's mean (18.95 per cent) was much larger than its median value (14.57 per cent), but both were greater than in 1970–2.

In contrast to conditions earlier in the century, the upper parts of the distribution are quite varied. The sectoral allegiances of the out-performing companies are not straightforward. Companies are financial and non-financial, services and manufacturing, old and new. What is clear is that car manufacturing (Renault España) is no longer a profit leader—and neither is steelmaking (Aceralia Corporación Siderúrgica). Also, commercial companies such as Centros Comerciales Carrefour and, to a lesser extent, El Corte Inglés generated a lower profitability than the other firms of the Large Sample. In the Small Sample, the leading performers by a large margin were the telecommunications company Telefónica International España and the two national bank giants Banco Santander Central Hispano (BSCH) and Banco de Bilbao Vizcaya Argentaria (BBVA).

The comparative perspective suggests a number of issues. First, companies in the Small Sample (the top ten) were generally more profitable than those in the Large Sample. Second, the average ROEs of the Spanish Small Sample were on a level with those of the British and Swedish Small Samples—both of which had very high values. All three countries performed much better than Germany, and Germany much better than Italy.

COMPANY PERFORMANCE ACCORDING TO HOLDING RETURN

Table 9.2 shows the mean and median values of the holding return (HR) for Spanish companies. As for the ROE, the mean and median values are reported for each three-year benchmark period.

In contrast to ROE's relative stability, the HR values varied greatly over time. The highest values were achieved in 1954–6, while the lowest levels occurred at the beginning of the century for the Large Sample and at the end of the century for the Small Sample.

At the beginning of the twentieth century, the HRs of the corporations in the Large Sample had a median value of 0.85 per cent, not very different from the mean of 1.04 per cent, while in the Small Sample the difference between the median and mean values was higher. The variation in HR was enormous: from −23.10 to

Table 9.2. HR for Spanish companies in the Small and Large Samples (in %)

Period	HR (Small Sample)		HR (Large Sample)	
	Mean	Median	Mean	Median
1911–13	5.05	2.5	1.04	0.85
1927–9	13.01	11.63	17.39	16.72
1954–6	26.43	27.16	27.16	28.47
1970–2	2.91	0.76	4.12	2.37
1998–2000	−3.22	−2.85	3.75	2.25

+23.30 per cent in the Large Sample and from −4.60 to +23.30 per cent in the Small Sample. However, one must remember that we do not have HR data for many of the companies in the samples. There are two reasons for this lack of data. First, a number of the most profitable companies were foreign-owned and their shares were quoted only on their home stock market: this was the case for example for Peñarroya and Tharsis. Second, many others were not publicly listed limited companies, including some that were formally incorporated, such as Catalana de Gas y Electricidad and Fomento de Obras y Construcciones.

Compared with ROE values in 1911–13, the average HR for Spanish companies at the time was quite modest. The data correspond to only one year, but the available Barcelona and Madrid stock exchange indices paint an even more pessimistic picture. The weighted Madrid stock exchange index declined by 6.6 per cent, the unweighted by 0.3 per cent, and the Barcelona unweighted by 3.1 per cent.[33] The crisis of Banco Hispano Americano has been well studied, as have the high expectations of Duro-Felguera, to name only the two most extreme cases.[34]

The 1927–9 values for HR seem to show a radically changed economic environment. The average HR for the Large Sample reached 17.39 per cent, which is very high; and the HR for the Small Sample (13.01 per cent) was also much higher that it had been in 1911–13 (5.05 per cent) The only exception to the pattern of high positive HRs was CAMPSA, which was only created in 1927. The Banco de España yielded a low HR at the time, but this is easy to explain. In 1921, a new banking law was passed that assigned the role of central banker to the Banco de España yet prevented it from being involved in commercial credit. Thus, for a number of years, Banco de España experienced both over-profitability and diminished expectations. With these two exceptions, it is also worth remembering that the late 1920s was a very expansive and euphoric period in Spain—as in many other countries. Primo de Rivera's dictatorship was a pro-business regime, and profits and investments boomed. But the regime collapsed in January 1930. After this point, the combination of domestic political uncertainty and international economic crises radically altered the country's business climate.

In the early 1950s, in the middle of the autarkic period, HRs were on average extremely high: 27.16 and 26.43 per cent for the Large and Small Samples, respectively. The median values were not very different: 28.47 and 27.16 per cent, respectively. HRs were also quite homogeneous, with no recorded cases of negative returns. That there should be such high returns is no surprise. The good news of the 1953 US–Spain agreement, combined with the new geopolitical environment that brought Franco's Spain into the United Nations (1955), generated a strong confidence in the continuation of Franco's regime. Profit expectations boomed, and investments followed immediately. The Spanish stock exchange enjoyed some of its best years.

Compared with the 1927–9 and 1954–6 benchmarks, HRs in the early 1970s were quite disappointing. With a median and mean HR of 2.37 and 4.12 per cent, respectively, for the Large Sample and of 0.76 and 2.91 per cent for the Small

[33] X. Tafunell, 'Empresa y bolsa', in A. Carreras and X. Tafunell, eds., *Estadísticas Historicas de España* (Fundación BBVA, 2005).

[34] A. Carreras, and X. Tafunell, *Historia Económica de la España Contemporánea* (Crítica, 2003).

Sample, investors' prospects fell to levels not seen since before the First World War. Moreover, the variation was considerable, ranging from 29.9 per cent for Tabacalera to −11.1 per cent for CEPSA. These low HR performances suggest strongly that the market was increasingly worried about companies' future profitability. The economy was overheated, and a sudden adjustment seemed likely.

At the end of the twentieth century, economic prospects worsened further. HRs for the top ten corporations reached their lowest level of the century, with a median of −2.85 per cent and a mean of −3.22 per cent. HRs for the Large Sample did not sink so low, but they were still quite disappointing: a median value of 2.25 per cent and a mean value of 3.75 per cent, the second lowest ever. HRs reflect the stock market crash of early 2000.

CONCLUSIONS

According to the data presently available, the Spanish big business experience in the twentieth century seems to have been one of high profitability. This does not mean more than that the perceived risk was above average and that the returns were expected to be higher than normal. A simple comparison of the long-term interest rates in Spain with those in other Western European countries suggests that for most of the century there was a difference of two or three percentage points, always against Spain. The difference disappeared only with the arrival of the euro in 2002.

Spanish experience underlines the consistency of its profitability data with the flow of foreign capital. As Spain was a net importer of foreign capital for most of the century, it comes as no surprise to see that returns were higher in Spain than elsewhere. Precisely because of this fact, the recent combination of high returns, low long-term interest rates, and capital exports that occurred around 1998–2000 is intriguing and deserves further examination from a comparative, long-term perspective.

ACKNOWLEDGEMENT

We would like to express our thanks to Anna Aubanell for helpful comments on earlier drafts of this chapter.

10

Growth and Profits in Swedish and Finnish Big Business in the Twentieth Century

Riitta Hjerppe and Mats Larsson

INTRODUCTION

In this chapter, we compare the performance of big business in Sweden and Finland during the twentieth century based on the ten largest companies in each country (the top ten) and on the largest companies in specific industries. How does the development of big business compare with the structure of the national economy? Does it reflect the changing structure of the economy, or are they very different? What has been the business performance, return on equity (ROE) and holding return (HR) of these companies? How do these indicators develop over time? Do the chosen measures of business performance fit such comparative studies?

We start with the hypothesis that the big firms chosen do reflect the structures of the two countries' economies. Accordingly, the Swedish companies should be more modern and many-sided at an earlier time than their Finnish counterparts. Other expected results are that the top companies have, in general, generated relatively good profits that have enabled both the companies and their countries to achieve rapid economic development over the course of the twentieth century.

First, we sketch the economic growth and structure of Sweden and Finland in the twentieth century. We then analyse the development of the overall changes in ROE and HR as well as the development of the ten largest companies in each country. Finally, we compare the profitability of the various industries as well as the ROE and HR of the companies overall. We end with a brief discussion of similarities and differences between the two countries.

THE ECONOMIES OF SWEDEN AND FINLAND IN THE TWENTIETH CENTURY

Sweden and Finland have historically been closely related. The political unification of the two countries ended in 1809, but even when Finland was a part of the Russian Empire between 1809 and 1917 and then an independent country from

1917, economic contacts between Finland and Sweden continued, although they did gradually decline. After the Second World War, their political and economic contacts increased considerably as they and their neighbouring states of Denmark, Norway, and Iceland established a Nordic network of cooperation. At first, the development of closer regional political and economic relations arose out of the strong political ties between the social democratic parties that for longer periods held governmental power in these countries and was based on the countries' acceptance of a common Nordic model for the welfare state. Economic cooperation beyond the Nordic network increased in 1961 when Sweden and Finland, as well as Denmark, Norway, and Iceland, joined the European Free Trade Area (EFTA). The role of the Nordic network for the countries' economic cooperation was weakened somewhat in 1973 when Denmark acceded to the European Community (EC) and declined even further when Sweden and Finland joined the European Union (EU) in 1995. The common EU membership has intensified relations between Sweden and Finland, especially in business. Capital flows between the two countries have increased considerably since 1995. These have, for example, resulted in big mergers between Finnish and Swedish companies, such as the bank Nordea, the wood and paper company Stora Enso, and the Swedish–Finnish telecommunication company TeliaSonera.

Sweden and Finland today are modern economies with high standards of living. In both countries, the economies have grown exceptionally rapidly over the course of the twentieth century. In Sweden, the annual growth rate of gross domestic product (GDP) was 2.6 per cent and in per capita terms 2.1 per cent; in Finland, these rates were 3.2 and 2.5 per cent. These are very high figures internationally. In the early twentieth century, the Swedish economy expanded more rapidly than the Finnish economy, and the difference between the two countries' GDP per capita was some 30–40 per cent. In the 1970s, Finland's economy started to converge clearly on the Swedish level, and by the end of the 1990s, the gap was almost closed.[1] The Swedish and Finnish economic structures have followed the well-known patterns of developed countries over the twentieth century: the shares of agriculture and forestry in the workforce and GDP declined, while those of manufacturing and services grew. Sweden achieved a mature industrial and service economy clearly earlier than Finland.

The structures of the manufacturing industry in the two countries have shared many similarities as well as having differences. Both countries have and have had important forest-based industries, especially timber sawmills and paper production. In the early twentieth century, Finland was more dependent on sawmilling than its Nordic neighbour, and throughout the twentieth century, it has had a relatively stronger paper industry. Sweden has had more mining and metal industry, including electrical, electronic, and transport machinery production. In 2000, both economies had very similar manufacturing industries. Since 1950, the level of workforce concentration in Swedish and Finnish manufacturing industry has increased steadily. In Sweden in 1970, the ten largest companies—excluding

[1] R. Hjerppe, *The Finnish Economy 1860–1985: Growth and Structural Change*, Studies in Finland's Economic Growth XIII (Helsinki: Bank of Finland Publications, 1989); Statistics Finland Historical National Accounts Database; O. Krantz and L. Schön, *Swedish Historical National Accounts 1800–2000*, Lund Studies in Economic History 41 (Stockholm: Almqvist & Wiksell, 2007).

commercial activities and insurance companies—accounted for 25 per cent of the total Swedish employment in the manufacturing and building industries. By 2000, this share had increased to 35 per cent. In Finland, the process of concentration was even stronger. In the early 1970s, the ten largest Finnish companies—excluding commercial activities—employed about 15 per cent of the total manufacturing and building workforce. Three decades later, Finland's economy was more concentrated than Sweden's. Its large manufacturing and building companies employed about 40 per cent of the sector's workforce.

THE DEVELOPMENT OF PERFORMANCE INDICATORS IN FINLAND AND SWEDEN

The Swedish companies had a fairly stable average ROE of between 8 and 9 per cent at the first two benchmarks in the early decades of the twentieth century (see Table 10.1). However, after the Second World War, their profitability became more volatile. The high average ROE in the 1950s could perhaps be explained by the general upturn of the Swedish economy during the rebuilding of the European economy after the war. But if we scrutinize the figures more closely, we find that this high value also is explained by the extremely high ROE—141 per cent—for one company, the mining company Loussavaara-Kiirunavaara (LKAB). This high value can be explained by the ownership construction—divided between the state and a private company—which as a consequence resulted in the unwillingness of both owners to increase the firm's equity. In the middle of the 1950s, the state also used its long-standing well-known option to take over the privately owned shares in LKAB. The lower median rate of ROE in 1954–6 also confirms that the LKAB value had skewed the average. After this specific case is excluded, the ROE for the Swedish companies exhibits a remarkable stability—about 8 per cent—during the first four benchmark periods. However, with the increased market liberalization and international competition in the 1990s, both average and median ROE rose markedly by 2000. An important driving force behind this growth was also the boom in the Swedish economy, especially for IT companies and other high-tech firms, of which there were several in the sample.

Table 10.1. ROE for largest Swedish and Finnish companies by industry, 1911–2000 (in %)

	1911–13	1927–9	1954–6	1970–2	1998–2000
Average					
Finland	10.5[a]	7.34	8.88	5.18	16.01
Sweden	8.31	8.98	16.12	8.08	18.25
Median					
Finland	10.15[a]	7.58	8.96	6.15	12.94
Sweden	8.28	8.38	7.35	7.78	13.37

[a] Only one observation

Source: Database of large Finnish and Swedish companies

Table 10.2. HR for the largest Swedish and Finnish companies by industry, 1911–2000 (in %)

	1911–13	1927–9	1954–6	1970–2	1998–2000
Average					
Finland	—	−2.53	19.53	29.65	38.31
Sweden	4.81	17.03	8.10	5.47	28.18
Median					
Finland	—	−2.53	19.53	29.65	38.31
Sweden	4.72	16.03	6.31	5.65	20.22

Source: Database of large Finnish and Swedish companies

The returns generated by the Finnish firms mainly followed the same trend. The most remarkable exception occurred during the 1970s, when the ROE in Finland was clearly lower than in Sweden. In both countries, the ROEs also followed the European pattern rather closely throughout the century.

The Swedish companies' HRs developed along a similar line to that of the ROEs (see Table 10.2). The benchmark periods of the 1910s, 1950s, and 1970s all show values for HR of 5–8 per cent. However, the values in the 1920s and at the end of the twentieth century were much higher, reflecting periods of economic booms and rising share prices.

By contrast, average HRs in Finland were negative in the 1920s, perhaps reflecting the grim outlook of wood and paper sales on the international market. In the 1950s and the 1970s, the Finnish HRs were high compared with Swedish and European averages. These results could have been caused by the special business tax legislation in Finland and Sweden. Limited liability companies became used to a practice of transferring part of their annual earnings to the company share capital and distributing free or discounted shares to shareholders or owners instead of dividends. In both countries, such free shares were tax-free, while dividends were considered an addition to shareholders' personal incomes and taxed progressively.[2] Around 2000, the world-wide dot.com boom generated rising share prices—and hence high HRs—also in Finland and Sweden.

THE TOP TEN COMPANIES IN FINLAND

Finland is known for its forest resources and its wood and paper industry. This is also seen in the structure of the ten largest companies in the sample. Six to seven of the large companies were in forest industry (wood and paper products) during the first half of the twentieth century (see Table 10.3) when 60–80 per cent of the country's exports were also forest industry products. The dominance of forest industry decreased from the 1950s, but still in the 1970s four of the top ten

    [2] O. Ikkala, E. Andersson, and E. Nuorvala, *Uusi Elinkeinoverolainsäädäntö* [*New Business Legislation*], Suomalaisen lakimiesyhdistyksen julkaisuja B-sarja, No. 147 (Helsinki: Suomen lakimiesliiton kustannus Oy, 1981).

Table 10.3. The top ten in Finland, including financial intermediaries, 1913–2000

Industry	Company name	1913	1927	1954	1972	2000
Financial intermediation	Föreningsbanken i Finland/Ab Nordiska Föreningsbanken	1	1	1	2	
Financial intermediation	Kansallis-Osake-Pankki	2	2	2	1	
Wood and paper	Oy W. Gutzeit & Co./Stora Enso	3	3	4	4	4
Wood and paper	Kymin Oy–Kymmene Ab	4	4	10	10	
Textiles and leather goods	Finlayson & Co. Oy	5				
Textiles and leather goods	Tammerfors Linne- och Järn-Industri/Oy Tampella Ab	6	9	9		
Wood and paper	Oy H. Saastamoinen Ltd	7				
Wood and paper	Trävaruaktiebolaget Kemi/Ab Kemi Oy	8	7			
Wood and paper	A. Ahlström	9	6		8	
Wood and paper	Karhula Oy	10				
Wood and paper	W. Rosenlew & Co. Ab		5			
Food, drink, and tobacco	Suomen Sokeri Oy/Finnish Sugar		8			
Wood and paper	Kajaanin Puutavara Oy/Kajana Timber		10			
Utilities, electricity and gas	Imatran Voima Oy/Imatra Energy			3		
Wood and paper	Yhtyneet Paperitehtaat OY/United Paper Mills			5		
Transport equipment	Wärtsilä-Koncernen Ab			6	7	
Mechanical engineering	Valmet OY			7	9	
Wood and paper	Rauma-Repola Oy			8	5	
Commercial activities	Kesko Oy				3	8
Oil and rubber; electrical engineering	Oy Nokia Ab				6	3
Financial intermediation	Sampo-Leonia Oy					1
Financial intermediation	Merita Oy					2
Utilities, electricity and gas	Fortum OY					5
Mature industries	UPM-Kymmene Ltd					6
Mature industries	Metsäliitto Oy/Forest Union					7
Mechanical engineering	Metso Oy					9
Basic metal industry	Outokumpu Oy					10

Notes: Ranking based on assets (1913, 1927, and 1954) and turnover (1972 and 2000). Financial intermediation: assets in 1972 and 2000.

Source: Database of large Finnish companies

companies were paper and sawmill companies, in 1998–2000 three. Moreover, they were among the largest in the world.

The other top ten companies in the early twentieth century were two large banks, a few consumer goods companies in textiles (Finlayson & Co.) or textiles with metal and paper industry on the side (Tammerfors Linne- och Järn-Industri Ab), and a sugar production company (Suomen Sokeri Oy/Finnish Sugar).

In the 1950s, the consumer goods companies were replaced by firms in electricity production and distribution (Imatran Voima Oy/Imatra Energy), mechanical engineering, production of transport equipment, for example ships (Wärtsilä-Koncernen Ab and Valmet Oy). In these years, the expanding mechanical engineering and shipbuilding firms at first sold their products to the Soviet Union and gradually also to other countries.

In the 1970s, the top ten was more diversified as large wood and paper companies all had important side activities either in mechanical engineering or in transport, after diversifying their business activities. Besides mechanical engineering and shipbuilding came manufacturers of such products as tires, cables, and paper (Nokia Oy), as well as retailing. Kesko Oy, a retailing chain, started to replace privately owned small grocery stores in food retailing and wholesaling. Kesko was also the first service industry company among the manufacturing companies.

The 1998–2000, the top ten looks very different from earlier benchmarks. Only two of the companies had the same name as in the 1970s, Kesko and Nokia, but Nokia had completely changed its line of production to mobile phones and telecommunications infrastructure. The others were results of profound reorganization of the large companies through mergers, acquisitions, and sales. Typical of the companies was that they all had international production and/or important exports and that they all had relatively long histories, dating from at least the late 1940s and 1950s, and, in many cases, from the late nineteenth century.

All the big forest industry companies of 1913 still existed in 2000 as parts of present-day Stora Enso, UPM-Kymmene, or Metsäliitto/Forest Union because of mergers and acquisitions and sales of companies. On the one hand, a present-day paper factory challenges the definition of mature industries in the case of the Finnish and Swedish forest companies, which hold leading positions in world paper manufacturing. During the early years of the twenty-first century, the Finnish–Swedish Stora Enso was fourth, the Swedish SCA fifth, and the Finnish UPM-Kymmene and Metsäliitto/Forest Union sixth and seventh on the list of the largest paper companies in the world. The production of special papers is accomplished by huge, automatically controlled machinery. The biggest machines produce 120 kilometres of paper per hour, and the paper is 12 metres wide. On the other hand, if a large number of mature industries is a sign of backwardness, then Finnish industry is in serious trouble, with five of the country's ten largest companies in 1998–2000 being in mature industries—there were only two in Sweden.[3]

---

[3] PricewaterhouseCoopers, *Global Forest and Paper Industry Survey*, 2005 Edition, Survey of 2004 Results, p. 12.

Finland's two largest companies at every benchmark were financial intermediaries. Although the two big banks of 1911–13 retained their position until the 1990s, the sector nevertheless underwent some dramatic changes. Commercial banks financing industry and commerce have been a typical feature of the Finnish economy. There were big changes in the company structure of the Finnish banks in the 1920s and again in the 1990s. Until the 1990s, all the big financial intermediaries were commercial banks. At that time, economic depression and a severe banking crisis led to mergers and buyouts that completely shook up the long-standing spheres of interest. The two biggest banks and some smaller institutions were merged into Merita, which at the beginning of the twenty-first century became part of Nordea, a multinational Nordic financial group. The other big financial intermediary, Sampo-Leonia, resulted from a merger of Sampo Insurance and the state-owned Postal Savings Bank (Postipankki/Leonia).

THE TOP TEN COMPANIES IN SWEDEN

Swedish industry in the nineteenth century was heavily dependent on primary products and industries involved in the refining of raw materials. Towards the end of the century, the iron and the wood and paper industries totally dominated both production and employment. However, in the 1890s, a more general breakthrough for new technologies pushed Sweden's industrial sector into a transition, with the engineering industry—in a broad sense—being the prime mover of this process.

Several of these companies had already been established during the middle of the nineteenth century. It was not unusual that these industries had a broad selection of products in their catalogues, but from the 1870s, production underwent a specialization and at the same time the market grew owing to international demand. At the beginning of the twentieth century, several of the newly established so-called 'genius firms' within engineering developed quickly. Among these industries, we can find, for example, Separator (centrifuges for separating cream and milk) as well as SKF (Svenska Kullagerfabrikken) and L.M. Ericsson.

During the interwar period, as well as in the years following the Second World War, the importance of the engineering industry increased. The 'genius firms' were joined by new companies connected to transport (Volvo, Scania, and Saab) and electrical household appliances (Electrolux and ASEA). At the same time, the wood and paper industry managed to retain a strong position in both production and export, and by increased investments in foreign countries the leading companies in this sector managed to expand without overexploitation of Sweden's natural timber resources.[4]

Even though industrialization started in Sweden and Finland in different periods and with different types of industries, the industrial structures of the two countries today have important similarities. In both countries, engineering

[4] M. Larsson, *En svensk ekonomisk historia 1850–1985* [*A Swedish Economic History 1850–1985*] (Stockholm: SNS, 1993).

and the wood and paper industries are among the most important. This has opened the way for both cooperation and competition between Swedish and Finnish companies. For example, in the telecommunications sector, Swedish Ericsson and Finnish Nokia were competitors in more or less the same fast-growing market during the last two decades of the twentieth century. At the same time, both Swedish and Finnish companies have had strong positions in the international pulp and paper markets, which has resulted in both cooperation and close following of competitors' activities.

These overall changes in the Swedish economy have been reflected in the development of its ten largest companies. Wood and paper held a strong position during the first two benchmarks, with two companies among the top ten. However, the sector's share decreased after the Second World War , and there was only one company among the ten largest in the 1950s benchmark and in 1998–2000, and none in the 1970s benchmark. Several of the companies registered as wood and paper industries in this database were also conglomerates that included sawmills, production of electricity and of pulp and paper, as well as mining and steel production.[5]

Thus, the wood and paper industries have not been of the same importance for the Swedish economy as for the Finnish. Instead, in a long-term perspective, Sweden's top ten has been dominated by the engineering industry (see Table 10.4). In fact, the most well-known Swedish industrial companies, such as Volvo, ASEA, Ericsson, Electrolux, and Saab-Scania, were all represented among the top ten companies during at least one benchmark period.

When the composition of Sweden's top ten began to change, the newcomers were also predominantly engineering firms. In 1927–9, two of four new companies were engineering companies, and in 1954–6, three out of five. This predominance reflects no doubt the golden age of Swedish industry, when the engineering sector grew from around 20 per cent of total industrial employment to close to 50 per cent. Compared with the first benchmark 1911–13, engineering replaced industrial companies traditionally associated with an early industrial development—primarily the food industry, but also mining.

In a similar way, the inclusion of new companies in the top ten during the last benchmark 1998–2000 reflects both the development of services in the Swedish economy and the maturity of traditional manufacturing industry. Three of the new top ten companies at this time were connected with services and trade. The largest commercial company, the food giant ICA, was the seventh largest firm in the country.

Several of the top ten companies have been subject to mergers, with this sometimes being the direct reason for their disappearance from the group. In fact, ten out of fourteen of the companies introduced into the top ten during the first two benchmarks, 1911–13 and 1927–9, later disappeared as a result of mergers. This situation radically changed after the Second World War, when only two of the twelve companies included in the top ten during the three

[5] J. Glete, *Ägande och industriell omvandling* [*Ownership and Industrial Transformation*] (Stockholm: SNS, 1987) and *Nätverk inom näringslivet: Ägande och industriell omvandling i det mogna industrisamhället 1920–1990* [*Network in Industry: Ownership and Industrial Change in Mature Industrial Society 1920–1990*] (Stockholm: SNS, 1994).

Table 10.4. The top ten in Sweden, including financial intermediaries and railways, 1913–2000

Industry	Company name	1913	1927	1954	1972	2000
Financial intermediation	Skandinaviska Kreditaktiebolaget	1	2	2		
Financial intermediation	Stockholms Enskilda Bank	2				
Food, drink, and tobacco	Swedish sugar	3	4			
Mining	LKAB	4	5	5		
Wood and paper	Stora Kopparberg	5	6			
Engineering	Separator	6	7			
Engineering	Allmänna Tele	7				
Wood and paper	Uddeholm	8	8			
Food, drink, and tobacco	Svensk Tobak	9				
Food, drink, and tobacco	Stockholms Bryggeri	10				
Financial intermediation	Svenska Handelsbanken		1	1	1	
Financial intermediation	Skandinaviska Enskilda Banken				2	2
Chemical	Swedish Match		3		10	
Engineering	SKF		9	3	5	
Engineering	ASEA		10	4	6	
Engineering	L.M. Ericsson			7	8	3
Commercial activities	KF (Coop)			6	3	
Wood and paper; matured industries	SCA			8		4
Transport equipment	Götaverken			9		
Transport equipment	Volvo			10	4	5
Financial intermediation	Nordea					1
Transport equipment	Saab-Scania				7	
Construction	Skanska (Skånska Cement)				9	7
Engineering	Electrolux					6
Insurance	Skandia					8
Commercial activities	ICA					9
Post and telephone	Telia					10

Note: Ranking based on assets (1913, 1927, and 1954) and turnover (1972 and 2000).
Source: Database of large Swedish companies

benchmarks from 1954–6 had been bought up by other companies. There was thus a relative stability in the Swedish top ten for several decades after 1945, a period when Swedish and Finnish laws limited foreign ownership. In the 1990s, however, liberalization resulted in an increased role for foreign ownership even among the largest Swedish companies. For example, the one-time giant food concern Swedish Sugar (Svenska Sockerfabriks AB/Sockerbolaget) was bought up in 1992 by Danisco, a Danish multinational, which a few years later also took over Finnish Sugar (Finnsugar/Cultor).

The major changes in ownership of the Swedish top ten companies confirm the results of previous research.[6] Over this ninety-year period, banks and foreign owners have increased in importance, while state ownership and individual Swedish owners and shareholders have decreased. Mergers between Finnish and Swedish companies illustrate this trend. This process of concentration and internationalization during

[6] M.J. Iversen and M. Larsson, 'Strategic transformations in Danish and Swedish big business in an era of globalisation, 1973–2008', *Business History*, 53, 1 (2011), 119–43.

the last fifty years is hardly surprising. In fact, it confirms the development of the two countries' economies from being rather isolated on the periphery of Northern Europe to becoming part of the globalized world economy.

The top ten's stability is also evident in the financial sector. Svenska Handels-banken (previously Stockholms Handelsbank) and Skandinaviska Enskilda Banken (created by the merger between Skandinaviska Banken and Stockholms Enskilda Bank in 1971) were among the most important financial intermediaries during all five benchmarks. Also, Nordea (Kreditbanken in 1954–6 and PK-banken in 1970–2) has had a strong position since the Second World War and joined the top ten in 1998–2000.

PROFITABILITY IN DIFFERENT INDUSTRIES

The basis for this analysis of profitability by industries is the development of the largest companies in different industries. Company size was measured by assets in 1911–13, 1927–9, and 1954–6, and by turnover in 1970–2 and 1998–2000. This means that for each benchmark period, between fifteen and nineteen companies have been selected for analysis. However, since there is only one company for each industry, the basis for comparing performance by industry is insufficient, so we have grouped the companies according to market orientation: home-market-oriented, export-oriented, and mixed companies. Since statistics about the markets for different products are difficult to obtain, the distinction between the three categories is a bit vague. It is mostly based on knowledge about the general development for each country's export industries and about the role of each company within these production areas.

In Sweden, the home market industries were throughout the entire period of investigation dominated by companies dealing with internal trade and infrastruc-ture, but companies in food and textiles have also been included in this group (see Table 10.5). The export industries have included companies within mining, engineering, and wood and paper. The only exception is Swedish Match (chem-icals), which already in the 1920s had large export markets. The group of mixed

Table 10.5. The largest Swedish and Finnish companies according to sales markets, 1911–2000

	1911–13	1927–9	1954–6	1970–2	1998–2000
Sweden					
Home-market-oriented	9	7	6	7	6
Export-oriented	3	5	6	6	5
Mixed	3	4	3	4	8
Total	15	16	15	17	19
Finland					
Home-market-oriented	—	13	8	9	4
Export-oriented	—	1	1	5	3
Mixed	—	1	6	3	11
Total	—	15	17	18	18

Source: Databases of Swedish and Finnish large companies

companies includes companies that had considerable activities in both national and export markets. Over time, the number of mixed companies increased. This is hardly surprising, considering the gradual internationalization of the economy that has taken place during the last decades. Thus, during the last benchmark period, the home market group was dominated by public and infrastructural companies, while companies in traditionally home-market-oriented industries had become more export-oriented and were therefore transferred to the group of mixed companies.

The majority of Finnish top ten companies were classified as home market industries until the 1970s, because the country's exports were dominated to such a large extent by forestry products. (By definition, this sector has only one representative in this group.) From the 1950s to the 1970s, Finnish mining, metal, and textile companies were classified as mixed companies because they sold both to the home market and to the Soviet Union and gradually to the Western market too. In 2000, most Finnish companies had important export activities as well as home markets. Home market companies were active in energy supply or services.

The ROEs for the largest Swedish companies were fairly stable during the three first benchmarks (see Table 10.6). The development for the two later periods, however, is more varied. The drop in ROE in the 1970s was mostly an effect of the general downturn in economic activity. While the 1960s had been a strong decade for Swedish industry, its performance in the early 1970s was weaker even before the first oil crisis in 1973. The late 1990s was a period of economic growth in which rationalizations and general economic prosperity resulted in increased returns. Compared with the previous two benchmark periods, the late 1990s was also characterized by a growing importance for market solutions as well as the necessity to show profitable results in order to retain shareholders' interest. By contrast, in the 1950s and 1970s, company growth and returns were hampered by strong governmental intervention and public controls.

The analysis of ROE for the Finnish companies has a shaky foundation because of the small numbers in some groups. The beginning of the 1930s depression and worsening export possibilities are not yet visible in the ROEs of the late 1920s,

Table 10.6. ROE for the largest Swedish and Finnish companies according to sales markets, 1911–2000 (in %)

	1911–13	1927–9	1954–6	1970–2	1998–2000
Sweden					
Home-market-oriented	8.8	10.5	7.1	6.9	12.8
Export-oriented	12.1	10.0	8.7 (30.9[a])	8.4	13.5
Mixed	5.2	6.6	12.6	7.4	11.9
Average	8.7	9.4	8.9 (17.7[a])	7.6	12.7
Finland					
Home-market-oriented	—	7.4	9.4	7.3	27.3[b]
Export-oriented	—	8.1[c]	20.8[c]	1.6	13.9
Mixed	—	2.6[c]	8.9	7.1	12.1
Average	—	7.2	9.0	5.2	15.9[b]

[a] The figures in parentheses include also the mining company LKAB, which has otherwise been omitted because of its high ROEs, around 140%, which to a large extent were the result of the company's undercapitalization
[b] TTH Finland/Finnmatkat is not included, because of unusually large losses
[c] One company only

Source: Databases of large Swedish and Finnish companies

Table 10.7. HR for the largest Swedish and Finnish companies according to sales markets, 1911–2000 (in %)

	1911–13	1927–9	1954–6	1970–2	1998–2000
Sweden					
Home-market-oriented	4.3	13.8	4.7	2.3	—
Export-oriented	14.1	21.6	14.0	3.4	21.3
Mixed	6.6	17.3	6.5	14.5	24.9
Average	6.7	17.3	10.1	6.3	23.6
Finland					
Home-market-oriented	—	6.1	25.8	36.5	—
Export-oriented	—	−18.9[a]	20.8[a]	32.8	68.0
Mixed	—	−21.9[a]	17.4	16.0	22.1
Average	—	0.8	22.0	29.7	35.8

[a] One company only

Source: Databases of large Swedish and Finnish companies

except in the result for Finska Ångfartygs AB (The Finnish Steamer Company Ltd). The 1950s brought good profits generally, even though the country was plagued by many kinds of economic problems in the immediate post-war years. However, it appears that the government's various regulations and economic policy measures to favour industrial development obviously reached their goal.

The slacking ROE in the early 1970s may be due to increasing difficulties in export markets, but it may also reflect the effects of the largest companies adapting their payouts to the taxation policies of the country, as mentioned earlier. The high ROEs at the end of the century are a manifestation of the unusual worldwide stock market boom at the time.

Shifting attention to HR, we see that the Swedish export-oriented companies had the strongest market positions in 1911–13, 1927–9, and 1954–6 (see Table 10.7). However, except for the first benchmark, the differences between the three groups were fairly small and also diminishing. In three of the five benchmark periods, HR was higher than ROE for Sweden's largest companies. Especially during the stock market booms of the 1920s and 1990s, the difference between HR and ROE was quite considerable (see Tables 10.6 and 10.7). Generally speaking, HR was higher for export-oriented companies than for both home-market-oriented and mixed companies. This might have been an effect of high expectations on the Swedish stock market for export companies in general, but it can also be explained by the good assessment of some individual companies buoying up the group as a whole. For example, both ASEA and SKF—heavy export companies—had high HRs in the 1920s; ASEA's HR was also good during the first benchmark period. The high HRs for the mixed companies in the last three decades of the century can also be explained by the strong development of a few companies. In both benchmarks, the insurance company Skandia exhibited unusually high rates of HR, and in the 1990s, the shipping giant Broström as well as the security services firm Securitas also had strong HRs.

In contrast to the Swedish companies, Finnish big companies' HRs were low at the end of the 1920s, possibly as a result of poor expectations in the face of falling world and domestic prices and depressed economic outlook in general, especially in the forestry and forest industry. The high HRs of the 1950s and 1970s may have been the results of the taxation and other economic policy measures mentioned earlier. Also, relatively fast inflation could have boosted market expectations. The jump in HR in 1998–2000 was clearly a product of the worldwide dot.com boom.

RETURN ON EQUITY

Measured by the ROE of the country's ten largest companies, the performance of Finnish business appears to have been relatively low or mediocre throughout the twentieth century (see Table 10.8). Having said that, one must also add that the validity of this data has to be seriously questioned. For the 1920s and the 1950s, the average ROEs were around 7 per cent, with relatively small differences between the companies. In the 1970s, Finnish big business, especially the ship-building and mechanical engineering companies and the paper companies, were doing rather badly even before the oil crisis. In the 1980s, the state-owned Enso-Gutzeit (forest industry) and Valmet (mechanical engineering and shipbuilding) were making losses, and the other paper companies were not doing well either. This led to a radical restructuring of the wood and paper as well as the engineering companies by closures and mergers in the 1980s and the 1990s. The booming share prices of 1998–2000 also seemed to raise ROE, and led to big differences between the largest companies.

The ROEs for the Swedish top ten were generally a couple of percentage points higher than those for their Finnish counterparts, and the gap increased during the last decades of the twentieth century. Both in 1970–2 and in 1998–2000, the ROEs for the Swedish top ten companies were about 4–5 percentage points higher than for the Finnish top ten. The question is why did Finnish industry perform worse than the Swedish during all five benchmark periods?

This is not an easy question to answer. However, one reason might be found in the countries' differing institutional structures. Finnish tax legislation made it easier for companies to build up hidden reserves and even-out profits across several operating years. Such practices were also possible in Swedish industry, but were probably not used to the same extent. Between 1938 and 1956, it was also possible for companies to write off investments already during their first year, thus enabling them to accumulate hidden capital reserves. But there is no clear evidence that Swedish business used such a build-up of capital regularly to even-out annual

Table 10.8. ROE for the ten largest companies in Sweden and Finland, 1911–2000 (in %)

	Sweden	Finland
1911–13	9.2	11.0[a]
1927–9	8.0	7.1
1954–6	21.6 (8.3[b])	6.8
1970–2	8.7	4.3
1998–2000	16.3	15.3

[a] Only one observation
[b] The figure in parentheses excludes LKAB

Source: Database of large companies for Sweden and Finland

profits. Rather, they used the reserves to finance special investments or to tide over periods of extremely high losses. This conclusion can be confirmed if we look at the ranges of ROE in the top ten companies in Sweden and Finland. For example, during the period 1927–9, the average ROE for the Finnish top ten varied between 4.7 and 9.2 per cent, while the average ROE for the Swedish top ten during the same benchmark period fluctuated between 3.8 and 13.6 per cent.

It is difficult to draw definitive conclusions about ROE in different industries, since the number of companies in the sample is so small. However, in Sweden, it looks as if retailing companies, such as ICA and Coop, generally had lower ROEs than companies engaged in industrial production. During the last three benchmark periods, the ROEs for the retailers hovered between 2 and 6 per cent, while for engineering firms they fluctuated around 10 per cent and during the last benchmark period reached 20 per cent and higher. In addition to engineering, the mining group—with LKAB—generated a high ROE. But, as explained earlier, this was to a large extent due to a comparatively low equity for this state-owned company. In Finland, one could say that the construction and property industries have usually been among the best according to ROE and mechanical engineering firms the worst.

Banking was highly state-regulated in both Sweden and in Finland from the 1930s to the 1980s, and in the 1990s it was saved from total collapse by government intervention. In a way, the controls guaranteed the banks very even profits. In both countries, it appears that the detailed regulation of banking resulted in the sector's comparatively low ROEs. The average ROE for Swedish financial intermediaries in 1927–9 was about 9 per cent, but it fell to 6 per cent in 1954–6. At the last date, this return was considerably lower (more than two percentage points) than the average ROE for the top ten. In 1970–2, the ROE for financial intermediaries was almost three percentage points lower than for the other companies in the top ten. Thus, it seems that the stability of Swedish banking—regulated closely by legislation—came at the price of reduced profitability. This situation was more obvious in the last benchmark period. In the late 1990s, ROE for the five largest Swedish financial intermediaries reached 19 per cent, compared with 16.6 per cent for the top ten companies. In addition to being a reflection of the liberalization of banking legislation at this time, the high returns can also have expressed the banks' desire to compensate their shareholders for heavy losses at the beginning of the 1990s, when Swedish banks were hit by a severe crisis.

HOLDING RETURN

The other performance indicator, HR, proved to be not well suited for an analysis of big business in Finland. The problem is not that information on share prices cannot be found, but rather that, as in the case of Italy, listing companies on the stock exchange has not been widespread in Finland until very recently. Finnish big business has been characterized by a relatively large share of family-owned companies as well as state-owned companies, the latter particularly since the 1950s. In 1927–9, 69 per cent of the companies analysed were listed at the stock exchange and accordingly could be assigned an HR. In 1954–6, the share was 58 per cent, in 1970–2, 56 per cent, and in 1998–2000, 62 per cent. When a

Table 10.9. HR for the ten largest companies in Sweden and Finland, 1911–2000 (in %)

	Sweden	Finland
1911–13	5.4	—
1927–9	17.5	2.0
1954–6	8.0	15.2
1970–2	6.0	26.0
1998–2000	15.6	35.3

Source: Database of large companies for Sweden and Finland

company's share capital consisted of ordinary and preferential shares and the share volumes were available, a weighted average of ordinary and preference shares was used for measuring HR. If this was not the case, just ordinary share prices were used. The results can be seen in Table 10. 9.

HRs for the Finnish top ten companies were falling in the late 1920s. This could be due to the strong representation of forest industry in the top group and to tight international competition. The world economic crisis of the 1930s started early in Finland; prices of timber started falling already in 1927 and exports of Finnish forest products in early 1928. The high HRs of the 1950s and 1970s were discussed earlier in this chapter. In addition to being influenced by special taxation legislation, the HRs could have been buoyed by the prevailing high inflation—share prices tend to follow general price rises. This link can also been seen in the HR for 1998–2000. Although not all Finnish companies boomed at the time, the share prices—and thereby HR—of electronics and paper companies soared.

For Swedish big business, HR appears to be a better performance indicator than was the case in Finland. The use of the stock market as an arena for the evaluation of companies' performance and trading with shares was quite common for the country's large companies throughout the twentieth century. The breakthrough of the Swedish stock market came already in the 1910s; seventy years later, in the 1980s, a second boom followed when the stock market was reorganized and also opened to medium-sized companies.

In the Swedish case, each benchmark period contains at least one year of generally falling stock market prices—1913, 1929, 1955–6, 1970, and 2000. But these years of low HR were compensated by higher HR either before or directly after. Thus, weak and strong years cancelled each other out in the period averages. With the exception of the first benchmark period, HR was also higher than ROE for the top ten companies. During the 1920s and 1950s, this difference was 5–7 percentage points, but it increased to close to 10 percentage points towards the end of the century (see Tables 10.8 and 10.9).

Comparing Sweden with Finland, however, gives us another perspective. In the period 1927–9, HRs for the Finnish companies were very low, but, in the benchmark periods of both the 1950s and 1970s, HRs were higher (4–5 per cent) for the top ten Finnish companies. During the last benchmark period, this situation changed to the advantage of the Swedish top ten companies.

When HR is used as a performance indicator, several of the Swedish low-performing companies, as measured by ROE, fall out of the analysis group. The retailers ICA and Coop were for a long time not organized as joint-stock companies, and thus were not subject to share trading or the evaluation of the stock market. Companies in traditionally strong sectors such as engineering and the wood and paper industry at times had low HRs. In fact, the fluctuations in HR between benchmark periods and between years within each benchmark make it difficult to draw firm conclusions. The only thing that seems quite clear is that fluctuations in HR are linked to the business cycle and that these fluctuations affect different industries at different times. For example, the telecommunications company Ericsson showed an increase in HR of 186 per cent in 1999, but a decrease of 22 per cent the following year. Generally speaking, however, changes in HR were not that extensive and did not occur within such a short time.

The HR for Swedish banks was not directly connected to the performance of the other top ten companies. Instead, HR fluctuations were linked to changes in institutional settings and to banking crises. Thus, during the period 1954–6, the average HR was negative (−4.2 per cent) for the two banks in the top ten, whereas in the 1970s, their average HR was +11 per cent, considerably higher than for the other top ten companies. Also, during the last benchmark period, 1998–2000, after deregulation had opened the market for banking, the HR for the two largest financial intermediaries (over 25 per cent) was considerably higher than for the other top ten companies.

CONCLUDING REMARKS

In this chapter, we have examined the establishment and performance of Swedish and Finnish big business for five benchmark periods during the twentieth century. In the analysis, we have compared the development and persistence of these large companies and their performance as measured by ROE and HR. The results of these analyses are to some extent quite clear.

From a general perspective, Sweden's top ten companies were about twice the size of their Finnish counterparts. This could of course be explained by Sweden being the larger country with, consequently, a larger potential market. Sweden also industrialized earlier and had a higher income per capita. Finland's later economic development has meant that much information is lacking on the performance of Finnish large companies, especially in the first part of the twentieth century. During the last decades of the century, however, Finland's economy grew quickly and the country's GDP per capita rose to Western European levels.

Despite the difference in firm size and the time lag in company growth between the two countries, we can see great similarities in development that are connected to a more Nordic model for structure and profit development.

The top ten companies in both Sweden and Finland were heavily involved in merger activities. For example, the electrical engineering company ASEA merged with twenty-four other companies between 1913 and 1938.[7] Other countries

---

[7] M. Larsson, 'Storföretagande och industrikoncentration' ['Big business and industrial concentration'], in M. Isacson and M. Morell, eds., *Industrialismens tid* [*The Age of Industrialization*] (Stockholm: SNS, 2002).

exhibited similar developments, and this resulted in both an increased size for those companies surviving and a situation where companies of all sizes lost their own identity when taken over by competitors. Several of the top ten companies in both Sweden and Finland disappeared from one benchmark period to the next because of these mergers. However, in spite of this, several of the large companies were present among the top ten in three to five benchmarks, such as the Swedish engineering companies Ericsson, ASEA, and Volvo, and the Finnish wood and paper companies Enso-Gutzeit/Stora Enso, Kymin-Kymmene/UPM-Kymmene, Tammerfors Linne- och Järn-Industri/Tampella, and A. Ahlström. And the two biggest Finnish banks were unchanged from 1913 to the 1990s. The lists of the long-lasting large companies also underline the relatively stable structures of the manufacturing industries in Sweden and in Finland: more engineering industry in Sweden and more wood and paper industry in Finland.

Nevertheless, the similarities between the two countries' industrial structure are obvious. The wood and paper sector is important in both countries, as is the production of machinery. Both areas are of course closely connected to the natural resources in the two countries. We can also see similarities in the two countries' engineering industries. For example, especially in the 1990s, Finland's Nokia and Sweden's Ericsson dominated the fast-growing mobile phone technology. In the Swedish case, this was the result of long-range research development in electrical engineering, while in the Finnish case, telephone production was the consequence of the exploitation of new international market possibilities.[8]

In general, both ROE and HR were lower for the Finnish large companies than for the Swedish. This can be possibly explained by an long-established and more active stock market in Sweden, which listed a larger proportion of the Swedish big companies than did the newer and smaller Finnish stock market. The higher return for Swedish companies is also explained by institutional factors. For example, business tax regulations in both Sweden and Finland made it possible for companies to even-out annual results by building up hidden capital reserves. This practice was used in both countries, but it is difficult to say to what extent. The possibility of writing off all investments during the first year was also an important way to conceal high profits. This might explain why ROE was high into the 1950s. This vagueness about the real profits of the large companies makes it difficult to determine the extent to which they were the engines of fast economic development in these countries.

Without doubt, big business has been of great importance for both Finnish and Swedish economies in establishing the position of these countries not only as important traders on the international market but also as catalysts for national economic development. This can also explain why institutional setting sometimes has promoted rationalization and big business before small-scale production. The special position of big business in Sweden and Finland is also demonstrated by how these large companies were liquidated. They seldom went truly bankrupt; instead, they merged with stronger competitors or were liquidated under controlled circumstances with the help of the state or the financial sector or both.

---

[8] M. Häikiö, *Nokia, The Inside Story* (Helsinki: Edita, 2002), pp. 35–40.

Part III

Industries' Performance

11

Old Industries in Europe, 1911–2000

Toni Pierenkemper, Helma De Smedt, Frans Buelens,
Ludo Cuyvers, and Marc Deloof

INTRODUCTION

In pre-modern societies, sustainable economic development and steady economic growth are possible only in societies that possess the appropriate resources directly or can acquire them in exchange for other products or resources. Some countries may also be able to access foreign resources through colonial exploitation or by force or political subordination. In pre-modern agrarian societies, the autonomous resources in question would, first and foremost, exist in the form of the inhabitants' labour, the earning power of the land, or the area's natural raw materials. It is therefore not surprising that early industrialization in Europe was primarily shaped by industries that were able to draw heavily on the available workforce and large reserves of natural products and raw materials.

In the nineteenth century, there were a number of industries that fell into this category. The woodworking industries, textiles, and food industries were prime examples, as well as mining (coal and iron ore) and the iron and steel industries stemming from it. In the first three, production relied on native wood, native and imported raw textile materials (wool, flax, cotton, and silk), as well as manifold agricultural products. In this chapter, we define such industries as Old Industries; more precisely, our definition encompasses the following industries: basic and fabricated metals; food, drink, and tobacco products; mining, textiles and leather goods; and wood and paper products. From the 1970–2 sample onwards, we define some of these Old Industries (basic and fabricated metals, and wood and paper products) as Mature Industries to indicate that their production processes have completely changed.

The Old Industries of the Industrial Revolution were the leading sectors of the nineteenth century and responsible for the significant upturns that characterized numerous European national economies at the time. They continued to significantly shape European economies in the twentieth century. However, the geographic spread of the nineteenth-century economic upturns was uneven, and as a result the individual European national economies were in extremely different stages of development at the start of the twentieth century. Some countries on the European periphery had barely begun modern industrial development. Others

Table 11.1. Old Industries: size, ROE, and HR, 1911–2000

Benchmark years	Size (million US$)	ROE (%)		HR (%)	
		Median	Average	Median	Average
1911–13	22.30	9.12	11.12	3.77	5.70
1927–9	43.16	8.86	10.87	6.25	12.46
1954–6	111.41	7.43	10.31	13.53	20.72
1970–2	43,223.86	4.99	4.15	2.12	6.25
1998–2000	383,492.02	10.31	11.69	6.12	23.66

Note: For definitions and methodological questions, such as 'benchmark years', see Chapter 2

had made tentative progress in that direction, while a small number showed clear signs of industrial economic structures.[1]

This process of development was characterized by several factors. There was a clear increase in the macroeconomic growth rate from values considerably below 1 per cent to values over 2 per cent. There was also a shift in the structural composition of the economy in favour of the industrial sector. Above all, however, it was the emergence and expansion of big business that really began to shape this process of development, even in the nineteenth century. How these large businesses continued to develop in European national economies in the twentieth century is the focus of interest in the present chapter, more precisely, how big Old Industry was able to bear up against new industries.

Large businesses within the Old Industries were distinct from large businesses in other sectors of the national economy in several respects, as can be seen from the figures for the former in Table 11.1.

The enormous stability of the return on equity (ROE) is particularly striking: it remained at roughly 10 per cent throughout the whole of the century, with the clear exception of the 1970s, when profitability was more than halved. The second half of the century also stood out by the fact that the ROE of the Old Industries was now considerably lower than the profitability of all other European big business. Clearly, Old Industry big businesses underwent a structural crisis from the middle of the century onwards in which they lost some of their developmental dynamic. It was only from the 1980s onwards, and with some difficulty, that they found themselves back on the path of expansion.

Comparing a century's worth of ROE data for the Old Industries, it is indeed striking that the 1970–2 benchmark differs significantly from all the others. First, whereas average ROE for all of the other periods is between 10 and 12 per cent, the overall ROE average for 1970–2 is below 5 per cent. Second, in 1970–2, median ROE is higher than average ROE, implying that there were several companies with a relatively low ROE. All of the other periods show the reverse pattern. The low returns of the early 1970s already presaged the bad years to come: the severe crises

---

[1] Including first and foremost Great Britain as the model of industrial economic growth. See Peter Mathias, *The First Industrial Nation: An Economic History of Britain 1700–1914* (London: Methuen, 1969). Belgium, Germany, and France had also made good progress by the end of the nineteenth century.

of 1973–4 and 1980–2, the sharp rise in energy prices due to two oil crises, and the vast restructuring of the economies following the structural crisis in the Old Industries.[2]

By 2000, the Old Industries' average and median ROE were back to the more normal levels of 11.69 and 10.31 per cent, respectively. This remarkable recovery was the result of three decades of adjustment to new economic realities.

SIZE

The development of their size, measured by their assets and turnover, serves as a first measure of how Old Industries performed in the European economies of the twentieth century. In terms of assets, all Old Industry companies grew considerably in the first half of the century. Around 1913, their average capital resources amounted to no more than $22.3 million, which increased to $43.16 million in 1927–9 and $111.41 million by 1954–6. In just forty years, then, the average capital endowment of a large Old Industry firm had increased almost exactly fivefold. This growth spurt indicates that these companies, at least until the 1950s, by no means belonged to the losers of industrial growth in twentieth-century Europe. However, a closer look at the individual subsectors of Old Industry in European countries reveals clear differences.

Great Britain had by far the most financially sound big business throughout the entire period, with average assets twice as large as those found in the other countries at every time period analysed. Finland was at the other end of the spectrum, with no large businesses at all at the start of the century, and Finnish big business was clearly behind the European average in terms of number and strength of financial resources in all other years we have compared. Only Germany, and with certain qualifications also France and Belgium, could to a certain extent keep up with Great Britain in terms of the development of big business in the first half of the twentieth century.

A clear hierarchy of European industrial development had, then, already started to form in the nineteenth century and was reflected in the number and financial strength of large businesses. This also remained the case in the twentieth century. British large businesses were at the apex of this hierarchy. Although challenged and indeed overtaken by German competitors in the iron and steel industry, they were still, all in all, able to maintain their leading position in terms of the size of their capital assets. Belgian and French competitors also began to assert themselves more strongly during the course of the century, whereas big business in the northern and southern European periphery was only able to achieve tentative, delayed and painstaking development. Nevertheless, in 1970–2, Italy, represented by Italsider, emerged as an important player in the more restricted group of

---

[2] S. Houpt, P. Lains, and L. Schön, 'Sectoral developments, 1945–2000', in S. Broadberry and K.H. O'Rourke, eds., *The Cambridge Economic History of Modern Europe*, Volume 2: *1870 to the Present* (Cambridge: Cambridge University Press, 2010), pp. 345–7.

Mature Industries.[3] By the end of the twentieth century, both Italy and Spain had joined the upper range of the European big business hierarchy, the former with ENI and Montedison, the latter with Inditex.

However, within the different subsectors of Old Industry, a more nuanced picture emerges. While in Great Britain large businesses were found mainly in the food and textiles industries, in Germany they were in the iron and steel industry, as well as the hard coal mining industry, which dominated on the basis of high productivity.[4] The structure of big business in France and Belgium[5] was much the same as in Germany; here, as in Germany, it was principally companies in heavy industry that were able to considerably consolidate their financial strength considerably in the twentieth century.

The European economies on the northern and southern periphery were still at the start of their industrial development in 1911–13. This was also apparent in the structure of their large businesses. However, in these countries, the 'large' businesses, according to our definition, were also those of heavy industry with access to—in certain respects—excellent capital resources. Large businesses in Italy were predominantly in the iron and steel industry,[6] and in Spain primarily in mining.[7] A similar pattern of the development and expansion of large businesses is found in Sweden, albeit with a further lag in timing. There, thanks to the presence of local raw materials (mineral ores and wood), similarly noteworthy large businesses started to develop,[8] while Finland saw the emergence of a small number of large businesses solely on the basis of the country's abundance of timber.[9]

A closer look at individual large businesses also reveals clear gradations of size (Table 11.2). A small group of super-large companies, which we will call Giants, had four times the amount of capital resources of an average contemporary large business. After these came a somewhat larger but still restricted group of extra-large companies, the Bigs, with capital resources twice the sector average. Of 174 Old Industry firms in the first benchmark 1911–13, fourteen were Giants and eleven were Bigs. The Giants were largely to be found in Great Britain and Germany, which each had six of these super-large companies. There were also several Bigs in France; in the remaining European national economies there were not any such large enterprises in the Old Industries at this time. Until the middle

---

[3] See: Y. Meny and V. Wright, *The Politics of Steel: Western Europe and the Steel Industry in the Crisis Years* (Berlin, New York: De Gruyter, 1986), p. 479; H. Aszkenazy, *Les grandes sociétés européennes* (Bruxelles: Centre de Recherche et d'Information Socio-Politiques (CRISP), 1971), p. 118.

[4] S.N. Broadberry and C. Burhop, 'Comparative productivity in British and German manufacturing before World War II: Reconciling direct benchmark estimates and time series projections', *Journal of Economic History*, 67 (2007), 315–49.

[5] See J.A. de Jonge, 'Die Wirtschaft (II. Westeuropa. Großbritannien und Irland, Frankreich, Belgien und die Niederlande 1850–1914)', in *Handbuch der Europäischen Wirtschafts- und Sozialgeschichte, Band 5: Europäische Wirtschafts- und Sozialgeschichte von der Mitte des 19. Jahrhunderts bis zum Ersten Weltkrieg* (Stuttgart: Klett-Cotta, 1990), pp. 338–41, 343–4.

[6] See P. Hertner, 'Italien 1850–1914', in *Handbuch der Europäischen Wirtschafts- und Sozialgeschichte*, Band 5, pp. 705–76, esp. 749–50.

[7] See S. Pollard, *Peaceful Conquest: The Industrialisation of Europe 1760–1970* (Oxford: Oxford University Press, 1981), p. 243.

[8] Pollard, *Peaceful Conquest*, p. 233.

[9] Y. Kaukiainen, 'Finnland 1860–1913', in *Handbuch der Europäischen Wirtschafts- und Sozialgeschichte*, Band 5, p. 277.

Table 11.2. Giants and Bigs in the Old Industries, 1911–2000

	1911–13		1927–9		1954–6	
	Giants	Bigs	Giants	Bigs	Giants	Bigs
UK	6	5	4	11	6	4
Gemany	6	1	2	4	2	4
France		3		2		3
Belgium		1	2	1	1	
Italy				2		3
Spain	1			2	1	4
Sweden	1	1		3		3
Finland						
Total	14	11	8	25	10	21

	1970–2		1998–2000	
	Giants	Bigs	Giants	Bigs
UK	2	3		3
Germany		1		1
France				
Belgium				
Italy		1	1	2
Spain			1	
Sweden				
Finland				1
Total	2	5	2	7

of the twentieth century British and German large businesses continued to dominate the Old Industries. Large businesses in general were scarce in the other European economies, with Bigs infrequent and Giants rare.[10]

Looking at the distribution of large businesses in the European economies by subsector (Table 11.3), it becomes clear that in Great Britain the most financially sound businesses were those in the food industry and the textiles industry, i.e. producers of consumer goods.[11] In Germany, by contrast, businesses in the iron and steel industries and in the hard coal mining industry, i.e. the producers of primary products and producer goods,[12] were the most financially

[10] In both 1927–9 and 1954–6, there were only two Giants that were not in Great Britain or Germany. They were the Belgian Union Minière and Ougree-Marihaye (1926/1929) and, in 1954–6, the Spanish company Empersa National Siderurgica in addition to the Union Minière.

[11] British Giants in 1911–13 included two tobacco companies (British American Tobacco and Imperial Tobacco), both belonging to the food industry, a brewery (Watney, Combe, Reid & Co.), also in the food industry, and two textile companies (J&P Coats and The Fine Cotton Spinners). In 1927–9, British American Tobacco, Imperial Tobacco, and J&P Coats, as well as Courtaulds (textiles), were still Giants. In 1954–6, the Distillers Company (food) had joined the list. De Beers Consolidated Mines (mining) was also a Giant at all three timeframes, and, by the middle of the century, the Steel Company of Wales (iron and steel) had also—just—qualified as a Giant, with $300 million basic capital.

[12] The German iron and steel sector in 1911–13 included the following companies: Fried. Krupp, Deutsch-Luxemburgische Bergwerks, and Hütten AG. Mining companies included Hibernia, Gelsen-kirchener Bergwerks AG, and die Harpener Bergwerks AG. In 1927–9, there was only Krupp and

Table 11.3. Size of subsectors in the Old Industries, 1911–2000 (assets in million US$)

	Iron and steel	Food	Mining	Textiles	Wood and paper	Mean
UK						
1911–13	23.8	79.3	36.8	66.0	13.8	43.9
1927–9	81.65	165.14	54.4	150.34	40.92	98.49
1954–6	251.85	476.47	166.87	235.28	181.87	262.47
1970–2	4,352.33	3,759.58	2,910.10	2,309.85		3,332.97
1998–2000	13,177.64	60,984.39	51,665.43			41,942.49
Germany						
1911–13	87.44	8.61	56.57	10.87	12.98	35.28
1927–9	216.05	19.2	30.98	31.51	13.03	62.15
1954–6	258.65	51.13	292.27	62.29	38.24	140.52
1970–2	6,065.04	1,912.44	4,239.43	254.03		3,117.74
1998–2000	33,131.46	3,565.98	20,859.67	4,717.19		15,568.58
France						
1911–13	21.04	13.14	30.0	8.18	4.23	15.32
1927–9	26.51	11.33	39.25	14.89	7.69	19.93
1954–6	197.58	30.1	32.73	32.73	26.89	65.68
1970–2	3,784.86	622.98	716.63	335.42		1,364.97
1998–2000	15,259.15	3,478.84	394.71	3,760.39		5,723.27
Belgium						
1911–13	34.21	0.44	2.81	3.24	3.17	8.7
1927–9	115.69	17.79	187.13	24.0	11.68	71.26
1954–6	60.42	19.24	204.43	17.05	16.5	63.53
1970–2	1,174.74	38.62	25.33	115.16		338.46
1998–2000	1,493.22	54.93	2,026.23	98.98		918.34
Italy						
1911–13	24.11	10.54	6.77	8.59	1.9	10.4
1927–9	62.90	11.15	4.76	12.69	8.75	20.05
1954–6	206.01	54.08	82.55	101.44	19.16	92.65
1970–2	4,789.04	158.12	78.29	224.21		1,312.42
1998–2000	7,423.37	28,864.47	51,965.47	16,574.96		26,207.07
Spain						
1911–13	10.04	22.75	53.93	7.36	6.45	20.11
1927–9	25.46	64.79	33.16	16.03	14.62	30.81
1954–6	236.45	109.27	196.77	29.71	22.64	119.97
1970–2	2,060.78	499.60				1,280.19
1998–2000	4,410.38	7,233.61		15,905.42		9,183.14
Sweden						
1911–13	5.65	48.93	43.14	3.16	20.98	22.34
1927–9	41.78	52.2	44.67	7.3	31.88	35.57
1954–6	222.64	40.17	181.08	9.91	127.91	117.34
1970–2	1,491.73	252.32	272.60	62.32		519.74
1998–2000	9,159.75	622.66	1,310.18	157.30		2,812.47
Finland						
1911–13						
1927–9	1.84	7.62	3.92	4.69	17.17	7.05
1954–6	14.14	15.92	34.1	17.25	72.22	30.73
1970–2	458.72	51.27	165.44	42.72		179.54
1998–2000	19,841.05	666.23	2,998.07	125.28		5,907.66
Average						
1911–13	29.47	29.54	27.72	15.33	9.09	22.3
1927–9	71.49	43.65	49.78	32.68	18.22	43.16
1954–6	181.59	99.55	149.52	63.21	63.18	111.41
1970–2	1,611.81	521.06	764.35	257.21		815.54
1998–2000	8,788.46	7,533.65	10,934.98	3,758.14		7,826.36

sound.[13] The two countries thus clearly took different paths in industrial development: Great Britain had embarked on its path from the end of the eighteenth century onwards during the First Industrial Revolution and had based its economy on consumer goods. Germany's path developed in the second phase of industrialization around the middle of the nineteenth century and had its basis in production goods. These different paths were to become further entrenched in the twentieth century. The different paths of industrial development followed by both economies are also apparent in the overall structure of their big business.

Attempts made by other countries to follow in the footsteps of these two countries met with varying degrees of success. Belgium was the first, succeeding from about 1830 onwards in very rapidly building up an independent industry on the basis of coal and iron, its local raw materials. In contrast, France struggled in the same endeavour.[14] In the countries of the European periphery, this process only began at the end of the nineteenth century. The First World War disrupted and halted economic development. As a result, a slower growth was experienced in all European national economies; indeed, the European economy collapsed at times, and the resulting protectionist tariff increases and competitive devaluations between the currencies were further obstacles hindering economic expansion. Despite this, the economies of the European countries expanded in the course of this time period, and Finland, for instance, even experienced above-average growth based on its local raw materials. Spain, which at the beginning of the century had belonged to Europe's poorest countries, also found itself in the midst of an upturn, but the country was particularly hard hit by the world economic crisis of the 1930s, then by the consequences of the Civil War and the international isolation under the Franco dictatorship, only fully industrializing in the 1960s with support from international capital. Italy's industrialization was also more successful in the early twentieth century than it had been in the nineteenth. However, successes remained largely restricted to the North; in spite of encouragement from the state, the South (the Mezzogiorno) remained underdeveloped.[15]

In the 1970s, average assets for the whole of the Old Industries rose to $815.54 million. Evidently, the size was not the same for each country or for each subsector. The average assets in the Mature Industries ($1,611.81 million) were considerably higher than those in mining ($764.35 million), food, drink, and tobacco ($521.06 million), or textiles and leather goods ($257.21 million). In fact, the assets of food, drink, and tobacco companies fell to $330 million, leaving aside British American Tobacco, the only real Giant in the sample. British American Tobacco, which originated as a joint venture between the British Imperial Tobacco Company and the American Tobacco Company in 1901,

Vereinigten Stahlwerke AG and in 1954–6 Mannesmann AG (iron and steel) and Gelsenkirchener Bergwerks AG (mining).

[13] In 1927–9, there were two Giants in the European economies outside Germany and Great Britain, namely Rio Tinto (mining) in Spain and Svenska Sockerfabriken (food) in Sweden.

[14] On the history of the industrialization of these countries, see T. Pierenkemper, *Umstrittene Revolutionen: Die Industrialisierung im 19. Jahrhundert* (Frankfurt am Main: Fischer-Taschenbuch-Verlag, 1996), pp. 38–63 (Belgium) and 64–89 (France).

[15] For an overview, see Pollard, *Peaceful Conquest*, pp. 278–325.

diversified during the 1960s and 1970s into a broad conglomerate that encompassed sectors such as paper production, the food industry, cosmetics, and, in the 1980s, even insurance and financial services. This diversification was stopped in 1989, as British American Tobacco once again intended to claim its dominant place in the tobacco sector.

At the end of the twentieth century (see the 1998–2000 sample), average assets in the Old Industries as a whole rose to $7,826.36 million, but now the average assets for mining were the highest ($10,934.98 million), ahead of the average assets of the Mature Industries ($8,788.46 million) and food, drink, and tobacco ($7,533.65 million). Textiles and leather goods again ranked last, with average assets of only $3,758.14 million.

Throughout most of the twentieth century, the overall picture of European business ranking did not change much, not even in the 1970s: the UK, Germany, and France remained the countries with the largest Old Industry companies in terms of assets. In the Mature Industries, Italy was also on the list. Italsider, British Steel Corporation, and August Thyssen-Hütte AG were clearly the biggest companies in the Mature Industries. In the food subsector, the UK was way ahead of the other countries, with Germany and France following at a distance. The British American Tobacco Company came out on top in this category and the German Dr August Oetker KG and Deutsche Unilever GmbH followed as second and third, respectively. Britain was prominent in the textiles and leather goods subsector, with British Courtaulds way ahead. In the mining subsector, Deutsche Ruhrkohle AG and the British Rio Tinto-Zinc Corporation were the leaders.

Thirty years later, in 1998–2000, the UK and Germany still played an important role in the Mature Industries. In the food, drink, and tobacco subsector, the UK took the lead with British American Tobacco ($26 billion), Diageo ($24 billion), and Cadbury Schweppes ($9.9 billion). In contrast, Germany had slipped behind Italy, which came out second with Montedison ($19 billion) and Parmalat ($9.3 billion). Italy also claimed a leading position ahead of the UK and Germany in the mining sector. The textiles and leather goods industry was now dominated by Southern European companies, with Spain and Italy having the biggest.

At the end of the twentieth century, food, drink, and tobacco had considerably increased its average level of assets, indicating that this subsector, which had been characterized by so many small and medium companies in the 1970–2 sample, had matured. Illustrating the new dynamics of this industry, some of the companies involved were established in the course of the last decade of the century, such as Diageo, created in 1997 as a result of the merger between Grand Metropolitan and Guinness. Others, such as Parmalat, created in 1961 as a small pasteurization plant in Parma, experienced rapid expansion, becoming a multinational company within a few decades. Of course, some of these companies have mixed activities, such as Montedison, a holding company mainly active in agrobusiness through its participation in the French company Eridania Béghin-Say, one of the world's leading agro-industrial concerns. The same holds for the German companies, some of which were also in tourism, such as C&N Touristic AG and TUI Group GmbH.

As mentioned earlier, textiles and leather goods had the lowest average assets of all the subsectors: $257.21 million in 1970–2 and $3,758.14 million in 1998–2000. This may be partially due to the absence in the sample of UK companies such as

Courtaulds, Coats Patons, and Total Group, which had been so dominant in 1970–2. The major companies at this time were to be found in Southern Europe, such as Inditex from Spain, with assets of $15.9 billion, and Edizione SRL, the holding company of the Italian Benetton family, with $13.9 billion.

The assets of mining companies increased considerably during these years, and the sector now contained some very large companies, such as ENI ($51 billion), Anglo American ($30 billion), Rio Tinto ($19 billion), and RAG AG (formerly Ruhrkohle AG) ($17 billion). These high asset levels were due to two factors. First, there was the vast range of activities involved. For example, Italian ENI is a multinational, integrated energy company, engaged in activities such as oil, gas, and electricity. Second, there was global engagement: Rio Tinto and ENI were active in numerous countries, and Anglo-American's foreign operations even exceeded its domestic activities. In contrast, the chief assets of LKAB (Luossavaara-Kirunavaara Aktiebolaget), a Swedish mining company going back to 1890, remained concentrated in Sweden. The company's mines in Luossavaara and Tuolluvaara were opened in the 1920s and closed in the 1970s. But its principal mine at Kiruna, opened in 1901, is still in operation.

The Mature Industries in 1998–2000 had higher assets than ever before, with Giants in iron and steel, such as ThyssenKrupp AG ($33.13 billion), Usinor ($14.12 billion), and Corus Group ($12.57 billion). Wood and paper could also boast a couple of Giants: the Finnish Stora Enso, a paper, packaging, and wood products company, with assets of $19.8 billion, and SCA (Svenska Cellulosa Aktiebolaget), with $9.15 billion. In many cases, these Giants were the result of mega-mergers. Corus was born in 1999 out of the merger of Hoogovens from the Netherlands and British Steel from the UK. ThyssenKrupp AG was the result of the merger of Thyssen Stahl AG and Krupp Stahl AG in 1997. The merger movement continued in the twenty-first century, as demonstrated, for instance, by the merger of the Australian BHP and the British Billiton in 2001, which produced BHP Billiton.

In 1970–2, the Mature Industries comprised only two Bigs and no Giants: the assets of Italsider ($4,378.02 million) and the British Steel Corporation ($3,502.50 million) exceeded double the subsector average of $1,611.81 million. In the food, drink, and tobacco subsector, there was no Big company, but there was one Giant: the British American Tobacco Company with assets amounting to $2,999.45 million, more than four times the subsector average of $521.07 million. In mining, two Bigs can be mentioned: the British Rio Tinto-Zinc Corporation ($2,533.52 million) and the German Saarbergwerke AG ($3,016.62 million). In both cases, company assets were clearly more than double the subsector average of $764.35 million. Indeed, the German company almost qualified for the status of Giant. In textiles and leather goods, average company assets amounted to $257.21 million, and the subsector contained one Giant and one Big, both British: Courtaulds ($1,516.26 million) and Coats Patons ($793.60 million).

By the end of the century, the home locations of several Giants were to be found in Southern Europe. The assets of the Spanish Inditex ($15,905.43 million) clearly surpassed four times the average company size of $3,758.14 million in the textiles and leather goods subsector. In mining, the assets of the Italian ENI ($51,887.01 million) also exceeded four times the subsector average of $10,934.98 million. Seven Bigs were spread over four sectors. In textiles and leather goods, the Italian Edizione (Benetton) had assets of $13,920.80 million that far surpassed twice the sector's average of $3,758.14 million and almost qualified the company as a Giant. Mining contained only one Big at this time: Anglo American, with assets of $30,692.27 million. However, two other companies in the subsector—the British Rio Tinto ($19,478.45 million) and the German RAG AG ($17,160.27 million)— were close to Big status; double the average company assets in the sector amounted to $21,869.97 million. Average size in food, drink, and tobacco was $7,533.65 million, and the subsector contained three Bigs, namely the Italian Montedison ($19,481.17 million) and the British firms Diageo ($24,520.69 million) and British American Tobacco ($26,559.76 million).

RETURN ON EQUITY

A remarkable stability in ROE is a particularly striking feature of the Old Industries in Europe; with the exception of the 1970s, ROE hovered around 10 per cent throughout the entire century (Table 11.4). Clearly, not only did the large businesses of the Old Industries continue to grow steadily in the twentieth century, as they had done in the nineteenth, but they did so with considerable profitability. Their stock yields at the start of the century (1911–13) were not greatly different, ranging from a high of 14.06 per cent in wood and paper to a low of 9.27 per cent in textiles. In 1927–9, the range of subsector profits remained limited: from 7.04 per cent in iron and steel to 15.49 per cent in wood and paper. However, by 1954–6, the differences in profitability between the subsectors of the Old Industries had considerably increased. In the most profitable subsector, mining, ROE was 18.53 per cent, almost four times larger than the 5.73 per cent in the least profitable subsector, textiles. Clearly, the general growth conditions for European large businesses had steadily worsened in the first half of the twentieth century, placing greater demands on individual companies. These demands were successfully met only with difficulty. The starkly varying political systems in interwar Europe no doubt also played a part. The development opportunities of the individual subsectors of the Old Industries differed widely, competition became more intense, and the subsectors developed quite differently over the course of the twentieth century. These conditions were also reflected in the varying fortunes of individual firms.

A first glance at the development of the profitability (ROE) of individual companies in the European Old Industries in the first half of the twentieth century shows notable differences that contrast with the overall picture of a stable average ROE. Large businesses in countries that had already embarked on successful industrialization in the nineteenth century (the UK, Germany, France, and Belgium) showed, by and large, slightly higher and slightly more stable returns than businesses in the trailing countries of the European periphery, at least at the beginning of the twentieth century. For these countries (Italy, Spain, Sweden, and Finland), the success of the large businesses seems to have been strongly influenced by foreign investors and interests.

In Great Britain, profits in the Old Industries remained surprisingly stable at between 11.44 and 10.6 per cent until the middle of the century, while in Germany, the ROE in the Old Industries fell from 10.4 per cent in 1911–13 to

Table 11.4. ROE in subsectors of the Old Industries, 1911–2000 (in %)

	Iron and steel	Food	Mining	Textiles	Wood and paper	Mean
UK						
1911–13	8.7	11.74	14.78	10.1	11.8	11.44
1927–9	1.75	18.04	7.97	10.17	15.42	10.67
1954–6	14.84	10.2	12.24	7.41	8.33	10.6
1970–2	0.17	13.01	8.27	11.28		7.90
1998–2000	9.85	26.34	12.78			16.32
Germany						
1911–13	15.75	10.73	8.5	9.97	7.03	10.4
1927–9	10.41	12.45	6.13	3.94	11.87	8.96
1954–6	2.42	12.79	2.96	4.84	4.8	5.56
1970–2	8.23	16.68	−12.63	−0.97		1.57
1998–2000	4.66	15.40	8.84	14.54		10.86
France						
1911–13	16.48	7.83		7.1	34.5	16.48
1927–9	8.85	18.72	7.66	11.42	20.6	13.45
1954–6	1.69	8.95	2.56	4.33	15.19	6.4
1970–2	4.01	6.38	2.79	−1.61		2.90
1998–2000	5.12	10.71	9.01	10.47		8.83
Belgium						
1911–13	6.79	19.77	38.37	16.29	12.61	18.77
1927–9	14.6	36.68	25.09	16.34	50.07	28.56
1954–6	10.05	11.05	30.34	4.54	8.84	12.96
1970–2	1.98	8.01	1.30	3.85		3.79
1998–2000	12.73	25.86	7.92	8.89		13.85
Italy						
1911–13	6.37	11.21	−19.0	5.47	13.67	3.54
1927–9	3.77	5.93	6.24	4.28	6.68	5.38
1954–6	2.81	9.68	7.69	1.95	9.05	6.34
1970–2	−6.95	4.93	2.01	1.80		0.47
1998–2000	7.32	4.28	11.78	14.55		9.48
Spain						
1911–13	9.65	15.5	37.8	10.0	6.45	20.11
1927–9		6.75	5.64	6.32	7.87	6.65
1954–6	4.14	10.62	12.75	22.09	12.55	12.43
1970–2	2.54	10.49	3.53	25.76		8.97
1998–2000	7.11	14.99		24.05		15.38
Sweden						
1911–13	6.05	6.73	18.79	8.36	8.51	22.34
1927–9	3.84	3.75	12.55	7.92	6.22	6.68
1954–6	6.71	8.78	141.78	10.66	14.77	35.88
1970–2	9.30	10.16	7.01	11.13		9.40
1998–2000	13.37	33.67	3.18	9.33		14.89
Finland						
1911–13						
1927–9	1.84	7.62	3.92	4.69	17.17	7.05
1954–6	10.71	9.23	12.56	5.97	5.08	8.71
1970–2	2.75	6.15	3.06	2.43		3.60
1998–2000	10.93	2.27	9.53	−2.68		5.01
Average						
1911–13	11.34	11.03	9.93	9.27	14.06	11.12
1927–9	7.04	14.02	9.3	8.51	16.49	10.87
1954–6	6.52	10.39	18.53	5.73	9.45	10.31
1970–2	2.85	9.73	0.59	3.33		4.15
1998–2000	8.54	16.29	9.78	12.11		11.69

5.56 per cent in 1954–6, while in France in the same period, it declined dramatically from 16.48 to 6.4 per cent. This decline in average returns can certainly be interpreted as an indicator of the Old Industries' structural problems in the twentieth century. The decline in ROE in iron and steel is particularly striking: it fell in Germany from an above-average 15.75 per cent in 1911–13 to 2.42 per cent in 1954–6, and in France from 16.48 to 1.69 per cent. During these years, the profitability in mining was so low in both countries that we can conclude that despite the growth observed in these subsectors, the profitability of their large businesses was extraordinarily hampered. European heavy industry, which suffered from massive overcapacity in the interwar period, attempted to counter this problem by mergers and the formation of cartels, although with limited success.[16] In these years, Vereinigte Stahlwerke AG[17] was established in Germany, whereas in Great Britain the United Steel Company came into being in 1918 in a more haphazard manner.[18] In Belgium, however, where this subsector played just as important a role, this observation is not applicable.[19] Here, the Old Industries' were not only able to realize higher than average yields in the first half of the twentieth century, but in iron and steel profitability also increased from below average in 1911–13 (6.79 per cent) to above average in 1927–9 (14.6 per cent). Other subsectors in Belgium also held up well and were able to attain consistently high returns, particularly in mining (ROE between 25 and 38 per cent). It was the large companies whose main activity was foreign-based as well as those controlled by foreign capital that particularly contributed to the performance of ROE in Belgium. Companies of this sort could also be found in other European states, for example in Spain, where the mining company Rio Tinto played a prominent role, and in Great Britain, with its numerous multinational companies.

The construction of a local iron and steel industry in Italy and Spain, countries on the southern periphery of Europe, is reflected in a considerable increase in capital in the businesses in this Old Industry subsector; profitability, however, remained disappointing. In Italy, the profitability of companies in iron and steel fell from 6.37 per cent in 1911–13 to 2.81 per cent in 1954–6, and in Spain, during the same period, it fell from 9.65 to 4.14 per cent. Subsequent industrialization in these countries came after the industrialization of the core European countries, but it proved only to have limited success. An industrial strategy based on the exploitation of local natural resources, such as was taking place in Sweden, held more promise. Here, rich woodland resources provided the foundations for the emergence and expansion of a significant paper industry, and the exploitation of rich ore deposits (iron and copper) allowed the successful expansion of mining and copper smelting. Similarly, in Finland, local natural resources were the basis

[16] U. Nocken, 'International cartels and foreign policy: The formation of the International Steel Cartel 1924–1926', in C.A. Wurm, *Internationale Kartelle und Aussenpolitik: Beiträge zur Zwischenkriegszeit* (Wiesbaden: Steiner, 1989), pp. 33–82.

[17] A. Reckendrees, *Das 'Stahltrust'-Projekt: Die Gründung der Vereinigten Stahlwerke AG und ihre Unternehmensentwicklung (1926–1933/34)* (München: C.H. Beck Verlag, 2000).

[18] D.S. Landes, *The Unbound Prometheus: Technological Change and Industrial Development in Western Europe from 1750 to the Present* (Cambridge: Cambridge University Press, 1969), p. 467.

[19] Here, as in other Continental European national economies, the iron and steel industry continued to grow in the 1920s. It was only in the 1930s that the appropriate capacity adaptations were undertaken. See Landes, *The Unbound Prometheus*, p. 477.

for the expansion of large businesses, although their capital endowment was comparatively modest.

As previously mentioned, the 1970s brought a structural crisis to the European Old Industries. The experience of the steel industry was typical. The need for structural change in the iron and steel industry had become apparent in the second half of the 1960s. The US was still the largest producer worldwide, but the USSR, Japan, and the European Coal and Steel Community (ECSC) produced increasing quantities for the international market. Although world demand for iron and steel was still growing in these years, there was a clear risk that further expansion in production capacity would lead to an overproduction crisis, which duly happened in the mid 1970s. In response, the European Community (EC) launched a programme to save its steel industry.[20] This programme reduced capacity and introduced a pricing system, aiming at preventing further price decreases. The restructuring of the European steel industry would reduce employment, increase productivity, and induce several mergers in the years to come. It was only one of the many subsectors that would get into deep difficulties. The general pattern for the 1970s was, however, not the same for all subsectors in the Old Industries.

Despite the rather low overall ROE performance in 1970–2, some subsectors of the Old Industries performed better than others. The food, drink, and tobacco subsector, for example, performed well, while several others, such as mining, textiles, and the Mature Industries (steel, metal, and paper) performed poorly. In food, drink, and tobacco, the average ROE was 9.73 per cent, while in mining, textiles, and the Mature Industries, it was 0.59, 3.33, and 2.85 per cent, respectively. The extremely low minimum ROE of −102.85 per cent in mining indicates that some companies in the subsector were in deep trouble.

A closer examination of subsectors, particularly at the company level, indicates that each subsector had some companies that performed rather well even if the subsector overall did not. In the Mature Industries, one company (out of sixteen in the group) had an ROE of at least 10 per cent in 1970–2, namely Mannesmann, a German steel company founded in 1885–90, which originally produced seamless steel tubes. From its foundation, Mannesmann was an international company, with headquarters in Düsseldorf. Over time, it became a diversified conglomerate.[21] In mining, there was also only one company (out of fourteen) that generated an ROE of at least 10 per cent. In textiles, there were three (out of fourteen) with this level of ROE. By contrast, in the food, drink, and tobacco subsector, six of fifteen companies, or over one-third, yielded an ROE of at least 10 per cent.

The European food, drink, and tobacco industry thus performed rather well. The subsector was dominated by companies such as Unilever (UK/the Netherlands), Nestlé (Switzerland), and BSN Gervais-Danone (France). The last named

[20] I.M. Evans, 'Aspects of the steel crisis in Europe, with particular reference to Belgium and Luxembourg', *The Geographical Journal*, 146, 3 (1980), 396–407; European Communities Commission, *Trouble over Steel*, Background Report (31 October 1977); European Communities Commission, *Steel Crisis Measures Extended*, Background Report (16 January 1978).

[21] H.G. Schröter, 'Continuity and change: German multinationals since 1850', in Geoffrey Jones and Harm G. Schröter, eds., *The Rise of Multinationals in Continental Europe* (Aldershot: Edward Elgar, 1993), pp. 28–48.

was the subsector's most important company on the European continent, although its operations in the glass subsector contributed to this leading position. That the sector was performing remarkably well is evidenced by the fact that only two of fourteen companies had an ROE lower than 5 per cent. Deutsche Unilever GmbH (ROE 24.62 per cent) and Associated British Foods (ROE 14.95 per cent) were the subsector's most profitable companies at this time.[22] But British American Tobacco was the real Giant, with assets of $2,999 million and an ROE of 12.67 per cent.

The textiles and leather industry was one of Europe's oldest industries. Nevertheless, the average company size was rather low compared with other subsectors. The Giant was Courtaulds (UK), a European leader in the field of synthetic fibres, with assets of $1,516 million and a ROE of 13.25 per cent. However, the vast majority of the companies in the industry performed much worse, with ten of fourteen companies having an ROE below 5 per cent. This indicates that textiles and leather would become one of the industries to suffer severely in the years to come. At the multilateral level, the Multi-Fibre Arrangement (MFA) was introduced in 1974 as a short-term measure intended to allow developed countries to adjust to imports coming from the developing world, where textiles were produced with low labour costs. On 1 January 1995, the MFA was replaced by the WTO Agreement on Textiles and Clothing, starting a transitional process for the ultimate removal of these quotas. Nevertheless, until the end of 2004, quotas were imposed on the amount developing countries could export to developed countries.[23]

In mining, several older enterprises were in deep trouble in this period. Two German companies—Ruhrkohle AG (with an ROE of −44.5) and Saarbergwerke Aktiengesellschaft (−7.82 per cent)—were in the red, while the Italian AGIP Gruppo ENI (0.7 per cent) and the Belgian Helchteren en Zolder (1.30 per cent) barely made it into the black. The best performer in 1970–2 was the German Rheinische Braunkohlen AG, with an ROE of 14.57 per cent, while four other companies turned a profit of 7 per cent or more: Swedish Boliden AB (7.06 per cent), British-owned Lonrho (9.66 per cent), Rio Tinto-Zinc Corporation (8.08 per cent), and Consolidated Gold Fields (7.06 per cent). The British companies were international mining companies, whereas the less profitable companies were mainly in the European coal mining business. In the years to come many of them would take the path of closing down their old coal mines.

The Mature Industries category was dominated by companies in steel and metallurgy, with some in paper production (Bowater and Enso-Gutzeit Oy). Overall, performance was extremely poor, with ten of sixteen companies earning an ROE below 5 per cent. Such poor profitability would force nearly all of these companies to merge with other firms. For example, in 1997, two of the Spanish steel producers in the 1970–2 sample—Endisesa (0.09 per cent ROE) and Altos Hornos de Viscaya (5.0 per cent ROE)—were absorbed into a new firm, Aceralia, which in 2001, together with the Belgian Cockerill (1.98 per cent ROE) and the

---

[22] See Aszkenazy, *Les grandes sociétés européennes*, pp. 205–31.

[23] C.B. Hamilton, *Textiles Trade and the Developing Countries: Eliminating the Multi-Fibre Arrangement in the 1990s* (Washington, DC: World Bank, 1990); A. Silberston, *The Multi-Fibre Arrangement and the UK Economy* (London: HMSO, 1984).

French Usinor (7.41 per cent ROE), merged into Arcelor, one of the world's largest steel producers at the time of establishment.

When examining the data at country level, it seems that the British companies in the sample performed best. They were, in general, the real super-large companies and had a critical advantage in some sectors because of their dominant position. For example, in food, drink, and tobacco as well as in textiles and leather, they had the best positions. However, many of these companies, for example those in mining, had substantial international operations, implying that UK performance did not represent a typical European business experience. Apart from Sweden, in nearly all other European countries, the levels of ROE were so low that it was taken for granted that nearly all of the companies involved would have to undertake considerable efforts to stop their declining rates of profit.

By 1998–2000, the collective profitability of the Old Industry companies in our sample was turned around. Both the average and median ROE were restored to their historically normal levels: 11.69 and 10.31 per cent respectively. This remarkable recovery was due to three decades of adapting to new economic realities. First, increasing competition prevailed owing to a global wave of globalization. Actually, as trade barriers vanished under the new WTO agreements, the world economy restored pre-1914 globalization. This evidently increased competition and induced companies to respond to this new environment. In Europe, the process was further strengthened by the rapidly evolving process of European unification. One of the key instruments in responding to this challenge was the enormous number of mergers and acquisitions, which increased assets per company, improved productivity, and exploited increasing returns to scale. Second, governments favoured more market-oriented policies with laws that improved access to capital for companies and deregulated capital markets. As a result, the stock market boomed: in 1998–2000, average HR was 23.66 per cent. Third, macroeconomic conditions with regard to price stability and government budgets improved considerably. Inflation rates, which had been at historically high levels in the 1970s and early 1980s, were reduced to relatively low rates, and government deficits were brought down to more manageable levels. Fourth, technological change was evolving rapidly, one of the most important developments being the rapid application of computer technology at the company level.

Old Industry companies participated in this adaptation and recovery. As a group, they succeeded in increasing average ROE to more attractive levels. Food, drink, and tobacco even attained an ROE of 16.29 per cent, followed by textiles and leather goods with 12.11 per cent. By contrast, profitability in mining (9.78 per cent ROE) and the Mature Industries (8.54 per cent ROE) was a little below the overall average in the Old Industries. The majority of the companies were, however, in good condition. In food, drink, and tobacco, eight of thirteen companies had generated an ROE above 10 per cent, in textiles and leather goods six of eleven, in the Mature Industries six of thirteen, and in mining five of thirteen. Really poorly performing companies were clearly a minority. In food, drink, and tobacco, there were only two companies with an ROE under 5 per cent, in textiles and leather goods three, in the Mature Industries four, and in mining three.

The overall picture at the subsector level becomes more diverse once we look at individual companies.

Company profitability in the food, drink, and tobacco subsector was extremely good, with four companies achieving an ROE higher than 20 per cent and four with rates between 10 and 20 per cent. This indicates clearly that in highly developed economies, food and drink processing can be a highly remunerative business with vast potential for new markets. The best performing company was British American Tobacco, with an ROE of 37.47 per cent. Diageo and Cadbury Schweppes, both British as well, also earned attractive returns of 22.10 and 19.46 per cent, respectively. But the Swedish AB Vin & Sprit (33.67 per cent) and the Belgian Spadel (25.86 per cent) had even better earnings.

Textiles and leather goods had the second highest overall ROE, and several of the subsector's companies were very profitable. The German-owned Hugo Boss AG was the top company, with an ROE of 29.29 per cent, followed by the Spanish Inditex, with 24.05 per cent. Four companies, among them the Italian companies Benetton Group and Edizione (Benetton), returned between 10 and 20 per cent on equity. Only three companies in the subsector had an ROE below 5 per cent.

Mining companies had recovered their profitability by the end of the century, with five of thirteen companies having an ROE above 10 per cent and only three having earnings below 5 per cent. The German K+S AG topped the list with an ROE of 18.89 per cent, followed by the Italian ENI (17.27 per cent), and two British companies, Rio Tinto (14.87 per cent) and Lonmin (14.05 per cent).

In the Mature Industries, there was only one company with a really high ROE, namely Bunzl from the UK (27.54 per cent), followed at a fair distance by SCA from Sweden (13.37 per cent), Bekaert from Belgium (12.73 per cent), Stora ENSO from Finland (10.93 per cent), Riva Acciaio from Italy (10.84 per cent), and the British Billiton (10.21 per cent).

From a country perspective, it seems that the Old Industries in the UK were the most profitable in Europe, with a 16.32 per cent ROE. This performance is probably the consequence of the international character of the British companies in the sample, which raises the question of whether they are generally representative of European enterprise. However, the Old Industries in several other countries—Belgium, Germany, Spain, and Sweden—also had a collective ROE above 10 per cent in 1998–2000. Italy and France were not far behind, with ROEs of over 8 per cent, while Finnish Old Industry companies clearly struggled (5.01 per cent). Thus, by the end of the twentieth century, the Old Industries in five of eight countries studied had succeeded in restoring ROE to historically average levels.

HOLDING RETURN

Whereas ROE is a short-term measure of business success relating to current business trends, the holding return (HR), which also encompasses the change in a business's share prices, should be considered a measure of the capital market's expectations of a company's future business performance. Data on the levels of HR at different times (Table 11.5) thus complement our findings on the profitability of European large businesses, in particular regarding whether a business's

Table 11.5. HR in subsectors of the Old Industries, 1911–2000 (in %)

	Iron and steel	Food	Mining	Textiles	Wood and paper	Mean
UK						
1911–13	12.15	22.34	−1.2	7.09	5.32	11.44
1927–9	−12.83	10.51	−17.5	−1.64	−3.79	−5.05
1954–6	20.35	13.12	5.22	6.78	6.29	10.35
1970–2	8.57	8.42	−3.58	19.59		8.25
1998–2000	5.37	13.99	111.59			43.65
Germany						
1911–13	−0.3	6.35	2.23	−0.56	−0.22	1.5
1927–9	8.56	−9.84	−6.31	0.21	5.49	−0.37
1954–6	13.48	42.83	10.38	10.38	26.27	21.87
1970–2	5.39	14.23		25.84		15.15
1998–2000	−42.98		32.04	4.02		−2.31
France						
1911–13	6.74	22.46	4.23	0.39	10.61	8.9
1927–9	61.29	8.35	47.9	37.71	30.01	37.05
1954–6	13.45	22.57	23.33	12.45	44.07	27.77
1970–2	0.13	2.16	−26.93	8.31		−4.08
1998–2000	32.04	8.59	1.67	7.18		12.37
Belgium						
1911–13	30.96	1.16	−0.10	6.28	−9.12	5.84
1927–9	39.82	20.34	7.93	54.41	44.93	33.49
1954–6	48.98	16.93	32.45	22.24	22.24	29.6
1970–2	−1.57	27.52	28.09	25.73		19.94
1998–2000	1.57	11.32	−6.79	78.02		28.04
Italy						
1911–13	4.82	2.71	11.63	−10.95	5.35	2.72
1927–9	15.33	32.93	5.27	−7.75	−35.0	2.16
1954–6	36.99	19.24		10.82		22.35
1970–2	−24.50		19.00	4.10		−0.47
1998–2000	19.29	32.88	6.03	17.59		18.95
Spain						
1911–13	13.35	2.8			9.0	8.38
1927–9		17.97				17.97
1954–6	41.19	12.77			20.9	27.29
1970–2	16.67	29.91				23.29
1998–2000	−8.59	19.72				5.57
Sweden						
1911–13	−10.7	2.7			6.6	−2.27
1927–9	16.03	1.67			11.2	9.63
1954–6	−0.33	6.33			30.2	12.07
1970–2	−6.97		−6.30	−13.40		−8.89
1998–2000	6.55	−8.30		14.40		4.22
Finland						
1911–13						
1927–9	15.8	17.4	26.77	10.5	−18.9	4.0
1954–6		11.2		37.27	20.73	23.07
1970–2	37.60	22.97		8.33		22.97
1998–2000	40.13		5.27			22.70
Average						
1911–13	8.85	11.62	1.05	0.53	4.94	5.7
1927–9	17.59	10.97	11.79	10.05	11.42	12.46
1954–6	25.34	19.9	16.29	15.12	25.32	20.72
1970–2	0.56	13.77	−2.98	13.34		6.25
1998–2000	17.20	15.65	43.19	17.03		23.66

profitability, as expressed in its ROE, was perceived as sustainable by the capital markets or not.

During the period covered, the capital markets seem to have remained optimistic in spite of the economic and political crises and catastrophes in the first half of the twentieth century: the HRs of all large businesses in the Old Industries grew on average from 5.7 per cent (1911–13) to 12.46 per cent (1927–9), and even to 20.72 per cent (1954–6). However, this overall trend clearly varies over time as well as by subsector and country. While it is true that the HR mostly increased in many national economies in Europe between the beginning and the middle of the century, the interwar period in the respective countries reveals an extremely conflicting picture. On average, the HRs of large businesses in German and British Old Industry were negative.[24] Capital markets evidently had pessimistic expectations of the sector's chances of development in general. For the iron and steel industry in Great Britain, the HR of −12.83 per cent in 1927–9 indicates that the markets' expectations were clearly low, if not negative. The pessimism also applied to the mining subsector in Britain and Germany with HR of −17.5 and −6.31 per cent, respectively. Clearly, these two leading sectors of industrialization in Europe's largest economies were no longer considered capable of profitable development. This lack of investor confidence coupled with growing international competition plunged these two subsectors into a serious crisis.

Such was evidently not the case in Belgium and France, where energetic efforts to modernize the mining industry were undertaken after the First World War. The interwar HR of the Old Industries in both countries was high: 33.49 per cent in Belgium and 37.05 per cent in France. These high HR levels were not reached again until the middle of the century. The capital market signalled extremely positive expectations with regard to the development of the Belgian and French Old Industries, with high HR values in several subsectors. They were particularly high for iron and steel and for mining in France and for iron and steel and for wood and paper in Belgium.

A less uniform picture emerges when we move from the core European countries to the countries on the northern and southern periphery. The increased variability is partly due to less developed national capital markets, which were therefore unable to completely fulfil their function of indicating the profitability of capital investments. Moreover, the limits of our data collection become particularly clear here, since for several companies and subsectors there is no HR to measure. Investments in British stocks and shares were therefore valued rather prudently before the middle of the twentieth century, and appropriate HRs were only seldom achieved. HR figures remained in single digits for the large part, occasionally reaching negative values, and did not evolve according to any pattern or regularity. It was only by the middle of the twentieth century (1954–6) that Old Industry companies in the European periphery attained HRs of similar levels to those in the core countries.

---

[24] D.L. Burn, *The Economic History of Steelmaking 1867–1939* (Cambridge: Cambridge University Press, 1961), p. 433, calls the 1920s a 'Black Decade' for British industry. The years of the Weimar Republic in Germany were also shaped by numerous economic crises; see A. Ritschl, *Deutschlands Krise und Konjunktur 1924–1934: Binnenkonjunktur, Auslandsverschuldung und Reparationsproblem zwischen Dawes-Plan und Transfersperre* (Berlin: Akademie Verlag, 2002).

How did investors expect the future to pan out from the 1970s onwards? Although HR data are highly dependent on short-run perspectives of the business cycle as well as on long-term perspectives regarding long-run performance, they can give some indications. Table 11.5 gives clear indications of the market's view of the economic prospects. Mining shows the darkest HR figures, with −2.98 per cent for the average HR (the median HR is −11.80 per cent); the figures for the Mature Industries were similarly grim, with 0.56 per cent for the average HR (the median HR is −4.08 per cent). By contrast, the food, drink, and tobacco and the textiles and leather goods industries had rather good HR figures.

At the end of the century, HR performance was also unusually high, with an average HR for the mining subsector at 43.19 per cent. The median HR was, however, generally speaking, rather low, indicating that high performances were due to the limited number of companies in the sample. The extremely high HR volatility points to the exceptional circumstances on the stock exchange during the 1990s, with booming returns. As investors' expectations of the future stock returns were extremely optimistic at the time, the high HR performances come as no surprise. Rather soon, however, the high hopes would prove to be an enormous bull market bubble that collapsed in the early twenty-first century.

CONCLUSIONS

Since the picture presented in this chapter is based on samples, it is by no means complete. Nonetheless, some prudent conclusions can be drawn. With due caution, it can be stated that the average ROE consistently fluctuated around 10 per cent throughout the entire twentieth century. Only the 1970–2 period was characterized by a low average ROE of only 4.15 per cent. Around that time, the abnormally high economic growth rates of the post-Second World War decades came to an end and were followed by stagnation and recession in the 1970s and 1980s. By the turn of the century, the average ROE had recovered its customary level of around 10 per cent, thanks to both sectoral and economy-wide adjustment. The 1990s brought important changes to the European economies, with an enormous number of mergers and acquisitions and rapid technological change being only a couple of examples. Although British big business generally performed best, the leading edge in entrepreneurial performance undeniably shifted from Northern to Southern Europe (particularly to Italy and Spain). The performance of the HR, which reflects expectations in the stock markets, showed a high degree of volatility.

12

The Performance of 'Chandlerian Enterprises'

Harm G. Schröter

This chapter deals with enterprises in chemicals and pharmaceuticals, oil and rubber and other non-metallic industries, electrical engineering and electronics, mechanical engineering, and transport equipment. In *economic* history, these branches are customarily associated with the Second Industrial Revolution that commenced around 1870. In calling them 'Chandlerian enterprises', we underline that our perspective here derives from the concerns of *business* history: the label also honours the late Alfred D. Chandler, whose pioneering work so excellently described and explained the processes of growth and performance in these groups of enterprises: 'Chandler is *the* historian of the Second Industrial Revolution' [my emphasis, H.G.S.][1]—Chapter 2 of this volume provides the necessary information on the definition and selection of these enterprises, and it need not be repeated here. Still, the reader may be reminded that our selection of the so-called 'new industries' represents the largest single group in the study's database: 1,013 out of 3,366 valid observations.

For brevity, we will use only one year to express the results of the three-year average always provided in the figures, consequently '1913' stands for the average of 1911, 1912, and 1913, and so on. For the same reason, we use slightly abbreviated group designations: 'oil' stands for the whole group of 'oil and rubber' and 'chemicals' for 'chemicals and pharmaceuticals'. We decided not to distinguish between chemical and pharmaceutical firms because the overall sizes of the groups of firms within the samples used here and those used elsewhere in this book should correspond and also because in Europe these firms were often identical, being active in both fields at least up to the 1990s. Similar considerations led to the inclusion of oil, rubber, and other non-metal industries in a single group; before 1914, business statistics grouped these activities together, so we had no choice but to treat them as one group up to that date.

---

[1] Amatori, Franco, 'Business history: state of the art and controversies', *Entreprises et Histoire*, 55 (2009), 11–23 (p. 15). A.D. Chandler, Jr, *Scale and Scope: The Dynamics of Industrial Capitalism* (Cambridge: Cambridge University Press, 1990); A.D. Chandler, F. Amatori, and T. Hikino, eds., *Big Business and the Wealth of Nations* (Cambridge: Cambridge University Press, 1997).

Our project has focused on enterprises rather than on countries. Consequently, especially in the chapters in this book on European branches of industries, the reader will receive much more information at the level of companies than at the level of countries. Concerning this last dimension, we can answer such questions as the extent to which our sample mirrors business development in individual countries—for instance first-movers versus latecomers: Were the leading countries of 1913 still the leading ones in 2000? However, in the context of our project, such country leadership in fact means leading enterprises operating in or registered in the specific states in question. Thus, our answer is much more specific: namely, to what extent were the leading Chandlerian firms in 1913 still playing in the top league in 2000? In short, the core of information provided here concerns the performance of enterprises and not that of countries.

THE CHANDLERIAN INDUSTRIAL GROUP

Our Chandlerian industrial group comprises mainly enterprises that grew particularly during the Second Industrial Revolution. This phase of industrialization was characterized by the application of science and scientific methods to both production and management. In several seminal tomes, Alfred D. Chandler analysed this transformation in both North America and Europe, pointing out the importance of innovation and technology. Over time, not only specific products but also entire branches of industries, such as the textile industry, experienced phases of rapid growth, stagnation, and relative decline. Within this Chandlerian group, electrical engineering and chemicals in particular enjoyed vigorous upswings during the first half of the twentieth century. In industrial chemicals, the 1960s marked the end of earlier major breakthroughs such as high-pressure chemistry and artificial fibres, but the related area of pharmaceuticals entered a phase of rapid growth from the 1980s. Electrical engineering followed a parallel trend. Here it was telecommunications and electronics that revived a certain part of the industrial group, also from about the 1980s. A third example is the transport equipment sector, where the focus changed from production of sea transport (shipbuilding) to that of road and air transport (motor vehicles and airplanes). Mechanical engineering and oil did not experience similar technological shifts of their centre of gravity. Thus, the Chandlerian group in the twentieth century contains two branches with roughly stable product development and three with a substantial change of focus. The contrast provokes several questions: Is the longevity of enterprises a function of product stability; in other words, do firms in the two more stable branches have a greater longevity than those in the changing ones? Is the business performance of enterprises in the three branches characterized by product transformation more volatile than that in the two more stable ones?

ULTIMATE PERFORMANCE: LONGEVITY

'Longevity' here means, of course, continued presence of an enterprise in our sample.[2] If the relative size and importance of a specific enterprise in its country's economy declined to such an extent that it no longer qualified for inclusion in our sample, it ceased to exist for the project even though in fact it continued in operation. Thus, in our study, 'longevity' reflects an enterprise's capability to maintain its ranking in the respective *national* environment. Our method does not allow sharp pan-European comparisons: a given company included in one country sample might be much smaller in fact than three parallel firms in another country which were excluded from that country's sample. The reason would be that in the second country there were other enterprises which were even larger than the three first mentioned. What we want to compare is not so much size per se but relative performance in the varying environments of different European countries. Table 12A.1 in the Appendix to this chapter provides an overview of the enterprises contained in each benchmark. It shows that sixteen enterprises were included in four of the project's five benchmarks, while five enterprises appeared in all of them. Thus, we have twenty-one Chandlerian firms that managed to stay in leading economic positions through much of the twentieth century. Because of the different nature of the industrial branches in which these firms operated, we presume that longevity would be unevenly distributed among them. At the same time, we expect longevity to be evenly distributed across countries on the assumption that economic competition evens out political differences. How do these hypotheses fare when confronted by the data?

The transport equipment branch contains two enterprises that figured in each benchmark between 1913 and 2000: namely, Fiat and Peugeot. Two other well-known firms, Daimler-Benz and Vickers, showed up four times. Yet a closer look at the sector's productive activities reveals profound changes over time. In 1913, eight of twelve firms were engaged in the construction of ships, both naval and mercantile. In 1927, the number of firms producing cars and lorries equalled the number of shipyards, and in all later benchmarks the production of land vehicles dominated the sector, with airplane construction gaining in importance in 1972 and 2000. There are no shipbuilding companies in our sample at the end of the twentieth century. Thus, in this sector longevity characterized exclusively the producers of motor vehicles, which at the beginning of twentieth century made up a very small part of the group.

Economic logic suggests that stability, and hence firm longevity, should dominate in the oil (i.e. oil and rubber) branch. The branch's operations are capital-intensive with large barriers to entry, and its companies offer relatively similar products. Under these conditions, it is not easy for newcomers to establish themselves and even harder for them to become large players—and thus be included in our samples. In 1913, we have to distinguish between firms engaged in the production of oil, rubber, and non-metal products and those in chemicals.

---

[2] According to Cassis, survival is one of the most relevant non-financial measurements of efficiencies: Y. Cassis, *Big Business: The European Experience in the Twentieth Century* (Oxford: Oxford University Press, 1997), p. 102.

Our sample of enterprises in that year is entirely dominated by chemical companies; in 1913, this branch and the economy as a whole were still based on coal and its derivatives. By 1927, the picture had changed markedly: oil companies were now in the majority, joined by a few rubber producers. This distribution remained stable until 2000. Taking into account forerunners of later companies—such the Deutsch-Amerikanische-Petroleum Gesellschaft, the German branch of Esso—the composition of enterprises in the branch also remained relatively unchanged. Shell (UK), Total (Cie Française des Pétroles) (France), BP (UK), and Petrofina (Belgium) remained stable in the sample, although only Shell counted as large in each of the benchmarks. Rubber companies also exhibited considerable longevity. Michelin (France) qualified for inclusion in four of five benchmarks. Because the branch lumped oil and rubber producers together, the significance of Pirelli appearing more often than Dunlop should not be over-stressed. The UK's position in oil was so strong that Dunlop's inclusion was trumped by oil companies. The notion that the group of oil, rubber, and other non-metallic mineral products was totally dominated by oil firms is not entirely correct though, for there were as many as eight rubber companies in our sample over time. As for companies in 'other non-metallic mineral products', however, there are only a few, such as Glaces Nationales Belges Saint-Roch Auvelais or Saint-Gobain.

The perhaps most stable group of Chandlerian enterprises was chemicals. Many well-known names—Bayer, BASF, and ICI, including those who changed names by merger—appeared in benchmark after benchmark. However, this stability was broken after 1972, and in 2000 the disruption was mirrored by the newcomers AstraZeneca, Aventis, and GlaxoSmithKline, all pharmaceutical companies. Indeed, pharmaceutical and cosmetic enterprises accounted for one-third of the group in the 2000 sample. Only one of the traditional chemical companies, Bayer, managed the full switch from industrial chemicals to pharmaceuticals. Still, despite the rapid expansion of pharmaceuticals, enterprises in the chemicals group, as in the oil group, exhibit a substantial degree of longevity.

In electrical engineering, though, we would presume longevity to be less marked. This group's activities are probably more differentiated than in oil and rubber or in chemicals and pharmaceuticals. From the beginning, there were three large sectors—generation and distribution of high-voltage energy, low-voltage telecommunications, and electrochemistry—to which came a fourth sector—electronics—in the last quarter of the twentieth century. Except for Siemens (Siemens-Schuckert Werke and Siemens & Halske) and Alcatel (Alcatel Alsthom Compagnie Générale d'Electricité), which managed to combine the first two sectors, all other enterprises operated exclusively or primarily in only one field of the two. Although the composition of the sample was unaffected by the introduction of nuclear power in the 1950s, it does reflect the surge in information technology from the 1980s. The break is particularly clear in the sectors of energy generation and telecommunications, whose firms had remained fairly stable to 1972. Between then and the end of the century, a major shake-up occurred. In 2000, only Alsthom, Bosch, General Electric Company (since 1999 Marconi), and Siemens were carry-overs from earlier benchmarks; the large majority of the sample consisted of newly included firms. The newcomers were partly established firms that previously had not qualified for the sample, such as Ericsson. But the majority consisted either of completely new companies, such as Logica, or of older firms that had been reconstructed so thoroughly that few traces of the former enterprise remained, such as Nokia. In sum, our presumption regarding longevity was partly right: there was a profound break in company continuity during the last quarter of the twentieth century, although up to 1972 the sample's membership was quite stable.

In the mechanical engineering branch, we find, as anticipated, a lot of variation. No company made all the benchmarks, although Gutehoffnungshütte/MAN came close. It was included in 1913, 1927, 1972, and 2000, but not in 1954. However, between 1913 and 1972, there was considerable longevity. Four companies made it into all benchmarks during this period: Ansado, Vickers, Fives-Lille, and Babcock & Wilcox. Babcock's inclusion was complex. In 1913, 1929, and 1954, it appeared as a British company, but in 1954, it also appeared as a German firm, Deutsche Babcock & Wilcox; in 1972, it also had two inclusions: as a foreign direct investment in Spain and an independent French firm. In the century's last two benchmarks, the companies included in the branch's sample fluctuated a good deal.

Longevity seems to have been unrelated to a company being a national champion in a particular industrial branch. There were exceptions of course, but the majority of enterprises could not maintain the same level of performance over the entire century. Even the largest enterprises were exposed to the pressures of competition, which could force even large dinosaurs into decline and eventual extinction. But the economic and technological differences between the branches of Chandlerian enterprises did not result in accompanying differences in firm longevity as we had anticipated. The number of long-term survivors in electrical engineering was six, in oil five, in chemicals and in transport equipment four, and in mechanical engineering three. This is quite an even distribution. Thus, the initial proposition that a profound change in a branch's technological base—or its absence—would be decisive for enterprise longevity in the branch cannot be sustained. At the level of enterprise, there were considerable turnover in all branches. Although new technologies in electrical engineering and in chemicals brought many new companies into the branch samples, the proportion of newcomers in mechanical engineering was roughly similar despite the absence of any technological breakthrough. In the latter branch, it was incremental change and competition that limited longevity. It seems that, with a very few exceptions, the sands of time wear down everything.

Our second thesis of an even distribution of long-lived large enterprises between countries is also not supported by the evidence. In Table 12A.1 in the Appendix at the end of this chapter, which lists all enterprises' dates of inclusion by name and country of origin, we find seven French, six German, five British, three Italian, and one Swedish entries. At first glance, it seems clear that company longevity is a function of country size, but the actual order of distribution cannot be easily explained. Logically, France should follow Germany and the UK. Were French firms protected by their country's well-known étatist economic policies? Were German enterprises protected by the power of the German universal banks (so-called Deutschland AG)? Was there more competition in the UK than on the Continent? The smaller number of long-lasting Italian firms might be related to their smaller total number in our sample, but this fact itself could be a derivative of the country's smaller size. Clearly, much more research on the basis of much more data needs to be done before these questions can be answered and related to the perennial conundrum of the 'varieties of capitalism'.[3]

FINANCIAL PERFORMANCE

First some methodological remarks: in this section we discuss only substantial differences; for instance, the difference in mean return on equity (ROE) of all Chandlerian firms in 1913 (12.08 per cent) compared with that of mechanical engineering (12.36 per cent) is considered to be insignificant and hence will not be presented here.[4] Unless stated otherwise, all means and medians mentioned in this chapter refer to the Chandlerian firms—not to the averages for all enterprises of the economy. Finally, the discussion integrates the presentation of ROE and holding return (HR) according to benchmark years and then in long-term comparison rather than having a section on ROE followed by one on HR. We will focus on contrasts and contradictions, but also point out what confirms traditional views and interpretations.

Average ROE for all Chandlerian companies in 1913 was 12.08 per cent, but the ROE for individual firms varied considerably (Table 12.1). ROE for the glass producer Glaces Nationales Belge (Belgium) was by far the highest. Belges Saint-Roch Auvelais (Belgium), Air Liquide (France), Fabrique Nationale (Belgium), Bayer (Germany), Hoechst (Germany), and Minerva Motors (Belgium) also earned returns that were at least double the group average. It is noteworthy that one-half of the most profitable firms were located in Belgium. HR is by definition much more volatile than ROE; to identify outliers, we therefore look for deviations that were at least three times greater (or less) than the average HR of 8.01 per cent. British Westinghouse (UK) clearly stands out with an HR nearly ten times the average! Alais Froges (France) and Société Alsacienne de constructions mécaniques (France) were also top performers in HR. Only one company, the Belgium mechanical engineering firm Fabrique Nationale, achieved outstanding results in both ROE and HR. On the other hand, we find five enterprises with a negative HR that was three times lower than the average: Babcock & Wilcox (UK), Officine Sesto (Italy), Saint Gobain (France), United Alkali (UK), and Vulkan-Werke (Germany). United Alkali stands out with a very negative HR of −36.45 per cent. On the eve of the First World War, it was well known that the British company's outdated technology doomed it to lose out to the Belgian Solvay.

In 1927, the group average ROE stood at 8.86 per cent, a decline of roughly one-quarter compared with 1913. Interestingly, the top performer was substantially unchanged. Again by far the highest ROE was generated by a Belgian glass producer (Glaces Nationales Belges-Glaces de Saint Roch Auvelais) (Table 12.2). Only three other firms earned twice the average ROE: the French Michelin and Rhône Poulenc and the German Siemens & Halske. HR presented a more composite picture, even when limiting our view to results that deviated more

---

[3] P.A. Hall and D. Soskice,eds., *Varieties of Capitalism: The Institutional Foundations of Comparative Advantage* (Oxford: Oxford University Press, 2001); R Whitley, ed., *Competing Capitalisms: Institutions and Economies*, Vol. 2 (Edward Elgar: Cheltenham, 2002).

[4] For fuller information on these issues, the reader should consult the Appendix to this volume.

Table 12.1. ROE and HR for Chandlerian companies in 1911–13 (in %)

Country	Company	Branch	ROE	HR
Italy	A.E.G. Thomson Houston	Electrical engineering	5.41	
Sweden	AB Separator	Mechanical engineering	10.11	6.07
France	Air Liquide	Oil, rubber	24.90	4.90
France	Alais, Froges, Camargue	Oil, rubber	8.40	51.10
Germany	Allgemeine Elektricitäts-Gesellschaft (AEG)	Electrical engineering	12.96	2.21
France	Alsacienne de constructions mécaniques	Mechanical engineering	12.99	49.17
Sweden	ASwedenA	Electrical engineering	7.37	22.00
Spain	Astillero del Nervión	Transport equipment		
Belgium	Ateliers Construction Electriques de Charleroi	Electrical engineering	6.43	10.33
France	Ateliers et chantiers de Saint Nazaire (Penhoët)	Transport equipment	11.89	11.13
UK	Babcock & Wilcox	Mechanical engineering	20.33	−13.06
Germany	BASF	Oil, rubber	22.74	8.18
UK	British Thomson-Houston Company	Electrical engineering	5.16	
UK	British Westinghouse Electric & Manufacturing Company	Electrical engineering	4.01	79.17
France	Chantiers de la Loire	Transport equipment	8.59	1.48
France	Compagnie Générale d'Electricité	Electrical engineering	12.46	3.07
Belgium	Fabrique Nationale	Mechanical engineering	28.46	28.09
Germany	Bayer AG	Oil, rubber	26.72	6.09
Germany	Höchst AG	Oil, rubber	26.71	9.80
Italy	FIAT (Fabbrica italiana automobili Torino)	Transport equipment	8.42	−0.59
France	Fives-Lille	Mechanical engineering	13.34	6.80
Belgium	Glaces Nation. Belges Saint-Roch Auvelais	Oil, rubber	56.93	4.17
Sweden	Höganäs-Billesholm AB	Oil, rubber	7.40	1.57
UK	Howard & Bullough	Mechanical engineering	12.65	17.09
France	Jeumont	Electrical engineering	6.39	
UK	John Brown & Company	Transport equipment	7.59	5.10
Sweden	Kockums Mekaniska verkstadaktiebolag	Transport equipment	−1.76	
UK	Kynoch	Mechanical engineering	7.85	13.66
UK	Lever Brothers	Oil, rubber	7.15	6.24
Germany	Mannesmannröhren-Werke	Mechanical engineering	11.83	5.92
Germany	Maschinenbau-Anstalt 'Humboldt'	Mechanical engineering	15.09	−0.19
Germany	MAN/Gutehoffungshütte	Mechanical engineering	10.54	13.39
UK	Metropolitan Carriage Wagon & Finance Company	Electrical engineering	13.13	11.61
Belgium	Minerva Motors	Transport equipment	32.85	11.85
Italy	Officine meccaniche Stigler	Mechanical engineering	8.18	
Italy	Officine Sesto San Giovanni & Valsecchi Abramo	Mechanical engineering	3.95	−13.57
France	Peugeot	Transport equipment	11.87	4.74
France	Saint-Gobain	Oil, rubber	7.32	−13.23
UK	Shell Transp. & Trading Comp.	Oil, rubber	13.24	15.28
Germany	Siemens & Halske AG	Electrical engineering	20.05	1.89
Germany	Siemens-Schuckertwerke, GmbH	Electrical engineering	14.25	
UK	Sir W.G. Armstrong, Whitworth & Co.	Transport equipment	8.20	6.98
Spain	Sociedad Española de Construcciones Metálicas	Mechanical engineering	6.50	
Italy	Società anonima italiana Gio. Ansaldo & C.	Transport equipment	5.70	
Italy	Società italiana per il carburo di calcio	Oil, rubber	7.68	4.24
Belgium	Société des Glaces Nationales Belges	Oil, rubber	10.95	5.08
France	Société française de constructions mécaniques	Mechanical engineering	11.17	8.08
Italy	Tecnomasio italiano Brown Boveri	Electrical engineering	5.37	
France	Thomson-Houston	Electrical engineering	4.53	0.90
Spain	Unión Española de Explosivos	Oil, rubber	15.90	−2.10
Italy	Unione ital. fra consum.... chimici	Oil, rubber	5.24	1.24
UK	United Alkali Company	Oil, rubber	4.93	−36.45
Belgium	Val-Saint-Lambert a Seraing	Oil, rubber	8.33	6.37
UK	Vickers	Transport equipment	9.30	7.81
Germany	Vulkan-Werke, Hamburg und Stettin	Transport equipment	4.61	−13.06

Source: Data set

Table 12.2. ROE and HR for Chandlerian companies in 1927–9 (in %)

Country	Company	Branch	ROE	HR
Finland	Ab Crichton-Vulcan Oy	Transport equipment	4.00	−35.62
Sweden	AB Separator	Mechanical engineering	8.05	20.63
Germany	Adam Opel AG	Transport equipment	−3.71	
Germany	Allgemeine Elektricitäts-Gesellschaft (AEG)	Electrical engineering	7.80	11.54
UK	Anglo-Persian Oil	Oil, rubber	14.38	−0.62
Italy	Ansaldo	Mechanical engineering	−3.24	9.21
UK	Armstrong, Whitworth Securities	Transport equipment	−2.26	20.00
Spain	Arrendataria del Monop. de Petrol. 'Campsa'	Oil, rubber	7.68	−2.55
Sweden	ASEA	Electrical engineering	5.52	27.77
UK	Associated Electrical Industries	Electrical engineering	4.43	9.81
Belgium	Ateliers Constructions de Charleroi	Electrical engineering	9.34	27.42
UK	Babcock & Wilcox	Mechanical engineering	12.10	9.76
UK	British Thomson-Houston	Electrical engineering	3.70	
UK	Cammell Laird	Mechanical engineering	−1.24	−20.48
Italy	Cantiere Navale Triestino	Transport equipment	4.90	1.42
France	Citroën	Transport equipment	3.16	63.55
Italy	Compagnia Italiana Italcable	Electrical engineering	7.49	2.35
Belgium	Compagnie Belge pour les Industries Chimiques	Chemicals and pharmaceuticals	8.82	27.82
France	Compagnie Française des Pétroles	Oil, rubber	−0.32	
France	Compagnie Générale d'Electricité	Electrical engineering	12.72	33.36
Germany	Daimler-Benz AG	Transport equipment	1.56	−21.73
Germany	Demag AG	Mechanical engineering	6.30	
Germany	Deutsch-Amerikanische-Petroleum Gesellschaft	Oil, rubber	11.30	
Germany	Deutsche Erdöl-AG	Oil, rubber	7.37	−12.92
UK	Dunlop	Oil, rubber	11.26	−14.52
Spain	Espanola de Construccion Naval, Sociedad	Transport equipment	9.20	22.96
Spain	Espanola de Construcciones Electromecanicas, Soc.	Electrical engineering	4.03	
Italy	FIAT	Transport equipment	10.37	9.67
Belgium	Fabrique Nationale d'Armes de Guerre	Mechanical engineering	7.07	72.93
Finland	Finska Färg och Fernissfabriks A.B.	Chemicals and pharmaceuticals	10.25	
France	Fives-Lille	Mechanical engineering	11.19	20.26
UK	General Electric Company	Electrical engineering	9.09	12.82
Belgium	Glaces Nationales Belges (Saint Roch Auvelais)	Oil, rubber	61.38	23.10
Sweden	Götaverken	Transport equipment	9.68	15.57
UK	Harland and Wolff	Transport equipment	1.39	−8.36
Germany	Henschel & Sohn AG	Transport equipment	−4.13	
Sweden	Höganäs-Billesholm AB	Oil, rubber	4.34	22.80
France	Huiles de Pétrole/BP	Oil, rubber	3.45	
Germany	IG Farbenindustrie AG	Chemicals and pharmaceuticals	10.41	−13.79
UK	Imperial Chemical Industries	Chemicals and pharmaceuticals	7.26	16.83
France	Jeumont	Electrical engineering	8.50	52.51
Germany	Kali-Industrie-AG	Chemicals and pharmaceuticals	11.17	33.53
Finland	Kone- ja Siltarakennus Oy	Mechanical engineering	5.85	−0.27
UK	Lever Brothers	Chemicals and pharmaceuticals	9.42	14.74
Germany	M.A.N.–Maschinenfabrik Augsburg-Nürnberg	Mechanical engineering	11.56	−14.04

(*continued*)

Table 12.2. Continued

Country	Company	Branch	ROE	HR
Belgium	Man. Liégoise de Caoutchouc . . . Englebert	Transport equipment	16.42	204.4
France	Michelin	Oil, rubber	26.41	
Italy	Montecatini	Chemicals and pharmaceuticals	10.37	19.54
Italy	Officine Elettriche Genovesi	Electrical engineering	7.29	75.89
France	Peugeot	Transport equipment	12.88	27.79
UK	Platt Brothers	Mechanical engineering	1.30	−36.32
France	Produits chimiques et électrométallurgiques d'Alais	Chemicals and pharmaceuticals	15.64	40.56
UK	Reckitt	Chemicals and pharmaceuticals	17.18	0.99
Germany	Rhenania-Ossag Mineralölwerke AG	Oil, rubber	1.53	
France	Rhône Poulenc	Chemicals and pharmaceuticals	25.22	28.40
Italy	Romsa	Oil, rubber	6.34	
Germany	Rütgerswerke-AG	Chemicals and pharmaceuticals	5.03	−15.15
France	Saint Nazaire Penhoët	Transport equipment	1.69	18.20
France	Saint-Gobain	Chemicals and pharmaceuticals	9.53	21.30
UK	Shell Transp. & Trading Comp.	Oil, rubber	16.67	6.76
Germany	Siemens & Halske AG	Electrical engineering	19.98	21.14
Germany	Siemens-Schuckertwerke AG	Electrical engineering	12.82	48.02
Germany	Singer Nähmaschinen Aktienges.	Mechanical engineering	5.82	
Italy	Snia-Viscosa	Chemicals and pharmaceuticals	4.97	−12.08
Spain	Sociedad Espanola de Construcciones Metalicas	Mechanical engineering		
Italy	Societa Ital. Ernesto Breda per Costr. Meccaniche	Mechanical engineering	5.06	5.66
Italy	Societa Italiana Pirelli	Oil, rubber	10.57	14.45
France	Société alsacienne de constructions mécaniques	Mechanical engineering	15.90	160.49
Belgium	Société Financière des Caoutchouc (Socfin)	Oil, rubber	11.87	−15.13
Finland	Suomen Gummitehdas Oy	Oil, rubber	9.78	
Finland	Suomen Sähkö Oy Gottfr. Strömberg	Electrical engineering	5.60	−4.87
Sweden	Svenska Tändsticksaktiebolaget	Chemicals and pharmaceuticals	10.12	10.40
France	Thomson-Houston	Electrical engineering	4.88	49.95
Spain	Union Espanola de Explosivos, S.A.	Chemicals and pharmaceuticals	16.40	59.07
UK	Vickers	Transport equipment	5.95	2.36

Source: Data set

than three times the average value of 19.49 per cent. The HR of the French rubber company Manufacture Liégeoise de Caoutchouc Souple, Durci et Gutta-Percha O. Englebert fils et Cie, exceeded this average tenfold, while the French mechanical engineering firm Société alsacienne de constructions mécaniques recorded an HR that was eight times higher than the group average! This last firm was surely a crown jewel for investors, since its HR was very high in both 1913 and 1927. Four other enterprises also recorded an HR that exceeded the average threefold: Citroot (France), Officine Elettriche Genovesi (Italy), Union Espanola de Explosivos, S.A. (Spain), and Fabrique Nationale (Belgium), repeating its performance in 1913. However, in 1927, there were more bad performers than in 1913. Investors in AB Crichton-Vulcan Oy (Finland), Cammell Laird (UK), Daimler-Benz (Germany), and Platt Brothers (UK) had to settle for an HR that was three times lower than the group average.

Looking for outlying performances in the post-war decade (Table 12.3), we discover that the leaders and losers of 1913 and 1927 no longer appear. Out of a total of seventy-seven enterprises, only four stood out with regard to ROE. Opel (Germany) was the top earner, with an ROE nearly eight times greater than the average, followed by Unilever (UK) with an ROE three and a half times better. Two oil companies, Petrofina (Belgium) and BP (UK), also generated twice the average ROE. There were also few positive HR outliers, but one company, Esso Standard Oil (France), performed absolutely brilliantly: its HR exceeded 300 per cent! An additional four companies—Magneti Marelli (groups Ercole Marelli and Fiat) (Italy), Shell (UK), Pechiney (France), and Pétroles BP (France)—earned twice the average HR. It should be noted that four of these five enterprises were in the oil business. On the negative side, there were two losers in both ROE and HR. Ansaldo (Italy) and Cantieri Riuniti Adriatico (IRI-group) (Italy) had an ROE two times lower than the average, and the HR for Ansaldo (Italy) and Dunlop (UK) was three times lower than the average. And for the first time, one company—Ansaldo—was a loser in terms of both ROE and HR.

In 1972, the number of deviations from the average ROE of 6.82 per cent as well as from the average HR of 8.80 per cent exceeds that found in earlier benchmarks (Table 12.4). At the same time, the range of deviation was smaller. The highest company ROEs—for Standard Electrica (Spain) and Pieux Franki (Belgium)— were only three and a half times the group average. The returns earned by Thorn Electrical Industries (UK), Boots Company (UK), Opel (Germany), L'Oreal (France), Hawker Siddeley (UK), and Air Liquide (France) were roughly similar. Both Compagnie d'Entreprises C.F.E. (Belgium) and Daimler-Benz (Germany) earned two times the average ROE. Deviations from the average ROE were higher on the negative side, with three Italian firms—Montedison, Pirelli, and Industrie A. Zanussi—having earnings that were respectively 7.6, 5.3, and 4.6 times lower than average ROE. Structurally, HR was similar to ROE, with many more deviations than earlier but of diminished size. The leading HR performance—6.8 times the group average—was achieved by the Finnish electrical engineering firm Strömberg. In five cases, the HR was about five times better than average: Hawker Siddeley (UK), Boots (UK), Magneti Marelli (Fiat group) (Italy), Nokia (Finland), Petrofina (Belgium), and Tube Investments (UK). And three companies registered an HR more than three times the average: British Insulated Callender's Cables (UK), Peugeot (France), and Thorn Electrical Industries (UK). On the negative side, the biggest losers were the Italian companies Olivetti (Italy) and Montedison (Italy), each with an HR three times lower than average. For five companies—AEG (Germany), Anic (ENI group) (Italy), CESPA (Spain), Hoechst (Germany), and Volkswagen (Germany)—the HR was two times lower than average. All told, there were thirty outliers in ROE and HR in 1972: thirteen positive (above average) and seventeen negative (below average). Almost two-thirds of the positive outliers, eight in all, were British firms. Three British companies—Boots, Hawker Siddeley, and Thorn—were positive outliers in both ROE and HR. German companies accounted for three negative and two positive outliers. But among the Italian enterprises there were six negative outliers and only one positive one. Moreover, the single positive outlier was part of the much larger Fiat-group,

Table 12.3. ROE and HR for Chandlerian companies in 1954–6 (in %)

Country	Company	Branch	ROE	HR
Germany	Adam Opel AG	Transport equipment	61.39	
Germany	AEG	Electrical engineering	4.93	25.80
France	Alsacienne de constructions mécaniques	Mechanical engineering	5.06	26.77
France	Alsthom	Electrical engineering	−0.73	10.30
Italy	Anic (Gruppo ENI)	Chemicals and pharmaceuticals	5.74	31.65
Italy	Ansaldo (Gruppo IRI)	Mechanical engineering	−10.56	−20.31
Sweden	ASwedenA	Electrical engineering	10.53	14.87
UK	Associated Electrical Industries	Electrical engineering	9.06	24.35
Belgium	Ateliers de Constructions et Electricité de Charleroi (ACEC)	Electrical engineering	6.80	−2.88
UK	Babcock & Wilcox	Mechanical engineering	7.68	22.35
Germany	BASF	Chemicals and pharmaceuticals	6.22	29.80
Sweden	Bofors AB	Mechanical engineering	7.34	18.90
UK	British Motor Corporation	Transport equipment	13.85	17.91
UK	British Oxygen	Chemicals and pharmaceuticals	7.57	−6.79
UK	British Petroleum Company	Oil, rubber	16.99	22.52
Italy	Cantieri Riuniti Adriatico (Gruppo IRI)	Transport equipment	−14.74	−5.17
France	Citroën	Transport equipment	2.81	48.73
Belgium	Compagnie Belge de Chemins de fer et d'Entreprises	Transport equipment	12.05	12.42
France	Compagnie Française des Pétroles	Oil, rubber	9.51	57.76
France	Compagnie Générale d'Electricité	Electrical engineering	5.02	14.13
Germany	Daimler-Benz AG	Transport equipment	7.50	47.17
Germany	Demag AG	Mechanical engineering	5.49	25.30
Germany	Deutsche Babcock AG	Mechanical engineering	5.13	30.40
Germany	Deutsche Shell AG	Oil, rubber	4.10	
UK	Dunlop Group	Oil, rubber	6.35	−28.94
Spain	E.N. Bazan de Construcciones Navales Milit	Transport equipment	10.37	
Spain	E.N. Calvo Sotelo (Encaso)	Oil, rubber	2.83	
UK	English Electric Company	Electrical engineering	7.74	15.16
Italy	Ercole Marelli	Electrical engineering	4.43	14.47
Spain	Espanola de Construccion Naval, Sociedade	Transport equipment	10.25	
Germany	Esso AG	Oil, rubber	2.64	
France	Esso Standard	Oil, rubber	8.79	311.12
Belgium	Fabrique Nationale d'Armes de Guerre	Mechanical engineering	9.58	15.49
Germany	Farbenfabriken Bayer AG	Chemicals and pharmaceuticals	6.24	31.11
Germany	Farbwerke Hoechst AG	Chemicals and pharmaceuticals	5.85	29.31
Italy	Fiat (Gruppo IFinland)	Transport equipment	7.21	53.58
France	Fives-Lille	Mechanical engineering	6.77	5.89
UK	Ford Motor Company	Transport equipment	14.93	
Germany	Gelsenberg Benzin AG	Oil, rubber	−0.21	
UK	General Electric Company	Electrical engineering	5.91	16.82
Belgium	Gevaert Photo Producten	Chemicals and pharmaceuticals	15.93	15.29
Sweden	Götaverken AB	Transport equipment	10.77	
UK	Guest, Keen & Nettlefolds	Mechanical engineering	10.41	15.11
UK	Hawker Siddeley Group	Transport equipment	12.79	34.39
Sweden	Höganäs-Billesholm AB	Oil, rubber	7.05	6.60

UK	Imperial Chemical Industries	Chemicals and pharmaceuticals	7.82	−4.52
Germany	Klöckner-Humboldt-Deutz-AG	Mechanical engineering	5.52	47.42
Spain	La Maquinista Terrestre y Maritima	Mechanical engineering	10.29	
Italy	Magneti Marelli (gruppi Ercole Marelli e Fiat)	Electrical engineering	7.22	102.63
Italy	Montecatini	Chemicals and pharmaceuticals	6.59	36.27
Belgium	Nationales Belges (Glaces)	Oil, rubber	8.07	59.31
Finland	Oy Strömberg Ab	Electrical engineering	13.67	38.15
France	Pechiney	Chemicals and pharmaceuticals	4.41	68.86
Belgium	Petrofina	Oil, rubber	17.71	7.14
France	Pétroles BP	Oil, rubber	2.88	82.87
Italy	Pirelli	Oil, rubber	6.64	31.71
France	Pont à Mousson	Mechanical engineering	4.76	24.83
France	Régie Renault	Transport equipment	9.70	
Italy	RIV—Officine di Villar Perosa	Mechanical engineering	3.81	
France	Saint Gobain	Chemicals and pharmaceuticals	14.46	38.49
UK	Shell Transp. & Trading Comp.	Oil, rubber	5.93	84.10
Germany	Siemens & Halske AG	Electrical engineering	5.67	−9.80
Germany	Siemens-Schuckertwerke AG	Electrical engineering	5.70	
France	SNECMA	Transport equipment	7.08	
Spain	Standard Electrica, s.a.	Electrical engineering		
Italy	Stanic (Gruppi ENI e Esso Italiana)	Oil, rubber	7.30	
Sweden	Svenska Tändsticksaktiebolaget	Chemicals and pharmaceuticals	7.64	6.03
France	Thomson-Houston	Electrical engineering	3.33	14.81
UK	Tube Investments	Mechanical engineering	7.63	5.37
Finland	Typpi Oy	Chemicals and pharmaceuticals	2.80	
France	Ugine	Chemicals and pharmaceuticals	5.59	59.02
UK	Unilever	Chemicals and pharmaceuticals	27.70	18.17
Spain	Union Espanola de Explosivos, S.A.	Chemicals and pharmaceuticals	12.80	33.56
Finland	Valmet Oy	Mechanical engineering	0.13	
UK	Vickers Group	Transport equipment	6.79	12.86
Germany	Volkswagenwerk GmbH	Transport equipment	5.16	
Finland	Wärtsilä-yhtymä Oy	Transport equipment	8.68	20.87

Source: Data set

which might had allocated profits in that particular company. Thus, it seems that the early 1970s were good years for British firms, whereas Italian large enterprise struggled.

Although the number of enterprises included in the 2000 sample is about the same as in 1972, the number of outliers fell from thirty to seventeen (Table 12.5). Of these, fourteen were positive and only three negative. This is a considerably better balance sheet than in 1972, the end of the so-called 'golden age', when over half of the outliers were negative. So was the golden age less gilded than thought?

Table 12.4. ROE and HR for Chandlerian companies in 1970–2 (in %)

Country	Company	Branch	ROE	HR
Belgium	A.C.E.C. (At. Constructions Electr. Charleroi)	Electrical engineering	6.82	17.09
Italy	A.P.I.—Anonima Petroli Italiana	Oil, rubber	−4.43	
Germany	Adam Opel AG	Transport equipment	19.05	
France	Air Liquide	Chemicals and pharmaceuticals	22.10	−3.93
Sweden	Alfa Laval AB	Mechanical engineering	4.89	6.73
Italy	Alfa Romeo (Gruppo IRI)	Transport equipment	3.57	
Germany	AEG-Telefunken	Electrical engineering	5.20	−10.01
Italy	Anic (Gruppo ENI)	Chemicals and pharmaceuticals	−0.86	−14.09
Italy	Ansaldo Meccanico-Nucleare (Gruppo IRI)	Mechanical engineering	−2.98	
Germany	Aral AG	Oil, rubber	6.19	
Sweden	ASEA	Electrical engineering	7.66	17.50
France	Ateliers de constructions de Roanne	Mechanical engineering		
Spain	Babcock & Wilcox	Mechanical engineering	0.04	
France	Babcock Fives	Mechanical engineering	6.07	13.07
Germany	BASF AG	Chemicals and pharmaceuticals	8.05	−0.85
Germany	Bayer AG	Chemicals and pharmaceuticals	9.78	−6.76
UK	Boots Company	Chemicals and pharmaceuticals	19.35	44.79
France	Bréguet aviation (avions Dassault)	Transport equipment	11.18	9.54
UK	British Insulated Callender's Cables	Electrical engineering	8.74	22.07
UK	British Leyland Motor Corporation	Transport equipment	5.33	1.05
UK	British Petroleum Company	Oil, rubber	7.15	16.14
Spain	Campsa	Oil, rubber	13.58	13.23
Spain	CEPSA	Chemicals and pharmaceuticals	7.02	−11.12
France	Cie des compteurs (groupe Schlumberger)	Electrical engineering	11.04	15.28
France	Cie Française des Pétroles	Oil, rubber	11.26	9.16
France	Citroën	Transport equipment	9.85	−7.95
Belgium	Compagnie d'Entreprises C.F.E.	Transport equipment	14.99	10.03
France	Compagnie Générale d'Electricité	Electrical engineering	7.88	4.46
Germany	Daimler-Benz AG	Transport equipment	14.55	−0.21
Germany	Demag AG	Mechanical engineering	7.74	8.34
Germany	Deutsche Shell AG	Oil, rubber	9.69	
France	Elf-Erap	Oil, rubber		
Germany	Esso AG	Oil, rubber	8.01	
UK	Esso Petroleum Company	Oil, rubber	2.69	
Germany	Farbwerke Hoechst AG	Chemicals and pharmaceuticals	9.73	−9.54
Italy	Fiat (Gruppo IFI)	Transport equipment	3.10	−2.30
UK	Ford Motor Company	Transport equipment	3.89	
UK	General Electric Company	Electrical engineering	9.64	10.26
UK	Guest, Keen & Nettlefolds	Mechanical engineering	8.50	9.52
Germany	Gutehoffnungshütte Aktienverein/ MAN	Mechanical engineering	8.79	−4.18
UK	Hawker Siddeley Group	Transport equipment	19.32	46.15
UK	Imperial Chemical Industries	Chemicals and pharmaceuticals	9.65	6.28
Italy	Industrie A. Zanussi	Electrical engineering	−24.79	
Italy	Industrie Pirelli	Oil, rubber	−29.23	
Italy	Ing. C. Olivetti & C.	Mechanical engineering	5.95	−17.67
Finland	Kemira Oy	Chemicals and pharmaceuticals	4.64	

Germany	Klöckner-Humboldt-Deutz AG	Mechanical engineering	6.53	−7.45
France	L'Oreal	Chemicals and pharmaceuticals	18.10	−0.02
Italy	Magneti Marelli (Gruppo Fiat)	Electrical engineering	1.30	48.51
Italy	Montedison	Chemicals and pharmaceuticals	−45.24	−23.10
Finland	Oy Nokia Ab	Oil, rubber	6.72	36.53
Finland	Oy Strömberg Ab	Electrical engineering	4.28	59.50
Finland	Oy Wärtsilä Ab	Transport equipment	−1.81	1.50
Belgium	Petrofina	Oil, rubber	10.17	44.86
France	Peugeot	Transport equipment	7.47	28.59
Belgium	Pieux Franki	Mechanical engineering	23.33	8.96
France	Poclain	Mechanical engineering	11.89	3.20
France	Renault	Transport equipment	−2.20	
France	Rhône-Poulenc	Chemicals and pharmaceuticals	5.05	−4.97
Germany	Robert Bosch GmbH	Electrical engineering	8.63	
France	Saint-Gobain Pont-à-Mousson	Oil, rubber	9.10	5.95
Spain	SEAT	Transport equipment	10.93	
UK	Shell Transp. & Trading Comp.	Oil, rubber	9.07	2.62
Germany	Siemens AG	Electrical engineering	11.33	9.16
Belgium	Solvay	Chemicals and pharmaceuticals	4.89	10.45
Spain	Standard Electrica	Electrical engineering	24.22	
Sweden	Svenska Tändsticksaktiebolaget	Chemicals and pharmaceuticals	8.83	4.30
France	Thomson CSF	Electrical engineering	9.10	8.57
UK	Thorn Electrical Industries	Electrical engineering	22.46	26.30
Sweden	Trelleborgs Gummifabrik AB	Oil, rubber	4.60	−2.33
UK	Tube Investments	Mechanical engineering	7.56	48.39
Spain	UERT	Chemicals and pharmaceuticals	9.76	−5.24
UK	Unilever	Chemicals and pharmaceuticals	11.60	15.36
Finland	Valmet Oy	Mechanical engineering	−0.27	
UK	Vickers	Mechanical engineering	5.34	−6.11
Germany	Volkswagenwerk AG	Transport equipment	5.92	−9.02
Sweden	Volvo	Transport equipment	12.70	5.07

Source: Data set

At the moment, we cannot answer this question—more and broader research is necessary. Returning to 2000, the most profitable company was Imperial Chemical Industries (UK), with an ROE 5.8 times greater than the group average of 15.70 per cent. GlaxoSmithKline (UK) and the Smiths Group (UK) also performed outstandingly, with earnings more than 3.5 times and 3.3 times the average ROE. Besides these three British firms, there were an additional five companies whose profits were double the group average: Deutsche Shell (Germany), DOW Chemical Iberica (Spain), Guest, Keen & Nettlefolds (UK), Nokia (Finland), and Tomkins (UK). The single negative outlier was Italtel (Olivetti Group) (Italy), which incurred an ROE of about −20 per cent. In HR, the mobile phone producer Nokia (Finland) was by far the top performer, with a result 11.5 times the average HR. Other exceptionally good performers for investors were Alcatel (France), CIR (Italy), Logica (UK), and Pirelli (Italy). The single negative HR outlier was Invensys (UK). As in 1972, the country with the most outliers was the UK, having six leaders and one loser. In 2000, only one firm, Nokia, achieved outstanding results in both ROE and HR.

Table 12.5. ROE and HR for Chandlerian companies in 1998–2000 (in %)

Country	Company	Branch	ROE	HR
France	Airbus industrie	Transport equipment		
France	Alcatel	Electrical engineering	11.89	84.36
UK	AstraZeneca	Chemicals and pharmaceuticals	21.98	19.77
Sweden	Atlas Copco	Mechanical engineering	12.64	48.57
France	Aventis	Chemicals and pharmaceuticals	−0.88	
UK	BAE Systems	Transport equipment	12.70	−1.98
Belgium	Barco	Electrical engineering	8.54	−7.40
Germany	BASF AG	Chemicals and pharmaceuticals	10.11	20.35
Germany	Bayer AG	Chemicals and pharmaceuticals	12.39	21.54
Germany	Bayerische Motoren Werke AG	Transport equipment	−11.57	34.83
UK	BBA Group	Transport equipment	22.93	−2.35
UK	BG Group	Oil, rubber	25.06	2.78
UK	BP Amoco	Oil, rubber	11.57	−9.02
Italy	CIR	Mechanical engineering	8.93	81.85
Germany	Continental AG	Oil, rubber	12.23	−2.69
Germany	Daimler Chrysler AG	Transport equipment	16.69	−2.23
Germany	Degussa AG	Chemicals and pharmaceuticals	12.72	−4.63
Germany	Deutsche Shell GmbH	Oil, rubber	38.35	
Spain	Dow Chemical Iberica	Chemicals and pharmaceuticals	33.88	
Italy	Enichem (ENI Group)	Chemicals and pharmaceuticals	−14.53	
Sweden	Ericsson	Electrical engineering	20.37	12.27
Spain	Ericsson Espana	Electrical engineering	22.16	
Italy	Fiat (IFI Group)	Transport equipment	3.64	−1.20
Finland	Fortum	Oil, rubber	9.57	−2.60
UK	GKN	Mechanical engineering	34.58	−11.58
UK	GlaxoSmithKline	Chemicals and pharmaceuticals	57.72	13.81
Spain	Hewlett Packard Espanola	Mechanical engineering	25.96	
Germany	Hewlett-Packard GmbH	Electrical engineering		
Italy	IFI (Agnelli)	Transport equipment	1.07	15.42
UK	Imperial Chemical Industries	Chemicals and pharmaceuticals	91.58	−6.22
UK	Invensys	Electrical engineering	3.76	−53.80
Italy	Italtel (Olivetti Group)	Electrical engineering	−19.88	
Finland	Kemira	Chemicals and pharmaceuticals	10.02	−10.00
France	L'Oreal	Chemicals and pharmaceuticals	15.16	−9.30
France	Lagardere Groupe	Electrical engineering	12.20	32.85
France	l'Air Liquide SA	Chemicals and pharmaceuticals	11.07	−11.09
UK	Logica	Electrical engineering	23.22	85.06
Italy	Magneti Marelli (Fiat Group)	Mechanical engineering	8.50	
Germany	MAN AG	Mechanical engineering	14.10	17.33
UK	Marconi	Electrical engineering	14.77	34.88
Finland	Metso	Mechanical engineering	11.48	2.27
France	Michelin	Oil, rubber	8.61	−8.22
Finland	Nokia	Electrical engineering	35.21	158.43
Sweden	Perstorp	Chemicals and pharmaceuticals	7.10	−1.40
Belgium	Petrofina	Oil, rubber	25.23	25.15
France	Peugeot	Transport equipment	8.85	8.57
Italy	Pirelli & C.	Oil, rubber	10.36	54.40
Italy	Pirelli SpA	Oil, rubber	30.04	23.06
Sweden	Preem	Oil, rubber	22.25	33.80
France	Renault	Transport equipment	10.75	10.16
Spain	Renault Espana	Transport equipment	6.15	
Spain	Repsol-YPF	Oil, rubber	12.86	−18.34
Germany	Robert Bosch GmbH	Electrical engineering	7.04	
UK	Rolls-Royce	Transport equipment	10.98	8.20

Germany	RWE-DEA AG	Oil, rubber	26.54	3.79
Belgium	Sabca	Transport equipment	6.45	−11.98
Belgium	Sait Electronics	Mechanical engineering	3.81	−0.67
France	Schneider Electric	Electrical engineering	12.02	
Spain	SEAT	Transport equipment	10.77	
UK	Shell Transp. & Trading Comp.	Oil, rubber	12.11	11.89
Germany	Siemens AG	Electrical engineering	14.90	23.09
UK	Smiths Group	Mechanical engineering	51.55	0.10
Italy	Snia	Chemicals and pharmaceuticals	2.46	15.86
Belgium	Solvay	Chemicals and pharmaceuticals	8.33	10.15
Italy	Stmicroelectronics (Finmeccanica Group)	Electrical engineering	7.37	
UK	Tomkins	Mechanical engineering	31.89	−14.55
France	Total Fina Elf	Oil, rubber	13.48	22.60
Germany	Volkswagen AG	Transport equipment	13.08	7.39
Sweden	Volvo	Transport equipment	16.83	−12.10
Germany	Würth-Gruppe	Mechanical engineering	16.78	
Germany	ZF Friedrichshafen AG	Mechanical engineering	22.58	

Source: Data set

CAN WE IDENTIFY LEARNING CURVES IN MANAGEMENT?

Shifting from a cross-sectional to a longitudinal focus, we can ask whether company managements were able to obtain better ROE or HR over the course of time. If so, this would indicate that the professionalization of management, the investment in management schools, and the organization of in-house lifelong learning were worthwhile. The mean of all ROEs in the Chandlerian group from 1913 to 2000 is 10.06 per cent, while that of HR amounts to 16.54 per cent. Could skilful management improve these figures over the course of the century? Indeed it could, for the average ROE was at its highest value in 2000. Strangely enough, however, its lowest value came in 1972, which was one of the peak years of the post-Second World War boom! Overall, though, the trend in ROE would support a hypothesis of steadily better business management. But HR shows a different picture. In 1954, during the first years of the post-war boom, the mean HR was nearly twice as high as in 2000: namely, 30.34 versus 13.73 per cent. Yet the last decade of the twentieth century was marked by the vogue of shareholder-value policies in corporate management, which aimed in particular at maximizing the value of the enterprise on the stock exchange. Good management at the time was defined as success in stimulating high share prices. The Chandlerian group's HR in 2000 stood at 13.73 per cent, up from 8.80 per cent in 1972, but a lower value than in all earlier benchmarks. This is not a very impressive argument for the improved-management thesis.[5] A sceptic might argue that stock market trends

[5] It is just a footnote to history that the prominent German chemical enterprise Hoechst was no longer part of our sample after it was merged into the short-lived enterprise of Aventis. Under the

effectively overrule all managerial efforts. So, was investment in management education not rewarded? Perhaps not, but in any case it should not be abandoned. The competitive environment of enterprise demands educated management. No enterprise nowadays can fall back in this respect. Even if management education turns out to be little more than a zero-sum game for the enterprise, companies cannot afford to simply opt out, for the competitive challenges remain even as the level of managerial education rises.

Given our long-term data on enterprise performance, what companies or branches should an investor have chosen in order to achieve the best returns? We have to split up the question, because the very long-term investor would bet less on HR and look more to ROE. We define a very long-term investor as a person who thinks in terms of decades or as families in which shares were inherited for a centenary (this indeed happened on the Continent!). A markedly higher than average ROE was to be found in oil/chemicals in 1913, in oil and in chemicals in 1927, in transport equipment in 1954, and in mechanical engineering, chemicals, and oil in 2000; in 1972, no branch had a significantly better ROE (Table 12.6). In other words, the very long-term investor should have put capital into oil or chemicals. Clearly underperforming branches in terms of ROE were transport equipment in 1927, mechanical engineering in 1954, oil in 1972, and transport equipment in 2000. Long-term ROEs for the individual branches varied considerably, and, with the possible exception of oil, there was no clear-cut winner. As far as underperformers are concerned, transport equipment's ROE was below average at several benchmarks—the growth of the motor vehicle industry could not always compensate for the problems in shipbuilding and the railway and aviation sectors.

But what about the short-term investor, looking not only for dividends but also for the growth in share value (HR)? In 1913, this person should have invested in electrical engineering companies, for the branch's HR at the time was twice the group average. The same branch would have been the best choice also in 1927 (an HR of 28.29 per cent versus a group average HR of 19.49 per cent). In 1954, short-term investment capital should have been ploughed into the oil branch, whose HR of 63.42 per cent clearly outperformed the group mean of 30.34 per cent. Oil was also a good bet in 1972; in that benchmark, the HR of both the oil and the electrical engineering branches was twice as good as the mean. In 2000, the short-term investment of choice was again electrical engineering, whose HR was three times higher than the mean! Underperformers in terms of HR were transport equipment and oil/chemicals in 1913, oil in 1927 (2.38 per cent HR versus a mean of 19.49 per cent!), mechanical engineering in 1954 (an HR of about one-half the mean), chemicals in 1972 (0.10 per cent HR versus a mean of 8.80 per cent), and transport equipment and chemicals in 2000 (both branches having an HR less than 50 per cent of the group mean). If the investment choice was determined by finding out which branch had the best earnings, it would differ according to which measurement of performance—ROE or HR—was given priority. Among the

chairmanship of J. Dormann, Hoechst was the first large German firm to embark on the new management idea of shareholder value. Dormann's determination earned him the label of 'the German Mr Shareholder Value', but his policies cost the company its existence.

Table 12.6. Financial performance of Chandlerian industries by branch

Benchmark	Branch	Year	Assets (US$)	Revenue (US$)	ROE (%)	HR (%)
1	Electrical engineering	1913	26,697,456		9.04	16.40
1	Mechanical engineering	1913	11,446,421		12.36	10.12
1	Transport equipment	1913	21,771,942		9.75	3.94
1	Oil, rubber, chemicals	1913	20,447,978		15.91	4.53
1	All Chandlerian industries	1913	19,927,777		12.08	8.01
2	Electrical engineering	1927	38,871,283		8.21	28.29
2	Mechanical engineering	1927	23,347,175		6.59	20.71
2	Transport equipment	1927	46,262,117		4.74	24.63
2	Chemicals	1927	144,644,106		11.45	16.58
2	Oil and rubber	1927	55,279,905		12.75	2.38
2	All Chandlerian industries	1927	56,106,687		8.86	19.49
3	Electrical engineering	1954	138,593,546		6.38	21.45
3	Mechanical engineering	1954	88,961,289		5.27	18.13
3	Transport equipment	1954	183,132,179		10.98	26.97
3	Chemicals	1954	256,522,254		9.16	27.59
3	Oil and rubber	1954	217,975,486		7.11	63.42
3	All Chandlerian industries	1954	177,195,269		7.88	30.34
4	Electrical engineering	1972	1,074,604,307	1,496,041,510	7.57	19.06
4	Mechanical engineering	1972	598,714,790	608,199,108	6.67	5.71
4	Transport equipment	1972	1,219,202,582	2,157,926,396	8.62	7.50
4	Chemicals	1972	1,575,852,613	2,319,548,823	5.40	0.10
4	Oil and rubber	1972	2,726,936,374	2,802,487,899	4.61	15.77
4	All Chandlerian industries	1972	1,453,336,707	1,901,299,600	6.82	8.80
5	Electrical engineering	2000	16,861,182,031	14,778,801,753	12.04	41.08
5	Mechanical engineering	2000	4,691,200,277	4,723,776,640	20.23	15.41
5	Transport equipment	2000	52,666,670,604	35,892,523,429	9.24	4.40
5	Chemicals	2000	13,707,141,938	11,065,715,977	18.61	4.90
5	Oil and rubber	2000	29,089,325,962	31,889,435,510	18.45	10.51
5	All Chandlerian industries	2000	23,317,789,373	19,904,293,011	15.70	13.73

Source: Own calculations from data set

Chandlerian group of enterprises in the twentieth century, the best choice according to ROE would have been oil, whereas the best choice according to HR would have been electrical engineering. However, both measures pointed to the same branch as being the worst investment: namely, transport equipment.

How much capital was necessary for doing business is also an important question for potential investors. Unfortunately, the relationship between assets and sales—capital turnover ratio—can be analysed only for the years 1972 and 2000, because in earlier benchmarks there are too few observations to calculate the measure.

The data in Table 12.7 reveal that the relationship between company sales and capital employed generally deteriorated in the last quarter of the twentieth century. Whereas in 1972 capital turnover was less than one year, in 2000 it needed more than twelve months to achieve it. In other words, in 2000, companies typically needed more capital to achieve the same volume of sales. If we have a closer look at the branch level, the picture is much more differentiated. We see

Table 12.7. Capital turnover ratio in Chandlerian companies,
1972 and 2000

Branch	1972	2000
Chemicals	1.5	0.8
Electrical engineering	1.4	0.9
Mechanical engineering	1.0	1.0
Oil	1.0	1.1
Transport equipment	1.8	0.7
All Chandlerian companies	1.3	0.9

Source: Own calculations from data set

first of all that the oil branch bucked the trend by increasing its capital turnover ratio and thus its profitability. In maintaining its ratio at unity, mechanical engineering also was exceptional. Chemicals and transport equipment suffered the biggest declines in capital turnover. In the transport equipment branch, the drop was over 50 per cent, which underscores earlier statements about its relatively low performance.

GROWTH OF ASSETS

In 1913, the mean assets of all Chandlerian enterprises amounted to about $20 million. The average size of firm assets varied, of course, from branch to branch. In transport equipment and oil/chemicals, company assets matched the overall average, while in electrical engineering they were much larger and in mechanical engineering only about half the average size. The distribution of assets size according to country was very concentrated: six of the ten largest enterprises were registered in the UK, while the rest were from Germany. No other country figured in the top ten (Table 12.8). The ten largest enterprises came from only three branches: oil and chemicals (four), transport equipment (three), and electrical engineering (three).

In 1927, the mean assets of all Chandlerian enterprises had grown to about $56 million. Oil firms' assets again equalled the overall average, while transport equipment fell below and mechanical engineering continued to be 50 per cent smaller than the group as a whole. Between 1913 and 1927, an enormous change occurred in the size of the other two branches—electrical engineering and chemicals. Electrical engineering lost its exceptional position of 1913 and was no longer the largest branch by assets; its average company size amounted to no more than 70 per cent of the group mean.[6] Its dominant role was taken over by the chemicals branch, whose mean assets of $115 million exceeded the Chandlerian group mean by more than 50 per cent. The country distribution of the top ten,

---

[6] W. Hausman, P. Hertner, and M. Wilkins, *Global Electrification: Multinational Enterprise and International Finance in the History of Light and Power, 1878–2007* (Cambridge: Cambridge University Press, 2008).

Table 12.8. The ten largest Chandlerian companies in 1911–13 ('Small Sample')

Rank	Country	Company	Branch	Assets (US$)
1	Germany	AEG	Electrical engineering	110,250,578
2	Germany	Siemens-Schuckertwerke, GmbH	Electrical engineering	77,027,145
3	UK	Lever Brothers	Oil, rubber	68,075,805
4	UK	Vickers	Transport equipment	58,720,286
5	UK	Shell Transp. & Trading Comp.	Oil, rubber	55,016,738
6	UK	Sir W.G. Armstrong, Whitworth & Co.	Transport equipment	53,241,952
7	Germany	Siemens & Halske AG	Electrical engineering	45,157,340
8	UK	United Alkali Company	Oil, rubber	34,465,352
9	UK	John Brown & Company	Transport equipment	31,407,400
10	Germany	Bayer AG	Oil, rubber	30,362,249

Source: Data set

Table 12.9. The ten largest Chandlerian companies in 1927–9 ('Small Sample')

Rank	Country	Company	Branch	Assets (US$)
1	Germany	IG Farbenindustrie AG	Chemicals and pharmaceuticals	431,727,669
2	UK	Lever Brothers	Chemicals and pharmaceuticals	343,491,303
3	UK	Imperial Chemical Industries	Chemicals and pharmaceuticals	339,678,133
4	UK	Anglo-Persian Oil	Oil, rubber	218,895,489
5	UK	Shell Transp. & Trading Comp.	Oil, rubber	180,264,910
6	Sweden	Svenska Tändsticksaktiebolaget	Chemicals and pharmaceuticals	156,402,252
7	UK	Dunlop	Oil, rubber	118,493,364
8	UK	Armstrong, Whitworth Securities	Transport equipment	117,852,489
9	UK	Vickers	Transport equipment	117,045,007
10	Germany	AEG	Electrical engineering	110,435,308

Source: Data set

however, was largely unchanged (Table 12.9). Also, in 1927, the largest European enterprises came mainly from the UK (seven) with two from Germany and one from Sweden. With five companies among the ten largest enterprises, the chemicals branch clearly dominated. Next came oil with three enterprises, transport equipment with two, and electrical engineering with one.

In 1954, the group's mean assets stood at $177 million. Firm size in both engineering branches was now smaller than average, but transport equipment companies were typically larger than average. The largest firm sizes were to be found in oil and chemicals; in both branches, average company assets exceeded $200 million. The previously noted continuity of country distribution was largely maintained in 1954. Also, in 1954, six of the ten largest Chandlerian firms were British, but now there were also newcomers: two each from Spain and Italy (Table 12.10). The combined effects of wartime destruction and post-war corporate de-concentration (for example, the dismantling of IG Farben) meant that, for the time being, there were no German companies in the European top ten. The branches most frequently found in 1954 were chemicals and oil, as in 1927, but their relative positions were exchanged. The oil branch now had four representatives, and chemicals and transport equipment three each. There was none from electrical engineering.

Table 12.10. The ten largest Chandlerian companies in 1954–6 ('Small Sample')

Rank	Country	Company	Branch	Assets (US$)
1	UK	Imperial Chemical Industries	Chemicals and pharmaceuticals	1,470,552,598
2	UK	British Petroleum Company	Oil, rubber	998,530,753
3	Italy	Fiat (Gruppo IFI)	Transport equipment	502,745,600
4	UK	Unilever	Chemicals and pharmaceuticals	464,210,674
5	UK	Dunlop Group	Oil, rubber	431,895,292
6	Spain	E.N. Bazan de Constr. Navales Milit	Transport equipment	422,072,742
7	Italy	Montecatini	Chemicals and pharmaceuticals	363,225,600
8	Spain	E.N. Calvo Sotelo (Encaso)	Oil, rubber	344,660,831
9	UK	Vickers Group	Transport equipment	324,951,466
10	UK	Shell Transp. & Trading Comp.	Oil, rubber	315,522,576

Source: Data set

Table 12.11. The ten largest Chandlerian companies in 1970–2 ('Small Sample')

Rank	Country	Company	Branch	Assets (US$)	Turnover (US$)
1	UK	Shell Transp. & Trading Comp.	Oil, rubber	20,785,392,696	14,364,682,341
2	UK	British Petroleum Company	Oil, rubber	8,694,097,049	8,582,291,146
3	Germany	Bayer AG	Chemicals and pharmaceuticals	4,755,646,173	4,021,329,987
4	Germany	Farbwerke Hoechst AG	Chemicals and pharmaceuticals	4,671,580,928	4,254,391,468
5	Germany	Siemens AG	Electrical engineering	4,283,286,445	4,751,254,705
6	Italy	Montedison	Chemicals and pharmaceuticals	3,799,695,049	1,410,351,208
7	Germany	Volkswagenwerk AG	Transport equipment	3,508,705,742	5,280,112,923
8	Germany	BASF AG	Chemicals and pharmaceuticals	2,941,412,070	3,720,514,429
9	UK	General Electric Company	Electrical engineering	2,852,826,413	2,559,824,912
10	Italy	Fiat (Gruppo IFI)	Transport equipment	2,666,959,054	3,669,559,705

Source: Data set

By 1972, the group average assets size grew (and was inflated) more than eightfold to $1,453 million. Company size in electrical engineering and mechanical engineering again declined relatively, amounting in the first branch to no more than 75 per cent of the general average and in the second branch to merely 40 per cent. In chemicals and transport equipment, firm size had fallen back to the group mean, whereas in oil, average company assets now stood at 187 per cent, almost double the group mean! In other words, the bulk of investment in Chandlerian firms between 1954 and 1972 was swallowed up by the oil branch. We can surmise that during the same period, we have a matching disinvestment in coal mining, for these were the years when the energy base of the Western economy switched from coal to oil, a move that is well reflected in our figures. A first glance at Table 12.11 gives a noteworthy finding: the Germans are back. Half of the ten largest Chandlerian firms in 1972, come from Germany; for the first time in the twentieth century, Germany had more representatives than the UK. That country had three enterprises and Italy two. These ten firms come from four different branches and thus are a good mix of the Chandlerian firms. Four companies belong to chemicals and two each to oil, transport equipment, and electrical engineering. For the first time, we have full information on both assets and turnover (sales), so the relationship between the two can be examined. Although this relationship does not give precise information on actual profits, it is assumed to be advantageous for an enterprise to maximize its capital turnover ratio: high sales with low assets. There are substantial variations: while BP, Bayer, Hoechst, Siemens, and the British General Electric Company achieved a capital turnover ratio of about 1.0, Shell managed no better than 0.7 and Montedison less than 0.4. By contrast, BASF, Volkswagen, and Fiat had considerably higher (and better) ratios: 1.5, 1.5, and 1.4, respectively. Capital turnover for the companies in transport equipment and electrical engineering was roughly similar, while it varied in chemicals and oil.

Between 1972 and 2000, the group mean assets size mushroomed sixteenfold to reach $23.3 billion. The relative size of mechanical engineering firms fell to no more than 20 per cent of the group mean, and, in spite of all the investment in the IT sector, the typical size of electrical engineering companies surprisingly remained at its 1972 level of about 72 per cent! A second surprise is the decline of company size in the chemicals branch. In 1972, it was a bit above the group mean, but in 2000 it had fallen to less than 60 per cent. Perhaps the branch could not match the growth of other Chandlerian firms during these years because of the shift from industrial chemicals to pharmaceuticals that occurred at this time.[7] The largest surprise, however, is the above-average growth of assets by transport equipment companies, a performance that even exceeded that of oil companies in their heyday. Only three firms in transport equipment had assets lower than the group average. In 2000, five countries were represented in the list of ten largest enterprises, more than ever before (Table 12.12). Germany took the lead with three firms, followed by the UK, Italy, and France with two each, and Spain with one. On the other hand, the number of branches represented declined. Five of the ten largest enterprises were in transport equipment, four in oil, and one in electrical engineering. Chemicals, the leading branch in 1972, was no longer present. When the relationship between turnover and assets is considered, only two firms, Total Fina Elf and Shell—both in oil, achieved a capital turnover ratio substantially larger than one. However, the two other oil firms in the list, BP Amoco and Repsol-YPF, had ratios less than one. Thus, as in 1972, capital turnover in the oil branch varied a good deal. By contrast, in the transport equipment branch, this indicator was rather uniform: four out of the five enterprises in this sector needed substantially more assets to achieve their sales results. Volkswagen had the best capital turnover with a ratio of 1.05; Fiat was second best with 0.88, while Daimler Chrysler had 0.81, Renault 0.76, and IFI 0.62.

Turning to the development of company assets over the entire twentieth century, we can identify changes in leading branches, but also one steady underperformer.

---

[7] The decline of the chemical industry is well explained in L. Galambos, T. Hikino, and V. Zagmani, eds., *The Global Chemical Industry in the Age of Petrochemical Revolution* (Cambridge: Cambridge University Press, 2007).

Table 12.12. The ten largest Chandlerian companies in 1998–2000 ('Small Sample')

Rank	Country	Company	Branch	Assets (US$)	Turnover (US$)
1	Germany	Daimler Chrysler AG	Transport equipment	183,967,872,969	149,911,373,708
2	UK	BP Amoco	Oil, rubber	144,296,580,066	148,431,342,831
3	Italy	IFI (Agnelli)	Transport equipment	99,188,515,510	61,648,818,316
4	Italy	Fiat (IFI Group)	Transport equipment	88,353,951,256	49,115,583,456
5	France	Total Fina Elf	Oil, rubber	76,124,193,651	105,757,939,531
6	Germany	Volkswagen AG	Transport equipment	75,325,886,263	78,983,567,208
7	Germany	Siemens AG	Electrical engineering	73,167,466,765	72,374,446,086
8	UK	Shell Transp. & Trading Comp.	Oil, rubber	49,144,296,721	59,675,659,291
9	France	Renault	Transport equipment	48,596,343,750	37,003,551,600
10	Spain	Repsol-YPF	Oil, rubber	48,392,532,537	40,660,080,697

Source: Data set

Table 12.13. The ten largest Chandlerian companies by industrial branch, 1913–2000

Year	Oil and rubber	Chemicals	Transport equipment	Electrical engineering	Mechanical engineering
1913	1	3	3	3	0
1927	3	4	2	1	0
1954	4	3	3	0	0
1972	2	4	2	2	0
2000	4	0	5	1	0
Total	14	14	15	7	0

Source: Own calculations from data set

The latter was without question mechanical engineering, which attracted relatively fewer and fewer assets in each benchmark (Table 12.13). By contrast the 'winning branch' shifted almost every time: in 1913, it was electrical engineering; in 1927 and 1954, chemicals; in 1972, oil; and in 2000, transport equipment. Not only is the changing leadership in this size race noteworthy, but also the extent of the gaps. In each benchmark the average assets size of companies in the outstanding branch amounted to at least 50 per cent above the general mean—with a large distance to the number two branch. In other words, competition for assets periodically resulted in massive fluctuations of investment between the individual branches of Chandlerian enterprises.

Thus, the industrial distribution of the largest European enterprises during the twentieth century was more uneven than commonly thought. It was not that 'big oil' dominated all the time. Until the 1970s, oil's position was countervailed by the strength of 'big chemicals'. The position of transport equipment was stable over time, and then, in the last quarter of the century, it surged to the top of the chart in 2000. After leading in 1913, electrical engineering declined, although it continued to maintain a steady presence in the top echelon, while mechanical engineering languished relatively and never produced an enterprise that belonged to the European top ten.

The geographical distribution of the largest European enterprises across the century gives somewhat surprising results (Table 12.14). Out of fifty entries,

Table 12.14. The ten largest Chandlerian companies by country, 1913–2000

Year	UK	Germany	Italy	Spain	France	Sweden	Belgium	Finland
1913	6	4	0	0	0	0	0	0
1927	7	2	0	0	0	1	0	0
1954	6	0	2	2	0	0	0	0
1972	3	5	2	0	0	0	0	0
2000	2	3	2	1	2	0	0	0
Total	24	14	6	3	2	1	0	0

Source: Own calculations from data set

the UK accounted for twenty-four, or roughly one-half. Recalling Chandler's proposition that organizational capabilities are learned foremost in big enterprise, it is thus logical that British companies regularly dominant the top ten lists, even though this challenges his suggestion of a British type of 'personal capitalism'.[8] Also remarkable is that a century of French dirigisme produced only two companies that qualified for the top ten. Belgium and Finland never had a company in this elite category, and Sweden only once. On the basis of these findings, one might postulate a class hierarchy for European big business according to country of origin: first class, UK; second class, Germany and Italy; third class, the rest.

GIANT AND LARGE FIRMS

Giant firms were rare among Chandlerian companies. Here 'Giant' means a company having assets more than four times the respective category average, while 'Big' is defined as being twice the average size. It is important to note that the term 'average' here does not refer to the group mean of Chandlerian enterprises as previously used, but to the mean of the respective branch or industrial activity, such as oil or chemicals. In 1913, there was a single Chandlerian Giant: AEG (Allgemeine Elektricitäts Gesellschaft), the German electrical engineering firm based in Berlin. Its branch rival Siemens could have qualified as a Giant as well, but the owners had split the enterprise into Siemens & Halske and Siemens-Schuckert Werke, which individually did not make the cut. The 1927 sample lacks a Giant, but there is one again in 1954: ICI (Imperial Chemical Industries, UK). In 1972, there are two Giants: BP and Shell, both oil companies and both British. In 2000, the first company, now called BP-Amoco, is still a Giant, the only one at this time. Since these Giants—with the single exception of BP-Amoco in 2000—represented each given year's leading branch in terms of assets, perhaps they were more characteristic than initially thought.

There are, of course, many 'Big' firms in each benchmark year, too many to be listed here. But if we establish a class of 'Very Big' enterprises, defined as three times a branch's average assets, we can identify firms that might embody developmental trends. In 1913, there are four 'Very Big' enterprises: Siemens-Schuckert

---

[8] Chandler, *Scale and Scope*.

Werke (electrical engineering), Sir W.G. Armstrong and Vickers (both transport equipment), and Lever Brothers (oil and chemicals). In 1927, the number rises to six: AEG, Anglo-Persian Oil, Shell, IG Farben, ICI, and Lever Brothers—is this perhaps a sign of the oft-mentioned concentration movement during the interwar period? In the 1954 benchmark, there are only three 'Very Big' firms: GKN ('Very Big' according to the mean size of its branch of mechanical engineering), ICI, and BP. By the end of the post-war boom in 1972, the number of 'Very Big' Chand-lerian companies has risen again to seven: Shell, BP, Bayer, Hoechst, ICI, Unilever, and Gutehoffnungshütte/MAN.[9] Finally, in 2000, there are three firms that qualify as 'Very Big': Daimler-Chrysler, Siemens, and Aventis (pharmaceuticals, France). A quick look at the context of these 'Very Big' firms shows that they do not especially reflect the leading branches at the time; rather they represent the position of individual companies in their respective industrial activity. All told, we can identify five Giant and twenty-three 'Very Big' companies over the course of the century. This is not an impressive quantity in a data set of 359 enterprises! Perhaps the role of big enterprise is overestimated?

FINDING TRACES OF WARS?

While such international economic shocks as the World Economic Crisis of the 1930s or the oil price crises of 1973/4 and 1979/80 affected business life in all countries, the consequences of the First and Second World Wars differed consid-erably, depending on which country an enterprise was based in. Being situated in a winning state—Belgium, France, UK, or Italy (in the First World War)—presumably gave advantages over firms in a defeated state—Germany or Italy (in the Second World War). For German enterprises, the two-time military defeat of their country brought loss of foreign investment, whether direct or portfolio, royalties for patents and trademarks, and market shares, losses that accrued to foreign competitors in the victorious states, which meant practically the rest of the world. It is hardly credible that such losses left no traces on company development, individually and collectively. If we recall that the First World War transformed the US economy from being the world's biggest debtor into the world's primary lender, we can surmise that enterprise growth in neutral states, here Spain and Sweden, might have exceeded that in winner states. We can test this hypothesis by examining the development of company assets registered in our data set. The relevant years to compare are 1913, 1927, and 1954. In the latter two years, the respective war had ended nine years before. Since our data set contains just one loser of both wars, Germany, we will define the assets of the German firms as the index '1' and relate the assets of other countries' companies to this base. If German enterprises suffered relatively excessive war-related losses—as we can presume they did—the assets of enterprises based in winning or neutral states should have jumped compared with those of German firms. In 1913, before the

---

[9] The figures for ICI and Unilever are missing in our data set, but I am confident that they qualify as 'Very Big'.

Table 12.15. Electro-technical industry: assets of the three largest national enterprises, 1913–54 (Germany = 1)

Year	Germany	UK	France	Sweden
1913	1	0.1	0.2	0.02
1927	1	0.5	0.3	0.1
1954	1	1.7	0.6	0.3

Source: Own calculations from data set

Table 12.16. Chemicals: assets of the three largest national enterprises, 1913–54 (Germany = 1)

Year	Germany	UK	France	Sweden
1913	1	1.8	0.5	0.08
1927	1	1.4	0.09	0.3
1954	1	2.7	0.6	0.1

Source: Own calculations from data set

two wars, German enterprise was exceptionally strong in electrical engineering and chemicals, both branches having considerable direct investment abroad and royalties from patents and registered trademarks. We therefore imagine finding the deepest traces of war in these two branches.

The data on the electro-technical industry in Table 12.15 offer a degree of support for our hypothesis. In 1927, following their country's defeat in the First World War, the German firms—AEG and Siemens—still dominated, but their British and French rivals had made up considerable ground. In 1954, after the destruction and unconditional defeat of the Second World War, German dominance in the branch was fractured, and its leading position taken over by British firms. In both post-war years, however, the relatively largest increase in assets occurred in neutral Sweden.

However, to determine if developments in electrical engineering were typical or exceptional, we must examine comparative asset growth in the second branch in which German firms excelled in 1913, namely chemicals (see Table 12.16).

First, we see that German chemical companies were not as dominant in 1913 as much of the literature suggests; the common impression of German dominance derives from the country's position in organic chemicals (dyestuffs) and overlooks British strength in all other industrial chemicals. The 1927 data contain no victors' benefit for British or French chemical firms; in fact, they lost ground to their German competitors. On the other hand, the chemicals branch in neutral Sweden grew tremendously between 1913 and 1927, which could be a war-related surge. The 1927 situation, however, was completely reversed in 1954: this time, firms from the two winning countries had recovered and increased their positions, while the branch in neutral Sweden had slumped.[10] To sum up: we find no traces of war-related relative shrinking of German chemical firms' assets in 1927—indeed,

---

[10] The Swedish slump was largely due to the collapse of Svenska Tändsticks AB in the 1930s, from which the company never fully recovered; it was thus not directly war-related.

Table 12.17. Mechanical engineering: assets of the three largest national enterprises, 1913–54 (Germany = 1)

Year	Germany	UK	France	Sweden
1913	1	0.9	0.8	0.4
1927	1	3.0	1.1	1.1
1954	1	3.0	0.9	0.5

Source: Own calculations from data set

Table 12.18. Transport equipment: assets of the three largest national enterprises, 1913–54 (Germany = 1)

Year	Germany	UK	France	Sweden
1913	1	4.9	1.8	0.07
1927	1	4.5	1.1	0.1
1954	1	3.4	1.4	0.4

Source: Own calculations from data set

rather the reverse—but there is a substantial confirmation of the hypothesis as regards the consequences of the Second World War.

Mechanical engineering was not a branch in which German firms were noticeably dominant in 1913. Did the two world wars affect their relative position? The findings are mixed (Table 12.17). After the First World War, British firms did indeed surge past their German competitors to establish a clear predominance. French and Swedish firms also seem to have experienced a war-related boom and gained ground on the Germans. In 1954, however, there is no evidence of such an effect. The relative position of British and German firms is the same as in 1927, while the French and Swedish positions have fallen back.

Although in 2000 the transport equipment industry was dominated by German car companies, this was not the case before the Second World War (Table 12.18). Up to that time, the British branch was overwhelmingly predominant. There is no indication of war-related benefits for non-German firms in 1927, and in 1954 the relatively stronger growth of French and Swedish firms is modest. The primary finding is in fact the relative decline of the largest British and French firms compared with German enterprise.

Finally, we take a look at the oil and rubber branch, which in 1913 was combined with the chemical branch (Table 12.19). At this date, British oil and rubber firms were already nearly twice the size of their German competitors, and after the First World War their growth left the Germans far behind. After the Second World War, however, they could add little to their lead. The position of French firms was unchanged after the First World War, but surged forward after the Second. The Swedish firms in oil and rubber remained very marginal throughout the entire period.

To sum up, the evidence supporting the hypothesis that the two world wars advantaged firms in the winning or neutral states is very mixed. While there some support with respect to electrical engineering, oil, and mechanical engineering in the UK, the indications in the French and Swedish cases are weak and unclear. On

Table 12.19. Oil and rubber: assets of the three largest national enterprises, 1913–54 (Germany = 1)

Year	Germany	UK	France	Sweden
1913	1	1.8	0.5	0.08
1927	1	5.2	0.6	0.1
1954	1	5.5	1.7	0.07

Source: Own calculations from data set

the other hand, there are no signs of the reverse, namely that the wars advantaged the firms in a defeated country. In other words, the wars may have had some effects on the assets of firms in belligerent states, but the significance is rather small. This evaluation corresponds with Cassis' observation on the 'stability of German big business'.[11] Although full resolution of the question requires more detailed investigation, this cursory review does contradict the popular Leninist rhetoric about capitalism and war: the wars were *not* good for European big business.

THE EFFECTS OF COUNTRY SIZE ON ENTERPRISE

Peter J. Katzenstein proposed some years ago that companies in small states were inevitably disadvantaged in the world economy.[12] Our data set includes three small states—Belgium, Finland, and Sweden, which gives us a chance to test this proposal a bit. A first glance at the data would seem to support Katzenstein's theory of small-state disadvantage: firm longevity was much more frequent in large states than in small ones. There were twenty-one examples of long-term survival among the Chandlerian companies, only one of which was based in a small state.

However, the indicators of ongoing economic performance—ROE and HR—clearly do not support Katzenstein's theory. Except for two benchmarks (HR in 1954 and ROE in 2000), enterprises based in small developed states—Belgium, Finland, and Sweden—outperformed their competitors based in large developed states—France, Germany, Italy, Spain, and the UK. As can be seen in Table 12.20, the difference was quite sizable. Unfortunately, we can only speculate about the reasons, since our data do not give a basis for more than this. The result, however, is in tune with others: in *Pathbreakers*, Margrit Müller showed that the small (West) European countries outperformed their larger competitors after the Second World War.[13] Perhaps large states tended to establish comprehensive, or

[11] Cassis, *Big Business*, pp. 46–54.
[12] P.J. Katzenstein, *Small States in World Markets: Industrial Policy in Europe* (Ithaca: Cornell University Press, 1985) and 'Small States and small states revisited', *New Political Economy*, 8, 1 (2003), 9–30.
[13] M, Müller, 'Introduction', in M. Müller and T. Myllyntaus, eds., *Pathbreakers, Small Countries Responding to Globalisation and Deglobalisation* (Bern: Peter Lang, 2008), pp. 11–35 (p. 15).

Table 12.20. ROE and HR according to size of country, 1913–2000 (in %)

Year	Large states		Small states	
	ROE	HR	ROE	HR
1913	10.11	7.36	16.71	10.61
1927	8.06	16.79	11.75	28.36
1954	7.54	31.58	9.25	17.68
1972	6.48	8.06	8.60	12.27
2000	16.40	11.82	13.92	19.74

Source: Own calculations from data set

interventionist, economic policies that restricted the managerial agility of enterprises, whereas small states did not command similar regulatory resources and hence companies there were forced (or enabled) to be more flexible and creative. In any case, the supposed advantage of a bigger home market in large states did not lead to better performance of the enterprises based there. This empirical result clearly upsets many general ideas about the disadvantages of small states,[14] as well as about transnational enterprise in general. The challenge concerns especially those theories based on a so-called home-market advantage versus a host-market disadvantage, such as Dunning's eclectic theory.[15] Unquestionably more research is needed here, but one thing is indisputable: there was no general disadvantage for small-state enterprises in twentieth-century Europe. On the contrary, in the Chandlerian industries, they outperformed their large-state competitors!

SUMMARY

In our sample of Chandlerian industries, longevity of individual companies varied greatly, mainly differing according to industrial branch. Longevity was very high in oil and chemicals, while it turned out to be very volatile in mechanical engineering. In the latter branch, the only stable sector was car production. In electrical engineering, the technological shift from power generation to telecommunication adversely affected company longevity. As regards actual economic performance of enterprises, ROE improved over the century, but HR did not. Oil companies generally were overperformers, companies in transport equipment generally underperformers. Oil companies also had the best capital turnover ratios. But the oil branch did not outperform all others in the growth of assets.

---

[14] Müller, 'Introduction', p. 12f.; M.L. Bishop, 'The political economy of small states: Enduring vulnerability?', *Review of International Political Economy*, 19, 5 (2012), 942–60; H.G. Schröter, 'Losers in power-plays? Small states and international cartelization', *Journal of European Economic History*, 39, 3 (2010), 527–55.
[15] J.H. Dunning, ed., *The Theory of Transnational Corporations*, United Nations Library on Transnational Corporations, Vol. 1 (London: Routledge, 1993); J.H. Dunning, 'The eclectic (OLI) paradigm of international production', in Jeffrey A. Krug, and John D. Daniels, eds., *Multinational Enterprise Theory*, Vol. 2: *Internationalization Process of the MNE* (Los Angeles: Sage, 2008).

In this performance category, the leading branch changed in each benchmark year, pointing to a high volatility of investment across branches and sectors. In contrast to traditional perceptions of German dominance in big business, nearly one-half of the top ten Chandlerian enterprises in Europe during the twentieth century were based in the UK, while France figured with no more than two. The number of 'Big' and 'Giant' firms in the Chandlerian group was quite limited. And also here, the enterprises and branches involved changed significantly, underlining once again the volatility of investors. Surprisingly, in the long run, wars had little effect on the relative size and performance of Chandlerian enterprises. And finally another surprise: firms based in small states consistently outperformed their competitors based in large states.

APPENDIX

Table 12A.1. Chandlerian companies by name and year of entry in the sample, 1913–2000

Country	Company	Branch	1913	1927	1954	1972	2000
Belgium	A.C.E.C. (At. Constructions Electr. Charleroi)	Electrical engineering				X	
Italy	A.E.G. Thomson Houston	Electrical engineering	X				
Italy	A.P.I.–Anonima Petroli Italiana	Oil, rubber				X	
Finland	Ab Crichton-Vulcan Oy	Transport equipment		X			
Sweden	AB Separator/Alfa Lava	Mechanical engineering	X	X		X	
Germany	Adam Opel AG	Transport equipment		X	X	X	
France	Air Liquide	Oil, rubber	X			X	
France	Airbus industrie	Transport equipment					X
Italy	Alfa Romeo (Gruppo IRI)	Transport equipment				X	
Germany	Allgemeine Elekricitäts-Gesellschaft (AEG)	Electrical engineering	X	X	X	X	
France	Alsacienne de constructions mécaniques	Mechanical engineering	X		X		
France	Alsthom	Electrical engineering			X		X
UK	Anglo-Persian Oil	Oil, rubber		X			
Italy	Anic (Gruppo ENI)	Chemicals, pharmaceuticals			X	X	
Italy	Ansaldo	Mechanical engineering	X	X	X	X	
Germany	Aral AG	Oil, rubber				X	
UK	Armstrong, Whitworth Securities	Transport equipment	X	X			
Spain	Arrendataria del Monop. Petrol. 'Campsa'	Oil, rubber		X			
Sweden	ASEA	Electrical engineering	X	X	X	X	

(*continued*)

Table 12A.1. Continued

Country	Company	Branch	1913	1927	1954	1972	2000
UK	Associated Electrical Industries	Electrical engineering			X	X	
Spain	Astillero del Nervión	Transport equipment	X				
UK	AstraZeneca	Chemicals, pharmaceuticals					X
Belgium	Ateliers Constr. Electr. de Charleroi (ACEC)	Electrical engineering	X	X	X		
France	Ateliers de constructions de Roanne	Mechanical engineering				X	
France	Ateliers et chantiers St. Nazaire (Penhoët)	Transport equipment	X	X			
Sweden	Atlas Copco	Mechanical engineering					X
France	Aventis	Chemicals, pharmaceuticals					X
UK	Babcock & Wilcox (UK)	Mechanical engineering	X	X	X		
Spain	Babcock & Wilcox (Spain)	Mechanical engineering				X	
UK	BAE Systems	Transport equipment					X
Belgium	Barco	Electrical engineering					X
Germany	BASF (Badische Anilin & Sodafabrik AG)	Chemicals, pharmaceuticals	X		X	X	X
Germany	Bayer AG (Farbenfabriken vorm. Bayer AG)	Chemicals, pharmaceuticals	X		X	X	X
Germany	BMW (Bayerische Motoren Werke AG)	Transport equipment					X
UK	BBA Group	Transport equipment					X
UK	BG Group	Oil, rubber					X
Germany	Bosch (Robert Bosch GmbH)	Electrical engineering				X	X
Sweden	Bofors AB	Mechanical engineering			X		
UK	Boots Company	Chemicals, pharmaceuticals				X	
UK	BP (BP Amoco)	Oil, rubber			X	X	X
France	Bréguet aviation (avions Dassault)	Transport equipment				X	
UK	British Insulated Callender's Cables	Electrical engineering				X	
UK	British Leyland Motor Corporation	Transport equipment				X	
UK	British Motor Corporation	Transport equipment				X	
UK	British Oxygen	Chemicals, pharmaceuticals				X	
UK	British Thomson-Houston	Electrical engineering	X	X			
UK	British Westinghouse El. & Man. Comp.	Electrical engineering	X				
UK	Cammell Laird	Mechanical engineering			X		
Spain	Campsa (Comp. Arrend. d. Monop. d. Petról.)	Oil, rubber				X	

Italy	Cantiere Navale Triestino	Transport equipment		X			
Italy	Cantieri Riuniti Adriatico (Gruppo IRI)	Transport equipment			X		
Spain	CEPSA	Chemicals, pharmaceuticals				X	
France	Chantiers de la Loire	Transport equipment	X				
France	Cie des compteurs (groupe Schlumberger)	Electrical engineering				X	
Italy	CIR	Mechanical engineering					X
France	Citroën	Transport equipment		X	X	X	
Italy	Compagnia Italiana Italcable	Electrical engineering		X			
Belgium	Comp. Bel. de Chemins de fer et d'Entrepr.	Transport equipment			X		
Belgium	Comp. Bel. pour les Industries Chimiques	Chemicals, pharmaceuticals		X			
Belgium	Compagnie d'Entreprises C.F.E.	Transport equipment				X	
France	Compagnie Générale d'Electricité (Alcatel)	Electrical engineering	X	X	X	X	X
Germany	Continental AG	Oil, rubber					X
Germany	Daimler-Benz AG (Daimler-Chrysler)	Transport equipment		X	X	X	X
Germany	Degussa AG	Chemicals, pharmaceuticals					X
Germany	Demag AG	Mechanical engineering		X	X	X	
Germany	Deutsche Babcock & Wilcox	Mechanical engineering			X		
Germany	Deutsche Erdöl-AG (DEA/RWE-DEA)	Oil, rubber		X			X
Germany	Deutsche Shell (AG; GmbH)	Oil, rubber			X	X	X
Spain	Dow Chemical Iberica	Chemicals, pharmaceuticals					X
UK	Dunlop	Oil, rubber		X	X		
Spain	E.N. Bazan de Constr. Navales Militares	Transport equipment			X		
Spain	E.N. Calvo Sotelo (Encaso)	Oil, rubber			X		
France	Elf-Erap	Oil, rubber				X	
UK	English Electric Company	Electrical engineering			X		
Italy	Enichem (ENI Group)	Chemicals, pharmaceuticals					X
Italy	Ercole Marelli	Electrical engineering			X		
Sweden	Ericsson	Electrical engineering					X
Spain	Ericsson Espana	Electrical engineering					X
Spain	Espanola de Construccion Naval, Sociedad	Transport equipment			X	X	
Spain	Espanola de Constr. Electromecanicas	Electrical engineering		X			

(*continued*)

Table 12A.1. Continued

Country	Company	Branch	1913	1927	1954	1972	2000
Germany	ESSO AG (Dt.-Am.-Petroleum Gesellschaft)	Oil, rubber		X	X	X	
UK	Esso Petroleum Company	Oil, rubber				X	
France	Esso Standard	Oil, rubber			X		
Belgium	Fabrique Nationale	Mechanical engineering	X	X	X		
Italy	FIAT (Gruppo IFI)	Transport equipment	X	X	X	X	X
Finland	Finska Färg och Fernissfabriks A.B.	Chemicals, pharmaceuticals		X			
France	Fives-Lille	Mechanical engineering	X	X	X	X	
UK	Ford Motor Company	Transport equipment			X	X	
Finland	Fortum	Oil, rubber					X
Germany	Gelsenberg Benzin AG	Oil, rubber			X		
UK	General Electric Company	Electrical engineering		X	X	X	X
Belgium	Gevaert Photo Producten	Chemicals, pharmaceuticals			X		
UK	GKN (Guest, Keen & Nettlefolds)	Mechanical engineering			X	X	X
Belgium	Glaces Nation. Belges Saint-Roch Auvelais	Chemicals, pharmaceuticals	X	X	X		
UK	GlaxoSmithKline	Chemicals, pharmaceuticals					X
Sweden	Götaverken AB	Transport equipment		X	X		
Germany	Gutehoffnungshütte Aktienverein/MAN	Mechanical engineering	X	X		X	X
UK	Harland and Wolff	Transport equipment		X			
UK	Hawker Siddeley Group	Transport equipment			X	X	
Germany	Henschel & Sohn AG	Transport equipment		X			
Spain	Hewlett Packard Espanola	Mechanical engineering					X
Germany	Hewlett-Packard GmbH	Electrical engineering					X
Germany	Hoechst (Farbwerke Hoechst AG)	Chemicals, pharmaceuticals	X		X		
Sweden	Höganäs-Billesholm AB	Chemicals, pharmaceuticals	X	X	X		
UK	Howard & Bullough	Mechanical engineering	X				
France	Huiles de Pétrole/BP	Oil, rubber		X			
Italy	IFI (Agnelli)	Transport equipment					X
Germany	IG Farbenindustrie AG	Chemicals, pharmaceuticals		X			
UK	Imperial Chemical Industries	Chemicals, pharmaceuticals		X	X	X	X
Italy	Industrie A. Zanussi	Electrical engineering				X	
Italy	Ing. C. Olivetti & C./Italtel	Mechanical engineering				X	X
UK	Invensys	Electrical engineering					X
France	Jeumont	Electrical engineering	X	X			
UK	John Brown & Company	Transport equipment	X				
Germany	Kali-Industrie-AG	Chemicals, pharmaceuticals		X			
Finland	Kemira Oy	Chemicals, pharmaceuticals				X	X

Germany	Klöckner-Humboldt-Deutz AG	Mechanical engineering			X	X	
Sweden	Kockums Mekaniska verkstadaktiebolag	Transport equipment	X				
Finland	Kone- ja Siltarakennus Oy	Mechanical engineering		X			
France	L'Oreal	Chemicals, pharmaceuticals					X
France	l'Air Liquide SA	Chemicals, pharmaceuticals					X
Spain	La Maquinista Terrestre y Maritima	Mechanical engineering			X		
France	Lagardere Groupe	Electrical engineering					X
UK	Logica	Electrical engineering					X
Italy	Magneti Marelli (Fiat Group)	Mechanical engineering			X	X	X
Germany	Mannesmannröhren-Werke	Mechanical engineering	X				
Belgium	Man. Liégoise de caoutch. Souple . . . Englebert	Transport equipment		X			
Germany	Maschinenbau-Anstalt 'Humboldt'	Mechanical engineering	X				
UK	Metrop. Carriage Wagon & Finance C.	Mechanical engineering	X				
Finland	Metso	Mechanical engineering					X
France	Michelin	Oil, rubber		X	X	X	X
Belgium	Minerva Motors	Transport equipment	X				
Italy	Montecatini	Chemicals, pharmaceuticals		X	X		
Italy	Montedison	Chemicals, pharmaceuticals				X	
Finland	Nokia	Electrical engineering					X
Italy	Officine Elettriche Genovesi	Electrical engineering		X			
Italy	Officine meccaniche Stigler	Mechanical engineering	X				
Italy	Offic. Sesto S. Giovanni & Valsecchi Abramo	Mechanical engineering	X				
Finland	Oy Nokia Ab	Oil, rubber				X	
France	Pechiney (Alais, Froges, Camargue)	Chemicals, pharmaceuticals	X		X		
Sweden	Perstorp	Chemicals, pharmaceuticals					X
Belgium	Petrofina	Oil, rubber			X	X	X
France	Pétroles BP	Oil, rubber			X		
France	Peugeot	Transport equipment	X	X	X	X	X
Belgium	Pieux Franki	Mechanical engineering				X	
Italy	Pirelli	Oil, rubber		X	X	X	X
UK	Platt Brothers	Mechanical engineering		X			
France	Poclain	Mechanical engineering				X	
France	Pont à Mousson	Mechanical engineering			X		
Sweden	Preem	Oil, rubber					X

(*continued*)

Table 12A.1. Continued

Country	Company	Branch	1913	1927	1954	1972	2000
France	Prod. Chim. et électrométall. d'Alais	Chemicals, pharmaceuticals		X			
UK	Reckitt	Chemicals, pharmaceuticals		X			
France	Renault	Transport equipment		X		X	X
Spain	Renault Espana	Transport equipment					X
Spain	Repsol-YPF	Oil, rubber					X
Germany	Rhenania-Ossag Mineralölwerke AG	Oil, rubber		X			
France	Rhone Poulenc	Chemicals, pharmaceuticals		X	X	X	
Italy	RIV–Officine di Villar Perosa	Mechanical engineering			X		
UK	Rolls-Royce	Transport equipment					X
Italy	Romsa	Oil, rubber		X			
Germany	Rütgerswerke-AG	Chemicals, pharmaceuticals		X			
Belgium	Sabca	Transport equipment					X
France	Saint-Gobain	Oil, rubber	X	X	X	X	
Belgium	Sait Electronics	Mechanical engineering					X
France	Schneider Electric	Electrical engineering					X
Spain	SEAT	Transport equipment				X	X
UK	Shell Transp. & Trading Comp.	Oil, rubber	X	X	X	X	X
Germany	Siemens AG (S&H, SWW)	Electrical engineering	X	X	X	X	X
Germany	Singer Nähmaschinen Aktienges.	Mechanical engineering		X			
UK	Smiths Group	Mechanical engineering					X
France	SNECMA	Transport equipment			X		
Italy	Snia	Chemicals, pharmaceuticals		X			X
Spain	Soc. Espanola de Construcciones Metalicas	Mechanical engineering	X	X			
Italy	Soc. Ital. E. Breda per Costruz. Meccaniche	Mechanical engineering		X			
Italy	Società italiana per il carburo di calcio	Oil, rubber	X				
France	Soc. alsacienne de constr. mécaniques	Mechanical engineering		X			
Belgium	Société des Glaces Nationales Belges	Oil, rubber	X				
Belgium	Société Financière des Caoutchouc (Socfin)	Oil, rubber		X			
France	Soc. française de constructions mécaniques	Mechanical engineering	X				
Belgium	Solvay	Chemicals, pharmaceuticals				X	
Spain	Standard Electrica	Electrical engineering			X	X	
Italy	Stanic (Gruppi ENI e Esso Italiana)	Oil, rubber			X		

Country	Company	Industry					
Italy	Stmicroelectronics (Finmeccanica Group)	Electrical engineering					X
Finland	Strömberg Oy Ab	Electrical engineering		X	X	X	
Finland	Suomen Gummitehdas Oy	Oil, rubber		X			
Sweden	Svenska Tändsticksaktiebolaget	Chemicals, pharmaceuticals		X	X	X	
Italy	Tecnomasio italiano Brown Boveri	Electrical engineering	X				
France	Thomson-Houston	Electrical engineering	X	X	X	X	
UK	Thorn Electrical Industries	Electrical engineering				X	
UK	Tomkins	Mechanical engineering					X
France	Total (Cie Française des Pétroles)	Oil, rubber	X		X	X	X
Sweden	Trelleborgs Gummifabrik AB	Oil, rubber				X	
UK	Tube Investments	Mechanical engineering			X	X	
Finland	Typpi Oy	Chemicals, pharmaceuticals			X		
Spain	UERT	Chemicals, pharmaceuticals				X	
France	Ugine	Chemicals, pharmaceuticals			X		
UK	Unilever	Chemicals, pharmaceuticals	X	X	X	X	
Spain	Union Espanola de Explosivos, S.A.	Chemicals, pharmaceuticals	X	X	X		
Italy	Unione ital. fra cons. e fabbr.... chimici	Oil, rubber	X				
UK	United Alkali Company	Oil, rubber	X				
Belgium	Val-Saint-Lambert a Seraing	Oil, rubber	X				
Finland	Valmet Oy	Mechanical engineering			X	X	
UK	Vickers	Transport equipment	X	X	X	X	
Germany	Volkswagen AG/GmbH	Transport equipment			X	X	X
Sweden	Volvo	Transport equipment				X	X
Germany	Vulkan-Werke, Hamburg und Stettin	Transport equipment	X				
Finland	Wärtsilä-yhtymä Oy	Transport equipment			X	X	
Germany	Würth-Gruppe	Mechanical engineering					X
Germany	ZF Friedrichshafen AG	Mechanical engineering					X

13

The Performance of European Transport and Utilities in the Twentieth Century

Anna M. Aubanell-Joubany and Terry Gourvish

The development of utilities has been strongly influenced by the changing ideology of governments during the nineteenth and twentieth centuries.[1] Indeed, it is fair to say that the role of governments, at the municipal, regional, national, and finally at the European level, has been a major determinant of the industry's ownership and profitability.

In some cases, like the airline industry, it was national security that encouraged state intervention.[2] However, the main factors underpinning the intervention of governments have been the public service and network technology characteristics of the several utilities, whether rail transport, electricity, gas, or water.[3] Until the mid 1970s, these economic activities had been considered a natural monopoly, that is, that the most efficient way to serve the market would be to have a single firm for each utility. Problems arose because a monopolistic firm tends to set high prices, and can exhibit inefficient management, making regulatory action justified. By the beginning of the 1980s, only parts of the production process enjoyed natural monopoly status and governments encouraged competition in the industry as part of the drive towards privatization.[4]

The importance of public ownership has varied in the several European countries and over the period studied. At the beginning of the twentieth century, municipal ownership was very important in the UK, Germany, and Belgium for the gas and electricity industries. After the Second World War, nationalization

---

[1] Robert Millward concluded that state enterprise in France and Britain was linked with socialist ideology, but this was not the case in Italy, Germany, and Spain: R. Millward, *Private and Public Enterprise in Europe* (Cambridge, 2005), pp. 3–11.

[2] Security reasons for intervention are also found in other industries: see R. Millward, 'Geo-politics versus market structure interventions in Europe's infrastructure industries *c*. 1830–1939', *Business History*, 53, 5 (2011), 673–87.

[3] Some authors point out that municipal or national governments regulated markets in response to the companies' requests: H. Platt, *The Electric City* (Chicago, 1991); T. DiLorenzo, 'The myth of natural monopoly', *The Review of Austrian Economics*, 9, 42 (1996), 43–58.

[4] W. Primeaux, 'A Reexamination of the monopoly market structure for electric utilities', in A. Phillips (ed.) *Promoting Competition in Regulated Markets* (Washington, 1975), 175–200. J. Clifton, P. Lanthier, and H.G. Schröter, 'Regulating and deregulating the public utilities 1830–2010', *Business History*, 53/5 (2011), 659–72.

took place in the UK, France, and Italy, resulting in state monopoly firms. With the ideological change that occurred in the 1980s, these state firms were privatized, resulting in some of today's large utilities. All these ownership changes resulted in the presence or absence of companies in our sample in response not only to the issue of private versus public ownership but specifically to the type of public ownership chosen by each government.

BUSINESS DEVELOPMENT

The transport and utilities (T&U) sector that is the focus of this chapter consists of three subsectors in the 1911–13 and 1927–9 benchmarks: (1) railways, (2) transport and communication, and (3) utilities (electricity, gas, and water).

In 1911–13, the T&U sector's average size was $137.4 million, twice the size of the average of the overall European sample. Fourteen T&U companies were among the fifty largest European firms. By 1927, the average size of the sector reached $232.7 million, 1.64 times larger than the average of the sample. In constant dollars, the size fell marginally between 1913 and 1927 (see Table 13.1). However, the number of T&U companies in the top fifty stayed the same.

The major fall in asset size occurred in 1954–6 owing to the nationalization process, which greatly affected the composition of the sector. There was only one railway company left in the sample, whereas railways were the largest firms in the first two benchmarks. The same phenomenon affected some of the largest electricity companies. The average size of the T&U sector was $196.9 million, 70 per cent of the average sample size. The number of T&U companies in the top fifty declined from fourteen to five, which demonstrates the big changes the sector underwent after the Second World War.

Between 1954–6 and 1970–2, the asset size of the T&U firms increased substantially: thirteen times when the assets are measured in current US dollars and seventeen times in constant dollars (base year 2000). In 1970–2, the average size of the T&U sector was 1.25 times larger than the average of the sample, higher than the relative size the sector had in 1954–6 but lower than the first two benchmarks. If instead of assets, turnover is considered, then the average size of the T&U firms is the same as the average turnover of the European sample. There were twelve T&U firms among the top fifty in assets terms and eight in the turnover ranking.

Table 13.1. Size in T&U, 1911–2000 (assets in million US$)

	T&U		European companies		Relative size
	Current US$	2000 US$	Current US$	2000 US$	T&U/all
1911–13	137.4	2,460.0	68.9	1,233.4	1.99
1927–9	232.7	2,306.4	141.8	1,405.3	1.64
1954–6	196.9	1,262.1	281.0	1,801.4	0.70
1970–2	2,695.8	21,620.0	2,164.5	15,482.8	1.25 (1.0)[a]
1998–2000	22,722.0	22,722.0	47,302.5	47,302.5	0.48 (1.0)[a]

[a] Figure in parentheses is relative size when turnover is considered

The asset size in current prices of the T&U firms increased almost 8.5 times between 1970–2 and 1998–2000 owing to the high inflation registered in this period. When the effect of inflation is excluded, the firm size in the sector had practically remained at the same assets level. As Table 13.1 shows, the average size in constant dollars increased by only 5 per cent in the twenty-eight-year period. The relative size of the T&U firms had fallen to its lowest level, less than half of the average of the European sample. This is because we lack some asset data from major companies and because the transport and telecommunications subsector is now split, with telecommunications firms studied separately in the knowledge industry sector in 2000. When turnover is considered, the relative size of the T&U firms is unchanged. There were six T&U companies among the top fifty European companies in assets and five companies among the fifty largest according to turnover.

The relative size of the T&U companies in the twentieth century declined. Before the First World War, the average asset size was almost double the average size of the largest European companies; by the end of the twentieth century, it was below that average. The number of large companies among the fifty largest also showed this trend. On the eve of the First World War, there were fourteen companies among the largest fifty, but by the year 2000, there were only six.

The large size of the T&U sector, $137.4 million in 1911–13, was due to the railways subsector. The average asset size of the railways companies was $328.4 million, while for transport and communication it was $32.2 million and for utilities $30.3 million, both below the European average size.

The six largest European companies in the 1911–13 sample were French and British railway firms: the Chemins de Fer de Paris à Lyon et à la Méditerranée (PLM), the Midland Railway, the Chemin de Fer Paris-Orléans, the Chemins de Fer de l'Est, the London & North Western Railway, and the Great Western Railway. They were 'Giant' firms, with assets four times the average of the T&U sector and almost eight times the average of the European sample. Railways made massive demands on the capital market, and their geographical spread made them large and complex businesses. When the London & North Western Railway was created in 1846, it was the world's largest company ranked by size of capital employed, although later the Midland Railway took over this distinction. Wardley's study of British companies in 1904/5 reveals that the top ten, ranked by the market value of assets, were all railway companies, led by the Midland, the London & North Western, and the Great Western.[5]

In 1911–13, shipping companies were the majority in the transport and communication subsector accounting for 97.2 per cent of assets. The only exceptions, out of the fifteen companies in the subsector, were the Swedish telephone company Stockholms Allmänna Telefonaktiebolag and the Belgium Canal de Blaton-Ath.

On the eve of the First World War, the shipping industry had evolved considerably in technological terms. The replacement of iron by steel for the construction of hulls, the adoption of the steam turbine, and the use of twin screws improved the efficiency of the industry considerably. Additionally, there was a

[5] P. Wardley, 'The anatomy of big business: Aspects of corporate development in the twentieth century', *Business History*, 33, 1 (1991), 278.

change towards specialized ships, increasing efficiency further.[6] The use of bigger ships required greater investment and also brought some overcapacity, which increased uncertainty in the business and encouraged protectionism. Two different ways to limit competition emerged. The first device was the creation of shipping conferences, instigated by the British companies. The shipping conference established unified rates on specific shipping lines and divided the trade by fixing the number of sailings or allocating a specific port to each company. The second way was the merger of companies in order to create quasi-monopolies in some areas. This was the strategy followed by J.P. Morgan with the International Mercantile Marine Co. and the German firms.

The two largest shipping companies, with assets that were double the subsector average, were Hamburg-Amerikanische Packetfahrt-Actien-Gesellschaft (Hapag) and Norddeutscher Lloyd (NDL). These two German companies were respectively in the twenty-eighth and thirty-third positions in the European ranking. Both companies were founded in the mid nineteenth century and expanded thanks to the massive emigration to America. The profits the two companies obtained from the transatlantic emigrant passages paid for the expansion of other routes.

The third company in size, thirty-eighth in the overall sample, was Messageries Maritimes, founded in 1871 to provide passenger and freight services and to carry mail, for which it received an annual payment from the French state. The company had profited from the increase in business created by the French colonial expansion, but not without some financial problems. Up to the First World War, the relationship between governments and the shipping companies was mainly confined to contracts to carry mail. It was not always advantageous for the companies, as the cases of Messageries Maritimes and NDL show. The conditions in terms of regularity and speed that the French government imposed on Messageries Maritimes were clearly incompatible with commercial operations—so much so that the company concentrated on passenger and freight services from 1912. Similarly, NDL lost 5.25 million Marks on mail-steamer lines to East Asia and Australia in spite of the 44.3 million Marks in subsidies that it received from the German government.[7]

In this period, the British steam mercantile fleet was the largest in the world, with 45.2 per cent of the total tonnage.[8] At the turn of the century, the British shipowners regarded the formation of American and German groups and conglomerates with dismay and decided to emulate this strategy. The best example was the Royal Mail Steam Packet Co., which was the fourth largest firm in the transport and communication subsector, forty-fifth in the overall ranking. Peninsular & Oriental Steam Navigation Company (P&O), in fifth place in the subsector and fifty-fourth in the general ranking, also embarked on a merger wave that extended well into the 1920s.

---

[6] P.N. Davies, 'British shipping and the world trade: Rise and decline, 1820-1939', in T. Yui and K. Nakagawa, eds., *Business History of Shipping* (Tokyo, 1985), p. 58.

[7] L.U. Scholl, 'Shipping business in Germany in the nineteenth and twentieth centuries', in *Business History of Shipping*, pp. 185–216.

[8] Davies, 'British shipping', p. 77.

The utilities subsector on the eve of the First World War was composed of a majority of electricity companies, 21 per cent of gas firms, and 7 per cent of water utilities. Electricity firms accounted for 55 per cent of total utility assets, gas companies for 37 per cent, and a single water company for 8 per cent. Among the five largest utility companies in 1911–13, there were three electricity companies, one gas company, and one water company. The biggest firm, with assets 4.5 times larger than the average utility firm, was the British Gas Light and Coke Co. It was the twenty-second largest company in Europe (the second largest if financial and railways companies are excluded) behind the German firm Krupp. The company was the first company to supply gas to London and became the largest gas company because it acquired many of the gas companies in London and the south-east of England, at that time the largest European urban conurbation.

The second, third, and fifth companies were electricity firms that were in the thirtieth, fifty-fifth, and eighty-eighth places in the ranking of European big business. These were in fact low places for an industry that was more capital-intensive than the railways. For example, in 1913 the capital/output ratio for the American electricity industry was 11, compared with 4.5 for the railways.[9] The high capital and low output are explained by the large fixed capital costs of the distribution network and the low-load-factor problem. The latter could only improve in time by combining lighting, power, and traction consumption, and this in turn could only be economically achieved in large cities. As long-distance electricity transmission technology was only available from the turn of the century, the industry was confined to the local level; electricity was generated, distributed, and consumed within the city. Thus, the size of the city determined the size of the business obtained. Up to 1913, the majority of the large utilities were companies that were based in the major metropolitan areas and that had bought other firms to avoid either direct or potential competition. This was the case with Berliner Elektricitäts Werke (the third largest utility), Società generale italiana Edison di elettricità Milan, and Newcastle-upon-Tyne Electric Supply.

From the very beginning of the electricity industry, electrical manufacturers created their own market by starting new businesses with the help of the banks. This was the case with the second largest company in the industry and the ninth largest European, the Deutsch-Ueberseeische Elektricitäts-Gesellschaft (DUEG), which was set up by AEG and the Deutsche Bank in 1898 in order to create electricity companies in Latin America, mainly Argentina. It can be argued that DUEG was more a financial company than an electricity one. The decision to include this conglomerate in the utilities sector lies in the fact that all its companies were electricity or tramway firms and that its investment strategy focused not only on the sale of electrical machinery but also on assisting the electricity firms to become more efficient by, for example, securing the demand for electricity from the tramways.

The use of long-distance transmission technology, which allows the generation phase to be located far from the consumption centres and the companies to expand at a regional level, was slow in coming. On the eve of the First World

---

[9] W. Hausman, P. Hertner, and M. Wilkins, *Global Electrification* (Cambridge, 2008), p. 22.

War, there were only nine regional power lines in Europe, with an average length of 158 kilometres. The greater financial requirements of hydroelectric power stations, where available, and of high-voltage power lines resulted in larger companies. An example is Riegos y Fuerzas del Ebro, the fifth largest utility.

The fourth largest utility in 1911–13 was the Compagnie Générale des Eaux, sixty-fourth in the European sample. Municipal ownership in the water supply industry was the norm in the countries considered in our study, except in Spain, where privately owned companies provided the service.[10] In spite of the fact that 75 per cent of the water undertakings in France were municipally owned, the only two water companies large enough to appear in our twentieth-century study were in fact French. The other company, Société Lyonnaise des Eaux et de l'Eclairage, was the tenth largest utility firm in 1927–9 and 1954–6. One might speculate that the greater size of this company was due to its diversification into the electricity business. However, this was not the case, because in 1954–6, when the company no longer owned the electricity part of its business, Lyonnaise des Eaux was still in tenth place.[11] These two companies became large because they held the concessions to supply the large French metropolitan areas and beyond. The Compagnie Générale des Eaux held the concession to supply water to Lyon, Paris, and Nantes, and before the end of the nineteenth century it also supplied water to Venice, Lausanne, Porto, and Constantinople, among others. The international strategy and the diversification into other public services explained the size and the success of Lyonnaise des Eaux, which was among the largest utility companies in 1970–2 and, after its merger with the multinational Compagnie de Suez in 1997, in 1998–2000 as well.

The average firm size in the T&U sector was $232.7 million in 1927–9. The railway companies were the largest, with an average asset size of $617.4 million, followed a long way behind by the utility firms with $65.2 million and the transport and communication companies with $52.4 million, which were smaller than the average European firm.

The largest European company continued to be a railway firm: the London, Midland & Scottish Railway, which was the product of a government-enforced merger (see below). Similar interventions in Germany and France reduced the number of large private sector railway companies. Thus, while in 1911–13 railway firms occupied the top five places in the European ranking, in 1927–9 there were only two in the top five. Finance companies had taken over their positions.

The 'Giant' firms with assets four times larger than the average of the T&U sector were all railway companies: London, Midland and Scottish Railway, the largest European company by asset size, Société Nationale de Chemins de fer Belges, established as a public company in 1926, the fifth largest, and the London and North Eastern Railway, the seventh largest. The 'Big' firms, with assets twice the average, were the Great Western Railway, in ninth place in Europe, and PLM, in eleventh place. The majority of the 'Giant' and 'Big' companies were concentrated in Britain; one was in Belgium and one in France.

---

[10] Millward, *Private and Public Enterprise*, pp. 18–19 and 41–55.
[11] The electricity part of the company had been nationalized in 1946.

Structural changes in Europe's railway industries produced a reduction in the number of independent private sector enterprises. In Germany, the railways were nationalized in 1920, although between 1924 and 1937 they were operated via a wholly government-owned private company, the Deutsche Reichsbahn Gesellschaft. France followed suit in nationalizing its railway companies in 1938. In Britain, the policy pursued by the government was to enforce the merger of 180 separate companies into four large regional monopolies, three of which appear in our sample.[12] Still privately owned, these companies operated under a strong government-imposed regulatory regime.

The shipping companies continued to dominate the transport and communication subsector in 1927–9. There was only one telephone firm out of the fifteen large companies considered. Shipping companies' assets amounted to 89.3 per cent of the subsector total. In 1911–13 four companies were among the fifty biggest European companies, while in 1927–9 there were only two, which shows the relative decline in size of the shipping industry. At this last benchmark, the assets of P&O, the thirty-ninth largest European firm and the largest in the subsector, amounted to only 27 per cent of the assets of the Vereinigte Stahlwerke AG, the biggest company in this study, excluding railways and financial firms.

The First World War devastated the majority of European shipping companies. The biggest three firms in 1911–13 experienced great losses. Hapag and NDL had hardly any fleet left because of wartime destruction, which was followed by confiscation of the remaining vessels over 1,600 GRT in reparation payments.[13] Messageries Maritimes had twenty-five fewer vessels and had fallen to 177th position in the ranking. In spite of such losses, however, the two German companies managed an exceptional recovery. By 1927–9, NDL was the fifth largest company in the subsector and the sixty-second in the European ranking, with assets bigger in nominal terms than in 1911–13. Despite a reduction of $12 million in assets, Hapag was the subsector's sixth largest company and seventy-third in Europe.

In the interwar period the supply of shipping exceeded demand. World trade grew at a significantly slower rate than before 1914 and after 1945. Overseas migration, which had been a major source of revenue, also declined owing to the restrictions set by the countries of immigration, especially the US. Given the fragile business circumstances, governments in Germany, France, and Italy supported their shipping industries with subsidies, construction loans, and flag discrimination. In other countries, such as Britain and the Scandinavian states, the shipping companies had to provide for themselves.[14]

The British shipping companies had become the subsector's largest firms. P&O, the largest shipping company, was in thirty-ninth place on the European ranking, Cunard Steam Ship in fiftieth, and the Royal Mail Steam Packet Co. in fifty-third. Although they were also affected by the war destruction, they had grown in size by buying up competitors in order to counter the oversupply of the interwar period.

---

[12] The fourth company was the Southern Railway.
[13] Gross Register or Registered Tonnage.
[14] J. Greaves, 'Managing decline: The political economy of British shipping', *Journal of Transport History*, 28 (2007), 57–74.

The only non-shipping firm big enough to appear in the transport and communication subsector was Compañía Telefónica Nacional de España (CTNE), the fourth company by asset size. Before the First World War, the telephone industry was limited to local networks; however, the technological advances in the industry in the interwar period pushed towards the establishment of national telephone networks. Many countries in our study—Britain, Germany, France, Italy, and Belgium—nationalized their telephone systems during these years.[15] In Spain, the telephone industry remained in private hands until 1945. The interest of Primo de Rivera's Military Directorate in creating a functioning national telephone network coincided with the strategy of the American firm International Telephone & Telegraph (IT&T) to create a holding company of telephone businesses outside the US. The result was the creation in 1924 of CTNE, an IT&T subsidy, with a contract signed with the government granting a monopoly concession.[16]

By 1927–9, the importance of the electricity companies had increased to 78 per cent of total utility assets, and four of the five largest companies were electric utilities. The proportion of assets represented by gas utilities had fallen to half that of the previous benchmark period. Out of the fifty largest European companies, four were utilities: one British, one Spanish, one German, and one Belgian.

The largest company in the subsector continued to be Gas Light and Coke, although it fell from twenty-second European place in 1911–13 to thirty-seventh in 1927–9. The company managed to reinvent itself by diversifying into the domestic heating and cooking market when faced with the strong competition from electricity utilities in the lighting market.

The second-largest utility, and in fortieth European place, was Compañía Hispano Americana de Electricidad (CHADE). By the end of the First World War, the economic position of the electrical holding company DUEG, the second-largest electricity company in 1911–13, was severely weakened, and its chief owner, Deutsche Bank, decided to sell it for three reasons. First, the bank did not have the capital necessary for the company to function efficiently; second, many company shares had fallen into foreign hands;[17] and third, it feared that the its shares would be seized for reparations. The buyer was a Spanish banking consortium that went on to create CHADE.

Countries with limited coal resources such as Italy, Spain, and Sweden had strong incentives to exploit their hydroelectric power resources from a very early stage. During the First World War, coal supplies fell everywhere, and prices increased sharply, causing major problems for the electricity companies in all countries. This helps to explain the large investments that electricity utilities made in the interwar years in hydroelectric power, increasing their need for larger amounts of capital. The war also made clear the need to interconnect the different

---

[15] Millward, *Private and Public Enterprise*, pp. 99–108. Italy nationalized its telephone network in 1907, privatized it in the 1920s, and nationalized it again in the 1930s.

[16] A. Calvo, 'State, firms and technology. The rise of multinational telecommunications companies: ITT and the Compañía Telefónica Nacional de España, 1924–1945', *Business History*, 50 (2008), 455–73.

[17] By 1920, as many as 50% of the shares were in foreign hands because the devaluation of the Mark had made them very attractive (shares were denominated in Marks). See Chapter 4 in Hausman, Hertner, and Wilkins, *Global Electrification*.

generating plants in order to guarantee a more stable electricity supply. A good example of this development is the third largest electric utility and the forty-first European company, Rheinisch-Westfälisches Elektrizitätswerk Aktiengesellschaft (RWE). RWE was founded in 1898 to serve the city of Essen, and the company expanded to embrace neighbouring industrial cities. In 1929, the first 220,000-volt line in Germany was finished, linking the coal fields in the Ruhr to the hydro-electric power in the Alps, connecting the north and south of Germany, and creating the world's largest power system. RWE is an example of the super-regional integration that occurred in many European countries before the Second World War.

The fifth largest utility, in forty-fifth European place, was the Belgian holding company Société Financière Transports et Entreprises Industrielles (Sofina). The company had been created by Union Elektrizitäts-Gesellschaft in 1892, which had in turn been set up by the American Thomson-Houston Electric Company with the objective of creating their own demand. In 1902, AEG bought Union Elektrizitäts-Gesellschaft and with it Sofina. The company's growth was spectacular; between 1913 and 1927, it experienced an accumulative annual growth rate of 17.4 per cent, and between 1927 and 1929, the capital increased 3.7-fold. By 1927, Sofina and other electrical holdings were highly interlinked, and their operations had expanded well beyond European boundaries. Electricity had become a global business.

In 1954–6, the average size of the T&U firms was $196.9 million, a 16 per cent fall in nominal terms compared with 1927–9. The big changes that the railway industry had undergone all over Europe explained the decline in the average firm size. In fact, there was only one railway company left in the sample, which justifies the decision not to make railway companies a separate subsector. The average firm size in the transport and communication subsector was $190.8 million, while in the utilities subsector it was $203.5 million. For the first time, the average utility size was larger than that of the transport and communication firms. There were no 'Giant' firms in the T&U sector in 1954–6. The 'Big' firms, with assets over twice the sector average, were geographically spread, with one German, one Belgian, one Italian, one British, and one Spanish: RWE, SNCB, Edison, P&O, and CNTE.

The composition of the transport and communication subsector had become more diverse. In asset terms, shipping companies represented 48.7 per cent, railways 26.9 per cent, and telephone companies 24.3 per cent. The shipping companies continued to provide the majority of firms, with 69.2 per cent of the subsector sample. The largest company in the subsector, eighteenth in the European ranking, was the railway firm Société Nationale des Chemins de fer Belges, with assets 3.2 times larger than the average. However, it was 57 per cent smaller than Imperial Chemical Industries (ICI), the largest non-financial company. There were no British or French railway companies in the sample, since Britain had followed France and Germany in nationalizing its railways in 1947. Until 1963, railways in Britain were owned and managed by a government body, the British Transport Commission.

Among the five largest subsector companies there were three shipping companies: P&O in twenty-fourth European place, Cunard Steamship Co. in sixty-fourth, and Messageries Maritimes in seventy-third. The post-war nationalization in the transport sector was not limited to the railways; some shipping companies were also nationalized, including Messageries Maritimes in 1948, and Hapag and NDL already in the late 1930s.

The only telephone company in the sample continued to be CTNE, the twenty-sixth largest European company and the third largest in the subsector, with assets 2.2 times larger than the subsector average. By this time, the company was controlled by the Spanish state, which owned a majority of its equity.

In 1954–6, the electricity companies were once again dominant in the utilities subsector, accounting for 97 per cent of all utility assets, but their size had fallen relative to Europe's largest companies. After the Second World War, the role of the state became more important in Western European economies. This was not new in the utility industry, where the role of local and/or regional governments had been present from the very beginning in all countries to varying degrees. The super-regional interconnections offered by advances in technology encouraged a merger wave that created regional monopolies and increased the interest of the state in controlling them.

RWE, the largest utility company, was the fifteenth European company, or the fourth largest European firm if we exclude the financial companies, and it provides an example of government participation before the Second World War. During the interwar years, the private ownership of electricity companies gave way to state or municipal ownership in Germany. By 1920, RWE's major shareholders were the Westphalian municipalities. State ownership increased in all electric utilities in the 1930s. RWE was the only large German electricity company with less than 30 per cent state ownership.[18]

State ownership increased in all the major countries after the war through nationalization or creation of state firms. From 1946 to 1948, the electricity and gas companies were nationalized in France and the UK, creating at the same time large state monopolies. Italian nationalization took place in 1962, when ENEL was created.[19] The French and British nationalizations affected more than a third of the largest utilities in 1911–13 and 1927–9. If we include the Italian firms, the affected companies rise to one-half. The Second World War accelerated the process of naturalization of the electricity industry in many countries, which ended in the 1970s.[20] This explains the disappearance of Sofina, which was reduced to a shadow of its pre-war existence by the nationalization and naturalization of its interests around the world.

The subsector's second, third, fourth, and fifth companies in 1954–6 were all major super-regional hydroelectric companies: the Italian Edison in twentieth position in the European ranking, the Spanish Iberduero in forty-third place, the Italian SIP in fifty-third, and the German Bayernwerk AG in eighty-fifth.

[18] U. Wengenroth, 'Rise and fall of state-owned enterprise in Germany', in P.A.Toninelli, ed., *The Rise and Fall of State-Owned Enterprise in the Western World* (Cambridge, 2000), pp. 103–27.

[19] R. Giannetti, 'Industrial policy and the nationalization of the Italian electricity sector in the post-World War II period', in F. Amatori, R. Millward, and P. A. Toninelli, eds., *Reappraising State-Owned Enterprise: A Comparison of the UK and Italy* (Abingdon, 2011), pp. 242–60.

[20] Naturalization is a process whereby foreign companies are bought by nationals of the country. Hausman, Hertner, and Wilkins named this process domestication: Hausman, Hertner and Wilkins, *Global Electrification*, p. 233.

In 1970–2, the average firm size for the T&U sector was $2,698.8 million. The average size of firms in the transport and communication subsector was $2,091.4 million, while for utilities it was $3,343.3 million. For the first time in the twentieth century, the average utility size was bigger (55 per cent) than the average size of the European firms. There were two 'Giant' firms in this benchmark—the Electricity Council Boards in the UK and ENEL in Italy—and two 'Big' firms—the (British) Post Office and British Gas. The concentration of the large firms in Britain is striking.

The transport and communication subsector had been completely transformed. The few telecommunications companies (12 per cent) had the largest proportion of assets (51.5 per cent) and turnover (37 per cent). The first, third, and fourth largest companies in asset terms were telecommunications firms: the Post Office, the twelfth largest European company, the Italian telephone company SIP in twenty-eighth place, and the Spanish CTNE in thirty-eighth. When turnover is considered, only the Post Office maintains its European ranking, while SIP falls considerably to seventy-third place and CTNE to 131st.

The railway companies represented 25 per cent of the firms in the subsector and accounted for 32.6 per cent of assets. The second and fifth companies in the subsector were the state-owned railway corporations SNCF in twenty-fifth European position and the British Railways Board in forty-third. The ranking by turnover was SNCF twenty-third and the British Railways Board forty-fifth. Although in the public sector, the British and French railway enterprises were encouraged to operate on a quasi-commercial basis, and employed accounting practices with balance sheets and profit-and-loss accounts as if they were private concerns. They thus generated data that make it possible for us to include them in our sample.

The shipping companies that held the majority of transport and communication assets in the preceding benchmark saw their importance drastically diminished, accounting in 1970–2 for only 4 per cent of assets and 14 per cent of turnover, although they were still the majority largest group in number of firms (31 per cent). From the early 1960s, the shipping companies faced increasingly strong competition in long-distance passenger transport from airlines. It took only ten years from 1958, when the first jet airliner crossed the Atlantic, for transatlantic ship liners to virtually disappear. Some shipping firms like the German Hapag did not even restart transatlantic passenger services after 1945 but concentrated instead on cargo business. The successful shipping companies diversified, expanding into short-haul sea ferries, logistics, offshore support vessels, and bulk carriers. By the end of the 1960s, the shipping companies were facing another enormous challenge, this time in the freight market, with the emergence of the container revolution.[21] In its first years, containerization created a merger movement in the European shipping industry; for example, Hapag and NDL formed Hapag-Lloyd in 1970, and Messageries Maritimes and Compagnie Générale Transtlantique created Compagnie Générale Maritime (CGM) in 1978.

---

[21] M. Levinson, *The Box: How the Shipping Container Made the World Smaller and the World Economy Bigger* (Princeton, NJ, 2002).

Airline companies appear for the first time in our sample in 1970–2 following their expansion in the 1960s. At this date, airlines represented 25 per cent of the sample, held 12 per cent of the subsector's assets, and accounted for 21 per cent of its turnover. The state intervened in the sector from early on. After the First World War, every country claimed sovereignty over its own airspace because of the high military importance. There were many reasons that explain why the majority of countries ended with a national carrier that was either state-owned (Air France and the British Overseas Airways Corporation (BOAC)) or in which the state held a controlling stake (Lufthansa, Alitalia, SAS, and Iberia). Among the most important reasons were the low profitability of the airline industry in the interwar period, the desire to guarantee access to colonial territories, and last, but not least, the fear that the economic superiority of the American airlines would overshadow the national industries.[22]

In 1970–2 the importance of the electricity companies had slightly diminished, representing 84 per cent of utility assets, with the gas companies making up the remaining 16 per cent. The largest utility, Britain's Electricity Council, was the twelfth largest European company but the second largest if financial companies are excluded. If turnover is considered, it was the sixth largest European company, the five above it being non-financial companies. The size of the utility companies had substantially increased since 1954–6 in relation to the rest of the Europe's companies. The picture in 1970–2 reflects the importance that nationalization had on the utilities, since four out of the five largest companies were state monopolies created with the British, French, and Italian nationalizations. The resulting companies were Electricity Council, the sixth largest European company in turnover terms, EDF the twenty-first, ENEL the thirty-first, and the British Gas Corporation the thirty-third.

The only large company in the utilities subsector that did not result from nationalization was also a state-owned company. VEBA (Vereinigte Elektrizitäts- und Bergwerks-Aktiengesellschaft), the nineteenth largest European company by turnover, was founded in 1929 by the Prussian government as a Berlin-based financial conglomerate for power and mining activities. In 1965, the Federal Republic of Germany placed the majority of its shares with private investors. VEBA's large size was due to its diversification, which extended beyond the initial electricity and mining business into chemicals, oil, glass, and transport.

The major technological change that took place in the electricity industry in this period was the use of nuclear power. The first nuclear plants were built in Britain and France in the late 1950s and early 1960s. In France, two-thirds of the electricity generated came from EDF nuclear plants; in Britain, nuclear plants produced about 26 per cent of the total and in Germany 23 per cent.

There were important changes in the gas industry also. The major technological change was the shift from gas manufactured by coal distillation to natural gas extracted from the gas fields under the North Sea and elsewhere. In Britain, the Gas Act of 1972 merged all the previously nationalized area gas boards into the British Gas Corporation, which then occupied the third position in asset size in the sample. The company was privatized in 1986.

---

[22] Millward, *Private and Public Enterprise*, pp. 231–41.

In 2000, the average T&U firm size was $22,722.0 million. In the transport and communication subsector, the average was $12,285.0 million, and in the utilities subsector, it was $31,071.6 million, both substantially below the European average of $47,302.5 million. German E.ON was the only 'Giant' firm, with assets four times the sector average. The 'Big' firms, with assets double the average, were Suez, RWE, Ferrovie dello Stato, Endesa, and ENEL. In contrast with the previous period, there were no British firms among the largest, and there were more countries represented: two German, two Italians, one French, and one Spanish.

When turnover data are considered, the average firm size in the T&U sector was $13,086.0 million, just below the European average of $13,185.3 million. The average turnover in the transport subsector was $7,563.2 million and in utilities $17,634.2 million, a third larger than the European average. E.ON continued to be the only 'Giant' company in the sector, while the 'Big' companies were RWE, Suez, and EDF. In this case, the largest companies were concentrated in Germany and France.

Airline companies provided the greater part of firms (40 per cent) in the transport subsector, accounting for 46 per cent of its turnover. The liberalization of the airline industry that took place in Europe from 1993 brought important changes to the market, the emergence of new players, and, with lower fares, an increase in the number of passengers. The second group in importance was the railway companies, with 35 per cent of the subsector's turnover. When assets are considered, the Italian, German, and French national railway monopolies account for 75 per cent of the total.[23] The size of the railways companies—the 'Giant' businesses in the nineteenth and early twentieth century—had relatively diminished by 2000. Ferrovie dello Stato was the forty-second largest European firm, followed by Deutsche Bahn in fifty-second position. In Britain, privatization in 1994 had fragmented the industry's structure. The largest company was Railtrack, a quasi-private company that was wound up (and replaced by Network Rail, another quasi-public company) after the Hatfield rail accident in 2000. However, Railtrack's asset base was a matter for debate throughout its brief existence.[24]

When turnover is considered, SCNF was the largest firm in the transport subsector and the fifty-sixth largest European company, British Airways the seventy-second, Deutsche Bahn the seventy-third, Lufthansa the seventy-sixth, and Stinnes AG the eighty-seventh. For the first time, there were two airlines among the top five companies in the transport subsector.

The average size of Europe's utilities was greater than that of transport firms. The five largest utilities occupied places above the transport firms in the turnover ranking. The structure of the utilities subsector remained unchanged after the 1970–2 benchmark, when electricity companies accounted for 75 per cent of the assets and gas firms for 17 per cent. However, the size of the utility companies had fallen in comparison with the largest European companies. E.ON was the largest utility in 2000, the twenty-seventh largest European company, and the eighth largest company if financial firms are excluded. No gas company was among the

[23] This figure is estimated because the SCNF asset data for this period were not available. Ferrovie dello Stato and Deutsche Bahn accounted for 59.4 per cent of total assets in the transport subsector.
[24] T. Gourvish, *Britain's Railways 1997–2005: Labour's Strategic Experiment* (Oxford, 2008), pp. 59–111.

top five utilities. The top five companies in asset terms were E.ON in twenty-seventh place, Suez in thirty-second, RWE in thirty-eighth, EDF in forty-sixth, and ENEL in forty-seventh. When turnover is considered, the utilities show a much larger size. E.ON was in seventh place, followed by RWE in twentieth, Suez in twenty-ninth, ENEL in forty-ninth, and Preussag in fifty-fifth.

The electricity industry experienced major changes from the 1970s owing to privatization, mergers, and globalization. The privatization of state-owned companies that usually enjoyed a national monopoly had different outcomes. British privatization avoided the creation of a private national monopoly by dividing the largest utility in 1972 into three companies: Powergen (the ninth largest utility in 1998–2000), National Power, and National Grid. The argument was that there was no need for an integrated industry since the technological changes had freed generation and retailing from the natural monopoly constraints.[25] On the other hand, although the Italian government privatized ENEL in 1992, the majority of its shares were still in hands of the government, and the company maintained its national monopoly until 1999.[26] In France, EDF's privatization in 2004 did not affect the size of the company.

In this period, electricity utilities sought to became larger. In those countries without a state monopoly, there was a merger wave. The largest utility company, E.ON, was the result of a merger between VEBA and VIAG in 2000. In the 1990s, both companies had directed their efforts to their core business of energy production. This was also the case of the Spanish Hidrola and Iberduero, which merged in 1992 to create Iberdrola. A larger size was crucial for international expansion in the era of globalization. Many European companies took the opportunity to enter the Latin American market when some of the state monopolies were privatized, or the US market after liberalization. The European Union's policy of encouraging market competition in order to break up national monopolies was another factor stimulating growth through foreign acquisitions.

PERFORMANCE BASED ON RETURN ON EQUITY

The performance of the transport and utilities sector based on the return on equity (ROE) was relatively poor over the twentieth century, with considerable fluctuations in benchmark periods.[27] In the first two benchmarks, the mean ROE was at roughly the same level—7.28 per cent in 1911–13 and 7.59 per cent in 1927–9. The companies' profitability suffered a drastic reduction in the aftermath of the Second World War, when the average ROE fell by half to 3.50 per cent in 1954–6, the lowest return in the century, and to 3.68 per cent in 1970–2. However, by 2000, the T&U companies had recovered to achieve their highest ever performance, with an average ROE of 11.11 per cent. In comparison with the

---

[25] M. Chick, 'The power of networks: Defining boundaries of the natural monopoly network and implications for the restructuring of the electricity supply industry', *Annales Historiques de l'Electricité*, (2004), 89–106.

[26] Toninelli, *The Rise and Fall*, p. ix.

[27] The ROE data are available for 94 per cent of the T&U firms.

Table 13.2. ROE of T&U sector, 1911–2000 (in %)

	T&U		European companies		Differential
	Mean	Median	Mean	Median	mean
1911–13	7.28	6.27	10.04	8.69	−2.76
1927–9	7.59	6.96	9.16	8.33	−1.57
1954–6	3.50	4.74	9.70	7.30	−6.20
1970–2	3.68	2.23	7.62	7.55	−3.94
1998–2000	11.11	12.41	14.24[a]	12.32	−3.13

[a] Excluding the outlier, the Finnish firm TIH Finland

Table 13.3. Geographical distribution of T&U firms in the top quartile of ROE, 1911–2000

	Germany	UK	France	Italy	Spain	Belgium	Sweden	Finland
1911–13	3		1	1	2	1	1	
1927–9	1	1	3	1	2	1	1	1
1954–6					2	1	1	2
1970–2	4				1	1		1
1998–2000	1	2			1	2	2	
Twentieth century	9/35	3/31	4/31	3/24	9/15	6/11	3/11	4/8
Success rate[a] (%)	25.7	9.7	12.9	12.5	60.0	54.6	27.3	50.0

[a] The success rate is the percentage of firms of a country with an ROE in the top quartile of the T&U sector

profitability of the whole sample of European big business, however, the performance of the T&U sector was disappointing throughout the twentieth century. The
ROE of the T&U companies was always below the average of the European firms.
In the last column of Table 13.2, we can see that the differential between the
average ROE of the sector and that of the whole sample was always negative.
The best period was in 1927–9, when the T&U's mean ROE was only 1.6
percentage points below the European mean. The worst period was 1954–6,
with an average ROE 6.2 percentage points below the European mean.

The performance of the T&U companies differed from that of the rest of the
European sample not only in the level of profitability but also in the trend. The
major difference occurred in the 1954–6 benchmark, when important changes
experienced in the sector, in particular the nationalization process, cut profitability in half while Europe's ROE increased.

The geographical distribution of the top 25 per cent of firms in the T&U sector
at each benchmark shows that the large countries did not dominate the best-
performing firms in the twentieth century (Table 13.3). Germany and Spain had
the largest number of such firms, while the UK, Italy, and Sweden had the lowest.
Given that the number of firms considered in this study depended on a country's
size, the more profitable countries—that is, those with a higher proportion of
firms among the most profitable of the sector—were Spain with 60.0 per cent of its
firms among the top 25 per cent according to ROE, followed closely by Belgium
with 54.6 per cent and Finland with 50 per cent of their firms in the top quartile.
The UK was the worst: only 9.7 per cent of the British firms in the T&U sector
reached a high enough profitability to be counted among the 25 per cent best.

Table 13.4. Geographical distribution of T&U firms in the lowest quartile of ROE, 1911–2000

	Germany	UK	France	Italy	Spain	Belgium	Sweden	Finland
1911–13	1	2	4	2				
1927–9	1	4	3	1		1		1
1954–6	3		2	1				
1970–2		3	2	1		1		
1998–2000	1	1	3	2				1
Twentieth century	6/35	10/31	14/31	7/24		2/11		2/8
Failure rate[a] (%)	17.0	32.3	45.2	29.2	0	18.2	0	25.0

[a] The failure rate is the percentage of firms of a country with an ROE in the lowest quartile of the T&U sector

Table 13.5. ROE of T&U subsectors, 1911–13 (in %)

	Mean	Median	Standard deviation
Railways	6.39	5.88	2.62
Transport and communication	7.33	6.92	3.87
Utilities	8.28	5.84	3.80
T&U	7.28	6.27	3.44
Highest and lowest performance: Oil, rubber, chemicals, and others Railways	15.91	9.68	13.45

France and Italy with 12.9 and 12.5 per cent, respectively, did not do much better. Germany did better than the other big countries, but still substantially worse than Spain. These data suggest that the dimensions of the country tended to act against firm profitability, although, given the monopolistic nature of the sector, a country's industrial policy highly influenced its companies' performance. The absence of top profitable firms in 1954–6 and 1970–2 in the UK, France, and Italy is explained by the effects of the industrial policies mentioned above. The high profitability of the Spanish firms in this sector is, on the other hand, indicative of the capture of the state by the private firms.

The larger countries thus had the most firms with the worst performance in the twentieth century. The country with the highest number of firms in the lowest quartile was France with fourteen companies, followed by the UK with ten, and Italy and Germany with seven and six respectively (Table 13.4). That meant that 45.2 per cent of the French firms in the T&U sector were among the lowest-performing firms, 32.3 per cent of the British, 29.2 per cent of the Italian, and 25 per cent of the Finnish. Germany, however, was an exception, with only 17.0 per cent of its firms in the bottom quartile, while Belgium had 18.2 per cent. There were two countries with no firms among the worst performers: Spain and Sweden.

The best-performing subsector within T&U in 1911–13 was utilities, with an average ROE of 8.28 per cent, while railways was the worst, with 6.39 per cent (Table 13.5). The average ROE for transport and communication was 7.33 per cent. This was a very poor performance; no other subsector in our study performed worse than the subsectors of T&U. Even the utilities' ROE—the best performance in the sector—was 7.63 percentage points below that of best-performing European subsector: oil, rubber, chemicals, and others. Railways was the worst performer of the whole study in this period. The T&U sector as a whole showed a lower dispersion of ROE in comparison with the whole sample, with a 3.44 standard deviation. Within the sector, railways showed the lowest dispersion, followed by utilities.

The poor aggregate performance is translated at company level, since only three firms, all utilities, were among the top 25 per cent of European companies by ROE. Berliner Elektricitäts-Werke was the twenty-fourth most profitable company, just one place behind was Stockholms Allmänna Telefonaktiebolag (twenty-fifth), while the Compagnie Générale des Eaux was in forty-third place.

The utilities subsector had the highest percentage of its firms in the top quartile, with 38.5 per cent, followed by transport with 23.0 per cent, and railways with only 6.6 per cent. Germany, had the most firms (three) in the top quartile of the T&U sector. Spain followed with two, whereas all other countries had one each except for the UK and Finland with none.

In 1911–13, no company in the T&U sector made losses. The subsectors with the highest number of firms in the bottom quartile were railways and transport and communication with four companies each; there was only one utility among the worst-performing. France had the most firms (four) in the bottom quartile. The UK and Italy had two each and Germany one. The remaining countries had none.

The utilities, the best-performing subsector, had a low performance compared with the rest of European big business. This can be explained by the high capital intensity, regulation of tariffs and/or profits, and the low load factor that affected the majority of companies in the sample. All network industries—electricity, gas, and water companies—needed large initial capital requirements. Industry prices were regulated by the municipalities from the beginning of the industry in most countries. The most important problem, especially for the electricity, was the low load factor. Those companies that could soften the peaks on the daytime demand curve by striking the right balance between lighting, power, and traction were able to obtain higher returns. The four best-performing utilities with ROEs above the average performance of all European leading companies were Berliner Elektrizitäts Werke, Compagnie General des Eaux, Transport and Entreprises, and Società Generale Italiana Edison. There was a positive correlation between the size of these companies and their profitability, with the exception of the subsector's largest firm, Gas Light and Coke, which was the penultimate worst performer.

The most profitable company in the transport and communication subsector was the already-mentioned Swedish telephone company. The performance of the shipping companies, the majority of the subsector, show opposed outcomes due to the strategies followed by the firms to deal with the increasing overcapacity, as mentioned in the previous section. Three French shipping companies were among the worst-performing, and two German shipping firms among the best-performing. In this subsector, there seems to be no clear correlation between the size of firms and their profitability. On the other hand, there was a strong correlation between their country and profitability. The best-performing shipping companies were the German firms, followed by the British, the Italian, and last the French.

Table 13.6. ROE of T&U subsectors, 1927–9 (in %)

	Mean	Median	Standard deviation
Railways	5.65	4.94	2.40
Transport and communication	5.52	6.06	2.39
Utilities	10.98	8.84	6.22
T&U	7.59	6.96	4.92
Highest and lowest performance:			
Wood and paper products	14.90	10.62	11.86
Commercial activities	3.31	11.49	39.46

The Spanish Ferrocarriles Andaluces was the only railway in the top quartile of the sector. Two out of the four worst performers were British: the Midland Railway and the Great Western, which were among the largest companies in Europe. By 1911, the industry was heavily regulated by government, and the prospect of nationalization was very real. On the other hand, many scholars have criticized railway managements for their sub-optimal operating policies. As Robert Millward has observed, most railway systems in Europe were 'on a knife edge'.[28]

Although T&U was still the worst-performing sector in 1927–9, its subsectors were no longer the least profitable ones in Europe: 'commercial activities' and 'transport equipment' had replaced them. Utilities continued to be the best-performing subsector within T&U, with an ROE of 10.98 per cent, double that of the railways with 5.65 per cent and transport and communication with 5.52 per cent (Table 13.6). Compared with the previous benchmark, this meant an improvement for the utilities' profitability of 2.7 percentage points and a deterioration for the transport and communication and the railways subsectors, which lost 1.8 and 0.7 percentage points, respectively. The improvement in the utilities' ROE also narrowed the gap with the best-performing subsector ('wood and paper products') to less than 4 percentage points. The utilities had become the fifth best-performing subsector out of the fifteen subsectors considered. This was the best time for the utilities in the entire twentieth century, with a much lower profitability data dispersion in comparison with the whole sample.

The marginal improvement was reflected in an increased number of firms among the top 25 per cent of European companies. The best-performing firms were electricity companies: in ninth place was Sofina, with an ROE of 29.91 per cent, the highest profitability any T&U firm reached in the twentieth century, followed by Sydsvenska kraftaktiebolaget in twentieth place with 19.83 per cent, Hamburgische Electricitäts-Werke AG in thirty-ninth place with 14.92 per cent, and Sydfinska Kraftaktiebolaget in fifty-ninth place with 11.79 per cent.

The utilities subsector had again the highest percentage of its firms in T&U's top quartile with 56.3 per cent, followed by railways with 16.7 per cent and transport and communication, which had no firm in the top quartile. France had the most companies (three) in the top quartile. Spain followed with two, while all the other countries had one each.

---

[28] Millward, *Public and Private Enterprise*, p. 148, and see also the work of J. Dodgson and N. Crafts.

Lloyd Triestino was the only company in the T&U sector that registered losses (−0.06 per cent) in 1927–9. Railways and transport and communication had 41.7 and 40.0 per cent, respectively, of their firms in the least profitable quartile. There was no utility firm in that group. The UK and France had between them more than half of the worst-performing firms, with four and three firms, respectively, in the sector's bottom quartile.

Sofina's very high profitability of 29.91 per cent—10 percentage points higher than the second most profitable company—may be explained by the fact that it was a holding company with interests around the world and therefore exposed to a higher country risk of their investments. In spite of Sofina's big size, there seems to be a weak negative correlation between the size of the utilities and their ROE in this period. The second and fourth most profitable companies, Sydsvenska Kraftaktibolaget (19.83 per cent ROE) and Sydfinska Kraftaktibolaget (11.79 per cent), were respectively the second smallest and the smallest companies in asset terms.

Hamburgische Elektrizitäts Werke (14.92 per cent ROE), Hidrola (11.32 per cent), and Energie Electrique du Littoral Méditerranéen (9.82 per cent) complete the list of the most profitable utilities. All these companies had experienced an increase in efficiency thanks to the interconnection of the regional systems made possible by long-distance electricity transmission technology.

Within the transport and communication subsector, the shipping companies performed particularly badly. In spite of the reduction in the number of vessels caused by the First World War, the decline in trade during the interwar period caused overcapacity in the industry. The negative effects of overcapacity on profitability would have been worse without the merger wave and the shipping conferences. The British firms had the lowest ROE, followed by the French. The best performance was by Stockholms Rediaktibolag Svea and the Compagnie Maritime du Congo.

The average ROE of T&U firms in 1954–6 was less than half that of the previous benchmark, the lowest of the whole century. Transport and communication was the worst-performing subsector, with an ROE of 1.69 per cent (Table 13.7). The utilities subsector performed much better, but, nevertheless, its average ROE of 5.64 per cent was the third lowest among all fourteen subsectors in the sample. Compared with the previous benchmark, the profitability of the utilities had fallen by one-half and that of the transport and communication by one-third. The disparity in performance between utilities and finance, the best-performing subsector, was an immense 15 percentage points, that is, an ROE almost four times higher. In this period, the T&U sector had a higher dispersion in the profitability data than the European sample

Table 13.7. ROE of T&U subsectors, 1954–6 (in %)

	Mean	Median	Standard deviation
Transport and communication	1.69	3.12	9.66
Utilities	5.64	4.97	1.72
T&U	3.50	4.74	7.35
Highest and lowest performance:			
Financial intermediation	20.69	10.32	31.44
Transport and communication			

(see Table 13.2). The utilities performance data distribution was more homogenous, with a standard deviation of 1.72, while that of transport and communication was more dispersed, with a standard deviation of 9.66.

The sharp decline in the profitability of the sector was reflected in the reduction to just one company in Europe's top 25 per cent. This was the Swedish shipping company Ångfartyg Tirfing AB, in sixteenth place with an ROE of 20.0 per cent.

The two subsectors had the same proportion of highly profitable firms. However, the worst-performing firms were all concentrated in the transport and communication subsector, with half of its firms in the first quartile. No utility was among the worst performers.

The best-performing firms in the top quartile were from the small countries: Spain and Finland had two and Belgium and Sweden one each. On the other hand, Germany had three of the worst-performing firms, followed by France with two and Italy with one.

The Second World War's devastation increased the demands that governments placed on the utilities. Price and profit regulation tightened, and profitability declined. Except for Intercommunale Belge d'Electricité, with an ROE of 9.67 per cent, all utility companies had an ROE below the average of European business. The concentration movement that took place in Belgium after the war prompted the creation of three companies, resulting in an increase in their efficiency. The other two utilities in the top quartile were the Finnish Imatran Voima and the Spanish Iberduero, which was the only large utility within the group.

In spite of the fact that the there were two shipping firms in the best-performing quartile—the above-mentioned Swedish firms and the Finnish Suomen Höyrylaiva—these were the exceptions in an industry that performed rather badly. The only two companies with actual losses were the German shipping firms: Hansa with a negative ROE of −22.11 per cent, and Hapag with −7.67 per cent. Italian and French shipping were the next worst performers, with very low profitability. Although there was a direct correlation between the size and the profitability of the company, the second most profitable company was thirty-five times smaller than the third. In this period, the country seems to matter for profitability, since the shipping companies of a given country have very similar ROEs. The third best-performing company in the T&U sector was the Spanish telephone company CTNE, now under state control.

In 1970–2, the performance of the T&U sector was practically unchanged and continued to be the worst of all the sectors in the European sample. There was, however, a reduction in the performance gap because the other sectors had experienced a sharp decline.

The utilities' mean ROE fell further, to 5.39 per cent, the worst rate of the twentieth century (Table 13.8). This was a marginal fall of 0.25 percentage points, negligible in comparison with the shock the industry had experienced in the previous period. The gap between it and commercial activities, the most profitable subsector, was almost 10 percentage points. Nonetheless, utilities performed better than the transport and communication subsector, which with an ROE of only 2.08 per cent was the second worst-performing subsector after mining. In the sector as a whole, ROE showed a low dispersion, with a standard deviation of 5.04.

Table 13.8. ROE of T&U subsectors, 1970–2 (in %)

	Mean	Median	Standard deviation
Transport and communication	2.08	1.00	3.69
Utilities	5.39	5.00	5.83
T&U	3.68	2.23	5.04
Highest and lowest performance:			
Commercial activities	14.84	14.34	10.35
Mining	0.82	3.43	14.05

Only two T&U companies, both large German utilities, made it into Europe's best 25 per cent at this benchmark: VEBA, with a 17.59 per cent ROE, was in twenty-fourth position and RWE, with 12.86 per cent, was in fiftieth place.

The utilities subsector had the highest percentage of its firms in the top quartile of the sector, with 35.7 per cent. For transport and communication, the percentage was 13.3. Germany had the most firms (four) in the top quartile of the T&U sector. Spain, Belgium, and Finland each had one.

In this period, there were seven firms with losses, the highest number in the twentieth century. The firm with the highest loss was Alitalia (−5.52 per cent), followed by Gaz de France, three railway companies (British Railways Board, SNCF, and SNCB), the British Electricity Council and Boards, and the British Post Office, all state-owned enterprises and the largest companies in the sector. The countries that housed the worst-performing firms were Britain with three firms, France with two, and Belgium and Italy with one each.

The top five performing firms were electricity companies. The two German firms just mentioned (VEBA and RWE) were joined by Spanish Hidrola (10.46 per cent ROE), Vereinigte Elektrizitätswerke Westfalen (9.49 per cent), and Intercom Belge (7.98 per cent). At the same time, this was the only period in the twentieth century in which utilities experienced losses. Gaz de France had an ROE of −3.35 per cent and the Electricity Council Board −0.51 per cent; we have no data for EDF and the South of Scotland Electricity Board. It was this dismal performance of the large state-owned companies that prompted privatization. But state-owned companies were not necessarily less efficient than privately owned ones. Between 1950 and 1973, productivity growth in the electricity and gas industry was higher in the UK than in the USA, where no state-owned enterprise existed.[29] The poor performance of the utilities derived from the non-commercial obligations laid on them by governments.[30] There was a negative correlation between the size of the utilities and their profitability.

As in the preceding benchmark, in 1970–2, there were two transport firms in the top quartile of best-performing firms. The German Hapag-Lloyd, which had made substantial losses in 1954–6, became the most profitable shipping company in the transport and communication subsector. This change of fortune was based on the merger of the two companies and the subsequent concentration on the

---

[29] M. O'Mahony, *Britain's Productivity Performance: An International Perspective* (National Institute of Economic and Social Research, 1999).

[30] Millward, *Private and Public Enterprise*, p. 295 and see Chapter 14 of this volume.

Table 13.9. ROE of T&U subsectors, 1998–2000 (in %)

	Mean	Median	Standard deviation
Transport	9.30	9.83	8.09
Utilities	12.60	13.39	6.24
T&U	11.11	12.41	7.21
Highest and lowest performance:			
Mechanical engineering	20.23	15.44	13.75
Food, drink, and tobacco products	8.49	9.54	8.19

cargo business. The Finnish Suomen Höyrylaiva Oy was again the second most profitable company. There seems to be a negative correlation between the size of the transport firms and their ROE in this period.

In 1998–2000, the T&U sector reached its highest profitability (11.11 per cent) in the twentieth century, but it continued to be the worst-performing sector in Europe.[31] Both the utilities and transport subsectors reached their higher performance, with 12.60 and 9.30 per cent ROE, respectively (Table 13.9). The improvement was impressive for the transport subsector, which experienced a 4.4-fold increase in returns, and substantial for utilities, with a 2.3-fold increase. Despite this improvement, the gap between utilities and the best-performing subsector, mechanical engineering, remained high at 9 percentage points, and the transport subsector remained the second lowest performer. The T&U sector as a whole showed a lower profitability dispersion in comparison with the whole sample: a 7.21 standard deviation against 19.40. Within the sector itself, utilities showed the lowest data dispersion.

The improved performance of T&U is reflected at the company level, with six firms among the top 25 per cent of European performers. Snam was the twenty-sixth most profitable firm, with an ROE of 27.67 per cent; Iberia (22.02 per cent) was in fiftieth place, and Lufthansa (18.57 per cent), CMB (18.48 per cent), Centrica (18.41 per cent), and Electrabel (18.38 per cent) were between sixty-first and sixty-fifth place. None of the above was among the very large companies of the sector.

The utilities subsector continued to have the highest percentage of its firms in the top quartile of the T&U sector, with 29.4 per cent, while transport had 21.4 per cent. There seems to be a weak negative correlation between the size of the utilities, measured either by assets or turnover, and their ROE in this period. The transport sector also shows a negative but stronger correlation between performance and size.

The countries with the most companies in the sector's top quartile were Belgium, Spain, and the UK with two each and Germany and Italy with one each. At the end of the twentieth century the 'Giant' and 'Big' companies of the sector were not the most profitable firms. Three of the top quartile utilities were gas companies, and for the first time two airlines were among the sector's most profitable companies.

---

[31] When the outlier TIH Finland is excluded from the 'Leisure and tourism' subsector. Otherwise the 'knowledge industries' was the worst performing sector.

In 1998–2000, there were two companies in T&U with losses, both Italian: Ferrovie dello Stato and Alitalia, which already had registered losses in the previous benchmark. The transport subsector had the highest proportion of their firms in the bottom quartile (35.7 per cent), while in utilities it was only 17.6 per cent. France had the most firms (three) in the bottom quartile, followed by Italy with two, and Germany, Great Britain, and Finland with one each.

PERFORMANCE BASED ON HOLDING RETURN

The study of performance based on the holding return (HR) complements the ROE analysis, since the former may be defined as the future expectations the market had for the development of the firm.[32] As is the case for the European sample overall, HRs in the T&U sector were higher than ROEs throughout the twentieth century except for the 1911–13 benchmark. The HR and ROE trends were also quite different. HR increased from an average of 4.80 per cent in 1911–13 to 18 per cent in 1954–6, the highest of the century (Table 13.10), while ROE was flat at 7.4 per cent in the first two benchmarks, reaching its lowest level (3.5 per cent) in 1954–6. In 1970–2, HR was a third of its previous value, but by the end of the century it had doubled. ROE remained essentially unchanged between 1954–6 and 1970–2, thereafter increasing threefold by 1998–2000. The gap between the two indicators was at its maximum in 1954–6, with 14.5 percentage points, the result of T&U stock values benefiting from the general optimism of the market at the time. In the following two benchmarks, the gap was reduced to less than three percentage points.

The performance of the T&U firms was inferior to that of the whole sample of European big businesses, as the last column of Table 13.10 shows. In the first two benchmarks—that is, before the Second World War—the average HR of the T&U firms was practically the same as the average HR for the whole sample. In 1954–6, the HR differential between T&U and the whole European sample reached almost seven percentage points, the highest of the twentieth century. On the other hand, the median HR of the T&U sector is three points higher than that of the whole

Table 13.10. HR of the T&U Sector, 1911–2000 (in %)

| | T&U | | European companies | | |
	Mean	Median	Mean	Median	Differential mean
1911–13	4.80	4.59	4.81	4.48	−0.01
1927–9	14.22	11.79	14.11	11.18	0.11
1954–6	18.00	23.85	24.94	20.90	−6.94
1970–2	6.59	6.30	8.22	7.80	−1.63
1998–2000	13.65	9.18	17.60	12.43	−3.95

[32] The HR data are available for the T&U firms in the following percentages: 84 per cent in 1911–13, 95 per cent in 1927–9, 68 per cent in 1954–6, 60 per cent in 1970–2 and 75 per cent in 1998–2000. Therefore, some caution should be applied to the 1954–6 and 1970–2 interpretations.

Table 13.11. Geographical distribution of T&U firms in the top quartile of HR, 1911–2000

	Germany	UK	France	Italy[a]	Spain	Belgium	Sweden	Finland[a]
1911–13	2	4	1	2			1	
1927–9		1	7	1		1	1	
1954–6	2	1			1		—[b]	
1970–2	1	—[b]	—[b]			1	1	1
1998–2000	1	1	1			1	2	
Twentieth century	6/32	7/26	9/26	3/16	2/14	3/12	5/9	1/5
Success rate[c] (%)	18.8	26.9	34.6	18.8	14.3	25.0	55.6	20.0

[a] Less than two-thirds of data are available for the twentieth century
[b] No data are available for Sweden and less than 15% for France and the UK
[c] The success rate is the percentage of firms of a country with an HR in the top quartile of the T&U sector

sample, which would indicate that the market had better expectations for a large part of the T&U firms than for European business generally. The HR differential between the T&U sector and the whole sample was substantially reduced in 1970–2 by the massive fall suffered by the majority of European companies. At the end of the century, despite the increase in the average HR for T&U firms, the differential had grown to almost four percentage points.

The analysis of the geographical distribution of the best-performing T&U firms has limitations, since the data are not fully available for all countries in all benchmarks. The data for Italy and Finland have to be used with caution because less than two-thirds of the HR data was available for those countries (Table 13.11).

The picture that emerges is quite different from that obtained by analysing ROE. The large geographical differences in success rate when ROE is considered are less pronounced when HR is taken into account. Sweden with 55.6 per cent of its firms among the top performers was the most successful country, followed by France with 34.6 per cent and the UK with almost 27 per cent. The success rate for the latter countries would probably be higher if data were available for the period 1970–2. The sound performance of France and the UK when HR is considered contrasts with the low success rate according to ROE (their success rate was the lowest). The case of Spain highlights this contrast in the other direction, because it was the most successful country in ROE terms and the least successful in HR terms, which could be explained by the less developed Spanish capital market.

The geographical distribution of the worst-performing firms shows that Germany was the country that contributed the most, though the bad performance is highly concentrated in the interwar benchmark, which indicates the low expectations the market had during the 1920s in particular. The countries with a higher failure rate were Finland with 40 per cent and Italy with 37.5 per cent (Table 13.12). Despite the fact that we do not have data for all the firms, we can assert with confidence that Italian firms' performance was very poor throughout the twentieth century. On the other hand, Sweden had no firm in this category, and only 7.1 per cent of the Spanish firms belonged to the worst performers.

In 1911–13, market expectations of the T&U sector were low in comparison with the other sectors. The transport and communication subsector had the highest HR (7.70 per cent), owing to the relatively good performance of the

Table 13.12. Geographical distribution of T&U firms in the lowest quartile of HR, 1911–2000

	Germany	UK	France	Italy[a]	Spain	Belgium	Sweden	Finland[a]
1911–13	1		3	2	1	2		
1927–9	6	2	1	1				1
1954–6		1	2			1	—[b]	
1970–2	3	—[b]	—[b]	2				
1998–2000	1	3		1				1
Twentieth century	11/32	6/26	6/26	6/16	1/14	3/12	0/9	2/5
Failure rate[c] (%)	34.4	23.1	23.1	37.5	7.1	25.0	0	40.0

[a] Less than two-thirds of data are available for the twentieth century
[b] No data are available for Sweden and less than 15% for France and the UK
[c] The failure rate is the percentage of firms of a country with an HR in the lowest quartile of the T&U sector

Table 13.13. HR of T&U subsectors, 1911–13 (in %)

	Mean	Median	Standard deviation
Railways	2.62	3.47	4.05
Transport and communication	7.70	9.86	11.59
Utilities	4.25	4.13	4.48
T&U	4.80	4.59	7.79
Highest and lowest performance:			
Electrical engineering	17.08	3.07	28.39
Textiles and leather	−0.36	0.30	9.99

shipping companies, although it was still 10 percentage points below electrical engineering, the best-performing subsector (Table 13.13). The T&U subsector with the worst expectations was railways, with an HR of 2.62 per cent, although this was still better than the prospects in textiles and leather, the subsector with the lowest HR in the entire study (−0.36 per cent).

In this period, there were nine T&U companies among the top 25 per cent of European firms. The five most profitable firms were shipping firms from the large countries. The Cunard Steamship Co. was the eighth most profitable firm in Europe, with an HR of 25.22 per cent, followed by Lloyd italiano in twelfth place with 21.11 per cent, the Royal Mail Steam Packet Company in thirteenth place with 19.42 per cent, Chargeus réunis in twenty-third place with 12.13 per cent, and Hamburg Südamerikanische Dampfschifffahrts-Gesellschaft in twenty-seventh place with 11.68 per cent. There were ten companies with a negative HR, the highest proportion of the twentieth century (27 per cent of the firms). The worst-performing was the Belgium Canal de Blaton-Ath, with an HR of −11.35 per cent, followed by the French shipping companies Messageries Maritimes (−10.47 per cent) and Compagnie Générale Transatlantique (−7.77 per cent).

The mean HR performance of the utilities subsector (4.25 per cent) was substantially lower than the subsector's mean ROE at the time (8.28 per cent), which shows the weak expectations investors had of a new sector with rapidly changing technology. The low market expectations of the electric utilities (5.07 per cent HR) contrasts with the high expectations of electrical engineering (17.08 per cent), indicating that electric utilities were not the main beneficiaries of the electrification process in this period. The Metropolitan Electric Supply Co. was the only utility among the top 25 per cent of European firms by HR, while there were two companies with a negative HR: Compagnie Générale du Gaz and Società generale italiana Edison di elettricità. There seems to be a correlation between the size of the utilities and the HR achieved.

The poor market expectations of railways were reflected in the negative HRs of a third of the companies. The two companies with better expectations were the Swedish Bergslagarnes Järnvägsaktiebolag with 9.93 per cent and the tramway firm Gesellschaft für elektrische Hoch- und Untergrundbahnen in Berlin with 8.57 per cent. The data indicate that there was a positive correlation between the size of the railway firms and their performance.

The market expectations of the T&U sector in 1927–9 improved substantially. It was the only period in the twentieth century when the average HR of the T&U sector was higher, though very marginally, than the average HR of the European sample. All subsectors benefited from the general optimism that accompanied the recovery from the long post-First World War recession, although this optimism came to an abrupt end with the Wall Street Crash of 1929. The average utilities HR of 24 per cent (Table 13.14) was the highest achieved in the twentieth century, a massive 20 percentage point increase on the previous benchmark. The subsector was the third best performer behind electrical engineering (28.29 per cent) and transport equipment (24.63 per cent). Railways, on the other hand, had the fourth worst prospects of all the subsectors. In this period, firm size does not seem to influence the HR in any of the three subsectors.

There were nine T&U companies among the top 25 per cent of firms in our study sample. In fourth place was Compagnie Générale Transatlantique, with an HR of 96.98 per cent. This was the company that in the previous period had shown the worst market expectations, with a negative HR (−7.77 per cent). Six electricity companies followed, with HRs ranging from the 77.71 per cent of the Belgium Sofina in fifth place to the 26.46 per cent registered by Società generale italiana Edison di elettricità in forty-seventh. Market expectations were high, and companies immersed in the globalization wave benefited the most.

An analysis of the top 25 per cent of the sector's firms shows a high concentration of firms in the utilities (six), followed by railways (three), and transport and communication (two). The distribution of companies with a negative HR complements this analysis, since, out of the nine firms with the poorest

Table 13.14. HR of T&U subsectors, 1927–9 (in %)

	Mean	Median	Standard deviation
Railways	7.91	7.27	11.39
Transport and communication	8.82	6.98	28.79
Utilities	24.00	13.30	23.55
T&U	14.22	13.30	23.80
Highest and lowest performance:			
Electrical engineering	20.29	27.42	23.14
Oil, rubber, and other non-metallic	2.38	−0.62	15.29

Table 13.15. HR of T&U subsectors, 1954–6 (in %)

	Mean	Median	Standard deviation
Transport and communication	17.73	20.18	17.37
Utilities	18.40	25.15	14.74
T&U	18.00	25.15	14.74
Highest and lowest performance:			
Oil, rubber, and other non-metallic	55.98	31.71	92.68
Textiles and leather	14.44	13.30	14.37

performance, six belong to the transport and communication subsector and three to railways. The utilities had experienced a substantial increase in demand and efficiency, and this was expected to continue in the future—hence the high HR. The data give a conflicting picture of the transport and communication subsector, with two high-performing firms, including the best performer, and six companies with negative HR. This disparity can also be seen with the high standard deviation (28.79). The same happened in the railway subsector. A closer look reveals that except for the Swedish railway Bergslagarnes Järnvägsaktiebolag, the best-performing companies in the subsector were French.

The market expectations of the T&U firms in 1954–6 reached the highest level of the twentieth century, and the gap between the average HR (18.0 per cent) and the ROE (3.5 per cent) was the biggest ever.[33] The subsector with the highest HR (18.40 per cent) was utilities (Table 13.15), even though this HR was almost six percentage points lower than in the previous period. On the other hand, the average HR of the transport and communication subsector increased to 17.73 per cent. The market expectations of all firms in the T&U sector had thus converged.

Compared with other subsectors in the European sample, the performance of utilities was poor, a huge 37 percentage points below the best-performing subsector, namely oil, rubber, and other non-metallic. Transport and communication was the third poorest subsector behind the textiles and leather and the mining subsectors. The HR data for utilities seem to be directly correlated with the size of the firms, whereas in transport and communication there is no correlation between the two variables.

Sector expectations seemed to be getting worse. Only four T&U firms were among the best 25 per cent of European firms by HR, a reduction to less than half of the number in the previous benchmarks; and the position those firms occupied was lower down the ranking. The best T&U firm, in thirty-fourth place, was Peninsular and Oriental, with an HR of 36.94 per cent. In fortieth, forty-first, and forty-second places came another shipping company, Hansa, with 35.48 per cent HR, the electric utility RWE with 35.39 per cent, and the telephone firm CTNE with 35.19 per cent. The close average HR between T&U's two subsectors was mirrored in the even distribution of firms between the best and worst performers. The best and the worst firms were shipping companies.

There seems to be no national pattern between the best- and worst-performing firms. France contained the worst-performing firms, including the only two firms

---

[33] In the 1954–6 period, HR data are available for 68 per cent of the T&U firms.

Table 13.16. HR of T&U subsectors, 1970–2 (in %)

	Mean	Median	Standard deviation
Transport and communication	8.00	9.04	10.76
Utilities	5.02	6.30	6.80
T&U	6.59	6.30	6.80
Highest and lowest performance:			
Electrical engineering	19.06	16.18	18.90
Mining[a]	−2.98	−2.24	20.91

[a] The lowest-performing sector was services to business, with an HR of −5.16, but since there were data for only one company, we took the second-lowest-performing subsector

with negative HRs: Messageries Maritimes with −14.49 per cent and Compagnie Générale des Eaux with −4.43 per cent.

The generally low market expectations of the 1970–2 period were clearly reflected in the low HR of the T&U sector: 6.59 per cent (Table 13.16).[34] The difference in performance between the two subsectors increased again; this time, the transport and communication subsector with an average HR of 8.00 per cent overtook the utilities with an HR of 5.59 per cent. Although the gap between the average HR of the entire European sample and that of the T&U sector was not so big, between the HR of transport and communication and that of electrical engineering, the best-performing subsector, there was a difference of 11 percentage points. On the positive side, there were other subsectors that had lower HRs than those in T&U; in mining, for example, the HR was −2.98 per cent.

The relation between the performance and the size of the firms was negative, with the highest correlation in the utilities subsector.

In this period, only one T&U company was among the top 25 per cent of European firms by HR: the shipping firm Suomen Höyrylaiva Oy occupied thirty-first place with an HR of 23.70 per cent. Besides this company, the best 25 per cent of firms by HR in the T&U sector were the Spanish telephone company CTNE (15.27 per cent HR), two shipping companies, Ångfartyg Tirfing AB (15.07 per cent) and Hansa (13.89 per cent), and the electric utility Intercom Belge d'Electricité (12.62 per cent).

There seems to be no correlation between country and the best-performing firms, but there is such a link for the worst-performing ones. The quartile of firms with the lowest HR were based in Germany (three) and in Italy (two). The German companies were electric utilities: VEBA (−6.20 per cent), RWE (−4.47 per cent), and Vereinigte Elektrizitätswerke Westfalen (1.97 per cent), which is striking since VEBA and RWE were the most profitable companies in ROE terms. The two Italian were Alitalia, the absolutely worst-performing firm, with an HR of −15.68 per cent, and the telephone company SIP (2.67 per cent).

At the end of the century, the average HR for the T&U sector had recuperated from its severe fall in the previous period.[35] The utilities subsector's HR was 15.82 per cent, while that for the transport subsector was 10.61 per cent (Table 13.17).

---

[34] In the 1970–2 period, HR data are available for 59 per cent of the T&U firms.
[35] In the 1998–2000 period, HR data are available for 75 per cent of the T&U firms.

Table 13.17. HR of T&U subsectors, 1998–2000 (in %)

	Mean	Median	Standard deviation
Transport	10.61	10.97	27.40
Utilities	15.82	9.01	16.90
T&U	13.65	9.18	21.50
Highest and lowest performance:			
Mining	45.09	14.86	86.55
Commercial activities	−3.12	−2.49	18.36

These performances were poor in comparison with the HR of the mining sub-sector, an impressive HR of 45.09 per cent, but substantially better than the negative HR of −3.12 per cent in commercial activities, the worst-performing subsector. In this benchmark, the sector's data show an inverse relation between a firm's HR performance and its size measured either in assets or in turnover.

In 1998–2000, there were four T&U firms in the top quartile of European companies according to HR: the Swedish transport firm Broströms Group was in ninth rank, with an HR of 74.40 per cent, followed by three utilities—Swedish Vattenfall in twenty-eighth place (48.00 per cent HR), French CEA Industrie in thirty-third place (42.52 per cent), and British Centrica in thirty-fourth place (42.00 per cent)

There were big differences in performance between the firms in both subsectors, as the large standard deviations show. Particularly striking is the 96.5 percentage point difference in HR between the best-performing firm, Broströms Group (74.40 per cent), and the worst-performing one, Alitalia (−22.16 per cent), both in the transport subsector. This performance gap also existed between firms involved in the same economic activity; in shipping, for example, the leading Broströms Group was far ahead of P&O, the subsector's second worst performer, with a dismal HR of −11.16 per cent.

Although the two best-performing firms were Swedish and three of the five worst-performing firms were British, there is no clear correlation between country and HR performance in this benchmark; the UK also had two companies with high HRs.

CONCLUSIONS

The performance of the T&U sector was disappointing throughout the century in comparison with the profitability of the whole sample of European big business. The ROE of the T&U companies was always below the average of the European firms. Before the Second World War, ROE was around 7.5 per cent, falling after 1945 to 3.5 per cent, where it stayed until the end of the century, when it reached 11 per cent. The performance of the T&U companies differed from that of the rest of the European sample not only in the level of profitability but also in the trend. The major difference was in the 1954–6 benchmark, when, owing to the important changes experienced in the sector, in particular the nationalization process, profitability fell to half, while ROE increased in other sectors of European business.

The more profitable countries, with a higher proportion of firms among the most profitable of the sector, were Spain, Belgium, and Finland. The worst-performing countries were France, the UK, and Italy. Germany did better than the other big countries, but still substantially worse than Spain.

The relation between the ROE performance of the T&U firms and their size in assets changed throughout the twentieth century, but it was almost always negative.

The railways subsector was the worst performer. Heavily regulated owing to its market dominance in inland transport during the nineteenth century, it suffered in the twentieth century as motor transport offered potent competition in both the passenger and freight markets. However, governments were slow to liberalize rail markets.

Utilities was the best-performing subsector. Its improved performance co-incided with periods when the industry became more global, and its worst performances occurred in periods when state intervention was at its strongest. Although regulation has always been present in the industry, the impact of the different types and intensity of regulation altered the amount of profits the companies made.

The transport subsector's profitability declined from the first benchmark until the middle of the century, after which it recovered by the end of the century to a slightly higher level. The high proportion of shipping companies with a declining profitability due to overcapacity problems explained the decline. The improvement at the end of the century was due to the increased importance of the airline firms, some with high profitability.

The future expectations the market had for the development of the firms in the T&U sector (HR) were generally higher than their actual returns (ROE). Nonetheless, in comparison with the overall European sample, the average HR achieved by the T&U firms was lower.

Geographical analysis of HR delivers a quite different picture from the one obtained by analysing ROE, with smaller differences in countries' success rates. Sweden was the most successful country, followed by France and the UK. Spain was the least successful in HR terms, which could be explained by the less developed Spanish capital market. The worst-performing countries were Italy and Germany, the latter with the majority of its worst-performing firms concentrated in the interwar period.

ACKNOWLEDGEMENTS

Financial support for parts of this contribution was provided by the Ministerio de Economía, Subprograma de generación de conocimiento, Proyectos de I+D, HAR2013-47182-C02-01.

14

Commercial and Financial Services

Mats Larsson, Edoardo Altamura, and Youssef Cassis

INTRODUCTION

Long-term economic development has made the service industries increasingly important. In this chapter, we concentrate on services from a wide perspective, including both financial services performed by banks and commercial activities performed by trading and retail companies. Banking and commercial activities are discussed in two separate sections.

The development of commercial and financial activities is closely related to improvements in living standards. The early industrial development of Great Britain and France had already opened the way for the commercialization of both wholesale and retail trade during the nineteenth century. The size of these countries also made it possible to make use of both economies of scale and economies of scope, even before a more general liberalization of international trade.

Differences in economic development between European countries and the size of the market—as a consequence of transportation requirements, the distribution of self-subsistent households, and the size of real wages—can explain many of the differences in the development of commercial activities. However, developments in the retail trade in particular differed between countries as a result of different national traditions. For example, in Sweden, the grocery trade was heavily concentrated in a small number of large retail chains as early as the inter-war period, and some of these companies also diversified their activities into both the wholesale trade and the production and retailing of other consumer products.[1]

Large-scale wholesale trade developed much earlier than large-scale retailing, which was an effect of economies of scale, especially in international trade. As is well known, international trade, especially the supply of oriental products, was a prerequisite for the economic development of several countries as early as the sixteenth and seventeenth centuries. These commercial activities could generate large profits, but also devastating losses. The risks were thus extensive. The diversification between wholesale and retail trade continued well into the twentieth

---

[1] For the history of the wholesale and retail trade, see for example R. Jessen and L. Langer, eds., *Transformations of Retailing in Europe after 1945* (Farnham, Surrey, 2012); N. Cox and K. Dennehahl, *Perceptions of Retailing in Early Modern England* (Aldershot, 2007).

century, and even today some of the largest commercial firms specialize in one product or another.

The improved profitability of companies and welfare of people opened the way for a growing number of transactions within the financial sector. However, this change occurred at different times in different countries. Thus, both Great Britain and France already had well-developed financial systems during the nineteenth century, at the same time as industrialization started, while this development came several decades later in the Mediterranean countries.[2] These prerequisites for development also explain both the size of banks and their profitability. However, the business of banking has changed considerably during the last few decades, from actors concentrating on collecting deposits and mediating loans to companies active in all types of financial markets—bonds, shares, insurance, real estate, and others—and working with new and different types of financial instruments. This change in the banks' business has been founded on strong tendencies to develop economies of scale and later also economies of scope.

COMMERCIAL SERVICES

Size and Domains of Activity

Commercial services include a variety of companies in terms both of activity and of size. But since our analysis deals with the sector's largest companies, several commercial activities are necessarily excluded. The sample includes wholesale companies (especially international trade), department stores, and super-/hypermarkets, as well as two hotels in the first benchmark period and one hotel chain in the last period. This means that products and services not suitable for economies of scale or scope will not be found among the sampled companies.

However, the type of commercial companies included in the sample accurately reflects the general development of the sector. The assets—as an indicator of size—of these companies have grown, especially after the Second World War, and thus at the same time as retail trade started to significantly increase in Western Europe. The growing size of these companies also reflects the development of transportation, which stimulated the expansion of the wholesale as well as the retail trade. With well-functioning transportation, it was possible to concentrate production and distribution, and this promoted larger companies. However, the most important explanation for the growing average size of these companies is the increased income and wealth of the population.

In both France and Great Britain, the size of the largest companies was considerably greater than in the other countries in 1913 (Table 14.1). However, already during the interwar period, the largest companies in both Italy and Germany could compete with those of France and Britain. In the four remaining countries, only Sweden shows a considerable development after the First

---

[2] C. Kindleberger, *A Financial History of Western Europe* (New York, 1993); Cox and Dennehahl, *Perceptions of Retailing in Early Modern England.*

Table 14.1. Average size of companies in commercial services (1913–54, assets; 1972–2000, turnover) (in thousand US$)

Country	1913	1927	1954	1972	2000
France	18,407	24,034	23,844	605,488	27,800,481
Germany	8,332	26,482	41,737	1,193,454	35,637,339
Great Britain	17,300	27,521	227,450	1,277,485	23,615,236
Italy	5,410	29,596	10,784	564,718	3,704,763
Belgium	1,968	4,977	16,176	153,129	2,746,619
Sweden	6,112	19,733	164,533	1,552,869	6,441,598
Spain	3,203	1,964	n.a.	265,023	2,332,694
Finland	n.a.	2,139	31,715	732,630	5,869,594

Note: The asset/turnover per country is based on an average of the largest three companies in France, Germany, and Great Britain, and on the two largest in Italy. The asset/turnover for companies in the remaining countries is based on only the largest company of the sector
n.a., not available

World War, owing to the expansion of the national consumer cooperative movement—the company KF (Kooperativa Förbundet). Another interesting observation is the small size of the Spanish company, probably an effect of the slow development of the Spanish economy.

In the aftermath of the Second World War (in the 1954 benchmark), the largest Swedish and British commercial companies continued to expand. In the case of Britain, three new companies were among the largest, while the leading company in Sweden was still the cooperative movement. The most astonishing feature is not the size of the British companies, but the assets of the largest Swedish firm—in a country with a tenth of the British population. However, the cooperative movement held a dominant position in both wholesale and retail trade in Sweden from the 1940s right up to the late 1970s.

If we concentrate on the five largest companies in each benchmark period, it is obvious that France, Great Britain, and Germany had and still have a leading position. During the first benchmark period, France and Great Britain were home to all five companies (Table 14.2). To some extent, this can be explained by the two countries' central position in the colonial trade, but it is also a result of their strong urbanization and growing consumer economy. The second benchmark period exhibits a more widespread distribution. The most surprising fact is probably that Italy is represented by two companies among the five largest—the Exxon subsidiary Societa Italo-Americana pel Petrolio and the textile trading company Societa Italia Commercia Materie Tessili.

After the Second World War, Great Britain had most representatives in the 'top five', followed by Germany. British companies included Great Universal Stores, Tesco, and Marks & Spencer[3] and the German ones Karstadt, Kaufhof, and Metro.[4]

[3] Great Universal Stores was established in 1900 as a mail order business with a wide range of products. Tesco started its business in 1919 and got its first permanent store in 1929, when the company became both a grocery and general merchandise retailer. Marks & Spencer was founded in 1884 and established its first permanent store in 1894. The company later concentrated on selling British-made goods.
[4] The Karstadt department store was founded in 1881and during the following decades branches were established all over northern Germany. Kaufhof was established in 1879 as a small store for

Table 14.2. Number of companies per country among the five largest in commercial activities

Country	1913	1927	1954	1972	2000
France	3	1			1
Great Britain	2	1	3	2	1
Germany		1	1	2	3
Italy		2			
Sweden			1	1	

Table 14.3. Type of activity of the largest commercial companies

	1913	2000
Department stores	6	
Specialist trading companies	6	5
Hotels	2	1
Hyper-/supermarket chains		11

As these were two of the largest economies in Europe, this is hardly surprising. However, the size of the population—the potential market—was not the only driving force behind the growth of commercial companies. This is also confirmed by the Finnish example Kesko, which was the eighth largest company in 1972, and the relative smallness of commercial companies in France and Italy in that year. One reason could be the early breakthrough in self-service shops in the Nordic countries, which led to the development of businesses with large retail shops and well-organized—and centralized—distribution chains.

In the year 2000, the turnover of the largest commercial companies was more commensurate with the size of each country's population. Even though recent decades have seen an increasing internationalization of commercial activities, a large proportion of these companies' business is still concentrated in their domestic markets.[5] However, there are some important exceptions, such as the French hypermarket chain Carrefour, which operates mainly in Europe but also has supermarkets in Africa, Asia, and America.[6]

Seen from an overall perspective, the large commercial companies gradually developed into hyper- or supermarkets including both wholesale and retail trade and often also production activities. In fact, these types of companies dominated the sample of commercial companies in 2000, while there were no comparable activities in 1913. Instead, the commercial sector in 1913 was dominated by department stores and specialist trading companies (Table 14.3). This development suggests an

textiles, but developed with branches before it was taken over by Metro AG in 1980 and totally merged in 1996.

[5] Jessen and Langer, *Transformations of Retailing in Europe after 1945*.

[6] The first Carrefour store was established in 1958, and the company opened the first hypermarket—combining a supermarket with a department store—outside Paris in 1963. In 1999, Carrefour merged with one of its major competitors, Promodès. In 2011, Carrefour was the fourth largest retail group in the world, with 1,452 supermarkets.

increasing efficiency in the commercial sector during the twentieth century, especially in the retail trade. Scale advantages are also seen in the specialized trading companies—for example the retailing of groceries or building materials.

The Long-Term Performance of Commercial Companies

The performance of commercial companies more or less corresponds to the average of Europe's leading companies, irrespective of industrial classification. Especially during the first and last benchmark periods, returns on equity (ROE) showed on average considerable similarities (Table 14.4). However, for the other three benchmark periods, there are some important differences.

During the second benchmark period, the mean ROE for commercial companies was heavily influenced by the extremely poor performance of the Italian company Societa Italiana Commercio Materie Tessili, which had an ROE of −131 per cent (see Table 14.6). The company with the best performance within this sector was the Grands Hôtels Belges, with a return of 36.1 per cent (see Table 14.5). Most companies within the sector achieved ROEs of between 10 and 15 per cent, and thus about the same level as the median return for the years 1927–9.

The mean ROE for the period 1954–6 is slightly higher than both the median value for the sector and the mean value for all sectors. This can to a large extent be explained by the high returns of two British companies: Woolworth and the Rank Organisation.[7]

The performance of the commercial companies seems to have been exceptionally strong in the early 1970s. ROE reached a level between 14 and 15 per cent, whereas the mean value for all sectors was about half of that (Table 14.4). The global downturn in the economy during the early 1970s obviously hit traditional industrial production harder than retail trade. Both the heavy and engineering industries, for example, faced much stronger global competition than the more domestically oriented commercial sector.

If we look at the long-term development of ROE from the perspective of the three best-performing companies in each of the five benchmark periods, the British companies held a strong position. Six of the fifteen companies were British, while three were French and only one came from Germany (Table 14.5). The

Table 14.4. Three-year average ROE for commercial companies (in %)

	1911–13	1927–9	1954–6	1970–2	1998–2000
ROE mean	9.0	3.3	11.9	14.8	10.7
ROE median	8.3	11.5	8.0	14.3	10.3
ROE mean, all sectors	10.1	10.1	10.4	7.7	14.2

---

[7] The British entertainment conglomerate the Rank Organisation was founded in 1937 and quickly became a vertically integrated film company. The company was a large film producer, but also manufactured radios, televisions, and photocopiers as one of the owners of Rank Xerox. The company was reorganized in 1996 to become the Rank Group Plc.

Table 14.5. The three best-performing commercial companies (in terms of ROE in %) in each benchmark period

Company	Country	1911–13	1927–9	1954–6	1970–2	1998–2000
Au Printemps	France	23.5				
Grands Hôtels Belges	Belgium	14.1	36.1			
Harrod`s Stores	Great Britain	11.9				
Deutsche-Russische Handels AG	Germany		22.4			
Au Bon Marché	France		15.2			
F.W. Woolworth	Great Britain			27.7		
The Rank Organisation	Great Britain			25.8		
Magazzini Standa	Italy			22.8		
Carrefour	France				41.8	
Marks & Spencer	Great Britain				26.3	
El Corta Ingles	Spain				21.2	
Kingfisher	Great Britain					17.3
Delhaize	Belgium					16.9
Tesco	Great Britain					14.1

British commercial companies were all dealing with the retail trade, originally concentrated on the domestic market but with their business gradually extending to other countries. Compared with the more general supermarket chains, the company Kingfisher stands out as an example of a modern specialized company. Kingfisher was established in the 1980s after a merger between the two British companies Woolworth and Paternoster. Kingfisher originally concentrated on home improvement products, but diversified into a wider range of products, though still connected to the fast-growing and profitable home improvement sector.

With the exception of Grands Hôtels Belges, no company appears among the 'top three' for more than one benchmark period. This is not that surprising, since commercial activities include a wide range of dynamic businesses. However, the tendency towards the increased importance of hyper- or supermarkets among the largest companies is also reflected in their share of the best-performing ones.

The strong performance of the British companies is in stark contrast with the poor performance of their Italian counterparts, especially during the two first benchmark periods (Table 14.6). During the latter benchmark periods, companies from several countries achieved a low ROE—between 2 and 3 per cent.

In contrast to the long-term stability of ROE, holding return (HR) displays far greater volatility. There were considerable fluctuations between the benchmark periods, especially after the Second World War, and more so for commercial companies than for the sample taken as a whole (Table 14.7). In 1954–6, companies from Italy and France exhibited high holding returns, with La Rinascente (70.9 per cent) and Galeries Lafayette (63.5 per cent) at the top. The three British companies, however, were at the bottom, with the Rank Organisation showing a negative return (−27.4 per cent). National trends in stock market prices appear to have played an important role in the development of HR, especially considering that the British companies had the largest ROE during the same benchmark period.

Table 14.6. The three worst-performing commercial companies (in terms of ROE in %) in each benchmark period

Company	Country	1911–13	1927–9	1954–6	1970–2	1998–2000
Compagnia Italiana grandi alberghi	Italy	0.9				
Lipton	Great Britain	5.9				
Au Bon Marché	France	7.6		2.0		
Società Italiana Commercio Materie Tessili	Italy		−131.1			
Società Italo-Americana pel Petrolio	Italy		2.2			
Stockman Oy	Finland		7.6			
Galaries Lafayette	France			4.8		
Emil Köster KG	Germany			4.9		
Nouvelles Galeries Réunies	France				2.1	
Kooperativa Förbundet	Sweden				2.3	
Kesko Oy	Finland				6.2	6.9
Centros Comerciales Carrefour	Spain					3.0
La Rinascente	Italy					5.6

Table 14.7. Three-year average HR for commercial companies (in %)

	1911–13	1927–9	1954–6	1970–2	1998–2000
HR mean	7.5	7.8	25.7	13.1	−3.1
HR median	6.9	4.9	27.7	9.9	−2.5
HR mean, all sectors	5.5	14.4	24.3	8.2	18.1

As in the case of ROE, HR was higher than the mean value for all sectors during the 1970–2 benchmark period. The most striking example was Carrefour, where HR reached 57 per cent. As many as eight commercial companies (out of twelve in the sample) posted an HR higher than the mean for all sectors. The situation was reversed during the 1998–2000 benchmark period, when eight out of ten companies had an HR lower than the mean for all sectors. In particular, companies from France and Great Britain presented low—even negative—rates, with Carrefour showing the poorest result (−31.5 per cent). The weak HRs achieved by commercial companies during this benchmark period can to some extent be explained by the information technology boom and the focus on knowledge-based industries on the stock market.

The examples given here have shown that the differences between the highest and lowest levels of both ROE and HR could be quite significant. The most conspicuous example is in 1927–9, when such a difference reached 192.8 for ROE (Table 14.8). This is mainly an effect of the poor performance of Societa Italiana Commercio Materie Tessili. However, from a long-term perspective, the gap between maximum and minimum levels is lower, and the standard deviation falls from 39.5 per cent in 1927–9 to 4 per cent in 1998–2000.

Table 14.8. Differences between highest and lowest levels of ROE and of HR for commercial companies, together with the respective standard deviations (SD) (in %)

	1911–13	1927–9	1954–6	1970–2	1998–2000
ROE	22.5	192.8	25.7	39.5	14.3
SD	5.3	39.5	8.4	10.4	4.0
HR	20.4	28.3	98.3	64.6	85.9
SD	6.2	10.1	28.8	16.9	18.4

Compared with ROE, HR exhibits a greater difference between the highest and lowest levels over the five benchmark periods and thus also a higher standard deviation. This development is probably connected to changes in the stock market, due to international openness, increased short-term trading, and greater volatility.

THE BANKING INDUSTRY

Banking Systems and Banks

A well-functioning financial system is of vital importance for economic progress and for the development of industry and trade. The traditional function of the financial system can be summarized as three basic tasks: transfer capital from savers to investors or for consumption; reallocate risks over time and in space; and provide effective liquid assets or other means of capital transfer.

These tasks can be fulfilled in different ways and with different institutions and actors, which are often related to a country's economic development. The financial system therefore often features specific national characteristics which are reflected in the structure and development of the market, the actors, and the financial instruments. Since financial transactions are based on stability and trust, long-term relationships have tended to be an important feature of the financial system in several European countries.

National financial systems can be described from different perspectives. However, one common definition is based on the organization of the financial market and its actors, particularly how credit relations are framed. The financing of industry and trade is of special importance in this context. Previous research has differentiated between bank- and market-oriented financial systems. In a bank-oriented system, the finance of industry and trade is primarily dependent on financial intermediaries—most often banks—which allocate capital from savers to those that seek it. A bank-oriented financial system can be found in, for example, Japan and traditionally also Germany and Sweden. In these countries, banks and industry have also developed through share ownership—especially banks' shareholding in industrial companies. Several countries in their early economic development also promoted a strong banking sector in order to finance the establishment of industry.

In market-oriented financial systems, on the other hand, companies rely on direct contacts with the market for the issue of bonds, shares, certificates, or other financial instruments. Since these transactions are made on the market, they do not necessarily require the intermediation of a bank. In a perfect world, this reduces transaction costs, compared with the bank-oriented financial system, where banks charge interest for the risks they take in lending money. The most refined example of a market-oriented financial system is to be found in the USA, and to a large extent also in the UK.[8] But, throughout their history, the majority of European countries have also made ample use of financial markets, and during the last three decades, bank-oriented financial systems have exhibited several features of the market-oriented ones.[9]

During the second half of the twentieth century, a growing portion of financial assets has been used for activities other than the financing of industry and trade—for example infrastructure investments and private consumption. This is an important reason why state intervention in the banking sector increased during and after the Second World War. Another explanation lies in the progress of left-wing movements, for whom state ownership or growing state control were important political objectives. In several countries, not least France, the state nationalized banks and other financial companies, while in others state control was strengthened through legislation and other regulations. In some countries and during short periods—for example in Sweden—one could almost talk of a state-oriented financial system, since the banks themselves could not decide upon the allocation of capital or the interest rate.[10]

The size and development of the national economy, as well as the structure of the financial system, can be expected to influence both the banks' growth and their profits. It is to be expected that large countries will have the biggest banks, but also that a bank-oriented financial system will produce larger and more diversified banks. This would probably mean that in the early twentieth century we will find the largest banks in the early industrialized countries—Great Britain, France, and Germany. But, as other countries develop, their financial systems will follow suit. It can therefore be expected that, for example, Swedish banks will be larger in the later than in the earlier part of the period under study.

The development of the financial sector is also strongly affected by general economic conditions, especially financial crises. Even though the selection of benchmark periods in this project has been made to avoid years of large economic fluctuations, it is difficult to totally eliminate the long-term effects of financial crises. A distinction should be made here between years of great financial distress, which affect business performance in the very short term, for a couple of years or so, and the structural changes brought about, in the longer term, by a major shock. Thus, the financial problems that hit several countries in the early 1920s are likely to have affected banks during the later part of the

---

[8] E. Berglöf, *SOU 1988: 38 bilaga 12 Ägande och inflytande i svenskt näringsliv* (Stockholm, 1988); J. Zysman, *Markets and Growth: Financial Systems and the Politics of Industrial Change* (London, 1990). The role of the City of London in the financial system is analyzed by Y. Cassis, *City Bankers 1890–1914* (Cambridge, 1994).

[9] Berglöf, *SOU 1988: 38*.

[10] M. Larsson, *Staten och kapitalet* (Stockholm, 1998).

decade. The Second World War can also be expected to have reversed financial development in several countries.[11]

The Structure of the Banking Sector

The measure of the banks' size has been based on their total assets for all five benchmark periods. The use of turnover is problematic from a methodological point of view. Not all banks declare their turnover, which is partly because turnover for banks does not supply relevant information about the company's business development.

On the eve of the First World War, the largest banks were located, not surprisingly, in Great Britain, France, and Germany. The median assets of the British banks included in the sample amounted to $379 million, compared with $363 million and $357 million for the French and German banks, respectively (Table 14.9). Nevertheless, the largest bank in 1913 was not British, but German: Deutsche Bank, with total assets of $534 million. Crédit Lyonnais was a close second with $532 million, while the third largest was London City and Midland Bank with $517 million. These three banks were followed by eight other banks from Great Britain, France, and Germany, all before the largest Belgian and Italian banks. This underlines the financial predominance of Great Britain, France, and Germany in the period before the First World War. Spain, Sweden, and Finland were far behind the other countries, with the largest bank being Skandinaviska Kreditaktiebolaget, with total assets of $97 million. This is in line with the sizes of these countries and the fact that industrial development had only just started there.

The First World War and the ensuing economic problems had considerable effects on the banking structure of some countries. Banks in France and Germany stagnated, while British banks continued to grow. France and Germany even fell behind Belgium and Spain. However, this was because only two Belgian and Spanish banks have been included in the sample, one of them being the countries'

Table 14.9. Average distribution of assets, 1913–2000 (in million US$)

Country	1913	1927	1954	1972	2000
France	363	300	702	13,644	378,942
Germany	357	430	510	13,035	553,867
Great Britain	379	1,823	4,179	15,349	489,708
Italy	241	528	936	19,451	218,221
Belgium	181	1,004	1,480	6,232	78,718
Sweden	74	296	784	5,382	169,379
Spain	31	1,348	4,481	9,889	299,734
Finland	44	74	303	1,641	56,824

Note: The assets per country are based on the average of the five largest banks in Germany and Great Britain, the four largest in France, the three largest in Italy, the two largest in Spain, Belgium, and Sweden, and the largest in Finland.

---

[11] Financial crises and their effects are analysed by C. Reinhard and K. Rogoff, *This Time is Different—Eight Centuries of Financial Folly* (Princeton, 2011).

central banks—the Banco de España and the Banque Nationale de Belgique—whose positions, including in terms of size, were very peculiar compared with private commercial banks.[12]

The largest bank in 1927 was the British Lloyds Bank, with total assets of just over $2 billion. If we do not include the central banks of Spain and Belgium, Lloyds was followed by three other British banks—Midland Bank, Barclays Bank, and Westminster Bank—with assets between $1.5 and $2 billion, while the French and German banks all had assets between $300 and $600 million. This was about the same size as banks from the other countries included in the analysis, except for Finland, where the average assets were only $74 million. Thus, the Spanish, Swedish, Italian, and Belgian banks grew significantly faster than the German and French banks after the First World War.

Not surprisingly, the Second World War took its toll on German banks, which were greatly reduced in terms of size compared with banks in the other countries. Their average assets totalled $510 million in 1954, only $80 million more than in 1927. After the Second World War and the dismemberment of the German three 'big banks' (Deutsche Bank, Dresdner Bank, and Commerzbank) by the Allies, the size of German banks decreased considerably. But in 1954, one of the successors of the old Deutsche Bank—the Rheinisch Westphälische Bank—was still the largest German Bank, with assets of $637 million, followed by Süddeutsche Bank with $605 million. Even though they were reunited in 1957-8, German banks had greater difficulties in expanding after 1945 than the banks of other warring countries. In France, the largest bank—Credit Lyonnais—had assets of just over $1.4 billion, while Italy's largest bank, Banca Nazionale de Lavoro (BNL), had around $1 billion in assets.[13]

The largest banks in Belgium and Spain were still the central banks, and they were still the only banks comparable in size to the largest British banks. With the exception of Banco de España, all five British banks in 1954 were larger than their European counterparts, the largest being Barclays Bank, with assets of over $6.1 billion. Undoubtedly, the British banks were in a position to develop during the first decade after the Second World War. This was of course partly an effect of the war being fought on the European continent, but also an effect of these banks' previous international contacts, which could be resumed after the war.

However, British banks lost their dominant position during the following decades. In 1972, the Italian banks emerged on top, with average assets of over $19 billion—and BNL as the largest bank with $23.5 billion. Barclays remained the largest British bank, with $25 billion in assets, followed by National Westminster Bank (NatWest) with $22 billion.[14] However the other British banks were

---

[12] Banque Nationale de Belgique was established with private capital in 1850, to perform the traditional tasks of a national bank. The Belgium government today owns 50 per cent of the shares. Banco de España was established as long ago as 1782 and has, in addition to its central banking tasks, been the supervisor of the Spanish banking system. After the Second World War, the bank was put under tight state control and was nationalized in 1962.

[13] BNL was founded in 1913 and was nationalized in 1929. It was re-privatized and listed on the Milan Stock Exchange in 1998 and was purchased by the French bank BNP Paribas in 2006.

[14] NatWest was formed by the merger of three banks: National Provincial Bank, Westminster Bank, and District Bank. The latter was taken over by National Provincial Bank in 1962, but could operate under its own name until the establishment of National Westminster Bank in 1970. After several

considerably smaller. The same holds true for France and Germany, where a couple of banks had grown faster than their competitors—especially BNP in France (assets $20.2 billion) and the merged and reorganized Deutsche Bank (assets $18.4 billion). Both of these banks were among the largest in Europe and had scale advantages over their national competitors.[15]

These examples demonstrate the important part played by concentration processes in the international financial system since the late 1960s. Especially since the 1980s, with the emergence of the global financial market, the need for large banks increased. Industrial activities required to a greater extent strong financial actors, which could support companies in their international development. This resulted in the establishment of bank subsidiaries in expanding national and regional markets all over the world, and increased competition.

In the last quarter of the twentieth century, the European banking sector was revolutionized in terms of scale and scope in a way that makes comparisons with previous periods difficult. Liberalization and deregulation fostered the creation of huge financial conglomerates operating across the globe over several sectors and line of products. This resulted in a spectacular growth of the size of the banks in all analysed countries. The assets of the largest banks in each country increased on average by between 1,000 and 4,000 per cent from 1972 to 2000. German banks experienced the fasted growth, at over 4,150 per cent. British, French, Swedish, and Finnish banks grew by around 3,000 per cent, while the Italian and Belgian banks increased their assets by just over 1,000 per cent (Table 14.9).

This increase in size was possible in part through an organic growth of the banks' business—but most of all through extensive merger activities. There are several examples of this process. For example, Midland Bank was acquired in 1992 by HSBC. The Italian bank Credito Italiano was privatized in December 1993 and Banca Commerciale Italiana in April 1994. After a series of mergers and acquisitions, Credito Italiano became Unicredito Italiano (now UniCredit) by the end of the 1990s, while Banca Commerciale Italiano merged with Banca Intesa to create IntesaBci (now Intesa Sanpaolo). The Swedish bank Nordea was the result of several mergers among Nordic banks from the early 1990s to the early 2000s.[16]

If we look at the largest banks for each of the five benchmark years, the importance of British banking becomes even more striking. As many as fourteen of the twent-five largest banks—for all bench mark periods—originated in Great

attempts, the Royal Bank of Scotland managed to take over NatWest in 2000, which made the Royal Bank of Scotland the second largest bank in the UK and Europe after HSBC.

[15] The four largest French banks had been nationalized, and remained so until privatization started in 1993. One of these banks—Comptoir national d'escompte de Paris—was merged with Banque nationale pour le commerce et l'industrie in 1966, creating Banque Nationale de Paris (BNP).

[16] The Swedish (Scandinavian) bank Nordea has its origins in the Swedish bank Jordbrukarbanken, which was taken over by the Swedish state in the 1920s. In the 1950s, the bank changed its name to Kreditbanken and its business was enlarged. The Swedish state was still the sole owner and all public financial activities were supposed to be handled by the bank. The bank merged with the Postal Savings Bank in the 1970s and formed the PK-bank, which was then expected to be an alternative to the private banks on the Swedish market. It was later merged with another Swedish bank, forming Nordbanken. With the deregulation of the financial market, a privatization of the bank started, and after mergers with other banks in the Baltic region—forming Nordea—the ownership of the Swedish state has been heavily reduced to around 7 per cent.

Table 14.10. Number of banks per country among the five largest

Country	1913	1927	1954	1972	2000
Great Britain	3	3	4	2	2
Germany	1				2
France	1			1	1
Spain		1	1		
Italy				2	
Belgium		1			

Britain (Table 14.10). Three banks each were established in Germany or France, two each in Italy and Spain, and one in Belgium. This underlines the importance of both national development and market size. For the first three benchmark periods, the banks' business was concentrated foremost in the country of origin and in colonized areas.[17] The number of alternative financial institutions was probably larger in Great Britain compared with, for example, Sweden, Finland, and Spain—especially with the active British stock market. But at the same time, the demand for capital in Great Britain was much larger than in, for example, Sweden and Spain, which facilitated the growth of British banks.

The deregulation of the national financial markets that began in the 1970s changed the situation for more or less all European banks, which can be seen especially during the last benchmark period. Globalization and international competition became a beacon for the financial market, and with deregulation it was increasingly difficult to uphold national restrictions and also keep to a bank-oriented financial system. Even though banks still play a major role in the financing of industry and trade, bank-oriented financial systems have become more market-oriented during the last decades. Those banks that were most ready to adjust to this new international order were those that already had international experience and a tradition of working in a 'free' market. It looks as if banks from Great Britain, France, and Germany had an advantage compared with banks from the other countries in this analysis.

The Business Performance of the Financial Sector

The global financial system went through a large number of financial crises during the twentieth century. The majority of these were very limited and only affected a national financial system or a few banks, without any systemic or long-term consequences. However, a couple of crises did have a global dimension. And even though the selection of benchmark periods has been made with this in mind, the long-term effects from financial disturbances can be quite considerable.

---

[17] The internationalization of European banking has been analysed in G. Jones, ed., *Banks as Multinationals* (London/New York, 1992) and by Y. Cassis, *Capitals of Capital: A History of International Financial Centres 1780–2005* (Cambridge, 2006).

Table 14.11. Three-year average ROE for banks (in %)

	1911–13	1927–9	1954–6	1970–2	1998–2000
ROE mean	10.3	12.8	17.9 (12.0)[a]	10.1	14.3
ROE median	9.6	9.9	8.9	10.3	13.3
ROE mean, all sectors	10.1	10.1	10.4	7.7	14.2

[a] The mean ROE of 17.9 per cent for 1954–6 includes all the banks in the sample, while the figure in parenthesis excludes Banco de Espana, which that year registered an ROE of 153.8%

Table 14.12. Three-year average HR for banks (in %)

	1911–13	1927–9	1954–6	1970–2	1998–2000
HR mean	3.2	12.1	20.8	10.3	12.7
HR median	3.8	11.2	10.7	9.5	12.5
HR mean, all sectors	4.0	13.7	24.3	7.3	18.2

Table 14.13. Differences between the highest and lowest levels of ROE and of HR for banks, together with the respective standard deviations (SD) (in %)

	1911–13	1927–9	1954–6	1970–2	1998–2000
ROE	11.7	30.5	149.1	12.7	53.7
SD	4.9	9.0	31.0	3.2	7.9
HR	31.2	69.8	73.4	35.4	89.9
SD	3.3	14.6	27.6	14.6	19.3

The long-term development of ROE in the banking sector reveals no significant differences with the sample as a whole (Table 14.11). ROE was impressively stable during all benchmark periods, and higher than the average for all sectors. ROE for 1954–6 was inordinately high (17.9 per cent) because of the result of Banco de España, which reached 154 per cent. A more realistic ROE for this year (12.0 per cent) is achieved if this bank is omitted. From the beginning of the 1970s, economic growth stagnated and the international financial market became increasingly unstable, especially as an effect of the travails of the Bretton Woods system. ROE decreased markedly for other sectors, while banks managed to keep it at a fairly stable level. Finally, the deregulation and globalization of the financial market, which commenced during the 1970s, resulted in a boom for banks during the last decades of the twentieth century.

The long-term stability of ROE is not matched by anything equivalent for HR, whether mean or median (Table 14.12). On the contrary, HR fluctuated considerably between periods, with the lowest levels in 1911–13 and 1970–2, and the highest in 1954–6, followed by the 1998–2000 period. The general changes in stock market prices had a strong influence on this development, which was closely related to that of all sectors.

As can be expected, there were wide differences between banks in both ROE and HR, and these differences were considerably higher than for the commercial companies (compare Tables 14.13 and 14.8). Differences between banks were more pronounced during the three last benchmark periods—also measured as standard deviation—especially in 1954–6 and 1998–2000. For the 1950s, this can be linked to large national differences, due to the reconstruction of national economies after the Second World War; for the last period, this can be an effect of differences in banks' competitiveness on the globalized financial market.

From the global point of view, financial crises do not seem to have had any serious long-term effects on the development of ROE and HR for banks during our benchmark periods. Instead, the general economic development and changes in the globalization of the financial system had a stronger impact. In the long run, HR seems to become increasingly volatile, as an effect of a more active market, with a large number of mergers in the last fifty years, globalization, and less formal regulations of the market. The growing role of market solutions also activated the stock markets, with an increased volatility for banks' shares.

Performances at National Level

The differences between ROE in different countries were considerable. This can to some extent be explained by the number of banks constituting the national samples. As discussed already, the small number of banks and the way they have been selected in Spain, Belgium, and Finland, and to a lesser extent Sweden, poses a problem, since individual banks can determine ROE at national level. However, the number of banks is also very small for the larger countries. The results must therefore be treated carefully, especially when analysing HR, since several banks were not listed on the stock exchange.

Considering first the banks from the four largest countries, those from Italy and Germany have tended to display the poorest performance. For three of the five periods, ROE for the Italian banks was a couple of per cent lower than for those of the other larger countries, while German banks were the poorest performers during the periods 1954–6 and 1998–2000. Both British and French banks showed better long-term results: their average ROE for all five benchmark periods was over 10 per cent (British banks came top with 12.2 per cent), while German and Italian banks managed only 9 and 8.7 per cent, respectively (Table 14.14).

The strong position of British banks—both as market leaders and performers— was established already during the late nineteenth century. The British position as a leader of industrial development and the global economy created highly favourable conditions for British banks, compounded by the higher degree of sophistication of the financial system and the business opportunities offered by

Table 14.14. Three-year average ROE for banks, national level (in %)

Country	1911–13	1927–9	1954–6	1970–2	1998–2000	Average
France	7.1	9.9	12.6	13.3	11.0	10.8
Germany	12.2	10.6	5.4	8.7	8.2	9.0
Great Britain	13.0	9.0	7.9	11.4	19.3	12.2
Italy	4.3	8.2	14.3	6.1	10.4	8.7
Belgium	10.8	18.4	37.5	11.3	12.6	18.1
Sweden	8.4	8.3	7.3	6.6	15.4	9.2
Spain	15.8	25.5	84.4	14.1	30.6	34.1
Finland	10.1	10.3	10.3	6.1	14.5	10.3

the City of London as the world's leading financial centre.[18] The strong general confidence in British banks was maintained during the interwar period, but as financial markets became increasingly national, the role of British banks was questioned. This tendency was further developed in the period after the Second World War, when competition on the international financial market increased.[19] It is therefore impressive that British banks managed to maintain a high ROE throughout all five benchmark periods.

Among the four remaining countries, the Spanish and Belgian banks stand out with a very high ROE. However, as already noted, the position of the central banks of Belgium and Spain complicates the analysis. Both banks demonstrate a high and even extremely high ROE during the three first benchmark periods. However, with substantial state ownership and the central banks' business being vital for the state, the risk of capital shortage in these banks was close to non-existent, making it more or less unimportant to increase share capital. These banks' equity ratios provide proof of this. For both the Banque Nationale de Belgique and the Banco de España, the equity/assets ratio was much lower than for comparable banks in 1927 and 1954 (Table 14.15; see also Table 14.17). This under-capitalization of the Spanish and Belgian banks enabled them to achieve higher ROEs than other banks.

The choice of financial system might also have affected the level of ROE. Thus, the two most prominent examples of a bank-oriented financial system—Sweden and Germany—display a comparatively low ROE both for individual benchmark periods and as an average for all periods, while British banks in a market-oriented system exhibit the highest ROE (Table 14.14). However, this might not necessarily be related to the financial system. Germany underwent several political and economic changes during the twentieth century that affected its banks' ROE. And in the Swedish case, both financial crises in the interwar period and extensive state control after the Second World War might have hampered ROE.

Compared with ROE data, it is more complicated to identify clear patterns in HR. Nevertheless, we can note larger fluctuations between the countries compared with ROE, especially after the Second World War (Table 14.14). There are also periods characterized by low general levels of HR, foremost the first benchmark period, and periods of higher levels—such as the recovery in the 1950s and the sharp increase during the globalization of the financial system in the last

Table 14.15. Equity/assets ratio for selected banks (in %)

Bank	1913	1927	1954
Lloyds Bank	6.7	6.3	2.3
Midland Bank	7.5	5.9	1.7
Banque Nationale de Belgique	6.7	2.2	0.6
Banco de Espana	n.a.	1.9	0.2

n.a., not available

---

[18] For a further analysis, see Cassis, *Capitals of Capital*, pp. 90–100.
[19] Jones, *Banks as Multinationals*.

Table 14.16. Three-year average HR for banks, national level (in %)

	1911–13	1927–9	1954–6	1970–2	1998–2000	Average
France	5.3	31.3	35.2	15.3	36.2	24.7
Germany	3.9	−0.7	53.5	−2.9	7.5	12.3
Great Britain	4.6	11.6	−0.7	31.1	13.2	12.0
Italy	1.2	15.2	n.a.	−1.7	26.3	10.3
Belgium	−1.1	4.9	10.5	11.8	16.3	8.1
Sweden	5.1	21.3	−4.2	6.6	25.2	10.8
Spain	−0.4	6.4	20.2	−6.9	−17.6	0.3
Finland	n.a.	11.7	2.4	19.8	n.a.	11.3

n.a., not available

benchmark period. This development indicates the growing interest and focus on shareholders' value.[20] The poor returns achieved by investors in the early 1910s might well be explained by the insecure political situation, while the strong development in 1927–9 is connected to the general economic recovery and speculation after the First World War.

Another interesting observation is the low HR for both Spanish and Belgian banks. Obviously, the dependence on the central banks' profits—with large state ownership—hampered the rise of stock market prices. Banks in the four largest countries—France, Germany, Great Britain, and Italy—all displayed an average HR of over 10 per cent, and as high as 24.7 per cent for French banks (Table 14.16). However, for all countries, HR fluctuates considerably between the benchmark periods, which renders conclusions more doubtful.

If we look at the three best- and worst-performing banks during the five benchmark periods, we can see—as already noted—the predominance of Banco de España and Banque Nationale de Belgique, in terms of ROE, during the first three periods. Besides these two central banks, German banks also did well (Table 14.17). It might look surprising that British banks were not among the best-performing banks during these periods, compared with those of other countries, but their ROE was still high and stable, even though they were outperformed by a couple of banks. During the latter two benchmark periods, several well-known banks achieved high ROE, including the British Lloyds Bank and the French Société Générale and Crédit Lyonnais. Among the best-performing banks in 1998–2000 were also the two Spanish banks BBVA and BSCH, both the result of mergers in the 1990s.[21]

---

[20] William Lazonick and Mary O'Sullivan, 'Maximizing shareholder value: A new ideology for corporate governance', *Economy and Society*, 29, 1 (2000), 13–35.

[21] The Spanish multinational banking group Banco Bilbao Vizcaya Argentaria (BBVA) was formed in 1999 through a merger between the two financial actors Banco Bilbao Vizcaya and Argentaria, and became the second largest bank in Spain. Banco Bilbao can trace its roots back to 1857. The Spanish bank Banco Santander was also founded in 1857, and as Banco Bilbao it grew through a merger (Banco Central Hispano) in 1999 and formed Banco Santander Central Hispano (BSCH). Even though the merger was supposed to be between two equals, the Santander part of the bank soon became dominant and the bank is known today as the Santander Group. Through international mergers, the Santander Group has grown to become one of the world's largest banks. In 2013, Santander also became the main owner (51 per cent) in the supermarket chain El Corte Inglés.

Table 14.17. The three best-performing banks (in terms of ROE in %) in each benchmark period

Company	Country	1911–13	1927–9	1954–6	1970–2	1998–2000
Banco de Espana	Spain	23.9	38.2	153.8		
Disconto-Gesellschaft	Germany	19.4				
Banque Nationale de Belgique	Belgium	15.4	24.2	60.2		
Darmstädter und Nationalbank	Germany		13.1			
Banco di Roma	Italy			20.4		
Banesto	Italy				16.3	
Société Générale	France				13.9	
Crèdit Lyonnais	France				13.4	
BBVA	Spain					35.3
Lloyds TSB Group	Great Britain					28.9
BSCH	Spain					26.0

Table 14.18. The three worst-performing banks (in terms of ROE in %) in each benchmark period

Company	Country	1911–13	1927–9	1954–6	1970–2	1998–2000
Società Italiana per le strada Ferrate Meridionali	Italy	0.7				
Société Générale	France	4.6	7.8			
Credito Italiano	Italy	6.0				
Skandinaviska Kreditaktiebolaget	Sweden		5.7			
Banco di Roma	Italy		7.1			
Rhein-Main Bank	Germany			5.2		
Deutsche Bank AG West	Germany			4.7		
Süddeutsch Bank AG	Germany			4.7		
Svenska Handelsbanken	Sweden				5.4	
BNL	Italy				3.6	
Bayerische Hypoteken- und Wechsel-Bank	Germany				5.6	
Westdeutsche Landesbank Girozentrale	Germany					2.6
Nationale Bank	Belgium					4.7
Bayerishe Hypo- and Vereinsbank AG	Germany					5.3

Several of the worst-performing banks were German—six of fourteen banks with the lowest ROE. Four others were Italian and two Swedish. No British or Spanish bank features in this group (Table 14.18). The poor results of these banks might be a little surprising. They can at least partly be explained, in the case of the Italian and German banks, by the financial situation around the two world wars and the interwar years. This was especially relevant for the three low-performing German banks in the 1950s, but also in the 1970s and 1990s. The business of the Bayerische Hypotheken- und Wechsel-Bank was primarily concentrated on mortgage lending, as was that of the Westdeutsche Landesbank Girozentrale, which also served as a central institute for the savings banks in North Rhine-Westphalia. This put obvious constraints on the possibilities to develop profitable areas of business.[22] But there were also specific problems connected with banks that explain a low ROE. For example, the Swedish bank Svenska Handelsbanken had extensive economic problems during the early 1970s.

CONCLUDING REMARKS

Commercial exchanges and financial transactions are activities of the greatest importance for every development process—during early industrialization as well as during globalization of markets. Companies in both sectors have undergone considerable concentration in all countries, but those from Great Britain, Germany, and France emerged as the largest companies in Europe—from the early twentieth century onwards. Most impressive, however, has been the expansion of the size and business of banks. The 'financialization' of the global economy has resulted in much larger companies, not only in the three leading European economies, but also in the smaller countries.

Great Britain held a dominant position among the large companies in both commercial and financial services during the early benchmark periods. British firms managed to uphold this position in banking, while German companies gradually became the largest in commercial activities. This could be a consequence of the enlarged market in Central Europe after the fall of the Berlin Wall, when German companies had an obvious advantage compared with companies from the other countries included in this analysis.

The concentration process in commercial activities is also reflected in the types of companies active in the field. During the early benchmark periods, both department stores and hotels could be found among the large commercial firms in several countries. But in the 1990s, hyper- or supermarket chains totally dominated the big companies in the sector. Banks as organizations have been more stable, and even though new financial instruments have developed and changed the business of banking, the banks' basic services have remained essentially the same.

ROE was overall higher and more stable for banks than for commercial companies. Only in the early 1970s did the latter perform on average better than the former. In the late 1920s and at the turn of the twenty-first century, banks performed considerably better than commercial companies. This is not surprising, since both decades were characterized by intense activity on the financial markets.

---

[22] Bayerische Hypotheken- und Wechsel-Bank was founded in 1835, and had already developed into the largest mortgage bank in Germany during the nineteenth century. The bank expanded internationally from the 1960s, and in 1998, it merged with Bayerische Vereinsbank to form Bayerische Hypo- und Vereinsbank Aktiengesellschaft. Through cooperation with the Austrian Creditanstalt and mergers with local banks, this bank increased its business in Central and Eastern Europe, still concentrating on mortgage affairs.

The results are not as clear cut for HR. Banks showed better results during the 1920s and 1990s, commercial firms during the other benchmark periods. The last benchmark period, in particular, stands out when banking and commercial activities are compared. Both ROE and, especially, HR were considerably higher for banks compared with commercial firms. Thus, despite increased competition on the financial markets, banks managed to make high profits.

The result of this analysis also confirms the strong performance of British banks compared with banks from other countries. The early internationalization of the British economy and the role of London as a centre for global finance can explain this strong position during the early benchmark periods. However, in order to maintain their lead, British banks had to be in the forefront in business development.

APPENDIX

Companies in the Large Sample

These are listed alphabetically for each benchmark period.

Benchmark	Country	Company	Sector	Year	Assets (US$)	Turnover (US$)	3-year average ROE	3-year average HR
1	DE	'Phoenix' Aktiengesellschaft für Bergbau und Hüttenbetrieb	Basic and fabricated metals	1913	53,330,474	70,247,621	22.30	6.36
1	IT	A.E.G. Thomson Houston	Electrical engineering	1913	4,152,511		5.41	
1	SE	AB Nordiska Kompaniet	Commercial activities	1913	6,112,267		8.28	
1	SE	AB Separator	Mechanical engineering	1913	14,093,600		10.11	6.07
1	DE	Actien-Gesellschaft für Maschinenpapier-Fabrikation	Wood and paper products	1913	10,020,340		9.42	1.07
1	DE	Adler & Oppenheimer Lederfabrik Aktien-Gesellschaft	Textiles and leather goods	1913	7,351,162		11.25	
1	IT	AEDES Società anonima ligure per imprese e costruzioni	Construction and property companies	1913	4,549,384		−3.18	−19.42
1	FR	Agence Havas	Wood and paper products	1913	4,231,560		9.78	18.19
1	FR	Air Liquide	Oil, rubber, chemicals, and other non-metallic mineral products	1913	4,559,215		24.90	4.90

(continued)

Continued

Benchmark	Country	Company	Sector	Year	Assets (US$)	Turnover (US$)	3-year average ROE	3-year average HR
1	FR	Alais, Froges, Camargue	Oil, rubber, chemicals, and other non-metallic mineral products	1913	13,297,014		8.40	51.10
1	DE	Allgemeine Elektricitäts-Gesellschaft (AEG)	Electrical engineering	1913	110,250,578		12.96	2.21
1	FR	Alsacienne de constructions mécaniques	Mechanical engineering	1913	12,671,288		12.99	49.17
1	ES	Altos Hornos de Vizcaya	Basic and fabricated metals	1913	7,940,036		15.40	3.40
1	GB	Amalgamated Press	Wood and paper products	1913	8,580,738		22.38	6.22
1	GB	Arthur Guinness & Son	Food, drink, and tobacco products	1913	46,571,548		11.22	-0.89
1	SE	ASEA	Electrical engineering	1913	6,752,533	4,584,000	7.37	22.00
1	ES	Astillero del Nervión	Transport equipment	1913	5,385,996		6.43	10.33
1	BE	Ateliers Construction Electriques de Charleroi	Electrical engineering	1913	6,766,260			
1	FR	Ateliers et chantiers de Saint Nazaire (Penhoët)	Transport equipment	1913	20,784,913		11.89	11.13
1	FR	Au Bon Marché	Commercial activities	1913	26,042,207		7.59	
1	FR	Au Printemps	Commercial activities	1913	15,432,316		23.45	11.84
1	GB	Babcock & Wilcox	Mechanical engineering	1913	15,014,429		20.33	-13.06
1	DE	Badische Anilin- & Soda-Fabrik (BASF)	Oil, rubber, chemicals, and other non-metallic mineral products	1913	30,062,450		22.74	8.18

1	IT	Banca Commerciale Italiana	Financial intermediation	1913	371,119,744	6.18	1.80
1	ES	Banco Hipotecario de España	Financial intermediation	1913	35,062,837	7.60	−4.60
1	ES	Banco Hispano-Americano	Financial intermediation	1913	14,416,517	3.70	−23.10
1	FR	Banque de Paris et des Pays-Bas	Financial intermediation	1913	138,220,849	7.64	0.13
1	BE	Banque Nationale de Belgique	Financial intermediation	1913	252,906,985	15.42	−2.80
1	DE	Bayerische Hypotheken- und Wechsel-Bank	Financial intermediation	1913	328,448,254	9.54	5.99
1	SE	Bergslagarnes Järnvägsaktiebolag	Railways	1913	21,312,533	9.62	9.93
1	DE	Bergwerksgesellschaft Hibernia	Mining	1913	31,406,137	9.49	
1	DE	Berliner Elektricitäts-Werke	Utilities; Electricity, gas, and water supply	1913	40,089,780	15.98	2.26
1	DE	Berliner Terrain- und Bau-Aktiengesellschaft in Berlin	Construction and property companies	1913	11,378,278	−42.19	−53.44
1	BE	Blaton-Ath (Canal de)	Transport and communication	1913	1,579,917	9.01	−11.35
1	GB	Bolckow Vaughan & Co.	Basic and fabricated metals	1913	23,573,052	8.33	18.80
1	GB	Borax Consolidated	Mining	1913	23,682,414	8.13	14.26
1	BE	Brasseries et Laiteries d'Haacht	Food, drink, and tobacco products	1913	442,821	19.77	1.16
1	GB	British American Tobacco Co.	Food, drink, and tobacco products	1913	69,221,567	19.11	4.14
1	GB	Calico Printers	Textiles and leather goods	1913	42,033,333	10.13	−9.29
1	ES	Caminos de Hierro del Norte de España	Railways	1913	184,786,715	5.00	0.50
1	BE	Carrières de Porphyre de Quenast	Construction and property companies	1913	3,872,562	10.08	3.02
1	IT	Cartiera italiana	Wood and paper products	1913	2,132,663	21.50	5.35

(continued)

Continued

Benchmark	Country	Company	Sector	Year	Assets (US$)	Turnover (US$)	3-year average ROE	3-year average HR
1	IT	Cartiere Pietro Miliani	Wood and paper products	1913	1,852,758		5.84	
1	ES	Catalana de Gas y Electricidad	Utilities; Electricity, gas, and water supply	1913	8,052,244		10.00	
1	FR	Chantiers de la Loire	Transport equipment	1913	14,845,560		8.59	1.48
1	BE	Charbonnages de Bascoup	Mining	1913	2,811,572		38.37	−0.10
1	FR	Chargeurs réunis	Transport and communication	1913	15,863,372		4.42	12.13
1	FR	Chemins de fer de l'Est	Railways	1913	583,011,583		9.63	4.84
1	FR	Cie Générale du Gaz	Utilities; Electricity, gas, and water supply	1913			5.78	−2.12
1	IT	Compagnia italiana dei grandi alberghi	Commercial activities	1913	3,847,468		0.92	6.93
1	IT	Compagnia reale delle ferrovie sarde	Railways	1913	18,150,665		5.25	0.63
1	FR	Compagnie Générale d'Electricité	Electrical engineering	1913	13,407,336		12.46	3.07
1	FR	Compagnie Générale des Eaux	Utilities; Electricity, gas, and water supply	1913	32,186,293		13.12	5.82
1	FR	Compagnie Générale Transatlantique	Transport and communication	1913	36,486,486		4.33	−7.77
1	BE	Compagnie internationale des Wagons-Lits	Railways	1913	35,585,395		7.24	−3.91
1	ES	Compañía Arrendataria de Tabacos	Food, drink, and tobacco products	1913	10,771,993		15.50	4.40
1	ES	Compañía Transatlántica	Transport and communication	1913	6,867,504			

1	FR	Comptoir de l'industrie linière	Textiles and leather goods	1913	6,138,996	6.46	−0.65
1	FR	Comptoir National d'Escompte de Paris	Financial intermediation	1913	359,824,903	7.20	7.67
1	GB	Consolidated Goldfields of South Africa	Mining	1913	30,892,848	6.98	−23.27
1	FR	Crédit Lyonnais	Financial intermediation	1913	532,493,822	8.65	8.05
1	IT	Credito italiano	Financial intermediation	1913	209,593,941	5.97	3.23
1	GB	Cunard Steamship company	Transport and communication	1913	31,894,886	7.87	25.22
1	GB	De Beers Consolidated Mines	Mining	1913	61,086,729	29.23	5.40
1	BE	De Naeyer	Wood and paper products	1913	3,172,394	12.61	−9.12
1	DE	Deutsche Bank	Financial intermediation	1913	534,684,594	12.61	2.87
1	DE	Deutscher Eisenhandel Aktien-Gesellschaft	Commercial activities	1913	8,689,285	9.12	4.77
1	DE	Deutsch–Luxemburgische Bergwerks- und Hütten-Aktien-Gesellschaft	Basic and fabricated metals	1913	66,247,689	8.20	−6.95
1	DE	Deutsch-Ueberseeische Elektricitäts-Gesellschaft	Utilities; Electricity, gas, and water supply	1913	72,537,646	9.91	3.29
1	BE	Dniéprovienne du Midi de la Russie (soc. metall.)	Basic and fabricated metals	1913	34,211,605	6.79	30.96
1	DE	Dresdner Bank	Financial intermediation	1913	366,220,529	9.71	2.94
1	IT	Elettricità Alta Italia	Utilities; Electricity, gas, and water supply	1913	10,471,347	5.84	
1	FR	Energie Electrique du Littoral Méditerranéen	Utilities; Electricity, gas, and water supply	1913	15,333,012	4.46	4.13
1	BE	Fabrique Nationale	Mechanical engineering	1913	3,176,539	28.46	28.09
1	DE	Farbenfabriken vorm. Friedrich Bayer & Co. (Bayer) (Börsenname Elberfelder Farbenfabriken)	Oil, rubber, chemicals, and other non-metallic mineral products	1913	30,362,249	26.72	6.09

(continued)

Continued

Benchmark	Country	Company	Sector	Year	Assets (US$)	Turnover (US$)	3-year average ROE	3-year average HR
1	DE	Farbwerke vorm. Meister Lucius & Brüning (Höchst)	Oil, rubber, chemicals, and other non-metallic mineral products	1913	27,218,717		26.71	9.80
1	ES	Ferrocarriles Andaluces	Railways	1913	28,188,689		10.00	−1.60
1	IT	FIAT Fabbrica italiana automobili Torino	Transport equipment	1913	6,514,103		8.42	−0.59
1	FI	Finlayson & Co. Oy	Textiles and leather goods	1913		2,155,000		
1	FI	Finska Ångfartygs Aktiebolaget	Transport and communication	1913				
1	FR	Fives-Lille	Mechanical engineering	1913	13,050,193		13.34	6.80
1	FI	Förenings-Banken i Finland	Financial intermediation	1913	43,828,111		10.15	
1	DE	Fried. Krupp Aktiengesellschaft (Krupp)	Basic and fabricated metals	1913	142,755,083		16.75	
1	GB	Gas Light and Coke Company	Utilities; Electricity, gas, and water supply	1913	137,148,976		4.64	
1	DE	Gebrüder Stollwerck Aktiengesellschaft	Food, drink, and tobacco products	1913	6,864,981		9.39	3.59
1	DE	Gelsenkirchener Bergwerks-Aktien-Gesellschaft	Mining	1913	94,030,609		8.71	1.16
1	ES	General Azucarera de España	Food, drink, and tobacco products	1913	34,738,779			1.20
1	BE	Germania (Glaces)	Oil, rubber, chemicals, and other non-metallic mineral products	1913	3,091,344		56.93	4.17
1	DE	Gesellschaft für elektrische Hoch- und Untergrundbahnen in Berlin	Railways	1913	40,482,247		6.27	8.57

1	BE	Grands Hotels Belges	Commercial activities	1913	1,968,268	14.11	9.01
1	FR	Grands Moulins de Corbeil	Food, drink, and tobacco products	1913		8.66	0.19
1	FR	Grands Moulins de Paris	Food, drink, and tobacco products	1913	11,476,834		
1	FR	Grands Travaux de Marseille	Construction and property companies	1913	13,317,123	6.83	−3.12
1	GB	Great Western Railway	Railways	1913	537,488,267	3.74	3.47
1	DE	Grosse Berliner Strassenbahn	Railways	1913	51,949,427	9.23	−0.21
1	GB	Guest, Keen & Nettlefolds	Basic and fabricated metals	1913	33,073,429	7.96	11.98
1	FR	Hachette	Wood and paper products	1913			0.66
1	DE	Hamburg-Amerikanische Packetfahrt-Actien-Gesellschaft (Hapag)	Transport and communication	1913	84,510,367	8.83	4.94
1	DE	Hamburg-Südamerikanische Dampfschiffahrts-Gesellschaft	Transport and communication	1913	19,291,169	10.74	11.68
1	DE	Handelsgesellschaft für Grundbesitz	Construction and property companies	1913	8,029,296	1.56	−5.30
1	DE	Hardt-Wülfing, Aktien-Gesellschaft in Berlin	Commercial activities	1913	5,399,768	10.38	
1	DE	Harpener Bergbau AG	Mining	1913	44,271,171	7.29	3.29
1	GB	Harrod's Stores	Commercial activities	1913	19,365,462	11.92	7.00
1	ES	Hilaturas Fabra y Coats	Textiles and leather goods	1913	7,360,862	10.00	
1	SE	Höganäs-Billesholm AB	Oil, rubber, chemicals, and other non-metallic mineral products	1913	7,226,133	7.40	1.57
1	GB	Howard & Bullough	Mechanical engineering	1913	9,437,400	12.65	17.09

(*continued*)

Continued

Benchmark	Country	Company	Sector	Year	Assets (US$)	Turnover (US$)	3-year average ROE	3-year average HR
1	IT	ILVA	Basic and fabricated metals	1913	27,816,919		−0.60	
1	GB	Imperial Tobacco Company [of Great Britain & Ireland]	Food, drink, and tobacco products	1913	110,994,467		13.28	2.17
1	GB	J. & P. Coats	Textiles and leather goods	1913	99,958,476		15.79	−2.97
1	FR	Jeumont	Electrical engineering	1913	12,823,630	5,501,931	6.39	
1	GB	John Brown & Company	Transport equipment	1913	31,407,400		7.59	5.10
1	DE	Kammgarnspinnerei Stöhr & Co. Aktien-Gesellschaft	Textiles and leather goods	1913	7,863,763		8.84	−3.71
1	SE	Kockums Mekaniska verkstadaktiebolag	Transport equipment	1913	2,149,067		−1.76	
1	FI	Kymin Oy	Wood and paper products	1913		4,358,000		
1	IT	Lanificio Rossi	Textiles and leather goods	1913	6,802,831		8.24	0.30
1	DE	Leonhard Tietz Aktien-Gesellschaft	Commercial activities	1913	10,907,417		9.18	0.82
1	GB	Lever Brothers	Oil, rubber, chemicals, and other non-metallic mineral products	1913	68,075,805		7.15	6.24
1	BE	Liniere La Lys	Textiles and leather goods	1913	3,241,343		16.29	6.28
1	GB	Lipton	Commercial activities	1913	19,352,324		5.94	4.16
1	IT	Lloyd italiano	Transport and communication	1913	6,986,018		3.93	21.11
1	GB	Lloyds Bank	Financial intermediation	1913	507,709,524		14.37	4.56
1	GB	London & North Western Railway	Railways	1913	579,833,943		5.53	3.82
1	GB	London City and Midland Bank	Financial intermediation	1913	517,066,667		11.05	4.04

1	GB	London County and Westminster Bank	Financial intermediation	1913	496,419,048		13.09	4.58
1	FR	Longwy	Basic and fabricated metals	1913	18,532,819		24.03	6.28
1	SE	Loussavaara-Kiirunavaara AB (LKAB)	Mining	1913	34,139,201		18.79	
1	SE	Malmö Yllefabriksaktiebolaget	Textiles and leather goods	1913	3,163,200		8.36	
1	DE	Mannesmannröhren-Werke	Mechanical engineering	1913	27,408,805	28,056,444	11.83	5.92
1	FR	Marine et Homécourt	Basic and fabricated metals	1913	23,301,158		12.13	6.05
1	DE	Maschinenbau-Anstalt 'Humboldt'	Mechanical engineering	1913	12,436,038		15.09	−0.19
1	DE	Maschinenfabrik Augsburg-Nürnberg Aktien-Gesellschaft (MAN)	Mechanical engineering	1913	27,978,094		10.54	13.39
1	FR	Messageries Maritimes	Transport and communication	1913	56,370,656		0.30	−10.47
1	GB	Midland Railway	Railways	1913	970,106,400		4.56	4.26
1	BE	Minerva Motors	Transport equipment	1913	2,772,003		32.85	11.85
1	FR	Mines d'Anzin	Mining	1913				−31.39
1	FR	Mines de Lens	Mining	1913	30,003,240			14.14
1	FR	Mines de Vicoigne-Noeuds & Drocourt	Mining	1913				4.56
1	IT	Navigazione generale italiana	Transport and communication	1913	22,813,688		6.22	8.11
1	DE	Neue Boden-Aktiengesellschaft	Construction and property companies	1913	19,367,194		5.30	−10.66
1	GB	Newcastle-upon-Tyne Electric Supply Company	Utilities; Electricity, gas, and water supply	1913	13,347,267		5.68	7.92
1	DE	Norddeutsche Wollkämmerei u. Kammgarnspinnerei ('Nordwolle')	Textiles and leather goods	1913	17,111,855		9.83	2.59
1	DE	Norddeutscher Lloyd	Transport and communication	1913	67,383,779		10.24	9.86

(continued)

Continued

Benchmark	Country	Company	Sector	Year	Assets (US$)	Turnover (US$)	3-year average ROE	3-year average HR
1	FR	Nouvelles Galeries Réunies	Commercial activities	1913	13,745,804		11.10	1.93
1	IT	Officine meccaniche Stigler	Mechanical engineering	1913	1,995,345		8.18	
1	IT	Officine Sesto San Giovanni & Valsecchi Abramo	Mechanical engineering	1913	1,814,596		3.95	−13.57
1	FR	Orléans	Railways	1913	596,236,737		8.97	4.59
1	DE	Ostafrikanische Eisenbahngesellschaft	Railways	1913	28,175,447		1.76	−1.62
1	ES	Papelera Española	Wood and paper products	1913	6,451,526		4.70	9.00
1	GB	Peninsular & Oriental Steam Navigation Company	Transport and communication	1913	40,331,852		6.54	10.11
1	FR	Petit Parisien	Wood and paper products	1913			68.99	12.98
1	FR	Peugeot	Transport equipment	1913	14,551,096		11.87	4.74
1	FI	Ph. U Strengberg & Co Ab	Food, drink, and tobacco products	1913		1,644,000		
1	FR	PLM	Railways	1913	1,242,053,285		5.88	7.01
1	FR	Raffinerie et sucrerie Say	Food, drink, and tobacco products	1913	14,797,297		6.99	44.72
1	FR	Revillon Frères	Textiles and leather goods	1913	10,215,882		7.74	1.42
1	ES	Riegos y Fuerzas del Ebro	Utilities; Electricity, gas, and water supply	1913	21,992,819			
1	ES	Rio Tinto	Mining	1913	53,929,084		37.80	
1	GB	Royal Mail Steam Packet Company	Transport and communication	1913	49,931,476		6.92	19.42

1	ES	S.A. Fomento de Obras y Construcciones	Construction and property companies	1913	1,346,499	7.90	
1	FR	Saint-Gobain	Oil, rubber, chemicals, and other non-metallic mineral products	1913	26,216,216	7.32	−13.23
1	FR	Schneider & Cie	Basic and fabricated metals	1913	21,274,131	13.28	7.09
1	DE	Schultheiss' Brauerei Actien-Gesellschaft	Food, drink, and tobacco products	1913	11,171,256	12.05	6.63
1	GB	Shell Transport and Trading Company	Oil, rubber, chemicals, and other non-metallic mineral products	1913	55,016,738	13.24	15.28
1	DE	Siemens & Halske Aktiengesellschaft	Electrical engineering	1913	45,157,340	20.05	1.89
1	DE	Siemens-Schuckertwerke, Gesellschaft mit beschränkter Haftung zu Berlin	Electrical engineering	1913	77,027,145	14.25	
1	ES	Singer Sewing Machine	Commercial activities	1913	3,203,232		
1	GB	Sir W.G. Armstrong, Whitworth & Co.	Transport equipment	1913	53,241,952	8.20	6.98
1	SE	Skandinaviska Kreditaktiebolaget	Financial intermediation	1913	97,685,864	7.27	3.37
1	SE	Skånska Cement AB	Construction and property companies	1913	4,300,534	9.16	2.17
1	ES	Sociedad Española de Construcciones Metálicas	Mechanical engineering	1913	4,503,232	6.50	
1	ES	Sociedad Metalurgica Duro-Felguera	Basic and fabricated metals	1913	12,145,601	3.90	23.30
1	IT	Società anonima delle miniere di Montecatini	Mining	1913	4,831,000	6.53	11.63
1	IT	Società anonima italiana Gio. Ansaldo & C.	Transport equipment	1913	21,881,804	5.70	

(continued)

Continued

Benchmark	Country	Company	Sector	Year	Assets (US$)	Turnover (US$)	3-year average ROE	3-year average HR
1	IT	Società anonima Riccardo Gualino	Mining	1913	8,705,901		−44.53	
1	IT	Società costruzioni A. Brambilla	Construction and property companies	1913	3,295,154		5.53	
1	IT	Società degli alti forni fonderie ed acciaierie di Terni	Basic and fabricated metals	1913	20,403,229		13.34	4.87
1	IT	Società della ferrovia sicula occidentale Palermo-Marsala-Trapani (A)	Railways	1913	9,278,237		3.09	−0.98
1	IT	Società generale italiana Edison di elettricità	Utilities; Electricity, gas, and water supply	1913	15,435,407		10.68	−1.98
1	IT	Società italiana E. De Angeli per l'industria dei tessuti stampati	Textiles and leather goods	1913	10,369,755		2.70	−22.19
1	IT	Società italiana per il carburo di calcio	Oil, rubber, chemicals, and other non-metallic mineral products	1913	9,401,625		7.68	4.24
1	IT	Società italiana per l'industria dello zucchero indigeno	Food, drink, and tobacco products	1913	9,914,488		13.48	2.33
1	IT	Società italo-americana pel petrolio	Commercial activities	1913	6,973,027			
1	IT	Società ligure-lombarda per la raffinazione degli zuccheri	Food, drink, and tobacco products	1913	11,175,065		8.94	3.09
1	BE	Société des Glaces Nationales Belges	Oil, rubber, chemicals, and other non-metallic mineral products	1913	3,817,985		10.95	5.08
1	FR	Société française de constructions mécaniques	Mechanical engineering	1913	7,412,493		11.17	8.08
1	FR	Société Générale	Financial intermediation	1913	420,187,645		4.57	5.52

1	FR	Société Générale d'Entreprises	Construction and property companies	1913	1,982,025		13.32	
1	GB	Stewarts & Lloyds	Basic and fabricated metals	1913	14,837,829 (assets as of 1912)		10.02	5.67
1	SE	Stockholms Allmänna Telefonaktiebolag	Transport and communication	1913	11,085,600		15.93	7.10
1	SE	Stora Kopparbergs Bergslagaktiebolag	Wood and paper products	1913	20,978,400		8.51	6.60
1	SE	Svenska Metallverken AB	Basic and fabricated metals	1913	5,650,133	5,710,133	6.05	−10.70
1	SE	Svenska Sockererfabriksaktiebolaget	Food, drink, and tobacco products	1913	48,240,531		6.73	2.70
1	SE	Sydsvenska Kraftaktiebolaget	Utilities; Electricity, gas, and water supply	1913	2,968,267		5.09	
1	DE	Tapeten-Industrie-Aktien-Gesellschaft (Tiag) in Berlin	Wood and paper products	1913	2,802,507		0.27	
1	IT	Tecnomasio italiano Brown Boweri	Electrical engineering	1913	2,686,826		5.37	
1	GB	The Bleachers Association	Textiles and leather goods	1913	43,531,052		7.42	17.44
1	GB	The British Thomson-Houston Company	Electrical engineering	1913	10,616,905		5.16	
1	GB	The British Westinghouse Electric & Manufacturing Company	Electrical engineering	1913	14,349,724		4.01	79.17
1	GB	The Fine Cotton Spinners' & Doublers' Association	Textiles and leather goods	1913	54,442,857		7.09	6.80
1	GB	The Metropolitan Carriage Wagon & Finance Company	Mechanical engineering	1913	13,241,829 (assets as of 1912)		13.13	11.61
1	GB	The Metropolitan Electric Supply Company	Utilities; Electricity, gas, and water supply	1913	12,546,843		4.87	11.19

(*continued*)

Continued

Benchmark	Country	Company	Sector	Year	Assets (US$)	Turnover (US$)	3-year average ROE	3-year average HR
1	GB	The Savoy Hotel	Commercial activities	1913	13,184,805		11.62	21.20
1	FR	Thomson-Houston	Electrical engineering	1913	29,834,311		4.53	0.90
1	BE	Transports et Entreprises	Utilities; Electricity, gas, and water supply	1913	12,025,002		11.52	7.77
1	ES	Unián Española de Explosivos	Oil, rubber, chemicals, and other non-metallic mineral products	1913	4,488,330		15.90	−2.10
1	IT	Unione italiana fra consumatori e fabbricanti di concimi e prodotti chimici	Oil, rubber, chemicals, and other non-metallic mineral products	1913	7,575,522		5.24	1.24
1	GB	United Alkali Company	Oil, rubber, chemicals, and other non-metallic mineral products	1913	34,465,352		4.93	−36.45
1	BE	Val-Saint-Lambert a Seraing	Oil, rubber, chemicals, and other non-metallic mineral products	1913	2,292,947		8.33	6.37
1	DE	Verein Deutscher Olfabriken	Food, drink, and tobacco products	1913	7,801,157		10.75	8.83
1	GB	Vickers	Transport equipment	1913	58,720,286		9.30	7.81
1	DE	Vulkan-Werke, Hamburg und Stettin	Transport equipment	1913	29,009,120		4.61	−13.06
1	GB	Wallpaper Manufacturers	Wood and paper products	1913	23,252,552		4.53	5.33
1	GB	Waterlow & Sons	Wood and paper products	1913	9,613,990		8.48	4.40

1	GB	Watney Combe Reid & Company	Food, drink, and tobacco products	1913	57,694,038		2.84	60.72
1	DE	Zellstofffabrik Waldhof	Wood and paper products	1913	26,119,332		11.41	−1.51
2	FI	A.B. Stockmann Oy	Commercial activities	1927	2,138,900		7.58	
2	DE	A.G. für Zellstoff- und Papierfabrikation	Wood and paper products	1927	8,578,196		12.46	1.28
2	FI	Ab Crichton-Vulcan Oy	Transport equipment	1927	1,728,992	6,409,225	4.00	−35.62
2	SE	AB Separator	Mechanical engineering	1927	36,194,421		8.05	20.63
2	FI	Ab Wärtsilä Oy	Basic and fabricated metals	1927	1,841,083		2.07	−15.80
2	DE	Adam Opel AG	Transport equipment	1927	23,561,721		−3.71	
2	IT	AEDES	Construction and property companies	1927	10,722,800		4.33	−14.93
2	FR	Agache Fils	Textiles and leather goods	1927	8,745,396		8.65	
2	FR	Agence Havas	Wood and paper products	1927	7,381,141		21.81	11.27
2	DE	Allgemeine Elektricitäts-Gesellschaft (AEG)	Electrical engineering	1927	110,435,308		7.80	11.54
2	GB	Allied Newspapers	Wood and paper products	1927	44,099,631		8.59	−3.05
2	ES	Almacenes Rodriguez s.a.	Commercial activities	1927	1,963,971			23.15
2	GB	Amalgamated Press	Wood and paper products	1927	51,523,534		11.31	−1.88
2	GB	Anglo-Persian Oil	Oil, rubber, and other non-metallic mineral products	1927	218,895,489		14.38	−0.62
2	IT	Ansaldo	Mechanical engineering	1927	34,777,125		−3.24	9.21
2	GB	Armstrong Whitworth Securities	Transport equipment	1927	117,852,489		−2.26	20.00

(continued)

Continued

Benchmark	Country	Company	Sector	Year	Assets (US$)	Turnover (US$)	3-year average ROE	3-year average HR
2	ES	Arrendataria de Tabacos Cia.	Food, drink, and tobacco products	1927	78,100,134		9.70	12.07
2	ES	Arrendataria del Monopolio de Petroleos, S.A., Cia., 'Campsa'	Oil, rubber, and other non-metallic mineral products	1927	103,411,276		7.68	−2.55
2	SE	ASEA	Electrical engineering	1927	28,053,634		5.52	27.77
2	GB	Associated Electrical Industries	Electrical engineering	1927	28,647,686		4.43	9.81
2	GB	Associated Newspapers	Wood and paper products	1927	27,129,052		26.35	−6.44
2	GB	Associated Portland Cement	Construction and property companies	1927	65,548,838		3.85	17.24
2	BE	Assurances Générales	Financial intermediation	1927	44,852,282		37.13	34.23
2	BE	Ateliers Constructions de Charleroi	Electrical engineering	1927	38,148,753		9.34	27.42
2	FR	Au Bon Marché	Commercial activities	1927	16,781,985		15.17	−3.10
2	GB	Babcock & Wilcox	Mechanical engineering	1927	36,465,795		12.10	9.76
2	IT	Banca Commerciale Italiana	Financial intermediation	1927	809,513,404		8.28	20.37
2	ES	Banco de Bilbao	Financial intermediation	1927	675,672,071		12.80	11.18
2	ES	Banco de Espana	Financial intermediation	1927	2,020,989,761		38.16	1.55
2	ES	Banco Hispano Americano	Financial intermediation	1927	573,027,691		12.22	16.82
2	FR	Banque de Paris et des Pays-Bas	Financial intermediation	1927	85,113,579		11.36	51.38
2	BE	Banque Nationale	Financial intermediation	1927	1,581,172,072		24.22	−18.42
2	GB	Barclays Bank	Financial intermediation	1927	1,737,055,702		7.95	2.88
2	SE	Bergslagarnes Järnvagsaktiebolag	Railways	1927	24,238,402		6.51	19.20

2	GB	British American Tobacco	Food, drink, and tobacco products	1927	190,461,089	19.39	10.70
2	GB	British Thomson-Houston	Electrical engineering	1927	39,131,877	3.70	
2	ES	Caminos Hierro del Norte de Espana Cia. De Los	Railways	1927	435,977,611		9.70
2	GB	Cammell Laird	Mechanical engineering	1927	37,020,049	-1.24	-20.48
2	IT	Cantiere Navale Triestino	Transport equipment	1927	12,962,688	4.90	1.42
2	IT	Cartiere Burgo	Wood and paper products	1927	7,544,828	7.37	
2	FR	Chargeurs réunis	Transport and communication	1927	25,116,714	6.55	-7.81
2	FR	Cie du Nord	Railways	1927	416,774,435	3.97	24.53
2	BE	Cimenteries Briquet. Bonne Esper. Raevels et Loen	Construction and property companies	1927	44,649,818	8.07	5.61
2	FR	Citroën	Transport equipment	1927	40,236,538	3.16	63.55
2	GB	City of London Real Property	Construction and property companies	1927	59,640,000	4.95	-0.73
2	BE	Cockerill	Basic and fabricated metals	1927	62,292,767	18.34	45.21
2	IT	Compagnia Italiana dei Cavi Telegrafici Sottomarini–Italcable (Soc. an. 'Compagnia italiana Italcable')	Electrical engineering	1927	12,015,352	7.49	2.35
2	BE	Compagnie Belge pour les Industries Chimiques	Chemicals and pharmaceuticals	1927	9,793,688	8.82	27.82
2	FR	Compagnie Française des Pétroles	Oil, rubber, and other non-metallic mineral products	1927	2,955,765	-0.32	
2	FR	Compagnie Générale d'Electricité	Electrical engineering	1927	32,751,056	12.72	33.36

(*continued*)

Continued

Benchmark	Country	Company	Sector	Year	Assets (US$)	Turnover (US$)	3-year average ROE	3-year average HR
2	FR	Compagnie Générale Transatlantique	Transport and communication	1927	41,107,774		4.48	96.48
2	BE	Compagnie Maritime du Congo Belge	Transport and communication	1927	23,013,452		8.28	16.40
2	FR	Comptoir National d'Escompte de Paris	Financial intermediation	1927	306,447,096		11.05	32.21
2	GB	County of London Electric Supply	Utilities; Electricity, gas, and water supply	1927	65,773,281		8.60	29.35
2	GB	Courtaulds	Textiles and leather goods	1927	223,347,948		11.30	−4.57
2	FR	Credit Lyonnais	Financial intermediation	1927	382,659,929		9.30	11.71
2	IT	Credito Italiano	Financial intermediation	1927	550,619,376		8.70	14.81
2	GB	Cunard Steam Ship	Transport and communication	1927	100,755,610		6.96	18.02
2	DE	Daimler-Benz AG	Transport equipment	1927	25,819,230		1.56	−21.73
2	DE	Darmstädter und Nationalbank	Financial intermediation	1927	438,652,999	40,380,047,506	13.05	0.97
2	GB	De Beers Consolidated Mines	Mining	1927	76,902,708		15.86	−10.36
2	BE	De Naeyer	Wood and paper products	1927	11,675,404		50.07	44.93
2	GB	Debenhams	Commercial activities	1927	39,325,459		11.18	2.68
2	DE	Demag AG	Mechanical engineering	1927	15,848,532		6.30	
2	DE	Deutsch-Amerikanische-Petroleum Gesellschaft	Oil, rubber, and other non-metallic mineral products	1927	22,741,904		11.30	
2	DE	Deutsche Bank und Disconto-Gesellschaft	Financial intermediation	1927	591,187,277	49,356,294,537	11.56	−3.45

2	DE	Deutsche Continental-Gas-Gesellschaft	Utilities; Electricity, gas, and water supply	1927	34,232,042		8.53	0.50
2	DE	Deutsche Erdöl-AG	Oil, rubber, and other non-metallic mineral products	1927	33,443,065		7.37	−12.92
2	DE	Deutsche Jurgens-Werke AG	Food, drink, and tobacco products	1927	13,889,085		8.52	30.15
2	DE	Deutsch-Russische Handels-Aktiengesellschaft	Commercial activities	1927	13,260,613		22.36	
2	IT	Distillerie Italiane	Food, drink, and tobacco products	1927	11,799,941		6.40	32.93
2	GB	Distillers Company	Food, drink, and tobacco products	1927	97,947,798		15.14	15.91
2	FR	Dollfuss Mieg & Cie	Textiles and leather goods	1927	12,174,776		16.12	39.59
2	GB	Dorman Long	Basic and fabricated metals	1927	75,342,732		1.09	−11.82
2	DE	Dresdner Bank	Financial intermediation	1927	464,636,636	43,942,992,874	9.61	−0.58
2	GB	Dunlop	Oil, rubber, and other non-metallic mineral products	1927	118,493,364		11.26	−14.52
2	FR	Energie Electrique du Littoral Méditerraneen	Utilities; Electricity, gas, and water supply	1927	29,082,738		9.82	53.41
2	FI	Enso-Gutzeit Oy	Wood and paper products	1927	17,167,330	11,139,521	8.11	−18.90
2	ES	Espanola de Construccion Naval Sociedad	Transport equipment	1927	82,181,930		9.20	22.96
2	ES	Espanola de Construcciones Electromecanicas Sociedad	Electrical engineering	1927	11,185,339		4.03	

(*continued*)

Continued

Benchmark	Country	Company	Sector	Year	Assets (US$)	Turnover (US$)	3-year average ROE	3-year average HR
2	IT	FIAT	Transport equipment	1927	66,968,894		10.37	9.67
2	BE	Fabrique Nationale d'Armes de Guerre	Mechanical engineering	1927	32,922,668		7.07	72.93
2	DE	Feldmühle, Papier- und Zellstoffwerke AG	Wood and paper products	1927	6,754,752		13.21	17.74
2	IT	Ferrovie Nord Milano	Railways	1927	8,211,333		7.29	
2	GB	Fine Cotton Spinners' & Doublers' Association	Textiles and leather goods	1927	75,793,802		6.19	−9.40
2	FI	Finlayson & Co Oy	Textiles and leather goods	1927	4,692,695		9.20	10.50
2	FI	Finska Ångfartygs Ab	Transport and communication	1927	4,059,511		3.58	−21.85
2	FI	Finska Färg och Fernissfabriks A.B.	Chemicals and pharmaceuticals	1927	332,620		10.25	
2	FR	Fives-Lille	Mechanical engineering	1927	17,481,240		11.19	20.26
2	ES	Fomento de Obras y Construcciones s.a.	Construction and property companies	1927	9,516,498		36.09	
2	DE	Fried. Krupp AG	Basic and fabricated metals	1927	102,438,014		5.55	
2	FR	Galeries Lafayette	Commercial activities	1927	31,284,733		14.05	−4.19
2	SE	Gamlestadens fabrikers AB	Textiles and leather goods	1927	7,296,594	1,609,010	7.92	
2	GB	Gas Light and Coke Co.	Utilities; Electricity, gas, and water supply	1927	154,227,676		5.15	11.79
2	ES	General Azucarera de Espana Sociedad	Food, drink, and tobacco products	1927	51,474,627		3.79	23.86
2	GB	General Electric Company	Electrical engineering	1927	61,818,051		9.09	12.82

2	DE	Gesellschaft für elektrische Hoch- und Untergrundbahnen in Berlin	Railways	1927	80,360,010		4.87	−4.21
2	BE	Glaces Nationales Belges (Glaces de Saint Roch Auvelais)	Oil, rubber, and other non-metallic mineral products	1927	13,070,218		61.38	23.10
2	SE	Götaverken	Transport equipment	1927	10,024,135	6,623,223	9.68	15.57
2	BE	Grands Hotels Belges	Commercial activities	1927	4,976,688		36.08	4.16
2	FR	Grands Moulins de Paris	Food, drink, and tobacco products	1927	11,358,030		7.19	13.28
2	FR	Grands Travaux de Marseille	Construction and property companies	1927	3,032,400		8.16	29.11
2	GB	Great Western Railway	Railways	1927	839,652,090		5.00	4.84
2	GB	Guest, Keen & Nettlefolds	Basic and fabricated metals	1927	92,547,628		6.18	3.70
2	GB	Guinness (Arthur) Son and Company	Food, drink, and tobacco products	1927	83,062,363		18.28	−9.57
2	FR	Hachette	Wood and paper products	1927	8,000,086		19.39	27.85
2	DE	Hamburg-Amerikanische Packetfahrt-Actien-Gesellschaft	Transport and communication	1927	72,698,895		7.27	−12.73
2	DE	Hamburger Hochbahn-Aktiengesellschaft	Railways	1927	37,466,126		5.18	−2.72
2	DE	Hamburgische Electricitats-Werke	Utilities; Electricity, gas, and water supply	1927	36,160,576		14.92	0.83
2	DE	Hamburg-Südamerikanische Dampfschifffahrts-Gesellschaft	Transport and communication	1927	18,658,418		6.06	1.00
2	GB	Harland and Wolff	Transport equipment	1927	104,642,158		1.39	−8.36
2	DE	Harpener Bergbau-Aktien-Gesellschaft	Mining	1927	39,215,621		3.86	−7.38

(*continued*)

Continued

Benchmark	Country	Company	Sector	Year	Assets (US$)	Turnover (US$)	3-year average ROE	3-year average HR
2	DE	Henschel & Sohn AG	Transport equipment	1927	25,682,385		−4.13	
2	ES	Hidroelectrica Espanola Sociedad	Utilities; Electricity, gas, and water supply	1927	30,294,160		11.32	12.61
2	ES	Hilaturas de Fabras y Coats Cia. anonima de	Textiles and leather goods	1927	16,030,324		6.32	
2	ES	Hispano-Americana de Electricidad, Cia., 'CHADE'	Utilities; Electricity, gas, and water supply	1927	130,719,246		10.13	18.92
2	SE	Höganäs-Billesholm AB	Oil, rubber, and other non-metallic mineral products	1927	14,962,456		4.34	22.80
2	GB	Home and Colonial Stores	Commercial activities	1927	21,072,440		9.95	16.40
2	FR	Huiles de Petrole/BP	Oil, rubber, and other non-metallic mineral products	1927	21,053,909		3.45	
2	DE	IG Farbenindustrie AG	Chemicals and pharmaceuticals	1927	431,727,669		10.41	−13.79
2	DE	Ilse Bergbau-Actiengesellschaft	Mining	1927	27,878,650		10.05	−3.69
2	IT	ILVA	Basic and fabricated metals	1927	49,984,680		3.05	21.37
2	GB	Imperial Chemical Industries	Chemicals and pharmaceuticals	1927	339,678,133		7.26	16.83
2	GB	Imperial Tobacco Company (of Great Britan and Ireland)	Food, drink, and tobacco products	1927	377,457,141		17.12	3.58
2	DE	Industriebau-Held & Francke Aktien-Gesellschaft	Construction and property companies	1927	4,092,168		−12.01	4.27

2	IT	Istituto di Fondi Rustici	Construction and property companies	1927	13,226,407		4.93	1.81
2	GB	J. & P. Coats	Textiles and leather goods	1927	151,878,843		13.03	9.06
2	DE	J.P. Bemberg AG	Textiles and leather goods	1927	13,775,738		10.52	10.47
2	FR	Jeumont	Electrical engineering	1927	14,032,755		8.50	52.51
2	GB	John Barker	Commercial activities	1927	24,452,567		11.79	7.19
2	DE	Kali-Industrie-AG	Chemicals and pharmaceuticals	1927	68,232,586		11.17	33.53
2	FI	Kansallis-Osake-Pankki	Financial intermediation	1927	73,922,981		10.30	11.53
2	FI	Kone-ja Siltarakennus Oy	Mechanical engineering	1927	2,735,945		5.85	−0.27
2	SE	Kooperativa förbundet	Commercial activities	1927	19,732,636	32,112,363	12.61	
2	DE	Leonhard Tietz AG	Commercial activities	1927	22,360,260		10.23	24.12
2	GB	Lever Brothers	Chemicals and pharmaceuticals	1927	343,491,303		9.42	14.74
2	IT	Linificio e Canapificio Nazionale	Textiles and leather goods	1927	13,825,477		5.98	−5.83
2	IT	Lloyd Triestino	Transport and communication	1927	22,783,414		−0.06	−11.02
2	GB	Lloyds Bank	Financial intermediation	1927	2,081,871,230		8.52	14.60
2	GB	London and North Eastern Railway	Railways	1927	1,667,329,509		2.97	3.02
2	GB	London Midland and Scottish Railway	Railways	1927	2,166,922,397		3.78	0.70
2	FR	Longwy	Basic and fabricated metals	1927	23,197,945		11.74	44.05
2	SE	Loussavaara-Kiirunavaara Ltd (LKAB)	Mining	1927	44,672,566		12.55	
2	DE	Lübeck-Buchener Eisenbahn-Gesellschaft	Railways	1927	17,291,006		4.19	−11.46
2	DE	M.A.N.-Maschinenfabrik Augsburg-Nürnberg	Mechanical engineering	1927	20,919,954		11.56	−14.04
2	IT	Manifatture Cotoniere Meridionali (bilancio 1926)	Textiles and leather goods	1927	11,574,740		2.58	−9.66

(*continued*)

Continued

Benchmark	Country	Company	Sector	Year	Assets (US$)	Turnover (US$)	3-year average ROE	3-year average HR
2	DE	Mannesmannröhren-Werke	Basic and fabricated metals	1927	53,311,444		19.08	−19.48
2	DE	Mansfeld Akt.-Ges. fur Bergbau und Huttenbetrieb	Mining	1927	25,843,179		4.48	−7.86
2	BE	Manufacture Liégoise de caoutchouc souple, durci et Gutta-Percha O. Englebert fils et Cie	Transport equipment	1927	21,646,740		16.42	204.44
2	FR	Messageries Maritimes	Transport and communication	1927	17,443,030		4.84	26.05
2	FR	Michelin	Oil, rubber, and other non-metallic mineral products	1927	39,242,423		26.41	
2	GB	Midland Bank	Financial intermediation	1927	1,951,650,350		9.05	11.25
2	ES	Minera y Metalurgica Penarroya Sociedad	Basic and fabricated metals	1927	25,456,357			
2	FR	Mines d'Anzin	Mining	1927	28,328,889		12.16	43.23
2	FR	Mines de Lens	Mining	1927	49,773,587		5.06	55.13
2	FR	Mines de Vicoigne-Noeuds & Drocourt	Mining	1927	39,662,676		5.77	45.34
2	BE	Minoteries et elevateurs a grains	Food, drink, and tobacco products	1927	17,789,135		36.68	20.43
2	IT	Monte Amiata	Mining	1927	4,084,087		24.39	5.27
2	IT	Montecatini	Chemicals and pharmaceuticals	1927	69,894,707		10.37	19.54
2	IT	Navigazione Generale Italiana	Transport and communication	1927	50,143,148		5.09	19.03

2	GB	Newcastle-upon-Tyne Electric	Utilities; Electricity, gas, and water supply	1927	57,208,644	5.17	4.65
2	FR	Nord Est	Basic and fabricated metals	1927	33,549,523	7.27	98.23
2	DE	Norddeutsche Wollkämmerei und Kammgarnspinnerei	Textiles and leather goods	1927	41,123,404	7.65	−7.41
2	DE	Norddeutscher Lloyd	Transport and communication	1927	82,260,001	7.51	−12.05
2	IT	Officine Elettriche Genovesi	Electrical engineering	1927	7,940,987	7.29	75.89
2	FR	Orléans	Railways	1927	423,143,799	9.40	21.71
2	DE	Ostwerke AG	Food, drink, and tobacco products	1927	21,698,132	10.45	−24.45
2	BE	Ougree-Marihaye	Basic and fabricated metals	1927	169,080,523	10.85	34.42
2	FI	Oy Tampereen Rakennuskonttori A.B.	Construction and property companies	1927	388,661	5.68	
2	FI	Paraisten Kalkki Oy	Mining	1927	3,921,914	10.05	26.77
2	GB	Peninsular & Oriental	Transport and communication	1927	134,532,961	4.19	6.98
2	FR	Petit Parisien	Wood and paper products	1927			50.91
2	FR	Peugeot	Transport equipment	1927	28,207,182	12.88	27.79
2	DE	Philipp Holzmann Aktiengesellschaft	Construction and property companies	1927	9,414,780	7.53	−15.43
2	GB	Platt Brothers	Mechanical engineering	1927	29,032,572	1.30	−36.32
2	FR	PLM	Railways	1927	730,249,608		17.49
2	GB	Powell Duffryn Steam Coal Company	Mining	1927	31,896,441	0.07	−24.63

(*continued*)

Appendix

Continued

Benchmark	Country	Company	Sector	Year	Assets (US$)	Turnover (US$)	3-year average ROE	3-year average HR
2	FR	Produits chimiques et électrométallurgiques d'Alais	Chemicals and pharmaceuticals	1927	30,373,146		15.64	40.56
2	FR	Raffinerie et sucrerie Say	Food, drink, and tobacco products	1927			30.24	3.42
2	GB	Reckitt	Chemicals and pharmaceuticals	1927	43,042,465 (assets as of 1928)		17.18	0.99
2	DE	Rheinisch-Westfälisches Elektrizitätswerk Aktien-Gesellschaft	Utilities; Electricity, gas, and water supply	1927	119,850,228		8.55	9.94
2	DE	Rhenania-Ossag Mineralölwerke AG	Oil, rubber, and other non-metallic mineral products	1927	42,993,610		1.53	
2	FR	Rhône Poulenc	Chemicals and pharmaceuticals	1927	39,281,684		25.22	28.40
2	ES	Rio Tinto Company	Mining	1927	31,243,652			
2	IT	Romsa	Oil, rubber, and other non-metallic mineral products	1927	3,216,556		6.34	
2	GB	Royal Mail Steam Packet	Transport and communication	1927	94,225,027		2.10	−17.71
2	ES	Royale Asturienne des Mines	Mining	1927	35,073,071		5.64	
2	DE	Rudolph Karstadt AG	Commercial activities	1927	43,825,116		14.12	5.69
2	DE	Rütgerswerke-Aktiengesellschaft	Chemicals and pharmaceuticals	1927	25,090,194		5.03	−15.15

2	FR	Saint Frères	Textiles and leather goods	1927	23,811,429	9.49	35.82
2	FR	Saint Nazaire Penhoët	Transport equipment	1927	15,254,421	1.69	18.20
2	FR	Saint-Gobain	Chemicals and pharmaceuticals	1927	46,185,297	9.53	21.30
2	FR	Schneider & Cie	Basic and fabricated metals	1927	22,782,304	7.53	41.58
2	DE	Schultheiss-Patzenhofer Brauerei AG	Food, drink, and tobacco products	1927	22,014,326	18.37	−15.54
2	GB	Selfridge	Commercial activities	1927	25,236,568	10.02	1.72
2	GB	Shell Transport and Trading Company	Oil, rubber, and other non-metallic mineral products	1927	180,264,910	16.67	6.76
2	DE	Siemens & Halske AG	Electrical engineering	1927	82,831,347	19.98	21.14
2	DE	Siemens-Schuckertwerke AG	Electrical engineering	1927	84,989,846	12.82	48.02
2	DE	Singer Nähmaschinen Aktienges.	Mechanical engineering	1927	19,225,835	5.82	13.99
2	IT	SIP	Utilities; Electricity, gas, and water supply	1927	90,079,238	8.45	13.99
2	SE	Skånska Cement AB	Construction and property companies	1927	7,200,858	12.07	13.70
2	IT	Snia-Viscosa	Chemicals and pharmaceuticals	1927	91,513,874	4.97	−12.08
2	ES	Sociedad Espanola de Construcciones Metalicas	Mechanical engineering	1927	5,123,473		
2	IT	Societa Anonima Stefano Pittaluga	Wood and paper products	1927	9,947,455	5.98	−35.00
2	IT	Societa Generale Italiana Edison di Elettricita	Utilities; Electricity, gas, and water supply	1927	96,942,196	8.08	26.46
2	IT	Societa Italiana Commercio Materie Tessili	Commercial activities	1927	26,832,901	−131.08	

(continued)

Continued

Benchmark	Country	Company	Sector	Year	Assets (US$)	Turnover (US$)	3-year average ROE	3-year average HR
2	IT	Societa Italiana Ernesto Breda per Costruzioni Meccaniche	Mechanical engineering	1927	18,774,743		5.06	5.66
2	IT	Societa Italiana Pirelli	Oil, rubber, and other non-metallic mineral products	1927	23,039,546		10.57	14.45
2	IT	Societa Italo-Americana pel Petrolio	Commercial activities	1927	30,359,352		2.20	
2	IT	Societa Mineraria e Metallurgia di Pertusola	Mining	1927	5,463,999		−11.92	
2	FR	Société alsacienne de constructions mécaniques	Mechanical engineering	1927	20,407,364		15.90	160.49
2	BE	Société Financière des Caoutchoucs (Socfin)	Oil, rubber, and other non-metallic mineral products	1927	47,284,126		11.87	−15.13
2	FR	Société Générale	Financial intermediation	1927	424,505,141		7.75	29.84
2	FR	Société Générale d'Entreprises	Construction and property companies	1927	3,983,451		3.43	61.69
2	FR	Société Lyonnaise des Eaux et de l'Eclairage	Utilities; Electricity, gas, and water supply	1927	38,169,152		9.08	51.14
2	BE	Société Nationale de Chemins de fer Belges	Railways	1927	1,792,527,381		3.91	12.09
2	BE	Soie Artificielle de Tubize	Textiles and leather goods	1927	24,002,866		16.34	54.41
2	SE	Stockholms Rediaktibolag Svea	Transport and communication	1927	15,542,505	7,546,795	8.38	14.80
2	SE	Stora Kopparbergs Bergslags AB	Basic and fabricated metals	1927	41,780,103	14,655,672	3.84	16.03

2	FI	Suomen Gummitehdas Oy	Oil, rubber, and other non-metallic mineral products	1927	2,374,736		9.78	
2	FI	Suomen Sähkö Oy Gottfr. Stromberg	Electrical engineering	1927	816,625		5.60	−4.87
2	FI	Suomen Sokeri Oy	Food, drink, and tobacco products	1927	7,618,183		6.21	17.40
2	SE	Svenska Handelsbanken	Financial intermediation	1927	330,625,363		10.97	22.77
2	SE	Svenska Sockerfabriks AB (Swedish Sugar Ltd)	Food, drink, and tobacco products	1927	52,198,979	26,525,074	3.75	1.67
2	SE	Svenska Tändsticksaktiebolaget	Chemicals and pharmaceuticals	1927	156,402,252		10.12	10.40
2	FI	Sydfinska Kraftaktiebolaget	Utilities; Electricity, gas, and water supply	1927	452,238		11.79	3.25
2	SE	Sydsvenska Kraftaktiebolaget	Utilities; Electricity, gas, and water supply	1927	18,569,590	2,057,388	19.83	11.60
2	ES	Telefonica Nacional de Espana Cia. 'CTNE'	Transport and communication	1927	83,923,539		7.51	16.72
2	DE	Tempelhofer Feld Aktien-Gesellschaft fur Grundstucksverwertung	Construction and property companies	1927	3,490,344		4.33	−3.87
2	IT	Terni	Basic and fabricated metals	1927	75,812,175		4.48	9.29
2	FR	Thomson-Houston	Electrical engineering	1927	30,347,571		4.88	49.95
2	BE	Transports et Entreprises Industrielles (Sofina)	Utilities; Electricity, gas, and water supply	1927	112,926,549		29.91	77.71
2	IT	U.N.I.C.A. (D)	Food, drink, and tobacco products	1927	10,493,289		5.46	
2	SE	Uddeholm AB	Wood and paper products	1927	31,877,984	10,698,579	6.22	11.20

(continued)

Continued

Benchmark	Country	Company	Sector	Year	Assets (US$)	Turnover (US$)	3-year average ROE	3-year average HR
2	FR	Union d'Electricité	Utilities; Electricity, gas, and water supply	1927	28,257,889		6.35	57.90
2	ES	Union Espanola de Explosivos S.A.	Chemicals and pharmaceuticals	1927	24,580,082		16.40	59.07
2	BE	Union Miniere	Mining	1927	187,127,597		25.09	7.93
2	ES	Union Resinera Española, S.A., LA	Wood and paper products	1927	14,615,907		7.87	
2	IT	Unione Italiana Tramways Elettrici	Railways	1927	3,587,657		10.76	
2	GB	United Steel	Basic and fabricated metals	1927	77,214,390		-2.03	-30.37
2	DE	Vereinigte Glanzstoff-Fabriken AG	Textiles and leather goods	1927	39,642,432		-6.35	-2.42
2	DE	Vereinigte Stahlwerke AG	Basic and fabricated metals	1927	492,393,367		6.59	-6.17
2	GB	Vickers	Transport equipment	1927	117,045,007		5.95	2.36
2	GB	Watney Combe Reid & Company	Food, drink, and tobacco products	1927	76,778,255		20.29	12.79
2	DE	Zellstofffabrik Waldhof	Wood and paper products	1927	23,764,605		9.94	-2.55
3	SE	AB Svenska Handelsbanken	Financial intermediation	1954	815,171,624		5.79	4.50
3	DE	Adam Opel AG	Transport equipment	1954	106,004,768		61.39	
3	FR	Agence Havas	Wood and paper products	1954	11,658,549		23.35	78.24
3	IT	AGIP (Gruppo ENI)	Mining	1954	94,852,800		6.38	

3	DE	Allgemeine Elektricitäts-Gesellschaft (AEG)	Electrical engineering	1954	182,073,895	175,446,961	4.93	25.80
3	FR	Alsacienne de constructions mécaniques	Mechanical engineering	1954	72,569,474		5.06	26.77
3	FR	Alsthom	Electrical engineering	1954	141,268,715		−0.73	10.30
3	ES	Altos Hornos de Vizcaya	Basic and fabricated metals	1954	225,508,233		8.28	41.19
3	GB	Amalgamated Press	Wood and paper products	1954	80,664,969		11.71	−3.93
3	SE	Ångfartyg Tirfing AB	Transport and communication	1954	65,182,102	2,150,203	20.04	
3	IT	Anic (Gruppo ENI)	Chemicals and pharmaceuticals	1954	23,961,600		5.74	31.65
3	IT	Ansaldo (Gruppo IRI)	Mechanical engineering	1954	129,188,800		−10.56	−20.31
3	IT	Arnoldo Mondadori Editore	Wood and paper products	1954	7,611,200		13.79	
3	GB	Arthur Guinness & Son Ltd	Food, drink, and tobacco products	1954	93,062,542		10.99	19.76
3	DE	Aschaffenburger Zellstoffwerke AG	Wood and paper products	1954	34,033,374	39,673,419	1.44	20.12
3	SE	ASEA	Electrical engineering	1954	201,814,414	202,010,439	10.53	14.87
3	GB	Associated Electrical Industries	Electrical engineering	1954	251,387,390		9.06	24.35
3	FR	Astra	Food, drink, and tobacco products	1954	33,654,504		7.58	13.65
3	BE	Asturienne des Mines	Mining	1954	49,173,355		15.61	26.11
3	BE	Ateliers de Constructions et Electricité de Charleroi (ACEC)	Electrical engineering	1954	104,814,122		6.80	−2.88
3	FR	Au Bon Marché	Commercial activities	1954	23,760,209		1.99	31.95
3	FR	Au Printemps	Commercial activities	1954	29,354,356		6.77	26.72

(continued)

Continued

Benchmark	Country	Company	Sector	Year	Assets (US$)	Turnover (US$)	3-year average ROE	3-year average HR
3	GB	Babcock & Wilcox	Mechanical engineering	1954	113,699,118		7.68	22.35
3	DE	Badische Anilin & Sodafabrik AG (BASF)	Chemicals and pharmaceuticals	1954	236,164,487	250,059,595	6.22	29.80
3	IT	Banca Commerciale Italiana (Gruppo IRI)	Financial intermediation	1954	904,980,800		14.94	
3	ES	Banco de Espana	Financial intermediation	1954	6,640,229,177	74,920,624	153.77	15.76
3	ES	Banco Hispano Americano	Financial intermediation	1954	2,187,883,293	96,700,080	17.97	30.95
3	FR	Banque de Paris et des Pays-Bas	Financial intermediation	1954	337,762,788		11.29	50.65
3	BE	Banque Nationale de Belgique	Financial intermediation	1954	2,234,924,552		60.18	18.87
3	GB	Barclays Bank	Financial intermediation	1954	6,141,343,958		8.44	6.59
3	DE	Bayerische Hypotheken- und Wechsel-Bank	Financial intermediation	1954	501,308,699		6.35	40.26
3	DE	Bayernwerk AG. Bayerische Elektrizitätsversorgung	Utilities; Electricity, gas, and water supply	1954	169,811,677		3.74	
3	DE	Bergwerksgesellschaft Hibernia A.G.	Mining	1954	263,895,123	162,097,735	2.43	
3	DE	Beton- und Monierbau AG	Construction and property companies	1954	7,420,739	23,837,902	7.62	34.53
3	IT	BNL (controllo pubblico)	Financial intermediation	1954	1,033,793,600		7.69	
3	SE	Bofors AB	Mechanical engineering	1954	84,635,993	53,740,576	7.34	18.90
3	GB	Bowater Paper Corporation & Subsidiaries	Wood and paper products	1954	283,831,267		8.60	26.02
3	GB	British American Tobacco	Food, drink, and tobacco products	1954	819,867,087		11.48	11.39

3	GB	British Celanese	Textiles and leather goods	1954	91,438,761		5.06	15.78
3	GB	British Oxygen	Chemicals and pharmaceuticals	1954	105,423,803		7.57	−6.79
3	BE	Brufina	Financial intermediation	1954	21,946,574		17.20	20.61
3	IT	Cantieri Riuniti Adriatico (Gruppo IRI)	Transport equipment	1954	106,667,200		−14.74	−5.17
3	FR	Celtex	Textiles and leather goods	1954	42,020,091		6.27	36.41
3	FR	Chargeurs réunis	Transport and communication	1954	41,987,843		3.12	23.85
3	DE	Chemische Werke Hüls AG	Textiles and leather goods	1954	96,231,228	92,038,142	4.95	
3	DE	Christian Dierig AG	Textiles and leather goods	1954	23,036,949	17,163,290	3.33	
3	BE	Ciments d'Obourg	Construction and property companies	1954	14,550,547		21.89	27.80
3	FR	Citroën	Transport equipment	1954	130,973,270		2.81	48.73
3	BE	Compagnie Felge de Chemins de fer et d'Entreprises	Transport equipment	1954	7,388,426		12.05	12.42
3	FR	Compagnie Française des Pétroles	Oil, rubber, and other non-metallic mineral products	1954	247,701,554		9.51	57.76
3	FR	Compagnie Générale d'Electricité	Electrical engineering	1954	106,301,480		5.02	14.13
3	FR	Compagnie Générale des Eaux	Utilities; Electricity, gas, and water supply	1954	28,325,276		6.08	−4.43
3	FR	Comptoir National d'Escompte de Paris	Financial intermediation	1954	763,365,210		14.49	31.25
3	IT	Cornigliano (Gruppo IRI)	Basic and fabricated metals	1954	196,953,600		3.36	
3	GB	Courtaulds	Textiles and leather goods	1954	388,734,374		9.07	5.38
3	FR	Crédit Lyonnais	Financial intermediation	1954	1,407,395,387		13.57	10.74
3	FR	Creusot	Basic and fabricated metals	1954	180,653,850		1.70	36.45

(*continued*)

Continued

Benchmark	Country	Company	Sector	Year	Assets (US$)	Turnover (US$)	3-year average ROE	3-year average HR
3	GB	Cunard Steamship Company	Transport and communication	1954	214,392,643		4.25	5.23
3	DE	Daimler-Benz AG	Transport equipment	1954	92,646,006	251,370,679	7.50	47.17
3	GB	De Beers Consolidated Mines	Mining	1954	354,852,174		20.08	0.64
3	DE	Demag AG	Mechanical engineering	1954	80,000,001		5.49	25.30
3	DE	Deutsche Babcock & Wilcox-Dampfkessel-Werke AG	Mechanical engineering	1954	40,648,392		5.13	30.40
3	DE	Deutsche Bank AG West (Rheinisch-Westfälische Bank)	Financial intermediation	1954	637,625,766	22,693,682,956	4.69	70.40
3	DE	Deutsche Dampfschifffahrts-Gesellschaft 'Hansa'	Transport and communication	1954	43,146,603		−22.11	35.48
3	DE	Deutsche Shell AG	Oil, rubber, and other non-metallic mineral products	1954	108,572,108	223,122,765	4.10	
3	GB	Distillers Company	Food, drink, and tobacco products	1954	333,019,663 (assets as of 1955)		9.08	20.90
3	DE	Dortmund-Hörder Huttenunion AG	Basic and fabricated metals	1954	183,604,284	159,952,324	−1.00	2.14
3	ES	Dragados y Construcciones s.a.	Construction and property companies	1954	35,710,631	3,939,928	12.31	
3	ES	E.N. Bazan de Construcciones Navales Militares	Transport equipment	1954	422,072,742	81,416,532	10.37	
3	ES	E.N. Calvo Sotelo (Encaso)	Oil, rubber, and other non-metallic mineral products	1954	344,660,831		2.83	

3	IT	Edison	Utilities; Electricity, gas, and water supply	1954	569,777,600		4.63	29.80
3	DE	Emil Koster KG a. A.	Commercial activities	1954	25,306,318	51,966,627	4.90	
3	ES	Empresa Nacional Siderurgica s.a. (Ensidesa)	Basic and fabricated metals	1954	301,391,287		-0.01	
3	GB	English Electric Company	Electrical engineering	1954	220,485,534		7.74	15.16
3	IT	ENI (controllo pubblico)	Mining	1954	70,251,200		8.99	
3	FI	Enso-Gutzeit Oy	Wood and paper products	1954	72,217,831	77,674,026	5.80	20.73
3	IT	Ercole Marelli	Electrical engineering	1954	24,876,800		4.43	14.47
3	IT	Eridania	Food, drink, and tobacco products	1954	77,195,200		7.54	16.14
3	ES	Espanola de Construccion Naval Sociedade	Transport equipment	1954	155,300,460		10.25	
3	DE	Esso AG	Oil, rubber, and other non-metallic mineral products	1954	118,560,187	265,554,231	2.64	
3	FR	Esso Standard	Oil, rubber, and other non-metallic mineral products	1954	170,249,606		8.79	311.12
3	GB	F.W. Woolworth	Commercial activities	1954	188,237,733		27.65	3.14
3	BE	Fabrique Nationale d'Armes de Guerre	Mechanical engineering	1954	28,528,247		9.58	15.49
3	DE	Farbenfabriken Bayer AG	Chemicals and pharmaceuticals	1954	314,190,710	288,200,238	6.24	31.11
3	DE	Farbwerke Hoechst AG vorm. Meister Lucius & Brüning	Chemicals and pharmaceuticals	1954	196,302,739	268,581,633	5.85	29.31
3	DE	Feldmuhle Papier- und Zellstoffwerke AG	Wood and paper products	1954	30,147,795	61,065,557	8.81	36.19

(*continued*)

Continued

Benchmark	Country	Company	Sector	Year	Assets (US$)	Turnover (US$)	3-year average ROE	3-year average HR
3	IT	Fiat (Gruppo IFI)	Transport equipment	1954	502,745,600		7.21	53.58
3	FR	Fives-Lille	Mechanical engineering	1954	72,664,933		6.77	5.89
3	GB	Ford Motor Company	Transport equipment	1954	271,618,149		14.93	
3	FR	Galeries Lafayette	Commercial activities	1954	18,418,903		4.82	63.48
3	FR	Gaz de France	Utilities; Electricity, gas, and water supply	1954	727,795			
3	DE	Gelsenberg Benzin AG	Oil, rubber, and other non-metallic mineral products	1954	90,684,151	93,682,956	-0.21	
3	DE	Gelsenkirchener Bergwerks-Aktien-Gesellschaft	Mining	1954	416,286,042		4.15	-4.08
3	ES	General Azucarera de Espana Sociedad	Food, drink, and tobacco products	1954	118,208,583		9.05	28.47
3	GB	General Electric Company	Electrical engineering	1954	227,317,320		5.91	16.82
3	IT	Generale Immobiliare	Construction and property companies	1954	45,515,200		6.99	39.90
3	GB	George Wimpey & Co.	Construction and property companies	1954	37,842,593		18.90	
3	FR	Georges Lesieur et fils	Food, drink, and tobacco products	1954	17,148,369		9.00	33.83
3	BE	Gevaert Photo Producten	Chemicals and pharmaceuticals	1954	37,448,141		15.93	15.29
3	FR	Givet-Izieux	Textiles and leather goods	1954	29,134,676		2.61	-5.37
3	SE	Gotaverken AB	Transport equipment	1954	112,187,313	48,463,174	10.77	

3	BE	Grands Magasins à l'Innovation	Commercial activities	1954	16,175,675		12.68	31.40
3	FR	Grands Travaux de Marseille	Construction and property companies	1954	62,042,137		11.01	2.79
3	GB	Great Universal stores	Commercial activities	1954	312,367,449		16.35	1.63
3	GB	Guest, Keen & Nettlefolds	Mechanical engineering	1954	275,926,596		10.41	15.11
3	FR	Hachette	Wood and paper products	1954	43,765,464		18.77	34.69
3	DE	Hamburg-Amerika-Linie (Hapag)	Transport and communication	1954	74,531,586		−7.67	29.55
3	DE	Hamburger Hochbahn AG	Transport and communication	1954	44,560,189		0.04	16.52
3	GB	Hawker Siddeley Group	Transport equipment	1954	181,552,222		12.79	34.39
3	ES	Hilaturas de Fabra y Coats Cia. Anonima de	Textiles and leather goods	1954	29,712,310	38,653,637	22.09	
3	DE	Hochtief AG für Hoch- und Tiefbauten	Construction and property companies	1954	14,967,819	29,797,378	6.04	44.53
3	DE	Hoesch Werke AG	Basic and fabricated metals	1954	266,817,652	292,872,461	3.99	0.14
3	SE	Höganäs-Billesholm AB	Oil, rubber, and other non-metallic mineral products	1954	23,577,422	11,869,322	7.05	6.60
3	ES	Iberduero	Utilities; Electricity, gas, and water supply	1954	302,866,347	47,546,123	7.30	27.34
3	FI	Imatran Voima Oy (IVO)	Utilities; Electricity, gas, and water supply	1954	82,658,498	24,689,177	6.42	
3	GB	Imperial Chemical Industries	Chemicals and pharmaceuticals	1954	1,470,552,598		7.82	−4.52

(*continued*)

Continued

Benchmark	Country	Company	Sector	Year	Assets (US$)	Turnover (US$)	3-year average ROE	3-year average HR
3	GB	Imperial Cold Storage and Company	Construction and property companies	1954	27,825,857		7.95	
3	GB	Imperial Tobacco of Great Britain and Ireland	Food, drink, and tobacco products	1954	659,921,725		9.25	0.43
3	BE	Intercommunale Belge d'Électricité (Société . . .)	Utilities; Electricity, gas, and water supply	1954	80,154,914		9.67	10.28
3	IT	Istituto Romano Beni Stabili	Construction and property companies	1954	26,400,000		2.86	6.55
3	IT	Italia di Navigazione (Gruppo IRI)	Transport and communication	1954	104,737,600		0.44	
3	IT	Italiana Industria Zuccheri	Food, drink, and tobacco products	1954	30,963,200		11.82	22.33
3	GB	J. & P. Coats	Textiles and leather goods	1954	225,669,862		8.11	−0.83
3	DE	Kaufhof AG	Commercial activities	1954	47,268,175	135,318,230	6.67	28.60
3	GB	Kemsley Newspapers	Wood and paper products	1954	61,133,177		4.69	−3.21
3	FI	Kesko Oy	Commercial activities	1954	31,714,667	171,645,887	15.13	
3	DE	Klöckner-Humboldt-Deutz-AG	Mechanical engineering	1954	67,308,697		5.52	47.42
3	SE	Kooperativa förbundet	Commercial activities	1954	164,533,543	291,127,006	5.11	
3	ES	La Maquinista Terrestre y Maritima	Mechanical engineering	1954	88,842,526	4,397,794	10.29	
3	ES	La Papelera Espanola s.a.	Wood and paper products	1954	27,635,971	17,764,109	12.55	20.90
3	IT	La Rinascente	Commercial activities	1954	16,776,000		7.91	70.94

3	FR	Le Nickel	Mining	1954	26,108,760		4.64	40.86
3	GB	Lloyds Bank	Financial intermediation	1954	3,961,969,879		6.70	3.37
3	SE	Loussavaara-Kiirunavaara AB (LKAB)	Mining	1954	181,080,029	110,032,865	141.78	
3	IT	Magazzini Standa	Commercial activities	1954	4,792,000		22.76	
3	IT	Magneti Marelli (gruppi Ercole Marelli e Fiat)	Electrical engineering	1954	21,800,000		7.22	102.63
3	IT	Manifatture Lane G. Marzotto	Textiles and leather goods	1954	77,102,400		0.44	
3	DE	Mannesmann AG	Basic and fabricated metals	1954	325,537,546	426,936,830	4.28	38.17
3	DE	Margarine-Union AG	Food, drink, and tobacco products	1954	93,408,821		26.84	
3	FR	Messageries Maritimes	Transport and communication	1954	189,666,595		1.85	−14.49
3	FR	Michelin	Oil, rubber, and other non-metallic mineral products	1954	60,410,531		9.78	−18.36
3	GB	Midland Bank	Financial intermediation	1954	5,063,187,910		9.14	0.21
3	SE	Mölnlycke Vaveri AB	Textiles and leather goods	1954	9,907,404	20,800,309	10.66	36.27
3	IT	Montecatini	Chemicals and pharmaceuticals	1954	363,225,600		6.59	36.27
3	BE	Nationales Belges (Glaces)	Oil, rubber, and other non-metallic mineral products	1954	14,066,891		8.07	59.31
3	GB	New Consolidated Gold Fields of South Africa	Mining	1954	64,561,169		10.32	13.06
3	DE	Nordsee Deutsche Hochseefischerei AG	Food, drink, and tobacco products	1954	14,541,120		5.62	36.52

(*continued*)

Continued

Benchmark	Country	Company	Sector	Year	Assets (US$)	Turnover (US$)	3-year average ROE	3-year average HR
3	FI	Outokumpu Oy	Mining	1954	34,092,606	26,823,377	12.56	
3	FI	Oy Finlayson-Forssa Ab	Textiles and leather goods	1954	17,245,675	18,582,684	5.97	37.27
3	FI	Oy Pohjoismaiden Yhdyspankki	Financial intermediation	1954	302,875,732		10.32	2.43
3	FI	Oy Rakennustoimi	Construction and property companies	1954	816,706	2,434,199	15.45	
3	FI	Oy StrömbergAb	Electrical engineering	1954	23,250,727	20,564,935	13.67	38.15
3	FI	Oy Vuoksenniska Ab	Basic and fabricated metals	1954	14,141,212	21,238,095	10.71	
3	BE	Papeteries de Belgique	Wood and paper products	1954	16,499,558		8.84	27.38
3	FR	Papeteries de France	Wood and paper products	1954	25,233,593		3.46	19.27
3	FR	Pechiney	Chemicals and pharmaceuticals	1954	161,387,475		4.41	68.86
3	GB	Peninsular and Oriental	Transport and communication	1954	462,634,955		4.86	36.94
3	BE	Petrofina	Oil, rubber, and other non-metallic mineral products	1954	73,517,621		17.71	7.14
3	FR	Pétroles BP	Oil, rubber, and other non-metallic mineral products	1954	131,736,504		2.88	82.87
3	FR	Peugeot	Transport equipment	1954	72,399,140		6.61	22.39
3	DE	Philipp Holzmann AG	Construction and property companies	1954	30,061,979		7.75	171.42

3	IT	Pirelli	Oil, rubber, and other non-metallic mineral products	1954	141,057,600		6.64	31.71
3	FR	Pont à Mousson	Mechanical engineering	1954	30,098,232		4.76	24.83
3	GB	Powell Duffryn	Mining	1954	81,212,640		6.33	1.96
3	DE	PreBische Elektrizitäts-Aktiengesellschaft	Utilities; Electricity, gas, and water supply	1954	159,666,266	46,841,478	4.06	
3	FR	Raffineries et sucreries Say	Food, drink, and tobacco products	1954	39,495,233		10.27	20.22
3	IT	Rai (Gruppo IRI)	Wood and paper products	1954	30,705,600		4.30	
3	ES	Real Compania Asturiana de Minas	Mining	1954	196,772,022		12.75	
3	FR	Régie Renault	Transport equipment	1954	187,840,149		9.70	
3	DE	Rheinische AG für Braunkohlenbergbau und Brikettfabrikation	Mining	1954	196,638,862		2.31	24.85
3	DE	Rheinisch-Westfälisches Elektrizitatswerk AG (RWE)	Utilities; Electricity, gas, and water supply	1954	698,553,023	102,097,732	5.96	35.39
3	FR	Rhone Poulenc	Chemicals and pharmaceuticals	1954	80,416,521		9.79	48.07
3	IT	RIV–Officine di Villar Perosa	Mechanical engineering	1954	35,944,000		3.81	
3	DE	Rudolph Karstadt AG	Commercial activities	1954	52,636,471		8.01	26.04
3	FR	Saint Frères	Textiles and leather goods	1954	27,041,671		4.10	6.30
3	FR	Saint Gobain	Chemicals and pharmaceuticals	1954	164,088,066		14.46	38.49
3	GB	Shell Transport and Trading Company	Oil, rubber, and other non-metallic mineral products	1954	315,522,576		5.93	84.10
3	FR	Sidelor	Basic and fabricated metals	1954	206,402,728		1.10	

(*continued*)

Continued

Benchmark	Country	Company	Sector	Year	Assets (US$)	Turnover (US$)	3-year average ROE	3-year average HR
3	DE	Siemens & Halske AG	Electrical engineering	1954	207,265,788	374,255,066	5.67	−9.80
3	DE	Siemens-Schuckertwerke AG	Electrical engineering	1954	222,092,966		5.70	
3	IT	SIP (Gruppo IRI)	Utilities; Electricity, gas, and water supply	1954	247,683,200		4.36	25.15
3	SE	Skånska Cement AB	Construction and property companies	1954	32,356,273	24,492,557	7.35	3.57
3	SE	SKF	Basic and fabricated metals	1954	227,644,898	55,287,067	6.71	−0.33
3	FR	SNECMA	Transport equipment	1954	97,735,387		7.08	
3	IT	Snia Viscosa	Textiles and leather goods	1954	125,784,000		3.46	10.82
3	FR	Société Générale	Financial intermediation	1954			9.09	10.60
3	BE	Société Generale de Belgique	Financial intermediation	1954	101,881,076		16.75	22.05
3	FR	Société Générale d'Entreprises	Construction and property companies	1954	84,664,145		6.86	5.25
3	FR	Société Lyonnaise des Eaux et de l'Eclairage	Utilities; Electricity, gas, and water supply	1954	39,634,370		4.88	5.25
3	FR	Société minière et métallurgique de Penarroya	Mining	1954	59,301,765		4.13	5.79
3	BE	Société Nationale des Chemins de fer Belges (SNCB/NMBS)	Transport and communication	1954	623,217,528		−3.29	2.97
3	ES	Standard Electrica, s.a.	Electrical engineering	1954	50,182,654			
3	IT	Stanic (Gruppi ENI e Esso Italiana)	Oil, rubber, and other non-metallic mineral products	1954	59,299,200		7.30	

3	GB	Steel Company of Wales	Basic and fabricated metals	1954	306,678,888		21.96	3.75
3	GB	Stewarts & Lloyds	Basic and fabricated metals	1954	227,280,899		14.00	31.94
3	IT	Stipel–Società Telefonica Interregionale Piemontese e Lombarda (Gruppo IRI)	Transport and communication	1954	177,424,000		5.31	
3	DE	Suddeutsche Bank AG	Financial intermediation	1954	604,989,257	30,154,946,365	4.70	73.60
3	DE	Suddeutsche Zucker-AG	Food, drink, and tobacco products	1954	45,585,219	75,327,771	5.92	49.15
3	FI	Suomen Höyrylaiva Oy (FÅA)	Transport and communication	1954	12,880,048	16,166,667	7.51	6.03
3	FI	Suomen Sokeri Oy	Food, drink, and tobacco products	1954	15,919,788	27,363,203	9.23	11.20
3	SE	Svenska Cellulosaktiebolaget (SCA)	Wood and paper products	1954	127,909,535	92,538,181	11.47	30.20
3	SE	Svenska Sockerfabriksaktiebolaget	Food, drink, and tobacco products	1954	40,169,920	675,236,806	8.78	6.33
3	SE	Svenska Tändsticksaktiebolaget	Chemicals and pharmaceuticals	1954	83,352,792	41,755,268	7.64	6.03
3	SE	Sydsvenska Kraftaktiebolaget	Utilities; Electricity, gas, and water supply	1954	62,018,556	18,383,916	4.97	
3	ES	Tabacalera s.a.	Food, drink, and tobacco products	1954	100,323,022	462,152,878	12.18	11.07
3	BE	Tabacofina	Food, drink, and tobacco products	1954	19,235,635		11.05	16.93
3	ES	Telefonica Nacional de Espana Cia, 'CTNE'	Transport and communication	1954	426,168,505	90,738,389	7.56	35.19
3	IT	Terni (Gruppo IRI)	Basic and fabricated metals	1954	215,070,400		2.25	36.99

(continued)

Continued

Benchmark	Country	Company	Sector	Year	Assets (US$)	Turnover (US$)	3-year average ROE	3-year average HR
3	GB	The Associated Portland Cement Manufacturers	Construction and property companies	1954	113,932,115		9.70	11.19
3	GB	The British Motor Corporation	Transport equipment	1954	257,445,626		13.85	17.91
3	GB	The British Petroleum Company	Oil, rubber, and other non-metallic mineral products	1954	998,530,753		16.99	22.52
3	GB	The Dunlop Group	Oil, rubber, and other non-metallic mineral products	1954	431,895,292		6.35	−28.94
3	GB	The Rank Organisation	Commercial activities	1954	181,744,949		25.76	−27.35
3	FR	Thomson-Houston	Electrical engineering	1954	93,971,391		3.33	14.81
3	GB	Tube Investments	Mechanical engineering	1954	171,443,073		7.63	5.37
3	FI	Typpi Oy	Chemicals and pharmaceuticals	1954	20,797,130		2.80	
3	FR	Ugine	Chemicals and pharmaceuticals	1954	103,571,799		5.59	59.02
3	GB	Unilever	Chemicals and pharmaceuticals	1954	464,210,674		27.70	18.17
3	BE	Union Cotonniere	Textiles and leather goods	1954	17,052,212		4.54	22.24
3	ES	Union Espanola de Explosivos s.a.	Chemicals and pharmaceuticals	1954	103,156,195		12.80	33.56
3	BE	Union Minière	Mining	1954	359,678,261		45.06	38.79
3	GB	United Steel Companies	Basic and fabricated metals	1954	221,587,051		8.57	25.36

3	FR	Usines de Kali-Sainte-Thérèse	Mining	1954	28,931,291		-1.09	
3	FR	Usinor	Basic and fabricated metals	1954	205,683,987		2.28	
3	FI	Valmet Oy	Mechanical engineering	1954	42,921,260	33,490,043	0.13	
3	DE	Vereinigte Glanzstoff-Fabriken AG (VGF)	Textiles and leather goods	1954	52,374,257	77,663,883	6.25	16.39
3	GB	Vickers Group	Transport equipment	1954	324,951,466		6.79	12.86
3	BE	Vieille Montagne	Basic and fabricated metals	1954	60,415,166		10.05	48.98
3	DE	Volkswagenwerk GmbH	Transport equipment	1954	108,938,975		5.16	
3	FI	Wärtsilä-yhtymä Oy	Transport equipment	1954	47,179,286	57,224,675	8.68	20.87
3	DE	Zellstofffabrik Waldhof	Wood and paper products	1954	45,544,695	58,402,861	4.17	22.51
4	BE	A.C.E.C. (At. Constructions Electr. Charleroi)	Electrical engineering	1972	209,065,302	275,684,427	6.82	17.09
4	IT	A.P.I.–Anonima Petroli Italiana	Oil, rubber, and other non-metallic mineral products	1972	83,068,357		-4.43	
4	DE	Adam Opel AG	Transport equipment	1972	1,083,948,535	2,035,727,698	19.05	
4	FR	Agache-Willot	Textiles and leather goods	1972	92,942,155	387,390,960	-9.09	-12.82
4	FR	AGF	Insurance	1972	728,351,319	440,146,709	-0.02	
4	IT	AGIP (Gruppo ENI)	Mining	1972	2,174,776,426		0.70	
4	FR	Air France	Transport and communication	1972	799,794,291	825,940,722	1.00	
4	FR	Air Liquide	Chemicals and pharmaceuticals	1972	496,318,451	616,970,658	22.10	-3.93
4	SE	Alfa Laval AB	Mechanical engineering	1972	448,959,418	400,399,401	4.89	6.73

(*continued*)

Continued

Benchmark	Country	Company	Sector	Year	Assets (US$)	Turnover (US$)	3-year average ROE	3-year average HR
4	IT	Alfa Romeo (Gruppo IRI)	Transport equipment	1972	612,201,473	480,003,426	3.57	
4	IT	Alitalia (Gruppo IRI)	Transport and communication	1972	649,364,400	475,831,763	-5.52	-15.68
4	DE	Allgemeine Elektricitäts-Gesellschaft AEG-Telefunken	Electrical engineering	1972	2,315,495,547	3,368,883,312	5.20	-10.01
4	DE	Allianz Lebensversicherungs-AG	Insurance	1972	3,433,586,705		11.78	35.89
4	ES	Altos Hornos de Vizcaya	Mature industries	1972	717,541,248	358,801,183	5.00	20.97
4	SE	Ångfartyg Tirfing AB	Transport and communication	1972	613,411,814	319,487,082	4.70	15.07
4	IT	Anic (Gruppo ENI)	Chemicals and pharmaceuticals	1972	998,615,727	363,004,968	-0.86	-14.09
4	IT	Ansaldo Meccanico-Nucleare (Gruppo IRI)	Mechanical engineering	1972	411,368,854	124,418,366	-2.98	
4	DE	Aral AG	Oil, rubber, and other non-metallic mineral products	1972	380,348,196	1,769,134,253	6.19	
4	IT	Arnoldo Mondadori Editore	Media	1972	104,985,438	147,186,911	5.94	23.96
4	SE	ASEA	Electrical engineering	1972	1,339,920,118	1,043,935,253	7.66	17.50
4	IT	Assicurazioni Generali	Insurance	1972	1,428,197,704	590,793,216	9.06	9.79
4	GB	Associated British Foods	Food, drink, and tobacco products	1972	760,132,566	1,822,126,063	14.95	16.72
4	FR	Ateliers de constructions de Roanne	Mechanical engineering	1972	n.a.	n.a.	n.a.	n.a.
4	DE	August Thyssen-Hutte AG	Mature industries	1972	2,512,796,400	3,723,964,868	6.15	-4.40

4	FR	Auxiliaire d'entreprise	Construction and property companies	1972	227,164,756	226,605,881	12.09	−11.78
4	DE	Axel Springer Verlag AG	Media	1972	127,755,647	346,612,296	22.52	
4	ES	Babcock & Wilcox	Mechanical engineering	1972	117,195,886	78,777,034	0.04	
4	FR	Babcock Fives	Mechanical engineering	1972			6.07	13.07
4	DE	Badische Anilin- & Soda-Fabrik AG (BASF)	Chemicals and pharmaceuticals	1972	2,941,412,070	3,720,514,429	8.05	−0.85
4	IT	Banca Commerciale Italiana (Gruppo IRI)	Financial intermediation	1972	20,292,941,580	724,038,033	7.00	−0.91
4	ES	Banco de Bilbao	Financial intermediation	1972	8,246,532,939		14.04	−1.04
4	ES	Banco Hispano Americano	Financial intermediation	1972	8,339,094,445		15.31	−6.55
4	ES	Banesto	Financial intermediation	1972	10,350,828,443		16.31	−7.66
4	BE	Banque de la Société Generale de Belgique	Financial intermediation	1972	6,878,790,763		11.49	8.09
4	GB	Barclays	Financial intermediation	1972	25,285,902,951		10.97	23.82
4	DE	Bayer AG	Chemicals and pharmaceuticals	1972	4,755,646,173	4,021,329,987	9.78	−6.76
4	IT	BNL (controllo pubblico)	Financial intermediation	1972	23,572,807,949	666,239,507	3.59	
4	FR	BNP	Financial intermediation	1972	20,169,316,812		13.42	
4	SE	Boliden AB	Mining	1972	272,608,797	263,863,769	7.01	−6.30
4	GB	Boots company	Chemicals and pharmaceuticals	1972	375,437,719	920,710,355	19.35	44.79
4	FR	Bouygues	Construction and property companies	1972	170,991,710	199,461,735	21.76	−10.11
4	GB	Bowater Corporation	Mature industries	1972	849,829,915	1,488,266,633	4.80	−2.29
4	FR	Bréguet aviation (avions Dassault)	Transport equipment	1972	1,221,703,176		11.18	9.54

(*continued*)

Continued

Benchmark	Country	Company	Sector	Year	Assets (US$)	Turnover (US$)	3-year average ROE	3-year average HR
4	GB	British Airways	Transport and communication	1972	1,597,981,491	1,348,924,462	0.92	
4	GB	British American Tobacco Company	Food, drink, and tobacco products	1972	2,999,449,725	5,096,173,087	12.67	−14.19
4	GB	British Gas Corporation	Utilities; Electricity, gas, and water supply	1972	5,136,568,284	2,243,121,561	0.51	
4	GB	British Insulated Callender's Cables	Electrical engineering	1972		1,153,076,538	8.74	22.07
4	GB	British Leyland Motor Corporation	Transport equipment	1972	944,472,236	3,204,102,051	5.33	1.05
4	GB	British Petroleum Company	Oil, rubber, and other non-metallic mineral products	1972	8,694,097,049	8,582,291,146	7.15	16.14
4	GB	British Railways Board	Transport and communication	1972	2,369,934,967	1,850,425,213	−1.16	
4	GB	British Steel Corporation	Mature industries	1972	3,502,501,251	3,696,348,174	−4.07	
4	FR	BSN Gervais Danone	Food, drink, and tobacco products	1972	438,954,734	1,564,234,709	6.65	−1.27
4	ES	Campsa	Oil, rubber, and other non-metallic mineral products	1972	374,785,187	444,468,648	13.58	13.23
4	FR	Carrefour	Commercial activities	1972	166,623,204	587,430,623	41.77	56.95
4	FR	Casino (Guichard Perrachon et Cie)	Commercial activities	1972	204,993,478	611,221,266	16.14	11.05
4	ES	CEPSA	Chemicals and pharmaceuticals	1972	533,931,041	378,319,371	7.02	−11.12
4	FR	Charbonnages de France	Mining	1972		832,474,239		

		Company	Industry	Year				
4	FR	Cie des compteurs (groupe Schlumberger)	Electrical engineering	1972	185,118,944	293,814,433	11.04	15.28
4	FR	Cie Française des Pétroles	Oil, rubber, and other non-metallic mineral products	1972	1,397,869,350	2,806,106,341	11.26	9.16
4	BE	Cimenteries et Briqueteries Réunies (CBR.)	Construction and property companies	1972	98,354,700		8.54	20.32
4	FR	Citroën	Transport equipment	1972	365,575,896	2,088,818,297	9.85	-7.95
4	FR	Club méditerranée	Leisure and tourism	1972	49,982,323	82,672,482	15.28	22.02
4	GB	Coats Patons	Textiles and leather goods	1972	793,601,801	875,415,208	9.30	18.95
4	BE	Cockerill Ougrée Providence Espérance Longdoz	Mature industries	1972	1,174,742,477		1.98	-1.57
4	IT	Cogefar	Construction and property companies	1972	158,646,565	98,346,753	2.83	
4	DE	Commerzbank AG	Financial intermediation	1972	11,082,984,532		9.34	-7.97
4	BE	Compagnie d'Entreprises C.F.E.	Transport equipment	1972	47,655,389		14.99	10.03
4	FR	Compagnie Générale d'Electricité	Electrical engineering	1972	364,853,720	2,163,560,755	7.88	4.46
4	GB	Consolidated Gold Fields	Mining	1972		536,285,643	7.06	1.81
4	GB	Consolidated Tin Smelters	Mature industries	1972	828,306,653		-0.23	-14.84
4	IT	Costruzioni autostrade italiane–SCAI	Construction and property companies	1972	50,282,679	88,783,622	4.88	
4	GB	Courtaulds	Textiles and leather goods	1972	1,516,258,129	1,943,721,861	13.25	12.78
4	FR	Crédit Lyonnais	Financial intermediation	1972	18,384,748,623		13.44	9.25
4	ES	CTNE	Transport and communication	1972	2,885,979,524	431,249,977	6.21	15.27
4	SE	Dagens Nyheter AB	Media	1972	67,395,419	96,699,601	12.78	6.23

(*continued*)

Continued

Benchmark	Country	Company	Sector	Year	Assets (US$)	Turnover (US$)	3-year average ROE	3-year average HR
4	DE	Daimler-Benz AG	Transport equipment	1972	1,627,328,066	3,435,037,764	14.55	−0.21
4	IT	Dalmine (Gruppo Finsider)	Mature industries	1972	411,024,499	271,403,118	−7.35	−28.96
4	DE	Demag AG	Mechanical engineering	1972	431,330,318	505,959,849	7.74	8.34
4	DE	Deutsche Bank AG	Financial intermediation	1972	18,431,039,004		9.69	−4.48
4	DE	Deutsche Dampfschifffahrts-Gesellschaft 'Hansa'	Transport and communication	1972	129,761,288	69,719,887	4.23	13.89
4	DE	Deutsche Lufthansa AG	Transport and communication	1972	687,968,294	718,874,827	2.10	3.24
4	DE	Deutsche Rhodiaceta AG	Textiles and leather goods	1972	76,638,331	95,881,119	−10.91	
4	DE	Deutsche Shell AG	Oil, rubber, and other non-metallic mineral products	1972	1,049,764,712	1,966,468,036	9.69	
4	DE	Deutsche Unilever GmbH	Food, drink, and tobacco products	1972	772,443,247	1,568,381,430	24.62	
4	GB	Dickinson Robinson Group	Media	1972		463,946,973	15.20	
4	FR	DMC (Dollfus Mieg)	Textiles and leather goods	1972	95,971,698	289,254,573	2.28	1.00
4	DE	Dr. August Oetker KG	Food, drink, and tobacco products	1972	970,868,081	811,427,328		
4	ES	Draconsa	Construction and property companies	1972	364,344,422	413,583,320	12.84	2.37
4	DE	Dresdner Bank AG	Financial intermediation	1972	15,186,612,884		10.31	−1.20
4	FR	EDF (Electricité de France)	Utilities; Electricity, gas, and water supply	1972		3,118,358,534		
4	ES	El Corte Ingles	Commercial activities	1972	265,022,561		21.20	

4	GB	Electricity Council and Boards	Utilities; Electricity, gas, and water supply	1972	13,794,397,199	4,829,914,957	−0.51	
4	FR	Elf-Erap	Oil, rubber, and other non-metallic mineral products	1972		1,854,282,303		
4	GB	EMI	Media	1972	888,271,636	802,831,416	6.37	−1.05
4	IT	ENEL (controllo pubblico)	Utilities; Electricity, gas, and water supply	1972	11,879,444,920	2,338,661,984	0.00	
4	ES	Ensidesa	Mature industries	1972	1,343,241,450	416,805,632	0.09	12.36
4	FI	Enso-Gutzeit Oy	Mature industries	1972	458,729,536	275,586,405	2.75	37.60
4	DE	Erba AG für Textilindustrie	Textiles and leather goods	1972	67,540,780	87,884,250	4.20	38.32
4	DE	Esso AG	Oil, rubber, and other non-metallic mineral products	1972	1,054,260,024	2,013,456,682	8.01	
4	GB	Esso Petroleum Company	Oil, rubber, and other non-metallic mineral products	1972	1,353,099,050	1,810,787,894	2.69	
4	DE	Farbwerke Hoechst AG	Chemicals and pharmaceuticals	1972	4,671,580,928	4,254,391,468	9.73	−9.54
4	BE	Femmes d+Aujourd+hui	Media	1972	20,521,654		−4.27	−33.80
4	IT	Ferrero	Food, drink, and tobacco products	1972	82,475,587	210,382,046	4.79	
4	IT	Fiat (Gruppo IFI)	Transport equipment	1972	2,666,959,054	3,669,559,705	3.10	−2.30
4	FR	Financière de Paris et des Pays-Bas	Financial intermediation	1972	477,515,030		3.87	−3.33
4	ES	Finanzauto y Servicios	Services to business	1972	37,108,106	11,408,558	9.16	−5.16
4	GB	Ford Motor Company	Transport equipment	1972	1,186,843,422	1,995,497,749	3.89	
4	DE	Friedrich Krupp GmbH	Mature industries	1972	1,900,836,787	2,408,406,524	7.58	

(continued)

Continued

Benchmark	Country	Company	Sector	Year	Assets (US$)	Turnover (US$)	3-year average ROE	3-year average HR
4	BE	G.B. Entreprises	Commercial activities	1972	153,129,430		10.88	5.76
4	IT	Galbani	Food, drink, and tobacco products	1972	75,645,023	213,270,516	5.07	
4	FR	GAN	Insurance	1972	811,534,104		0.44	
4	FR	GDF (Gaz de France)	Utilities; Electricity, gas, and water supply	1972	2,076,769,231	877,478,192	−3.35	
4	BE	General Biscuit Company	Food, drink, and tobacco products	1972	38,621,566		8.01	27.52
4	GB	General Electric Company	Electrical engineering	1972	2,852,826,413	2,559,824,912	9.64	10.26
4	FR	Generale Occidentale	Food, drink, and tobacco products	1972	66,353,370	998,612,251	4.10	
4	GB	George Wimpey	Construction and property companies	1972		605,302,651		−10.34
4	DE	Gerling-Konzern Versicherung-Beteiligungs-Gruppe AG	Insurance	1972	1,577,028,511		18.12	
4	GB	Grand Metropolitan	Leisure and tourism	1972	1,929,632,316	1,514,657,329	8.71	22.02
4	FR	Grands Travaux de Marseille	Construction and property companies	1972	14,707,509	305,115,001	9.19	10.36
4	GB	Great Universal Stores	Commercial activities	1972	1,196,668,334	1,510,800,400	10.56	8.40
4	DE	GroBversandhaus Quelle Gustav Schickedanz KG	Leisure and tourism	1972	336,601,497	1,477,728,984		
4	DE	Gruner + Jahr GmbH & Co. Druck- und Verlagshaus	Media	1972				
4	IT	Gruppo Finanziario Tessile	Textiles and leather goods	1972	90,657,872	119,508,309	3.60	

4	GB	Guest, Keen & Nettlefolds	Mechanical engineering	1972	1,442,421,211	1,558,779,390	8.50	9.52
4	DE	Gutehoffnungshutte Aktienverein	Mechanical engineering	1972	1,851,025,054	2,389,585,947	8.79	−4.18
4	FR	Hachette	Media	1972	169,990,662	582,672,495	13.85	−7.14
4	DE	Hapag-Lloyd AG	Transport and communication	1972	401,173,782	347,806,770	7.56	5.45
4	FR	Havas	Media	1972	85,508,661	289,254,573	8.30	−7.31
4	GB	Hawker Siddeley Group	Transport equipment	1972		1,165,582,791	19.32	46.15
4	BE	Helchteren et Zolder	Mining	1972	25,332,753		1.30	28.09
4	ES	Hidrola	Utilities; Electricity, gas, and water supply	1972	1,499,986,806	195,183,398	10.46	7.80
4	ES	Hilaturas Fabra y Coats	Textiles and leather goods	1972		31,865,567	25.76	
4	DE	Hochtief AG fur Hoch- und Tiefbauten	Construction and property companies	1972	281,387,712	636,762,861	14.32	15.52
4	DE	Horten AG	Commercial activities	1972	370,211,114	851,317,440	18.78	17.96
4	ES	Iberduero	Utilities; Electricity, gas, and water supply	1972	1,282,631,025	184,997,542	4.87	5.45
4	FI	Imatran Voima Oy (IVO)	Utilities; Electricity, gas, and water supply	1972	238,233,844	131,263,523	2.23	
4	GB	Imperial Chemical Industries	Chemicals and pharmaceuticals	1972		4,237,118,559	9.65	6.28
4	GB	Imperial Group	Food, drink, and tobacco products	1972		3,404,202,101	11.41	22.72
4	IT	Industrie A. Zanussi	Electrical engineering	1972	339,621,381	292,706,870	−24.79	
4	IT	Industrie Pirelli	Oil, rubber, and other non-metallic mineral products	1972	754,012,335	434,954,600	−29.23	
4	IT	Ing. C. Olivetti & C.	Mechanical engineering	1972	605,074,525	436,172,691	5.95	−17.67
4	BE	Intercom Belge d'Electricité	Utilities; Electricity, gas, and water supply	1972	925,506,460		7.98	13.68

(continued)

Continued

Benchmark	Country	Company	Sector	Year	Assets (US$)	Turnover (US$)	3-year average ROE	3-year average HR
4	IT	Italgas (Gruppo ENI)	Utilities; Electricity, gas, and water supply	1972	178,137,742	114,253,898	1.91	11.70
4	IT	Italsider (Gruppo Finsider)	Mature industries	1972	4,378,019,531	1,234,486,894	-6.34	-20.03
4	FR	Jacques Borel International (filiale groupe américain W.R. Grage)	Leisure and tourism	1972	43,922,410	76,526,566	22.00	
4	FI	Kansallis-Osake-Pankki	Financial intermediation	1972	1,641,400,910		6.24	19.80
4	DE	Karstadt AG	Commercial activities	1972	692,056,117	1,451,756,648	14.55	12.13
4	DE	Kaufhof AG	Commercial activities	1972	651,435,345	1,277,290,450	14.12	8.74
4	FI	Kemira Oy	Chemicals and pharmaceuticals	1972	176,831,020	141,596,697	4.64	
4	FI	Kesko Oy	Commercial activities	1972	183,896,841	732,630,924	6.23	27.90
4	DE	Klöckner-Humboldt-Deutz AG	Mechanical engineering	1972	756,792,363	671,894,605	6.53	-7.45
4	SE	Kooperativa förbundet	Commercial activities	1972	931,595,564	1,552,869,456	2.25	
4	IT	La Rinascente	Commercial activities	1972	284,558,849	504,956,313	7.81	-6.35
4	BE	La Royale Belge 'Vie Accidents'	Insurance	1972	812,394,424		38.89	15.62
4	ES	La Union y el Fenix Espanol	Insurance	1972	313,555,189	117,687,599	1.70	-8.75
4	FR	Lainière de Roubaix	Textiles and leather goods	1972	146,514,731	221,847,753	1.97	36.74
4	IT	Lanerossi (Gruppo ENI)	Textiles and leather goods	1972	133,558,335	104,044,886	0.00	4.10
4	FR	Le Nickel	Mining	1972	513,472,589	629,659,001	1.56	-29.80
4	GB	Lonrho	Mining	1972	376,588,294	542,521,261	9.66	7.75
4	FR	L'Oreal	Chemicals and pharmaceuticals	1972	294,622,374	402,458,366	18.10	-0.02

4	FR	Lyonnaise des Eaux et éclairage	Utilities; Electricity, gas, and water supply	1972	289,622,345	398,493,259	6.29	8.96
4	IT	Magazzini Standa (Gruppo Montedison)	Commercial activities	1972	209,719,034	624,480,041	15.05	
4	IT	Magneti Marelli (Gruppo Fiat)	Electrical engineering	1972	150,712,695	145,401,747	1.30	48.51
4	DE	Mannesmann AG	Mature industries	1972	1,651,407,775	2,244,353,827	10.97	15.18
4	GB	Marks & Spencer	Commercial activities	1972	712,431,216	1,376,343,172	26.34	5.12
4	ES	Melia	Leisure and tourism	1972		56,013,692		
4	FR	Michelin	Oil, rubber, and other non-metallic mineral products	1972	302,036,911	1,685,170,449	20.14	14.92
4	GB	Midland	Financial intermediation	1972	14,748,664,332		11.41	27.41
4	SE	Mölnlycke AB	Textiles and leather goods	1972	62,329,199	105,381,540	11.13	−13.40
4	IT	Montedison	Chemicals and pharmaceuticals	1972	3,799,695,049	1,410,351,208	−45.24	−23.10
4	GB	Natwest	Financial intermediation	1972	21,912,838,919		13.30	27.37
4	DE	Neckermann Versand KGaA	Leisure and tourism	1972	252,478,357	693,851,945	9.24	9.44
4	FR	Nouvelles Galeries Réunies	Commercial activities	1972	298,466,581	617,763,680	2.13	−7.62
4	FI	Outokumpu Oy	Mining	1972	165,447,583	123,141,934	3.06	
4	FI	Oy Finlayson-Forssa Ab	Textiles and leather goods	1972	42,724,988	43,926,041	2.43	8.33
4	FI	Oy Nokia Ab	Oil, rubber, and other non-metallic mineral products	1972	184,238,033	206,232,408	6.72	36.53
4	FI	Oy Strömberg Ab	Electrical engineering	1972	79,301,580	81,620,393	4.28	59.50
4	FI	Oy Wärtsilä Ab	Transport equipment	1972	472,781,953	187,123,025	−1.81	1.50
4	FI	Oy Yhtyneet Ravintolat Ab	Leisure and tourism	1972	11,263,763	17,938,248	6.46	
4	FR	Péchiney UK	Mature industries	1972	1,293,535,026	2,661,578,201	4.62	−6.37
4	FR	Penarroya	Mining	1972	203,162,440	133,683,804	4.01	−24.06

(continued)

Continued

Benchmark	Country	Company	Sector	Year	Assets (US$)	Turnover (US$)	3-year average ROE	3-year average HR
4	BE	Petrofina	Oil, rubber, and other non-metallic mineral products	1972	904,099,882		10.17	44.86
4	FR	Peugeot	Transport equipment	1972	725,570,761	2,134,218,810	7.47	28.59
4	DE	Philipp Holzmann AG	Construction and property companies	1972	294,626,406	668,130,489	20.84	21.14
4	BE	Pieux Franki	Mechanical engineering	1972	31,482,016		23.33	8.96
4	FR	PLM	Leisure and tourism	1972	34,051,575	34,694,687	6.54	
4	FR	Poclain	Mechanical engineering	1972	147,063,569	175,455,987	11.89	3.20
4	FI	Polar-Rakennus Oy	Construction and property companies	1972	40,971,757	46,673,049	11.96	
4	GB	Post Office	Transport and communication	1972	9,308,831,916	3,828,914,457	−0.31	
4	FR	Publicis SA	Media	1972	17,781,436	146,907,216	12.03	−16.54
4	IT	Rai (Gruppo IRI)	Media	1972	314,572,554		0.39	
4	GB	Rank Organisation	Leisure and tourism	1972	790,902,951	488,291,646	14.09	19.63
4	FR	RATP	Transport and communication	1972	2,339,059,633	456,260,904	0.20	
4	GB	Reed International	Media	1972	1,266,883,442	1,494,997,499	6.10	16.02
4	FR	Renault	Transport equipment	1972	1,636,777,175	2,429,305,599	−2.20	
4	DE	Rheinisch-Westfälisches Elektrizitätswerk AG	Utilities; Electricity, gas, and water supply	1972	3,709,056,668	1,433,814,304	12.86	−4.47
4	DE	Rheinische Braunkohlen AG	Mining	1972	553,039,210	300,371,393	14.57	

4	FR	Rhône-Poulenc	Chemicals and pharmaceuticals	1972	1,131,913,362	2,479,381,519	5.05	−4.97
4	ES	Rio Tinto Patino	Mining	1972		69,021,316	3.53	
4	GB	Rio Tinto-Zinc Corporation	Mining	1972	2,533,516,758	1,534,767,384	8.08	−20.31
4	DE	Robert Bosch GmbH	Electrical engineering	1972	827,566,417	1,808,343,789	8.63	
4	DE	Ruhrkohle AG	Mining	1972	3,016,617,491	2,096,988,769	−44.63	
4	DE	Saarbergwerke Aktiengesellschaft	Mining	1972	669,777,902	622,150,876	−7.82	
4	FR	SACILOR	Mature industries	1972	719,789,972	512,881,180	0.00	
4	IT	SAI	Insurance	1972	410,952,544	255,917,423	2.42	−15.87
4	FR	Saint-Gobain Pont-à-Mousson	Oil, rubber, and other non-metallic mineral products	1972	1,037,436,980	2,589,611,343	9.10	5.95
4	DE	Salamander AG	Textiles and leather goods	1972	109,859,787	153,074,659	3.81	13.36
4	FI	Sanoma Oy	Media	1972	20,732,887	33,565,342	6.62	
4	SE	Sara restauranger AB	Leisure and tourism	1972	13,727,140	76,119,404	1.72	
4	ES	SEAT	Transport equipment	1972	684,320,523	561,629,127	10.93	
4	GB	Shell Transport and Trading Company	Oil, rubber, and other non-metallic mineral products	1972	20,785,392,696	14,364,682,341	9.07	2.62
4	GB	Shipping Industrial Holdings	Transport and communication	1972		1,432,941,471		3.76
4	DE	Siemens Aktiengesellschaft	Electrical engineering	1972	4,283,286,445	4,751,254,705	11.33	9.16
4	IT	SIP (Gruppo STET)	Transport and communication	1972	3,955,173,891	1,161,502,484	5.69	2.67
4	SE	Skandia Försäkringsaktiebolag	Insurance	1972	2,282,867,271		7.53	30.93
4	SE	Skånska Cement AB	Construction and property companies	1972	563,317,206	649,527,023	12.76	1.50

(continued)

Continued

Benchmark	Country	Company	Sector	Year	Assets (US$)	Turnover (US$)	3-year average ROE	3-year average HR
4	SE	SKF	Mature industries	1972	1,491,738,532	1,047,551,019	9.30	−6.97
4	FR	SNCF	Transport and communication	1972	4,378,284,997	2,682,596,604	−1.04	
4	IT	Società Mineraria e Metallurgica di Pertusola	Mining	1972	78,295,357	49,429,501	3.32	19.00
4	FR	Société Générale	Financial intermediation	1972	16,113,570,918		13.88	26.92
4	BE	Société Nationale des Chemins de fer Belges (SNCB/NMBS)	Transport and communication	1972	1,135,378,447		−0.37	12.62
4	BE	Solvay	Chemicals and pharmaceuticals	1972	1,053,167,019		4.89	10.45
4	FR	Source Perrier	Food, drink, and tobacco products	1972	117,676,210	367,961,935	8.40	5.59
4	GB	South of Scotland Electricity Board	Utilities; Electricity, gas, and water supply	1972		370,165,083 (turnover as of 1971)		
4	ES	Standard Electrica	Electrical engineering	1972		264,446,865	24.22	
4	DE	Strabag Bau-AG	Construction and property companies	1972	153,622,329	400,564,617	41.93	
4	DE	Süddeutsche Zucker-AG	Food, drink, and tobacco products	1972	169,138,642	200,576,859	8.75	14.23
4	FI	Suomen Höyrylaiva Oy	Transport and communication	1972	118,757,300	70,347,056	6.95	23.70
4	FI	Suomen Sokeri Oy	Food, drink, and tobacco products	1972	51,272,858	80,435,376	6.15	22.97
4	SE	Svenska Handelsbanken	Financial intermediation	1972	5,570,107,210		5.44	9.97

4	SE	Svenska Tandsticksaktiebolaget	Chemicals and pharmaceuticals	1972	523,964,684	577,864,180	8.83	4.30
4	SE	Svenska Tobaksaktiebolaget	Food, drink, and tobacco products	1972	252,322,903	91,191,925	10.16	
4	SE	Sydsvenska Kraftaktiebolaget	Utilities; Electricity, gas, and water supply	1972	345,217,564	127,244,059	5.13	6.30
4	ES	Tabacalera	Food, drink, and tobacco products	1972	499,607,686	213,534,977	10.49	29.91
4	GB	Tarmac	Construction and property companies	1972	294,522,261	486,408,204	15.40	25.58
4	FR	Thomson CSF	Electrical engineering	1972	458,805,788	1,521,213,310	9.10	8.57
4	GB	Thorn Electrical Industries	Electrical engineering	1972	563,281,641	1,496,498,249	22.46	26.30
4	GB	Tootal	Textiles and leather goods	1972	n.a.	457,598,799	n.a.	27.03
4	DE	Touristik Union International GmbH KG	Leisure and tourism	1972	n.a.	n.a.	n.a.	n.a.
4	GB	Trafalgar House Investments	Construction and property companies	1972	722,388,694	591,525,763	11.26	33.59
4	SE	Trelleborgs Gummifabrik AB	Oil, rubber, and other non-metallic mineral products	1972	124,637,382	116,670,170	4.60	-2.33
4	GB	Trust House Forte	Leisure and tourism	1972	661,748,374	531,978,489	13.06	-7.88
4	GB	Tube Investments	Mechanical engineering	1972	795,547,774	839,762,381	7.56	48.39
4	FR	UAP	Insurance	1972	1,369,961,397		0.10	
4	ES	UERT	Chemicals and pharmaceuticals	1972	308,800,965	428,800,373	9.76	-5.24
4	GB	Unilever	Chemicals and pharmaceuticals	1972		10,840,420,210	11.60	15.36
4	BE	Union Cotonniere	Textiles and leather goods	1972	115,167,421		3.85	25.73

(continued)

Continued

Benchmark	Country	Company	Sector	Year	Assets (US$)	Turnover (US$)	3-year average ROE	3-year average HR
4	FR	Usinor	Mature industries	1972	1,771,536,430	1,045,598,731	7.41	6.62
4	FI	Vakuutus Oy Pohjola	Insurance	1972	170,099,090	172,666,348	13.36	58.67
4	FI	Valmet Oy	Mechanical engineering	1972	300,026,281	172,666,348	−0.27	
4	DE	VEBA AG	Utilities; Electricity, gas, and water supply	1972	3,821,639,191	3,240,906,451	17.59	−6.20
4	DE	Vereinigte Elektrizitätswerke Westfalen AG	Utilities; Electricity, gas, and water supply	1972	1,629,019,437	508,155,583	9.49	1.97
4	GB	Vickers	Mechanical engineering	1972	445,005,003	434,204,602	5.34	−6.11
4	ES	Victor Sagi Publicidad	Media	1972	n.a.	n.a.	n.a.	n.a.
4	DE	Victoria Lebens-Versicherungs-Aktien-Gesellschaft	Insurance	1972	1,467,378,892		50.20	0.24
4	DE	Volkswagenwerk AG	Transport equipment	1972	3,508,705,742	5,280,112,923	5.92	−9.02
4	SE	Volvo	Transport equipment	1972	1,503,195,332	1,544,250,578	12.70	5.07
4	BE	Wagon Lits	Leisure and tourism	1972	108,203,558		5.79	35.82
4	GB	Woolworths	Commercial activities	1972		946,393,197		17.23
5	SE	AB Vin & Sprit	Food, drink, and tobacco products	2000	622,663,106	622,554,096	33.67	−8.30
5	FR	Accor	Commercial activities	2000	1,580,716,974	908,413,829	10.15	−20.56
5	ES	Aceralia Corporacion Siderurgica	Mature industries	2000	4,410,381,292	3,698,015,216	8.52	−8.59
5	FR	Adecco Travail	Services to business	2000		15,752,484,619	−13.62	42.69
5	DE	Adidas-Salomon AG	Textiles and leather goods	2000	3,709,379,616	5,386,816,839	4.15	−17.16
5	GB	Aegis Group	Services to business	2000	2,266,646,264	8,663,231,282	8.66	49.80

5	FR	AGF	Insurance	2000	13,446,386,264	2,457,125,225	10.20	−27.44
5	FR	Air France	Transport	2000	n.a.	9,532,145,033	10.36	10.04
5	FR	Airbus industrie	Transport equipment	2000	n.a.	n.a.	n.a.	n.a.
5	FR	Alcatel	Electrical engineering	2000	40,379,980,469	28,928,626,000	11.89	84.36
5	DE	Alcatel SEL AG	Post and telecommunications	2000	1,694,977,843	1,845,457,903	0.48	22.50
5	IT	Alitalia	Transport	2000	4,338,995,569	4,976,920,236	−1.70	−22.16
5	DE	Allianz Aktiengesellschaft	Insurance	2000	406,199,224,520		15.45	20.56
5	BE	Almanij	Financial intermediation	2000	3,399,355,613	432,976	12.30	3.98
5	IT	Alpitour (IFI Group)	Leisure and tourism	2000	351,735,598	942,577,548	8.12	
5	FR	Alstom	Electrical engineering	2000	19,798,628,906	16,739,046,900	16.79	−5.18
5	ES	Altadis	Food, drink, and tobacco products	2000	7,233,617,897	7,022,082,526	14.99	19.72
5	GB	Anglo American	Mining	2000	30,692,270,945	14,860,563,807	9.43	264.66
5	IT	Assicurazioni Generali	Insurance	2000	196,611,890,694	41,003,508,124	10.24	24.84
5	IT	Astaldi	Construction and property companies	2000	972,119,645	663,774,003	8.67	
5	GB	AstraZeneca	Chemicals and pharmaceuticals	2000	18,479,923,001	15,842,679,600	21.98	19.77
5	SE	Atlas Copco	Mechanical engineering	2000	6,724,587,126	5,075,271,161	12.64	48.57
5	FR	Atos Origin	Services to business	2000	249,085,002	248,071,777	18.51	−53.72
5	FR	Aventis	Chemicals and pharmaceuticals	2000	39,633,035,156	20,543,303,400	−0.88	
5	FR	Axa	Insurance	2000		87,188,884,786	10.34	35.82
5	GB	BAE Systems	Transport equipment	2000	26,017,692,017	14,627,159,745	12.70	−1.98
5	GB	Barclays	Financial intermediation	2000	473,469,585,174	25,098,514,701	17.66	12.52

(*continued*)

Continued

Benchmark	Country	Company	Sector	Year	Assets (US$)	Turnover (US$)	3-year average ROE	3-year average HR
5	BE	Barco	Electrical engineering	2000	676,600,812	195,327,733	8.54	-7.40
5	DE	BASF Aktiengesellschaft	Chemicals and pharmaceuticals	2000	35,595,457,903	33,185,007,386	10.11	20.35
5	GB	Bass (Six Continents)	Leisure and tourism	2000	13,047,093,204	5,898,757,199	22.28	8.39
5	DE	Bayer Aktiengesellschaft	Chemicals and pharmaceuticals	2000	33,651,218,612	27,682,791,728	12.39	21.54
5	DE	Bayerische Hypo- und Vereinsbank Aktiengesellschaft	Financial intermediation	2000	661,478,951,256		5.31	1.52
5	DE	Bayerische Motoren Werke Aktiengesellschaft	Transport equipment	2000	33,119,460,857	32,640,324,963	-11.57	34.83
5	GB	BBA Group	Transport equipment	2000	2,724,408,012	1,958,169,142	22.93	-2.35
5	ES	BBVaseguros	Insurance	2000		2,707,182,372	27.23	
5	BE	Bekaert	Mature industries	2000	1,493,222,858	647,606,167	12.73	1.57
5	IT	Benetton Group	Textiles and leather goods	2000	2,654,172,821	1,862,998,523	16.07	17.59
5	ES	Berge y Compania	Services to business	2000		2,080,686,934	33.12	
5	DE	Bertelsmann Aktiengesellschaft	Media	2000	13,563,515,510	15,254,800,591	19.96	
5	GB	BG Group	Oil, rubber, and other non-metallic mineral products	2000	9,300,482,597	3,551,076,084	25.06	2.78
5	GB	Billiton	Mature industries	2000		4,252,803,880	10.21	50.88
5	FR	BNP-Paribas	Financial intermediation	2000	651,404,125,000	50,680,359,000	10.93	
5	SE	Bonnier AB	Media	2000	1,510,546,683	1,829,944,950	7.91	22.80
5	SE	Borås Wäferi	Textiles and leather goods	2000	157,300,921	167,111,789	9.33	14.40

5	FR	Bouygues	Construction and property companies	2000	19,901,144,531	17,555,752,000	4.67	65.90
5	GB	BP Amoco	Oil, rubber, and other non-metallic mineral products	2000	144,296,580,066	148,431,342,831	11.57	−9.02
5	GB	British Airways	Transport	2000	21,570,834,181	14,434,677,175	6.42	−10.61
5	GB	British American Tobacco	Food, drink, and tobacco products	2000	26,559,758,464	16,551,985,450	37.47	10.74
5	GB	British Telecom	Post and telecommunications	2000	59,992,934,817	30,218,247,954	16.03	32.01
5	SE	Broströms group	Transport	2000	481,931,651	272,415,109	7.15	74.40
5	ES	BSCH	Financial intermediation	2000	322,126,998,683		25.98	−24.16
5	GB	Bunzl	Mature industries	2000	602,303,728	3,778,417,702	27.54	21.55
5	DE	C&N Touristic AG	Food, drink, and tobacco products	2000	2,382,066,915	4,597,867,574	15.40	22.07
5	GB	Cable & Wireless	Post and telecommunications	2000	34,360,112,309	10,098,514,701	22.63	14.14
5	GB	Cadbury Schweppes	Food, drink, and tobacco products	2000	9,903,943,309	6,938,466,202	19.46	65.90
5	FR	Cap Gemini Ernest & Young	Services to business	2000	2,800,876,962	2,470,787,610	4.67	
5	FR	Carrefour	Commercial activities	2000	41,368,949,219	59,686,475,400	12.34	−31.51
5	FR	CEA-Industrie	Utilities; Electricity, gas, and water supply	2000	8,268,759,443	8,347,400,018	6.91	42.52
5	GB	Centrica	Utilities; Electricity, gas, and water supply	2000		15,062,140,042	18.41	42.00
5	ES	Centros Comerciales Carrefour	Commercial activities	2000	23,344,054,741	6,359,961,468	2.99	
5	FR	Charbonnages de France	Mining	2000	975,677,623			

(*continued*)

Continued

Benchmark	Country	Company	Sector	Year	Assets (US$)	Turnover (US$)	3-year average ROE	3-year average HR
5	FR	Christian Dior	Textiles and leather goods	2000	3,578,853,260	1,538,312,057	1.75	−25.03
5	IT	CIR	Mechanical engineering	2000	3,251,477,105	2,312,592,319	8.93	81.85
5	BE	CMB	Transport	2000	1,103,301,329	84,687,962	18.48	22.35
5	FR	CNP Assurances	Insurance	2000	124,396,835,938	22,504,944,100	11.09	5.12
5	BE	Cofinimmo	Construction and property companies	2000	1,218,748,154	64,655,650	6.68	5.12
5	DE	Continental Aktiengesellschaft	Oil, rubber, and other non-metallic mineral products	2000	7,030,096,012	9,338,072,378	12.23	−2.69
5	GB	Corus Group	Mature industries	2000	12,575,342,593	17,744,771,143	−8.20	−56.33
5	FR	Crédit Agricole	Financial intermediation	2000	64,558,335,084	3,950,066,994	8.57	52.39
5	BE	Creyf's	Services to business	2000	131,694,055	258,866,322	29.80	52.39
5	DE	Daimler Chrysler AG	Transport equipment	2000	183,967,872,969	149,911,373,708	16.69	−2.23
5	FR	Danone	Food, drink, and tobacco products	2000	2,278,750,354	1,852,015,205	9.05	8.59
5	DE	Debeka Lebensversicherungsverein auf Gegenseitigkeit	Insurance	2000	33,333,641,064		16.13	15.31
5	DE	Degussa AG	Chemicals and pharmaceuticals	2000	17,686,484,490	16,800,221,566	12.72	−4.63
5	BE	Delhaize	Commercial activities	2000	1,974,291,913	2,746,619,276	16.93	11.19
5	DE	Deutsche Bahn Aktiengesellschaft	Transport	2000	36,435,561,300	14,277,141,802	1.32	19.48
5	DE	Deutsche Bank	Financial intermediation	2000	867,829,579,025	14,032,496,307	12.96	18.35
5	DE	Deutsche Lufthansa Aktiengesellschaft	Transport	2000	13,672,451,994	14,032,496,307	18.57	18.35

5	DE	Deutsche Post AG	Post and telecommunications	2000	138,737,075,332	30,195,716,396	41.69	
5	DE	Deutsche Shell GmbH	Oil, rubber, and other non-metallic mineral products	2000	3,999,424,178	16,096,820,690	38.35	
5	DE	Deutsche Telekom AG	Post and telecommunications	2000	114,699,039,882	37,794,497,784	9.37	14.27
5	BE	Dexia	Financial intermediation	2000	123,728,449,040		20.46	18.25
5	GB	Diageo	Food, drink, and tobacco products	2000	24,520,690,637	16,097,302,213	22.10	17.10
5	ES	Dow Chemical Iberica	Chemicals and pharmaceuticals	2000	568,192,587	1,150,904,698	33.88	
5	DE	Dresdner Bank Aktiengesellschaft	Financial intermediation	2000	446,360,782,866		10.43	8.96
5	DE	E.On AG	Utilities; Electricity, gas, and water supply	2000	98,056,683,900	68,360,413,589	12.48	5.77
5	DE	ECE Projektmanagement G.m.b.H. & Co. KG	Construction and property companies	2000		6,608,280,875		
5	DE	Edeka-Gruppe	Commercial activities	2000		28,803,545,052		
5	FR	EDF	Utilities; Electricity, gas, and water supply	2000		31,779,962,426	3.90	
5	IT	Edizione (Benetton)	Textiles and leather goods	2000	13,920,790,251	6,592,503,693	13.02	
5	FR	Eiffage	Construction and property companies	2000	653,806,820	801,628,190	10.86	
5	ES	El Corte Ingles	Commercial activities	2000	9,968,897,807		9.64	
5	BE	Electrabel	Utilities; Electricity, gas, and water supply	2000	10,596,546,344	9,251,510,340	18.38	17.62
5	BE	Electrafina	Financial Intermediation	2000	2,415,066		0.71	24.99

(continued)

Continued

Benchmark	Country	Company	Sector	Year	Assets (US$)	Turnover (US$)	3-year average ROE	3-year average HR
5	GB	Emi Group	Media	2000	3,454,366,073	3,852,682,631	−21.72	10.75
5	ES	Endesa	Utilities; Electricity, gas, and water supply	2000	45,532,892,309	13,821,261,526	14.16	9.16
5	IT	ENEL	Utilities; Electricity, gas, and water supply	2000	47,324,593,796	22,790,805,022	12.41	4.63
5	IT	ENI	Mining	2000	51,887,001,477	44,255,908,419	17.27	14.86
5	IT	Enichem (ENI Group)	Chemicals and pharmaceuticals	2000	4,096,196,455	5,555,760,709	−14.53	
5	FR	Eramet	Mining	2000	394,711,876	296,462,433	4.90	1.67
5	DE	ERGO Versicherungsgruppe Aktiengesellschaft	Insurance	2000	97,729,874,446		9.84	20.51
5	SE	Ericsson	Electrical engineering	2000	27,286,640,868	29,821,660,217	20.37	12.27
5	ES	Ericsson Espana	Electrical engineering	2000	1,417,614,483		22.16	
5	FR	Eridania Beghin Say	Food, drink, and tobacco products	2000	331,597,635	247,669,923	16.69	
5	DE	ESCADA Aktiengesellschaft	Textiles and leather goods	2000	545,082,149	751,850,066	10.17	−15.42
5	IT	Esprinet (2)	Services to business	2000	308,345,643	652,695,716	27.78	
5	GB	Exel	Transport	2000	3,402,889,553	6,498,939,072	14.39	21.61
5	IT	Fiat (IFI Group)	Transport equipment	2000	88,353,951,256	49,115,583,456	3.64	−1.20
5	IT	Fincab	Leisure and tourism	2000	549,298,375	394,202,363	−76.18	
5	FI	Finnair	Transport	2000	1,432,039,500	1,542,769,000	14.40	−8.63
5	IT	Finsiel (Olivetti Group)	Services to business	2000	1,159,527,326	1,116,137,371	17.76	
5	ES	Fomento de Construcciones y Contratas	Construction and property companies	2000	5,159,943,037	4,124,649,126	18.01	−17.44

5	BE	Fortis AG	Insurance	2000	404,434,091,581		17.30	22.54
5	FI	Fortum	Oil, rubber, and other non-metallic mineral products	2000	13,797,454,000	10,259,693,000	9.57	−2.60
5	FR	France Telecom	Post and telecommunications	2000	121,751,585,938	31,015,746,000	12.33	19.22
5	IT	FS-Ferrovie dello Stato	Transport	2000	51,115,214,180	4,399,926,145	−5.32	
5	ES	Gas Natural SDG	Utilities; Electricity, gas, and water supply	2000	8,987,372,549	4,515,851,093	14.44	2.25
5	BE	GBL	Financial intermediation	2000	5,462,163,959		14.22	25.43
5	GB	GKN	Mechanical engineering	2000	5,850,424,329	5,901,788,421	34.58	−11.58
5	GB	GlaxoSmithKline	Chemicals and pharmaceuticals	2000	32,329,322,052	27,415,883,601	57.72	13.81
5	GB	Granada Compass	Leisure and tourism	2000		6,109,427,099		
5	FR	Groupe carrières du Boulonnais	Mining	2000		52,970,827	13.11	
5	DE	Gruner + Jahr Aktiengesellschaft & Co.	Media	2000	1,838,702,000	2,708,641,064	39.59	
5	ES	Grupo Iberostar	Leisure and tourism	2000		1,555,576,050		
5	GB	Hanson	Construction and property companies	2000	10,941,892,842	4,571,082,146	10.68	29.26
5	FR	Havas Advertising	Media	2000	689,226,167	1,552,483,187	8.16	
5	GB	Hays	Services to business	2000	2,241,144,993	3,207,032,434	53.57	−21.54
5	FR	Hermes Intl	Textiles and leather goods	2000	181,541,248	150,229,767	19.18	39.39
5	ES	Hewlett Packard Espanola	Mechanical engineering	2000		1,497,285,900	25.96	
5	DE	Hewlett-Packard GmbH	Electrical engineering	2000		4,531,390,192		
5	GB	Hilton Group	Leisure and tourism	2000	7,056,148,078	5,992,725,068	7.74	5.39
5	DE	Hochtief Aktiengesellschaft	Construction and property companies	2000	6,064,438,700	8,849,704,579	8.89	−11.42

(*continued*)

Continued

Benchmark	Country	Company	Sector	Year	Assets (US$)	Turnover (US$)	3-year average ROE	3-year average HR
5	GB	HSBC Holdings	Financial intermediation	2000	675,809,316,403	50,140,951,804	13.73	−5.67
5	DE	Hugo Boss Aktiengesellschaft	Textiles and leather goods	2000	462,733,569	852,494,458	29.29	44.63
5	ES	Iberdrola	Utilities; Electricity, gas, and water supply	2000	18,665,104,488	6,423,707,340	9.50	8.85
5	ES	Iberia Lineas Aereas de Espana	Transport	2000	4,164,588,869	3,985,681,376	22.02	
5	SE	ICA Group	Commercial activities	2000	2,758,816,155	6,441,598,081	9.64	
5	IT	IFI (Agnelli)	Transport equipment	2000	99,188,515,510	61,648,818,316	1.07	15.42
5	GB	Imperial Chemical industries	Chemicals and pharmaceuticals	2000	10,618,213,185	9,728,705,668	91.58	−6.22
5	IT	Impregilo	Construction and property companies	2000	3,691,838,996	1,747,599,705	−2.81	−2.00
5	ES	Inditex	Textiles and leather goods	2000	15,905,428,575	2,413,866,292	24.05	
5	DE	Infineon Technologies AG	Services to business	2000	8,173,005,908	6,723,596,750	−5.20	
5	IT	IntesaBci	Financial intermediation	2000	306,730,059,084	10,409,896,603	9.06	54.37
5	GB	Invensys	Electrical engineering	2000	11,373,567,457	11,295,847,226	3.76	−53.80
5	IT	Italtel (Olivetti Group)	Electrical engineering	2000	1,174,298,375	911,189,069	−19.88	
5	DE	K+S AG	Mining	2000	1,458,733,383	1,927,529,542	18.89	70.75
5	FI	Kemira	Chemicals and pharmaceuticals	2000	2,232,269,500	2,313,223,000	10.02	−10.00
5	FI	Kesko	Commercial activities	2000	2,391,385,000	5,869,594,000	6.88	4.50
5	GB	Kingfisher	Commercial activities	2000	11,531,757,663	17,640,193,998	17.34	−14.25
5	DE	KirchMedia GmbH & Co. KGaA	Media	2000	5,064,299,681	3,072,130,212	12.64	
5	DE	Kommanditgesellschaft Allgemeine Leasing GmbH & Co.	Construction and property companies	2000		8,307,549,210		

5	FR	L'Oreal	Chemicals and pharmaceuticals	2000	1,678,642,935	1,642,560,050	15.16	−9.30
5	IT	La Rinascente (IFI Group)	Commercial activities	2000	3,887,555,391	4,514,401,773	5.60	0.21
5	FR	Lagardere Groupe	Electrical engineering	2000	2,156,687,295	1,580,480,480	12.20	32.85
5	FR	l'Air Liquide SA	Chemicals and pharmaceuticals	2000	1,521,815,985	1,049,933,299	11.07	−11.09
5	GB	Land Securities	Construction and property companies	2000	12,435,111,215	853,288,875	4.10	6.59
5	GB	Legal & General	Insurance	2000	161,992,514,639	35,251,591,391	14.72	−3.87
5	FI	L-Fashion Group/Luhta	Textiles and leather goods	2000	125,283,451	168,420,500	−2.68	
5	SE	LKAB	Mining	2000	1,310,186,952	532,185,098	3.18	
5	GB	Logica	Electrical engineering	2000	905,697,277	1,351,924,826	23.22	85.06
5	GB	Lonmin	Mining	2000	1,494,714,397	759,321,006	14.05	49.03
5	IT	Maffei	Mining	2000	78,471,196	53,545,052	6.29	−2.81
5	IT	Magneti Marelli (Fiat Group)	Mechanical engineering	2000	3,374,261,448	4,109,121,123	8.50	
5	DE	MAN Aktiengesellschaft	Mechanical engineering	2000	10,333,271,787	13,461,041,359	14.10	17.33
5	GB	Marconi	Electrical engineering	2000	16,919,897,304	8,778,417,702	14.77	34.88
5	IT	Mediaset	Media	2000	3,714,918,759	2,136,262,925	15.89	56.99
5	FI	Merita	Financial intermediation	2000	56,824,144,339	3,677,410,343	14.52	
5	DE	Metro AG	Commercial activities	2000	20,617,614,476	43,325,332,349	9.62	31.17
5	FI	Metso	Mechanical engineering	2000	3,316,302,000	3,620,575,500	11.48	2.27
5	FR	Michelin	Oil, rubber, and other non-metallic mineral products	2000	15,958,196,289	14,180,231,000	8.61	−8.22
5	IT	Montedison	Food, drink, and tobacco products	2000	19,481,166,913	12,900,664,697	1.48	55.78

(*continued*)

Continued

Benchmark	Country	Company	Sector	Year	Assets (US$)	Turnover (US$)	3-year average ROE	3-year average HR
5	BE	Nationale Portefeuille maatschappij	Financial intermediation	2000	2,474,119,276		22.59	22.47
5	FI	Nokia	Electrical engineering	2000	18,507,645,000	28,264,868,000	35.21	158.43
5	SE	Nordea	Financial intermediation	2000	216,360,276,885	5,419,523,628	16.09	32.70
5	IT	Olivetti	Post and telecommunications	2000	87,029,172,821	27,503,692,762	7.44	42.64
5	GB	P & O Peninsular & Oriental	Transport	2000	4,620,281,297	2,429,524,098	12.32	−11.16
5	IT	Parmalat	Food, drink, and tobacco products	2000	9,383,308,715	6,784,527,326	7.07	9.97
5	GB	Pearson	Media	2000	13,192,280,096	5,594,119,430	22.24	32.86
5	FR	Pechiney	Mature industries	2000	1,067,507,188	1,384,312,330	9.54	58.53
5	SE	Perstorp	Chemicals and pharmaceuticals	2000	864,010,465	1,006,050,035	7.10	−1.40
5	BE	Petrofina	Oil, rubber, and other non-metallic mineral products	2000	7,719,225,443	7,532,135,340	25.23	25.15
5	FR	Peugeot	Transport equipment	2000	42,115,328,125	40,693,314,600	8.85	8.57
5	DE	Philip Morris GmbH	Food, drink, and tobacco products	2000	1,183,918,061	6,073,005,710		
5	FR	Pinault Printemps Redoute	Commercial activities	2000	29,415,285,156	22,806,554,600	11.56	
5	IT	Pirelli & C.	Oil, rubber, and other non-metallic mineral products	2000	12,713,257,016	7,067,946,824	10.36	54.40
5	IT	Pirelli SpA (Pirelli & C Group)	Oil, rubber, and other non-metallic mineral products	2000	11,580,502,216	6,849,150,665	30.04	23.06

5	FI	Pohjola	Insurance	2000	4,824,270,300	3,775,782,900	61.42	62.47
5	FI	Pohjolan Voima Oy	Utilities; Electricity, gas, and water supply	2000	2,009,880,000	472,767,510	0.97	
5	IT	Poste Italiane	Post and telecommunications	2000	24,804,283,604	6,368,168,390	−110.78	
5	GB	Powergen	Utilities; Electricity, gas, and water supply	2000	16,609,395,100	6,354,956,047	14.39	−1.85
5	SE	Preem	Oil, rubber, and other non-metallic mineral products	2000	1,604,403,990	5,035,700,660	22.25	33.80
5	DE	Preussag AG	Utilities; Electricity, gas, and water supply	2000	17,088,257,016	20,175,406,204	13.39	26.27
5	GB	Prudential	Insurance	2000	232,025,403,154	41,738,405,577	19.69	18.08
5	FR	Publicis Groupe	Media	2000	541,621,399	1,530,404,665	23.06	
5	BE	Quick Restaurants	Leisure and tourism	2000	244,702,733	47,668,944	7.33	−14.35
5	DE	RAG Aktiengesellschaft	Mining	2000	17,160,265,879	13,655,280,650	−0.17	
5	IT	Rai	Media	2000	2,635,709,010	2,596,011,817	8.86	
5	FR	RATP	Transport	2000				
5	FR	Renault	Transport equipment	2000	48,596,343,750	37,003,551,600	10.75	10.16
5	ES	Renault Espana	Transport equipment	2000	6,707,339,057	6,707,339,057	6.15	
5	ES	Repsol-YPF	Oil, rubber, and other non-metallic mineral products	2000	48,392,532,537	40,660,080,697	12.86	−18.34
5	GB	Reuters	Media	2000	5,795,019,747	5,447,105,183	70.02	22.84
5	DE	REWE Handelsgruppe	Commercial activities	2000	34,783,140,377			
5	GB	Rio Tinto	Mining	2000	19,478,453,972	7,882,691,725	14.87	21.09
5	IT	Riva Acciaio	Mature industries	2000	5,876,107,829	4,567,023,634	10.84	

(continued)

Continued

Benchmark	Country	Company	Sector	Year	Assets (US$)	Turnover (US$)	3-year average ROE	3-year average HR
5	GB	RMC Group	Construction and property companies	2000	7,957,260,079	6,935,434,980	10.50	−10.16
5	DE	Robert Bosch GmbH	Electrical engineering	2000	22,622,018,022	29,131,647,333	7.04	
5	GB	Rolls-Royce	Transport equipment	2000	10,513,371,090	9,025,462,261	10.98	8.20
5	GB	Royal Bank of Scotland	Financial intermediation	2000	479,180,749,338	31,330,706,275	17.00	32.73
5	GB	Royal Sun Alliance	Insurance	2000	3,162,928,160	72,932	2.72	3.99
5	DE	RWE Aktiengesellschaft	Utilities; Electricity, gas, and water supply	2000	59,997,024,874	39,167,260,490	14.18	1.96
5	DE	RWE-DEA Aktiengesellschaft für Mineraloel und Chemie	Oil, rubber, and other non-metallic mineral products	2000	5,589,918,759	12,016,248,154	26.54	3.79
5	BE	Sabca	Transport equipment	2000	194,293,759	138,152,696	6.45	−11.98
5	GB	Sainsbury [J]	Commercial activities	2000	15,992,725,068	22,779,630,191	10.43	−6.36
5	FR	Saint Gobain	Construction and property companies	2000	29,521,599,609	26,540,319,600	11.10	5.57
5	BE	Sait Electronics	Mechanical engineering	2000	152,184,269	3,038,497,046	3.81	−0.67
5	DE	Salzgitter AG	Mining	2000	2,240,675,775	5,151,316,659	7.81	−6.67
5	FI	Sampo-Leonia Insurance	Financial intermediation	2000	30,515,747,500	1,347,364,000	20.74	38.10
5	FI	Sanoma-WSOY	Media	2000	1,339,268,650	5,783,788,774	14.70	14.80
5	DE	SAP Aktiengesellschaft Systeme, Anwendungen, Produkte in der Datenverarbeitung	Services to business	2000	5,156,942,393		24.40	−15.56
5	SE	SCA	Mature industries	2000	9,159,753,638	7,320,760,887	13.37	6.55
5	FR	Schneider Electric	Electrical engineering	2000	1,518,404,426	1,256,821,815	12.02	

5	GB	ScottishPower	Utilities; Electricity, gas, and water supply	2000	24,764,721,459	5,021,218,551	17.17	9.20
5	ES	SEAT	Transport equipment	2000		5,863,626,424	10.77	
5	SE	Securitas	Services to business	2000	3,797,896,114	4,448,356,680	9.06	62.90
5	GB	Shell Transport and Trading Company	Oil, rubber, and other non-metallic mineral products	2000	49,144,296,721	59,675,659,291	12.11	11.89
5	DE	Siemens Aktiengesellschaft	Electrical engineering	2000	73,167,466,765	72,374,446,086	14.90	23.09
5	BE	Sioen Industries	Textiles and leather goods	2000	98,985,414	4,101,736	8.89	78.02
5	SE	Skandia Försäkringsaktiebolag	Insurance	2000	65,602,332,806	21,560,364,092	13.68	43.40
5	SE	Skanska	Construction and property companies	2000	8,413,473,592	12,125,143,075	25.64	9.25
5	IT	SMI	Mature industries	2000	1,547,267,356	2,179,652,880	3.80	19.29
5	GB	Smiths Group	Mechanical engineering	2000	6,003,624,133	4,866,626,250	51.55	0.10
5	IT	Snam (ENI Group)	Utilities; Electricity, gas, and water supply	2000	15,279,726,736	12,897,895,126	27.67	
5	FR	SNCF	Transport	2000		18,315,177,253	2.48	
5	IT	Snia	Chemicals and pharmaceuticals	2000	1,701,440,177	1,165,066,470	2.46	15.86
5	FR	Société Générale	Financial intermediation	2000	420,865,029,542	27,621,861,152	13.58	36.38
5	FR	Sodexho Alliance	Food, drink, and tobacco products	2000	868,501,959	1,445,639,169	6.39	
5	BE	Sofina	Financial intermediation	2000	1,176,214,919	1,556,499	26.15	12.34
5	BE	Solvay	Chemicals and pharmaceuticals	2000	4,950,906,573	903,648,449	8.33	10.15
5	FI	Sonera	Post and telecommunications	2000	9,066,792,000	1,914,038,500	28.25	139.35

(*continued*)

Continued

Benchmark	Country	Company	Sector	Year	Assets (US$)	Turnover (US$)	3-year average ROE	3-year average HR
5	BE	Spadel	Food, drink, and tobacco products	2000	54,934,453	31,225,997	25.86	11.32
5	DE	Stinnes AG	Transport	2000	5,082,163,959	11,102,289,513	9.31	11.90
5	IT	Stmicroelectronics (Finmeccanica Group)	Electrical engineering	2000	2,506,462,334	1,841,765,140	7.37	
5	FI	Stora ENSO	Mature industries	2000	19,841,051,500	12,112,318,500	10.93	40.13
5	FR	Suez	Utilities; Electricity, gas, and water supply	2000	80,329,273,438	31,884,304,800	7.83	5.07
5	IT	Supermarkets Italiani	Commercial activities	2000	2,034,711,965	2,895,125,554	13.17	
5	SE	Svenska Spel	Leisure and tourism	2000	535,673,407	1,541,178,394	99.97	87.60
5	ES	Telefonica	Post and telecommunications	2000	85,281,853,193	26,296,990,003	10.60	
5	ES	Telefonica Moviles Espana (Tele-Movile)	Post and telecommunications	2000	19,627,607,452	4,846,002,711	14.25	62.31
5	SE	Telia	Post and telecommunications	2000	13,377,118,875	5,893,497,575	16.14	
5	BE	Telindus	Post and telecommunications	2000	203,912,482	115,495,753	153.57	23.81
5	GB	Tesco	Commercial activities	2000	15,743,167,305	30,425,886,632	14.05	−2.49
5	DE	ThyssenKrupp AG	Mature industries	2000	33,131,462,334	34,350,997,046	4.66	−42.98
5	FI	TIH Finland /Finnmamtkat	Leisure and tourism	2000	22,362,458	116,309,930	−616.88	
5	ES	Timon	Media	2000	993,177,600		12.95	
5	GB	Tomkins	Mechanical engineering	2000	6,072,052,479	5,098,514,701	31.89	−14.55
5	IT	Toro Assicurazioni	Insurance	2000	13,112,075,332	4,152,511,078	5.38	25.53

5	FR	Total Fina Elf	Oil, rubber, and other non-metallic mineral products	2000	76,124,193,651	105,757,939,531	13.48	22.60
5	DE	TUI Group GmbH	Food, drink, and tobacco products	2000		9,750,830,511		
5	IT	UniCredito Italiano	Financial intermediation	2000	187,090,103,397	8,592,134,417	9.43	11.52
5	BE	Union Minière	Mining	2000	2,026,235,229	2,840,889,956	7.92	−6.79
5	FR	Usinor	Mature industries	2000	14,128,812,849	14,524,556,869	5.69	20.49
5	FI	Valio	Food, drink, and tobacco products	2000	666,238,000	1,285,951,000	2.27	
5	FR	Vallourec	Mature industries	2000	1,628,309,895	2,034,665,805	0.70	17.09
5	SE	Vattenfall	Utilities; Electricity, gas, and water supply	2000	12,564,342,944	3,455,060,773	8.08	48.00
5	DE	VEDIOR Personaldienstleistungen GmbH	Services to business	2000		5,077,548,006		
5	FR	Vinci	Construction and property companies	2000	2,444,621,878	1,831,248,544	21.06	
5	FR	Vivendi Universal	Media	2000		38,587,150,665	7.96	27.23
5	GB	Vodafone Group	Post and telecommunications	2000	244,785,474,603	12,711,427,705	59.76	52.60
5	DE	Volkswagen Aktiengesellschaft	Transport equipment	2000	75,325,886,263	78,983,567,208	13.08	7.39
5	SE	Volvo	Transport equipment	2000	21,882,923,639	14,178,884,831	16.83	−12.10
5	GB	WPP Group	Services to business	2000	13,644,501,275	21,153,379,812	43.16	60.74
5	DE	Wurth-Gruppe	Mechanical engineering	2000	2,689,161,653	4,741,691,465	16.78	
5	FI	YIT-yhtymä	Construction and property companies	2000	745,144,400	1,149,167,500	17.55	20.90
5	DE	ZF Friedrichshafen Aktiengesellschaft	Mechanical engineering	2000	3,835,856,721	6,000,738,552	22.58	

Index